The Cruising Chef Cookbook

Second Edition

The Cruising Chef Cookbook

By

Michael Greenwald

Edited by
Marcy Raphael

Illustrated by
Rebecca Thomson

Paradise Cay Publications
Arcata, California

Paradise Cay Publications P.O. Box 29 Arcata, California 95518-0029
(707) 822-9063 • fax (707) 822-9163 • (800) 736-4509 e-mail: paracay@humboldt1.com
www.paracay.com

Printed in the USA

Library of Congress Cataloging in Publication Data
Greenwald, Michael
Title: The Cruising Chef Cookbook, Second Edition
Includes index
1. Cookery, marine. I. Title.
ISBN0939837-00-5

Second Printing The Cruising Chef Cookbook, Second Edition May 1996

97 98 99 2000 2001 2002 2003 2004 2005 2006

2 3 4 5

Previous Titles:

The Cruising Chef ISBN 0-8306-6864-0 pbk

First printing The Cruising Chef January 1977
Second printing The Cruising Chef December 1978
Third printing The Cruising Chef February 1982

The Cruising Chef Cookbook, ISBN 0-931297-00-1 pbk
Copyright © 1984 by Michael Greenwald (The Cruising Chef)

First Printing The Cruising Chef Cookbook October 1984
Second printing The Cruising Chef Cookbook July 1986
Third printing The Cruising Chef Cookbook January 1988
Fourth printing The Cruising Chef Cookbook September 1990
Fifth Printing The Cruising Chef Cookbook June 1992
Sixth printing The Cruising Chef Cookbook August 1994
Seventh printing The Cruising Chef Cookbook March 2001

MICHAEL GREENWALD holds a 100 ton Master's license, power and sail and has 55,000 miles of cruising experience, including eight crossings of the Atlantic Ocean, two crossings of the Pacific and has crossed both the Atlantic and Pacific Oceans solo. Greenwald was a combat medic in the USA and USAR. He is an aircraft pilot with experience in Central and South America, has made several canoe voyages in the Canadian Arctic and traveled extensively in Africa. He is a Paris-trained chef and lives aboard his 36-foot sloop in southern California.

Special thanks to Marcy Raphael for the countless hours she spent editing this book and creating the cover. Without her help and advice this book would not have been possible.

Table of Contents

The dangerous person in the kitchen is the one who goes rigidly by weights, measurements, thermometers and scales.

X. Marcel Boulstein

Preface

I once knew two sailors who sailed around the world. They were great sailors but didn't like to cook. They were big on Spam, canned corn beef and sauerkraut. They bought cases of canned fish roe and ate it from the can. They fought constantly about whose turn it was to make a meal and often ate their eggs raw because they so hated to cook. Every pot, pan, cup and plate on the boat had an eye in it. When the meal was over they threaded a line through everything which was dirty and towed it until pronounced clean. These guys are my good friends but I never sent them a copy of this book. They had no use for it.

This is a cookbook for people who love good food and like to cook. It is intended to show you how to produce sumptuous, nourishing meals that satisfy the appetite and delight the soul—meals made predominantly from fresh ingredients, no matter how long the voyage. The great majority of recipes in this book are simple, one-pot affairs that can easily be made underway. Most require common ingredients, found in every port, that store well and last a long time. Every recipe has either been created by me during a lifetime of ocean cruising or is a simplification of classic recipes which are too complex for a boat.

The joy of having sailed far and eaten well linger in the mind long after the hard times are remembered with laughter. Only the essence of the adventure, the lust for life and the joy of it all remain islands in the mind's eye more green and scented than anything dreams can bring.

Michael Greenwald
The Cruising Chef

PERCENTAGE OF CALORIES FROM FAT IN YOUR FOOD

LESS THAN 10%

Bagels
Beans, peas, lentils
Cake, angel food
Consomme
Cereals, breakfast (except granola)
Cottage cheese
Fruits
Grains
Milk, skim
Tuna, in water

10-20%

Buttermilk
Bread: white, whole wheat
Scallops, grilled, poached
Turkey (white meat, no skin)
Shrimp
Yogurt (nonfat)

20-30%

Beef: sirloin (lean only)
Muffin: bran, corn, blueberry
Fish: cod, sole, bass (broiled)
Liver
Oysters, raw
Pancakes
Shake, thick
Soups: chicken noodle
Wheat germ

30-40%

Beef: flank steak, roast (lean)
Cake: yellow, white (without icing)
Chicken, roasted without skin
Cottage cheese, creamed
Fish: flounder, haddock (fried)
Granola
Ice milk
Milk, 2%
Pizza
Seafood: scallops (breaded, fried)
Soups: bean with pork
Tuna in oil (drained)
Turkey, roasted dark meat
Yogurt (low fat)

40-50%

Beef: T-bone (lean only), hamburger
Cake: devil's food with chocolate icing
Ice cream (regular)
Mackerel
Pumpkin pie
Salmon, canned
Sardines (drained)
Yogurt (whole milk)
Milk, whole

50-75%

Beef: corned
Bacon, Canadian
Cake, pound
Cheese: cheddar, American, Swiss, etc.
Chicken, roasted with skin or fried
Chocolate candy
Croissant
Eggs
Fried fish
Ice cream (rich)
Lake trout
Lamb
Oysters, fried
Pork (trimmed, lean)
Soups, creamed
Tuna salad
Tuna with oil
Veal

75% OR MORE

Avocado
Bacon
Beef: sirloin, hamburger (regular)
Cold Cuts: bologna, salami
Cream: heavy, light, half-and-half
Cream cheese
Coconut
Dressings: French, Italian, ranch, mayonnaise, Thousand Island, bleu cheese
Egg Yolk
Hot dogs
Nuts
Olives
Pork: sausage, spareribs
Peanut butter
Seeds
Sour cream

About Food and Health

We believe that in order to be happy one must eat well and exercise. We know that cholesterol—whatever that is—is supposed to be bad for you. We also know that Eskimos lived for centuries on a diet consisting of whale and seal blubber, that the Japanese eat less fat, more fish and rice than the French but do not live longer; that the French consume quantities of butter and wine but do not have a shorter life span than anyone else.

Today, the politically correct diet is very low in fat, but you will find many recipes in this book which call for politically incorrect ingredients such as cheese, cream, sour cream, bacon fat, salami and salt pork. If you do not like these ingredients do not cook with them. You can use safflower oil instead of peanut or olive oil, because safflower oil is lower in polyunsaturated fats. You can stir fry foods because stir frying uses little oil. Pressure cook and enjoy all kinds of beans and grains which require no oil at all. In some recipes you can use low fat yogurt or sour cream and skim cheese instead of full fat cheese. You can favor salsas, acid marinades, cucumber and yogurt dressings for salads because they contain less oil.

You can significantly reduce the animal product ingredients which many recipes include. One may achieve a pork flavor by rubbing a slice of ham hock through a pan of hot oil without cooking and using bacon; add lean smoked meat to food instead of using fatty trimmings; skim everything and remove all the oil; make a miso/vegetable stock and use it instead of a meat stock.

On the other hand, the physically active body, such as those engaged in ocean sailing, hauling up anchors and rowing needs and burns more saturated fat than the body which is engaged in watching TV. Our recipes are designed for the active body and, when that body "swallows the anchor", it will need and demand less fat. Having said all this we include a "fat chart" on the next page which we use when we are in port and indolent.

1 Provisioning & Planning

AVAILABILITY OF FOOD

Food does not end when you leave America. Trust me. People everywhere eat. Even in developing countries you will find everything you need in the larger ports. You will find healthy, well nourished people all over the world. The problem of the malnourished is generally a lack of money rather than a lack of access to food.

It is not necessary to buy every can of olives and box of salt which you think you will need for the entire voyage. You do not need to spend your weekends canning every meal you will eat for the next two years. You just need food reach the next major port.

Overstocking is in reality a much more common problem than hunger aboard most boats. **Overloading** affects the way the boat handles and its speed. In addition, shopping for food in strange places is part of the fun. Therefore, contain the natural desire to fill every available space with food. Buy just what you need plus a specific reserve, or you will invariably end up with a load of old tins you would be embarrassed to give away.

Keep in mind that best tasting meals come from **fresh ingredients**, not cans. Remember the role cans play in your home, where canned food is used to add an ingredient or provide an easy side dish. Think of cans as a supplement for an otherwise fresh diet.

Avoid the temptation to buy provisions in a **wholesale or commercial grocery**. The savings is surprisingly small. Commercial groceries often do not stock the brands with which you are familiar. You may end up with a lot of something you don't like. **Container sizes** are larger in a commercial grocery than in a supermarket. Cruisers in fact want smaller containers of many items to reduce spoilage. What will you do with an open gallon of tuna, for example?

STOCK UP ON LUXURY FOODS that will be hard to find in foreign ports such as maple syrup, fine vinegar, marinated artichokes, good salami, wild and exotic rice, dried mushrooms, curry paste, fancy cheese, special dressings and sauces.

Since you like them they will not endure a slow death in the storage locker. If you are going to have Thanksgiving you'd better take some turkey gravy, canned yams and cranberry sauce. Definite bargains in the USA are whisky, wine, cigarettes, clothing, fruit juices, bottom paint, line and yacht gear. There are very few countries in the world that offer lower prices and more variety than the USA.

STOCK UP ON BEVERAGES not because they are hard to find but because they are heavy and are consumed in quantity. Better to handle them in a place where you have a car. A good drink supply will also be a backup in the event that you run out of water

BUY WINE—plenty of that. It's cheap and available in America, like nowhere else. Even the French do not have the variety and low prices found in the USA. Truck it down. Varnish the labels. Put it in the bilge.

DO NOT BUY large quantities of pasta, sugar, flour, rice, oil, beans, tinned fish, soups, meat or tinned vegetables. These are found everywhere. Keep in mind that canned goods lose much of their flavor after about six months.

BRINGING PESTS ABOARD: Remove fresh vegetables from sacks or boxes before bringing aboard. Everything should be dumped on the dock or into the dinghy, so that rot and clinging pests can be found. Cartons and bags should not be brought aboard since they may contain pests or their eggs. This is extremely important. Items sold in cardboard containers such as cake mixes should be removed from their package and vacuum sealed to isolate potential pests. More about roaches later.

PROVISIONING STRATEGY

Think of food in terms of how long it will last without spoiling. At the beginning of a voyage you will be able to utilize many fruits and vegetables which do not require refrigeration. This will allow you to reserve the more perishable refrigerated foods for later in the voyage.

As the voyage progresses you can use more of the refrigerated foods as well as longer lasting unrefrigerated fruits which have ripened. Also use vegetables such as potatoes and onions which last for a long time without refrigeration.

Finally, when most of the more perishable foods have been consumed you will place greater emphasis on the long lasting food supply, those items which will last weeks or even months without spoiling. Read more about meal planning later in this chapter.

MEAL PLANNING STRATEGY

FIRST WEEK:

- Food prepared before the voyage
- Chicken
- Fresh fish
- Unrefrigerated perishable vegetables and fruits.

During the first week, eat unrefrigerated vegetables which only last a short time. Included are ripe tomatoes and avocados, summer squash, eggplant, broccoli, peas, green peppers and cauliflower; fruits such as melons, grapes, pineapple, peaches, pears.

SECOND WEEK:

- Fish of opportunity
- Meat
- Ripe fruits, longer lasting fruits like apples and pineapple
- Vegetables like cabbage and squash
- Some refrigerated items

The second week eat the ripened tomatoes and avocados which were purchased green. Unrefrigerated cabbage and carrots will also be good. You could add radishes and green onions from the fridge. The iceberg lettuce in the 'fridge will still be fresh.

THIRD WEEK:

- Fish of opportunity
- Meats, hot dog, bacon, salami
- Pasta
- Refrigerated vegetables and fruit
- Long lasting (base supply) fruits and vegetables, last of ripened fruit

By the third week most of the unrefrigerated perishables will be gone and you will be left with the base supply of **citrus fruit, potatoes, onions, carrots, yams, coconuts and apples**. The deep stored refrigerated vegetables start to deteriorate.

During the third week you might want to start your seed sprouter, so that when the lettuce is gone you will have fresh seed sprouts available. There is absolutely no reason why you should not be able to have a salad and/or fresh vegetables every day no matter how long the passage.

THEREAFTER: Ah, the Great Thereafter!

- Fish of opportunity
- Meat, processed meat
- Canned meat, fish and fowl
- Pasta
- Base supply fruits and vegetables
- Sprouts
- Hard cheese
- Bean soups, potato pancakes, curried lentils and rice with dried mushrooms.

MAKING LISTS

MAKE A MEAL PLAN to be sure you purchase everything you will need. Read more about meal plans later in this chapter.

MAKE A STOWAGE PLAN: Sketch a plan of the stowage spaces in the boat and assign a letter to each. The large, dry spaces are for items such as tins which would otherwise rust; wet places for vacuum sealed items; dark, cool spots for fruit and vegetables; hot areas for grains and cereals; and the bilge for glass, vacuum packs and plastic bottles. Keep a space near the galley for a miscellaneous handy reserve. Try to keep like items together and in the same location. With a little organization, you will have everything at your fingertips.

THE REFRIGERATOR

The refrigerator is the vessel's most coveted spot for storing food. It must be loaded carefully. Most marine refrigerators are **top loaders**. They do not lose their cold when the doors are opened as is the case in the home. Unfortunately, top loaders make food less accessible. The object is to get as much food into the 'fridge as possible without over packing it and without having to unpack it to reach items at the bottom. Drinks are the highest demand objects in the 'fridge. They should be kept as handy as possible.

Pack food in **wire trays** or **mesh sacks**. This keeps the food from touching the holding plate, reducing its efficiency. We try to layer the food in the order of use. For example each tray might have enough butter, cheese, vegetables and meat to last a few days. Try to put the chicken and meat closer to the cold and the veggies on the hull side. Durable fruits and vegetables like carrots and lemons go in color coded mesh sacks. Items needing the most cold or those which are to be consumed last go to the bottom of the refrigerator.

Marine refrigerators, unlike most modern home refrigerators are moist since they are not "frost free." This reduces the drying effect on fruits and vegetables but it also allows the buildup of mold.

When in port, occasionally defrost your fridge, wipe with a strong bleach solution. Sponge up any reserve liquid in the bottom (important) and allow to dry. It is particularly important to be sure the bottom of the fridge is clean and washed with a strong bleach solution.

SELECTION FOR REFRIGERATION: Allocate a certain amount of space in the refrigerator for fruits and vegetables, and plan what will be stored there. Resist the "buy and jam" technique. Select items which can be refrigerated for two or three weeks, such as herbs, certain lettuces, cucumbers, celery, carrots, turnips, beets, Brussels sprouts, cabbage, radishes, artichokes and fruit like apples and small melons.

Go easy on delicate stuff like peaches and papayas. Some items such as the radishes and herbs may be used frequently. Keep them handy. Some foods like the iceberg lettuce, turnips and beets, will be used when the unrefrigerated fresh stuff is gone.

We have a special bin where we keep fresh herbs like parsley, cilantro, basil, green onions, and also asparagus, whose bottoms will actually rest in containers of water. Rinse and cut off the bottom to get a fresh surface. Drop aspirin in the water to slightly acidify. Place herb and container in an open plastic sack. Read more about this in Chapter 16.

ICE

PURCHASING: Block ice lasts longer and stores better than cubes. Buy blocks and line the bottom of the 'fridge with THEM. Deep store chicken and meat near it. Buy a bag of ice cubes as a ready supply just for drinks. When your ready supply is exhausted, break off a big chunk from a block, break it up and use it for drinks. Resist the temptation to pour crushed ice over everything. When the compressor pulls the box temperature down the crushed ice freezes into an impenetrable mass. If you wish, break blocks into big chips and toss them into the refrigerator.

MAKING ICE: An easy way to make ice in a refrigerator without a freezer is to press a Ziploc half full of water against the holding plate.

CONSUMING ICE: Ice sold in fishing ports is made for commercial purposes such as chilling trawler fish. It may not be edible and is not intended for human consumption. This ice is often delivered by hose as a slush. Ask the fishermen if it can be consumed.

USING ICE: Do not allow fruit and vegetables to lie directly on the ice. Temperatures below 34° F. damage produce. Meat should be securely wrapped or it will impart its flavor to the ice and everything else it touches. Algae and some molds thrive in an ice chest. Clean when in port. Never let ice water stand in the bilge, even in a fiberglass boat. It is contaminated with bacteria.

LONG-LASTING UNREFRIGERATED BASE SUPPLY

Listed below are the "guts" of any galley, tough, long lasting fruits and vegetables which do not necessarily have to be refrigerated. Store base vegetables so that they will not be tossed around, abraded by other items or each other and be sure air circulates around them. They all like cool, dry, dark places.

Stacking flat vinyl coated mesh trays are best. Stack them at the end of a spare bunk or in the shower. Shallow plastic storage boxes are OK but lay newspaper in the bottom. In general you want very large vegetables for the base supply as the larger mass resists drying. These items should last a month or two depending on temperature. Examine them weekly. Learn more in Chapter 16.

APPLES are often sold with very shiny skins indicating that they have been waxed. The wax protects the fruit and slows drying. Buy select, big, very hard apples free of cuts, dents or soft spots. Wrap some in aluminium foil for unrefrigerated storage. Wrap some in paper, put in a vegetable Ziploc and store in the bottom of the fridge.

Apples are the longest-lasting fruit and may last a few months in the fridge. Store unrefrigerated apples in trays like potatoes. Never store apples near onions since the onions emit a gas which damages the apples. Tart apples such as pippins last longer than sweet, softer varieties such as Delicious.

CARROTS will last several weeks unrefrigerated if wrapped in a damp towel and kept cool. They need to be wiped with a clean cloth about every five days to keep them from developing mold. For the long lasting supply bigger carrots are better.

CITRUS FRUIT: test for freshness by hefting. Read more in Chapter 16. If in doubt, buy one piece and cut it open. The fruit must be fresh and full of juice. Wash in chlorinated water. Sun dry. Individually wrap in foil. This reduces moisture loss and isolates each fruit, reducing the spread of mold. Store in trays. Examine by squeezing and smelling.

COCONUTS: In addition to being tasty and thirst quenching, coconuts travel extremely well and may be stored under the dinghy or in the bilge if it is not oily. If possible, coconuts should be purchased green.

ONIONS: Buy select large yellow (Cepa) cooking onions with undamaged golden skins. Bermudas or Spanish onions are tasty but do not last as long. Cepa onions are tough enough to store in a sack.

POTATOES: We can't even tell you how long they last because we have never been on a cruise long enough to see them all go bad. Our longest sea voyage was 54 days.

WINTER SQUASH: Hard squash and small pumpkins will last for a month without refrigeration. Keep cool. Protect them from dehydration by enclosing in individual paper bags.

STORAGE OF POULTRY

Fresh, whole birds last about five days in the refrigerator. **Frozen birds** lose a bit of taste but may remain frozen for a long time. In isolated places only buy freshly killed fowl since frozen birds have often traveled far, been freezer burned, or defrosted and refrozen several times.

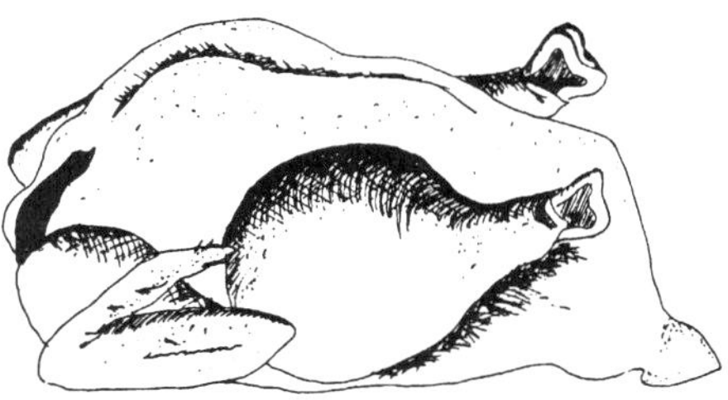

Rinse the bird before use and allow to reach room temperature. Then, wash and let your nose be your guide. If you are getting nervous about a chicken, pressure cook it in stock before it goes bad and Ziploc everything while it is hot. This will extend its life several days. Learn more in Chapter 13.

STORAGE OF MEAT

SELECTION: Selecting meat for a cruise is fundamentally different than buying meat for home use. When one purchases meat for home use it is used quickly. On a cruise it may have to last longer. When one buys a piece of meat for dinner it is usually purchased with a specific recipe in mind. On a boat, one or several pieces may have to serve in a variety of different dishes. At home size and waste are not serious considerations, so one may buy cuts which may require trimming or have a big bone. On a boat space in the 'fridge is much more important than saving a few cents and a cut bone is a source of contamination.

BEST CUT is the **fillet** (**tenderloin**) from a young animal. Famous recipes such as Chateaubriand, Tournedos and Filet Mignon come from this cut. The fillet is the most tender (and most expensive) cut and will come out tasting great if not overcooked.

THE TENDERLOIN is usually removed from the carcass intact. It has a tough, white membrane surrounding it which protects it from bacteria. In many butcher shops you can get the butcher to whack off whatever size piece you want from a virgin loin, further reducing the possibility of contamination. If you can get the end piece it will be completely surrounded by membrane except for where it has been cut. Last but not least, a loin is smooth and regular, making it easier to wash and sterilize.

PURCHASING: Tenderloins from young animals have a little marbled fat, are fine grained, light red in color and up to four inches in diameter. The loins from old critters are coarse grained, dark, almost brown and up to eight inches in diameter.

Pork and lamb loins are equally delicious. Select cuts are often available in sealed pouches which preserve them. Meat sold this way is usually select. Check the expiration date. Learn more in Chapter 12.

OTHER GOOD SELECTIONS include pieces without cut bones because bone ends are easily contaminated, hard to clean and can abrade a plastic bag, causing a leak. Therefore sirloins, rib eyes or any high quality piece which is surrounded as much as possible by fat or white tissue and free from cuts or flaps (which may harbor bacteria) are good choices. Fatty meat may not be good for you but the fat protects the meat from contamination. Trim before cooking.

PREPARATION: Wash thoroughly in vinegar or sear in a hot, dry pan. The object here is to kill off surface bacteria with a quick burst of heat, not seal or cook the meat. We have been known to hang the meat from a hook and flash it with a blowtorch. While hot, drop into a Ziploc. Fill with oil (we use a mixture of peanut and a little olive oil). Air is your enemy. Squeeze it out. Add a few whole, unskinned garlic cloves and peppercorns. Consider a little rosemary and thyme. Place in a plastic jar to avoid leaks. Store as cold as possible.

A tenderloin which I purchased in Tangier and stored in the bilge was served to guests at an arrival party sixty days later. It was a little thin in flavor but tender and very succulent after being marinated for two months in olive oil and rosemary. We served it with a zippy horseradish, lemon and sour cream sauce. Everyone loved it. No one died.

SALAMI is of particular interest to the yachtsman because it is so long lasting. Be sure to purchase it unsliced and whole. Salami is expensive, often equivalent in price to steak. We find it worth the extra expense, not only for flavor, but also for convenience. There are a number of reasons why salami lasts so long. First, it is cooked meat that is inserted into a protective jacket while still hot. Second, it is very oily, and the oil acts as a preservative. Finally, salami meat is often smoked, and frequently a preservative is added, usually sodium benzoate or nitrite.

All of these factors contribute to a long shelf life, measured in terms of months, or a year. Hang salami if possible, they crave fresh air. Some salami do not require refrigeration. They are full of preservatives and will probably be edible when your grandchildren inherit your boat. Salami should be turned occasionally (to prevent the oil from settling out) and examined for mold.

STORAGE OF AGED HAM: Country-cured ham, Spanish ham, and Italian prosciutto have been hung for several years in a cool, dry place. They may be eaten safely without cooking. In fact, they become tough and unpalatable if cooked. They will last additional years without refrigeration if handled properly.

These hams are expensive but extremely delicious. They have a very intense flavor and are therefore used sparingly, cut paper thin and traditionally served in antipasto or with fruit. A small ham lasts a long time. They must be purchased on the bone and not sliced. The best storage technique is to hang them inside a paper bag. The bag will catch the drips and you can add a few sheets of newspaper for added protection. These hams don't like damp places with poor air flow.

HOT DOGS AND OTHER HOUNDS: In terms of shelf life we are talking about immortality here. The unused packs can be saved for your children's inheritance. After all, we are talking about processed meat with at least twenty percent fat, loaded with stabilizers, coloring agents and preservatives. So bad for you and so delicious. Buy the best and deep-store in the 'fridge. This is the ultimate reserve meat. Do not be fooled into thinking that "turkey dogs" are lower in fat—read label.

EGGS: The best eggs come from free-ranging chickens. Their eggs have a thicker shell and tougher membrane which resists contamination. Read more about buying and storing eggs in the Chapter 6.

LONG LIFE MILK: Pasteurized milk takes up precious space in the refrigerator and spoils within a few weeks. Long life, ultra heat-treated milk is an unrefrigerated product which comes in a paper box. It tastes as fresh as pasteurized milk, contains more vitamins and lasts six months without refrigeration. It comes in half-quart and quart (liter) boxes which are slightly more expensive than refrigerated milk. This product is hard to find in the USA but is the most common way of buying milk in many parts of the world.

STORAGE OF PASTA, RICE, GRAINS: These items are best stored in a vacuum sealed pouch or a plastic jar. Once sealed, they may be stored in the bilge. We usually heat our grains in the oven (350 F. for twenty minutes stirring occasionally) to kill pests and their eggs. The microwave is very good for this purpose. If you fail to do this, one day you will be sorry.

CANNED GOODS

SIZE SELECTION: When you open a can or jar, the correct strategy is to use the contents as rapidly as possible to avoid spoilage. Therefore buy cans sized to be consumed in one meal. Keep my mother's dictate in mind: *A bargain isn't a bargain if you can't use it.* Resist the temptation to buy bigger cans and save, save, save.

SHELF LIFE AND NUTRITIONAL VALUE: Canned food will last for about two years but can last much longer under ideal conditions (such as in the Arctic). The taste of the food begins to deteriorate six to eight months after being canned. Because canned food is cooked in the can, preservatives are usually not added.

Nutritionally canned food is not significantly different from fresh food and in some cases vitamins have been added to replace those lost in the cooking process. In first world countries canned food is becoming healthier. Less sugar and salt are added.

CONTENTS SELECTION: Canning is a harsh process which damages the flavor and texture of some foods, while others survive almost intact. LOSERS include canned peas, asparagus and delicate vegetables. The texture of fruit is usually destroyed by cooking but flavor remains. WINNERS include beans, tomato products, corn, beets, potatoes, fish in oil or a rich sauce (not water), meat (discussed below), savory sauces like curry, fruit preserves, gourmet main courses.

CANNED MEAT: American winners include cuts of whole meat, hams, shoulders. Most US meat stews and spreads are second quality—or lower. American canned meat products like chili, meat and vegetable stews or spaghetti with meat sauce are usually extremely fatty and of low quality. European and Scandinavian products are much better. Asiatic fish and shellfish products are also usually quite good.

RESERVE CACHE

A reserve cache is a supply of food which is held for the time when you completely run out of everything else. This is an extremely unlikely event. Even if you are dismasted it is very likely that you will have an adequate supply of food to last a month, not to mention what you can catch. In any event, what you really want for such a disaster is a good radio or emergency locator.

SHELF LIFE: The first consideration when selecting a food for a reserve cache is shelf life. The size of a reserve is up to you and depends on your needs. For coastal cruising a week's supply is plenty since you will also be carrying bulk items such as pasta and rice which will keep you going.

FOOD IN PACKETS: Dehydrated food sold in foil packets lasts three or four years without loss of flavor. Fancy dehydrated selections are sold in camping stores. They are expensive but edible. Nourishing gourmet meals are sold this way. A wide variety of dehydrated soups are sold in most supermarkets. They are much cheaper than gourmet camping packets which is their soul virtue. They can be made more filling by adding cooked pasta.

CANNED GOODS: To extend the life of cans write the contents of the can on the lid. Spray lid with acrylic sealer and store. Store where the cans won't get knocked around. A can's contents may be immortal but its taste begins to deteriorate after six months.

PASTA AND RICE make very good reserves since they are virtually immortal if stored properly. Pasta and rice may not represent a balanced diet but people can last a long time with very little other food before vitamin deficiencies (scurvy) begin to appear.

TOBACCO: Smokers frequently underestimate how much tobacco they will need for a voyage. Some even say they plan to quit during the passage, an ominous thought. I suggest that you suggest they quit elsewhere. You have a choice: you can share a small area with someone undergoing tobacco withdrawal or you can carry tobacco in your cache. Individual packets of smoking tobacco along with rolling papers can be vacuum sealed and stored. They last longer and are cheaper than rolled cigarettes.

CHILLING WITHOUT REFRIGERATION

Citrus fruits last months, particularly if washed in the fruit and vegetable dip (see page 45). Citrus drinks, lemon favored tea, even soda pop with citrus always have a cool taste even if not chilled.

The temperature of bottled drinks usually can be lowered ten to twenty degrees by wrapping a wet dish towel around the bottle and standing it in a bowl of water in the shade. A breeze helps. The same procedure using alcohol instead of water is even more effective, but expensive.

Items chilled at night can be wrapped in a dry towel in the morning to insulate them. They will keep their cool for several hours. The sea is always cooler near the bottom, so try tying the items to be chilled to a long line and dropping them over the side. Cloth or blanket-covered canteens keep contents cool if the cloth is kept wet.

WINE AND BEER

WINE: Buy good wine for drinking and cooking. Do not buy bulk wine unless you have a very great thirst. Once wine is opened it begins to deteriorate. The process is subtle enough to make you suddenly realize you have been drinking vinegar for a week when you could have had something decent. The memory of good wine will linger long after the pain of spending the money for it is forgotten.

Wine ages more rapidly on a boat because of the motion. Wines do not like the lurching, frequent temperature changes and engine vibration of a boat. Robust reds usually last longer than whites. White wine more than three years old becomes thin after an ocean crossing. Buy young wines.

The bilge is the place for storing wine but the bilge is damp and mold eventually penetrates the corks. Six months is stretching it for tropical waters. For longer storage you can dip the heads of the bottle in paraffin wax to retard mold—or you can drink the wine faster and buy more.

BEER: As a beer lover I must admit to the satisfaction of having a lazarette bulging with a supply of beer that will last for months. Beer in metal cans, especially aluminum tends to develop corrosion holes. These holes are not only caused by salt moisture but, in some cases, by the motion of the boat and the vibration of the engine. Purchase beer for long voyages in bottles.

STORAGE TOOLS

VACUUM SEALER: This is a "must" item for a cruiser, useful for storing food, tools, books, medical supplies, even clothing. You can seal staples like pasta and flour, which makes them immortal, and allows you to store them anywhere. You can make stews and soups, seal while hot, allow to cool and store in the 'fridge. Get one.

ZIPLOC FREEZER BAGS: Buy different sizes, as strong and cheap as possible. These are expensive and hard to find in foreign countries. Use bags for short term storage of food since the bag eventually imparts its flavor to its contents.

VEGETABLE BAGS: These are Ziploc bags with tiny holes which allow fruit and vegetable metabolic gasses to escape and allow limited circulation of air. This reduces mold formation and increases the life of fruits and vegetables in the refrigerator.

PASTA AND RICE purchased in cardboard cartons should be repackaged immediately since the food assumes the taste of the container if not eaten promptly.

COOKING OIL: Meat and other foods are packed in oil for storage. You will need several gallons for this purpose.

THE TRASH PROBLEM

The word "trash" and the word "problem" seem to go together but on land the problem is usually someone else's. At sea the problem is yours. How you handle it is a matter of conscience and necessity.

It is no pleasure to sail into some isolated place only to find the litter of some thoughtless person fouling the beach. Even "organic" items such as citrus fruit skins and paper plates end up ashore. Bottles and cans litter the bottom of a pristine anchorage for years. If you are near land burn your trash, then bury it.

No matter how ecology-minded you are, there comes a moment on extended sea voyages when it is time to cope with the trash. Organic garbage is quickly eaten by sea creatures and can be dumped. Glass bottles and jars are inert and will eventually be reduced to sand. Cans rust away. Beer cans should have holes punched in them so they sink.

Plastic products, especially foam such as **styrene** and **urethane** should be not be thrown into the sea. They should be stored for disposal ashore. When thrown ino the sea styrene and urethane are eventually reduced to individual plastic bubbles which are sometimes consumed by fish affecting their reproduction. The next time you walk along a tide line, look carefully. You will be amazed at how many tiny plastic bubbles you will see.

The sea, once believed capable of absorbing unlimited pollution, is in reality a delicate organic solution. Do your part to keep it celan.

SHIPBOARD PESTS

You must be certain that there are no live pests aboard at the beginning of a cruise. In comparison to a house, the problem of ridding a boat of roaches is much greater because of numerous inaccessible places not reached by the gas. Sprays, baits, and residuals are merely methods of containing the problem. Large boats have more air pockets because of space between double walls, panels, ceiling and air conduits.

How many roaches constitute infestation? If you come aboard at night and see three roaches, you have a real problem. Two of them will probably be pregnant females. The first assault must be massive, for roaches are an adversary not to be underestimated. This is what you are going to have to do:

Remove every damned thing on the boat and put it on the dock. This sounds outrageous, unreasonable and excessive. It may be outrageous and unreasonable but it is not excessive. Examine everything carefully for egg cases.

Open the bilge, the engine compartment and every locker. Remove drawers, shake out sails, and destroy cardboard cartons Remove

Alfred the Gecko

and destroy paper bags. This is a favorite home of roaches. Seal air vents, tape refrigerator, and store exposed food on deck.

Wear a diving tank and mask, cover yourself with a suit of trash bags, use roach spray everywhere. This is not to kill the roaches, it's just to get them moving. Spray in electric outlets, light fixtures, drain holes, wire runs, vent tubes and dorades under the stove and also on deck.

Seal all vents and windows. Bomb the living hell out of the vessel using three or four times the recommended amount of cans. Be sure every compartment has its own bomb, no matter how small. Throw a separate can in the engine compartment and the lazarette. Turn on fans, if available, to swirl the poison around.

Open vessel the next day and air for a few hours. Buy baits or roach traps and put them everywhere. Make a roach poison mixture of sugar and boric acid about 1:10. Sprinkle this powder in all of the food lockers and the bilge, everywhere it will not be a nuisance. This powder is not toxic to people or pets.

There is now a slight possibility that you have killed off all the adult roaches on the vessel. Now let us talk about their eggs. In a few days or a week the eggs will hatch. If you were lucky enough to buy bombs in developing countries that have never heard of the EPA, you may get a poison which penetrates the egg cases in which case you may have solved your problem. If not, if you see a baby roach or two, be assured there are more. Your only hope is to repeat everything.

I once got roaches in Tahiti. I did everything just described. The roaches survived. They romped through the boric acid. They disdained the baits. They reproduced faster than I could kill them. Female guests hated them. Finally, after a long, dateless, roach infested Pacific voyage, I returned to San Francisco and hauled out. The next week it was very cold. I opened the boat and found about a hundred roaches belly up on the cabin sole. Those Tahitian roaches couldn't stand the cold.

We had a friend whose boat became infested with roaches in Thailand. He bought an eight-inch lizard called a **gecko** in the market place and he named it Alfred. Alfred ate roaches and eventually ate himself out of a job. I bought him for a bottle of wine. Alfred slept during the day. At night he quietly ate roaches. He was very good at this. Sometimes he hung from the ceiling. Sometimes he crawled along walls. Sometimes we would just drop him into a food locker for the day . Alfred was quite friendly, made great efforts to avoid being stepped on, and never kept union hours. However he eventually ate himself out of business and we then discovered why his previous owner decided to trade him for wine. When Alfred was hungry he barked. Hell, I don't know, maybe he was just horny. He barked until we got up, rolled a small amount of ground meat onto the end of a string and dangled it before him. Since Alfred worked only at night this operation was frequently performed at two a.m. Someone eventually stepped on Alfred. Not me.

MICE AND RATS

These little animals can cause much damage to your vessel because they gnaw everything, including electrical insulation and plastic tubing. Use traps and bait, but keep your toes out of the traps!

I once had a rat run down a dock line, through the anchor hawse hole and into the bilge. I could hear that critter but he was too fast for me. I went into the town but could only find traps for young mice. What to do? Finally I bought the little mouse traps and that night put out several. I sat in the darkness armed with a pizza spatula. In the middle of the night the trap snapped and I discovered an extremely large, rather annoyed rat trying to pull the trap off his head. I did him in with the spatula.

NATURAL PREDATORS

Cats sometimes eat insect pests (except roaches) and some may be willing to kill mice, but even a cat has real difficulty catching a mouse once it is aboard. Usually rodents avoid boats that smell of a cat.

GROCERY SHOPPING IN FOREIGN PORTS

If you love to cook there is nothing more enjoyable than shopping in native markets. Since there is not much refrigeration in such places, the food is much fresher than in "first world" countries where one could grow old and die looking for a fresh tomato.

There are supermarkets in most large ports which sell everything but are much less exciting than shopping in an open market. The supermarket's advantage is that you can buy many "first world" items not sold in the open-air markets and the price of everything is plainly marked. Many of these places take credit cards. In any event, you can see the total on the cash register and know how much to pay. Plan to make big purchases in the supermarket after visiting the open-air market and know what is available there.

WHEN VISITING AN OPEN-AIR MARKET: avoid the temptation of acquiring a guide, particularly young boys hanging about, who speak good English. They want to take you to their friends who will possibly add a guide's commission to your bill. These boys may be nice but you will be happier without them and will find everything you need regardless of whether you speak the language or not.

Before you buy anything, examine the entire market. You will then know what's available, the general prices and you will also spot the stalls with the best stuff.

Never wear jewelry or anything expensive. Wear plain clothes. If there is one bad guy hanging around he will be looking at you. Put your money in a fanny pack you wear in front or in a buttoned pocket. Never carry a purse or keep your cash in a pants pocket. Bring heavy carrying sacks and your own bags. You can buy these things in the market but they are not free. Bring a back pack or a hand cart if needed. A collapsible, good-quality cart is really useful since you will be doing a great deal of walking. Test the cart thoroughly before purchasing.

People who are food vendors are usually not crooks although, like everyone else, they aren't above cutting a good deal for themselves. In most cases prices are chalked up somewhere and, as is true in supermarkets, prices are extremely competitive. These people make their living selling food, not cheating tourists. This is not to say that someone won't try to sell you an old fish or a tough chicken—let the buyer beware! One does not haggle over the price of food since the prices are plainly marked and quite competitive.

Get the vendors to help you make selections. They know what is good and, considering the low price of food in such places, quality rather than price is of greatest importance. Speaking the language is not important but learn key phrases like "how much; is this the best; is this a young animal?"

Most fresh foods in "first world" countries are washed several times and wrapped in plastic. In native markets this is not the case. Wash everything you buy in chlorinated water and watch out for pests.

In developing country markets meat is usually hung on a hook in the open market. This may look disgusting but is not dangerous. Wash the meat in vinegar and water after purchase. If you plan to store it, rather than eat it immediately, hang it from a piece of wire and thoroughly blowtorch or scorch in a pan to kill fly eggs. You may now consider it safe for consumption.

SELECTING LIVE ANIMALS: In places where there is no refrigeration meat is frequently sold "on the hoof." See last section of Meat and Chicken chapters.

EGGS are frequently sold "loose" so you must bring your own container. These eggs are usually from free ranging chickens and are extremely fresh.

When in a market, only eat cooked food which is sold piping hot wrapped in newspaper or on disposable plates. Do not eat salads, cheese, pastries or pies.

MEAL PLANNING STRATEGY

CRUISE OF A WEEK OR LESS: You hardly need to plan differently than you would at home. Make a meal plan for the trip. Use the recipes in this book because they are simple and designed for a boat. Make up a grocery list from the meal plan (described later in this chapter). You can also bring food made ashore.

LONG COASTAL CRUISE: You will be going ashore frequently and will be able to purchase more fresh supplies, so do not overstock on basics. Buy them along the way. Learn more about your potential ports of call and what is available by reading cruising guides and talking to local chandlers.

You can also make enough cooked food for the first days. Knowing you have at least several days of prepared food is a great comfort in the beginning of a cruise, while you are getting your sea legs—and stomach.

OCEAN PASSAGE supplies must be balanced and complete. Buy everything you need for the estimated time of the passage plus a 10-15% surplus. Most ocean passages take thirty days or less.

CRUISE PREPARATION: Make a first week's menu and include everything you plan to bring aboard cooked. We will discuss planning the second week's menu and then the "Thereafter menu." The object is not to eat exactly as planned, it is to make sure that all the necessary supplies get aboard.

When making a meal plan, include everything, right down to the midnight snacks. Show this menu to everyone in the ship's company to make sure there are no strong objections. Then make a list of ingredients for each recipe.

For the "Thereafter" meal plan multiply by the number of weeks remaining in the voyage. Keep in mind that life under sail is more vigorous than ashore and food consumption will increase, especially breakfast.

BOTTLED DRINKS: If the weather is hot and the crew are not seasoned, the beverage consumption can be fantastic. Allow at least a six-pack of water and quart of juice per man, and if that doesn't do it make tea and powdered drinks. Most sailors love beer and wine but these beverages make you more thirsty. A little wine can be added to a fruit juice mix to make Sangria, which is quite thirst-quenching. Bottled and canned drinks plus powders which can be mixed with water provide beverage diversity and a hedge against water shortage.

Once we lost our entire fresh water supply four days out of the Canary Islands on a transatlantic delivery. We faced a four-thousand mile crossing to Miami with five gallons of emergency water and two gallons of battery water. Fortunately, we had a large reserve of bottled juice and wine—plenty of wine. Between the bottled liquids and a small amount of collected rain water, we honestly could say that we did not suffer for a moment. How different the picture would have been without bottled drinks!

SNACKS: Dried fruit, granola bars and oatmeal cookies are a great snack. Salami and cheese also make fine snacks. Oatmeal cookies are particularly good because they do not become stale quickly and are easily revived by heating. Hot chocolate and oatmeal cookies make a good night watch snack. Prepared snacks, such as hard boiled eggs, deviled eggs, stuffed celery, hot soup (kept in a thermos), or even more hefty snacks, such as ready-to-eat chili, beef stew, or chowder, are recommended.

PLANNING FOR THE BIG EATER

I once met a nice fellow named John who volunteered to crew for me without pay. All I had to do was feed him. At first this seemed like a good deal—until I fed him and discovered how much he could eat—which was as much as the rest of the crew combined. John was big but lean. It became obvious that he had a metabolism which was different from ours and possibly from everyone else on the planet.

I discovered this on the very first day of his employment, when I made a yard long sub sandwich, intended for the crew of four—a pound of salami, a pound of cheese, six tomatoes, six eggs, two onions, three ounces of mayo, three ounces of salad dressing, lettuce, onions and pickled peppers, plus of course a salad, potatoes, wine and dessert. John thought the sub was for him—he ate the whole thing—and also a serving of the pasta which I had to make to replace the vanished meal.

Our food bill instantly doubled. John could inhale three chicken halves. He could romp through a four-pound steak and in fact had two fillet mignons for two, a complete dinner for four, at our End-of-the-Crossing celebration. His idea of a good breakfast was four to six eggs, a half-pound of bacon and a stack of hot cakes plus fruit, milk and cereal. In the evenings John would quietly slip away to some bistro on the quay, to quickly inhale three or four hamburgers.

I developed an acute conflict. As a chef I love to feed people and after all, a cook's way of expressing love is to feed everyone. But the cost was overwhelming—and it looked like we would need a bigger stove. I was making three chickens for dinner! And John would eat the leftovers. Anything. He was great crew and I didn't want to lose him, but something had to be done.

Over the years I have frequently met dissatisfied crew who felt that they were being starved by the captain. Correspondingly, the captains were indignant because they were buying what they considered adequate, good-quality, nourishing food and the crew was being unreasonable in their demands. In the old days such conflicts often led to mutiny and murder. Today it leads to ill feeling and a spoiled passage.

My solution was to feed John a special first course about half an hour before the meal. The special course was usually something very bulky that I could make easily and inexpensively. In the morning John got gargantuan bowls of hot cereal with raisins and dried fruit—followed by breakfast. At noon he often started out with a bucket of rice with vegetables and a little chopped salami, followed by lunch. At night we usually served him a pre-antipasto pasta—he would get two or three quarts of spaghetti carbonara, fettuccine Alfredo or boiled potatoes with garlic mayonnaise, followed by our usual very complete dinner. I watched this and couldn't believe it. I couldn't believe it at every meal. I still can't believe it, but it happened. In conclusion, ignore logic and feed reality.

John inhaling the "sub"

TESTED TRANSATLANTIC MEAL PLANS

Make a menu for a week and show it to the crew to be sure there are no strong objections. Create a **tally sheet**. Multiply the quantities by the number of weeks in the voyage plus a 15% reserve. You now have a **provisions list**. The sample meal plans which follow are for hungry crews on long passages. Make your own plan taking into consideration the appetites and food restrictions of your crew and the season. Buy an extra sack of fresh provisions just before you sail.

CREATING A PROVISIONS LIST

How does a menu become a tally sheet and then a provisions list? We submit here two lunches as examples. Each meal serves four. When tallying ingredients, be sure to include everything you need to complete a week's menu.

I. **Curried lentil soup** with bacon
Sliced onions,
Carrot and raisin salad,
Fruit
Beer

II. **Spaghetti Carbonara**
Olives
Artichoke, pickled beets
Red wine

MEAT
Bacon (1/4 pounds) .... /

CARBOHYDRATES
Lentils (cups) .... ////
Spaghetti, pound .... /

VEGETABLES, TINS
Olives, black (tins) .... /
Artichokes (jars) .... /
Pickled beets (tins) .... /

FRUIT
Raisins (cups) .... /
Apples .... //
Oranges .... ///

BEVERAGES (multiply by number of crew)
Red wine (bottles .... /
Beer (tins) .... //
White wine (bottles) .... /

MISCELLANEOUS
Chicken bouillon cubes .... //
Olive oil (cups) 1/4
Eggs .... //
Parmesan, grated (cups) .... //
Honey (cups) 1/4
Mayonnaise (cups) 1/4

SPICES
Bay leaf .... /
Curry powder (tablespoons) .... //
Ginger (tablespoons) .... /
Salt & pepper ....

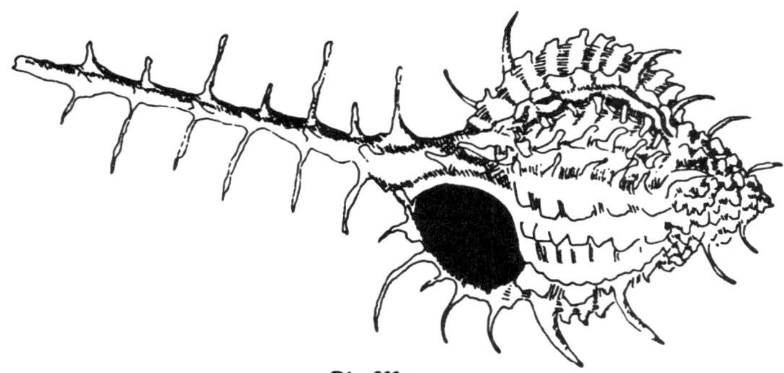

The Murex

A mollusk of the Mediterranean and Atlantic African coast collected in ancient times to use as a dye. Quantities of Murex were crushed in vats and cotton cloth was soaked in the mixture. When the cloth was exposed to sunlight it turned a permanent purple, called Royal Purple in ancient times.

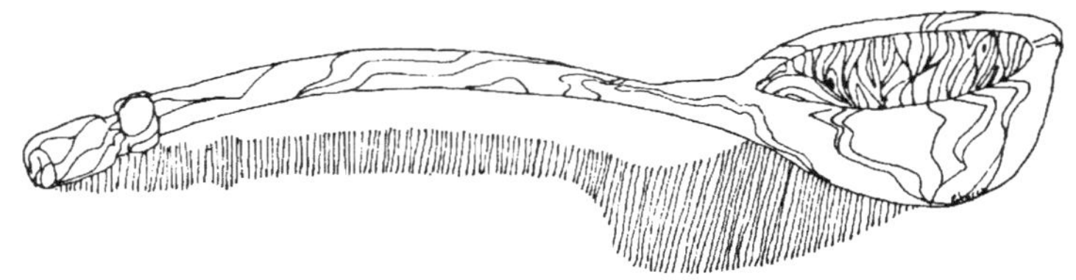

SEVEN-DAY MEAL PLAN

BREAKFAST	LUNCH	DINNER
Scrambled Eggs; Bacon; Toast; Butter, Jam, Oranges; Coffee with Cream; Drinks	Pessure-cooked Whole Chicken; Sliced Onion, Carrot & Raisin Salad; Bread; Cheese; Drinks	Curried Lentils Cooked in Chicken Broth with Carrots, Onions, Mushrooms; Bread, Rice, Leftover chicken; Cheese; Salami; Fruit; Beer/ Red Wine; Drinks
Mushroom & Onion Omelet; Toast; Jam; Cheese; Sliced Apples; Tea/Coffee.	Tuna Salad Sandwiches; Boiled Potatoes Tossed with Rosemary, Olives, Artichokes; Cheese; Drinks	Atria Beef/pasta; Steamed Carrots w/ Butter, Olives & Onions; Chocolate Chip Cookies; Red Wine; Drinks
Scotch Eggs; Fried Ham; Fried Toast; Butter; Jam; Coffee/Drinks	Split Pea Soup, Smoked Ham Hock, Ham; Croutons; Onion Slices;Cheese and Crackers; Beer; Drinks	Creamed Tuna Pasta; Steamed Turnips with Olives, Artichoke hearts, Parmesan Cheese; Fruit Salad; White Wine; Drinks
Pancakes with Maple Syrup; Sausages; Hard Boiled Eggs; Oranges; Hot Chocolate with Cinnamon	Leftover Pea Soup; Melted Cheese Sandwiches; Boiled Eggs; Cookies; Drinks	Stir Fried Beef with Vegetables in Mushroom Sauce; Bread; Fruit Slices; Nuts; Red Wine; Drinks
Hot Cereal with Dried Fruit; Bacon; Cinnamon Toast; Coffee	Potato Salad with Garlic Mayonnaise; Crackers; Apples; Cheese; Iced Tea	Artichokes with Hollandaise; Carrot & Raisin Salad; Sliced Fruit; Beer; Coffee
Cheese Omelet; Hash Brown Potatoes; Toast; Coffee	Ham Sandwiches with Onions, Mayonnaise, Mustard; Cole Slaw; Beer	Lentil Burgers; Steamed Cabbage or Sauerkraut; Pancake with Whipped Cream; Beer or Red Wine
Fresh Corn Bread with Syrup; Tinned Sausage; Orange & Apple Slices; Coffee	Bean Soup with Bacon & Onion; Cruising Salad Niçoise; Fruit Salad; V-8 Juice with Lemon	Spanish Fritatta Omelet; Melted Cheese on Crackers; Applesauce; White Wine

"THEREAFTER" MEAL PLAN

BREAKFAST	LUNCH	DINNER
Oranges; Cheese omelette; Bacon; Toast, Jam	Tomato Soup; Ham Sandwiches; Baked Beans; Candy	Beef stew with Peas, Carrots, Potatoes. Tinned Pineapple. Tinned Cake
Hot Applesauce; Soft-Boiled Eggs; Home Fries with Onions; Toast	Tuna Salad Sandwiches; Raw Vegetables; Boiled Eggs; Tinned Apricots	Hot Tuna Casserole; Buttered Noodles; Carrots; Peaches in Cream
Hot cereal with Raisins, Bananas; Fried Tinned Ham with Onions; Toast	Macaroni/Cheese; Antipasto of Olives, HB Eggs, Artichoke hearts, Cookies	Spaghetti with Tomato and Cheese Sauce. Green beans with Bacon; Garlic Bread
Pancakes with Syrup and Marmalade; Sausage; Grape Juice	Lentil Soup; Sardine Paté, Crackers; Antipasto: Salami and Cheese; Chocolate	Potato Pancakes; Apple Sauce; Sliced Cold Ham; Chocolate Pudding
Orange and Grapefruit Slices; Soft-boiled Eggs; Blueberry Muffins; Bacon;	Chile con Carne, Red Beans; Tomato Salad with Vinaigrette; Fruit; Cookies	Curried Chicken; Rice Pilaf; Turnips; Butterscotch Pudding; Oranges
Cold Cereal; Cheese Omelet; Toast with Melted Cheese and Tomato;	Chili Burgers; French fries; Tinned Peaches; Chocolate; Cheese; Mixed Nuts	Corned Beef Hash with Potatoes and Onions; Buttered Peas; Banannas Foster
Grapefruit; French Toast; Small Steak with Mushrooms	Salami and Cheese Sandwiches; Baked Beans; Olives; Carrot slices; Cookies	Candied Ham; Mashed Potatoes; Buttered Green Beans; Chocolate

SNACKS:
Mixed nuts; coconut chocolate; chip cookies; walnuts, parmesan; chunks & port; Fruit cake slices; apples tinned cheese; oatmeal cookies; dried apricots; sunflower seeds; oranges; artichokes on crackers; oatmeal cookies; oranges, grapefruit; hard-boiled eggs

BEVERAGES:
Beer (2 per person per day); red wine; white wine; port; V-8 juice; pineapple juice; grape juice; tea; coffee; Grand Marnier

Galley of Firewitch

2 The Galley

There's no use denying it, being a cruising chef is a demanding job. The galley is much smaller than your kitchen and all storage space is at a premium. The sink is much smaller than you are used to and often lacks hot water. Counter space is limited. You will have to develop the habit of washing and stowing galley gear as it is used, not just at the end of the meal.

WORK FLOW PLANNING is much more important than at home, where you have enough space to spread out and set half completed items aside. Your visits to the fridge or ice box must be carefully planned to avoid losing its precious cool. Good organization of icebox contents is important.

Make a list of what needs to come out of the box for the whole meal, then remove it all at once. Find a few spots where you can wedge things such as bowls of chopped food. When the vessel is underway lay a wet towel on the counter and set plates on it. This reduces slides.

Most of all, have patience. Don't be discouraged. With a few miles under your keel they will call you Master Chef.

DOING THE DISHES: When offshore or in a clean anchorage you can wash with sea water. **Coconut oil-based soap** works well with sea water because it lathers. Commercial dish soap does not lather but still works.

Sea water is hard water. It takes two or three times more sea water to rinse away soap and food particles than fresh water. Wash galley gear with hot sea water and if you can, rinse in fresh. The fresh water rinse reduces salt stains and corrosion.

If you have an adequate fresh water supply, you can wash with fresh water. Fill a kettle with fresh water and heat it. A gallon of fresh water is sufficient to wash the pots and plates of a meal for four. Pour the hot water on the sponge or rag, not on the plate. To avoid salt stains on plates, wipe them dry rather than air dry. Get them off the counter promptly.

ESSENTIAL EQUIPMENT

THE PRESSURE COOKER: If your vessel is big enough for just one pot, make it a pressure cooker. It may be used with the pressure valve on or as an ordinary pot with the valve off. Learn more about pressure cooking in Chapter 4. The pressure cooker will be mentioned again and again throughout this book. Learn to use it. I guarantee a whole new culinary vista will open to you both afloat and ashore.

THE STERN RAIL GRILL: Another extremely important galley tool is a good stern rail grill. If you do not own a home BBQ, I urge you to buy one so that you can begin to learn how to grill food. A grill is very useful on a boat, since it can produce wonderful food and keep the cooking heat and odor out of the main salon.

PLATES: Most yachtsmen use plastic plates because they are unbreakable but plastic plates scratch and become dull. Enamelware is tough but gets really hot! Heavy china plates break but they are cheap and easy to replace. They are our choice.

Paper Plates: Save a wash-up. Use paper cups and plates, particularly at sea. Paper plates can be thrown over the side at sea but at anchor they often float ashore or litter the bottom. Plastic or foam cups and plates should be stored for disposal ashore.

The most utilitarian drinking vessels for a boat are stainless thermal mugs, which cannot break, hold heat or cold and look good. You can buy plastic wine glasses but they look best in the chandler's showcase and go down hill from there. We prefer inexpensive glass wine glasses and replace them as they break.

POTS AND PANS: Pots and pans

coated with a non-stick surface are the cruising chef's first choice. They will save labor and water when cleaning up. Use wooden or plastic utensils to avoid scratching nonstick pots. Nonstick pots are inexpensive, found everywhere and are easily replaced. Stainless pots are not non-stick but last forever. Look for nesting pots if you have a stowage problem.

KNIVES: **Stainless steel** kitchen knives are also a best choice. They do not hold an edge as well as high carbon steel but they will not rust. Get a sharpening steel and file when you buy the knives.

FOOD PROCESSOR (BLENDER): You are really going to need a food processor for your boat. This means finding one that operates on DC or you will need a power inverter to supply AC. Do not leave port without a food processor.

OTHER IMPORTANT TOOLS

FOOD GRINDER: A food grinder is extremely useful to grind meat, tough mollusks, old chickens and to make chum for fishing.

VACUUM SEALER: A vacuum food sealer has many uses on a boat and allows you to store supplies in damp areas. It is also useful for protecting tools, electronic equipment, emergency supplies, even clothes. Get one.

COFFEE POT: Look for a squat stainless pot which will not easily tip. A good way to make filter coffee is with a funnel and thermos. Place the filter in the funnel and the funnel in the thermos. Wedge the thermos bottle in the sink to avoid tipping. Use a large funnel to avoid spills in rough seas.

If you are a cappuccino kind of person like myself buy a small espresso maker which will run off your inverter. A "moca maker" is a type of forced drip machine. It produces a slightly less intense coffee than espresso. It gets its heat from the stove.

POTATO BAKER OR STOVE TOP OVEN: If your galley lacks an oven, a potato baker can be used in its place. The type with a thermometer in the top is best.

GALLEY GEAR

POTS AND PANS

pressure cooker, 4-quart,
spare gasket and valve
twelve-inch skillet with lid
ten-inch fry pan with lid
one-quart covered double boiler set
three quart covered sauce pan
four-quart Dutch oven
twelve-inch wok (optional)
vegetable trivet
non-stick baking pan
non-stick muffin pan

KNIVES

paring knife, 5-inch (2)
chopping knife, 6 to 8-inch
filleting knife, 8-inch
serrated bread knife, 8-inch
cleaver or hatchet
sharpening steel, stone, file

MISCELLANEOUS
basting brush
bottle insulators, foam (4)
bottle stoppers,
can opener
cheese slicer
chopping block, wood, 10-inch
corkscrew/bottle opener
colander, plastic
crackers, crab (2)
grater, stainless, sheet type
ice pick
ladle, serving
meat hammer
measuring spoons
mixing bowls, nesting (3)
peeler, potato (2)
pot holders (2-4)
scaler, fish, plastic
scissors, heavy, stainless
salt and pepper shakers, flip top, two sets
spatula, straight blade
spatula, wok
scraper, rubber
spoon, drainer
spoon, large cooking (2)
striker and spare flints
whisk, medium

HERBS AND SPICES

The following list contains herbs, salts, and spices used in Cruising Chef recipes.

arrowroot
basil leaf, crushed
bay leaf
celery seed
chile powder
cinnamon
cloves, whole
cumin
curry powder
dill weed
fennel
garlic salt
ginger powder
marjoram, crushed
mint flakes
mustard, powdered
oregano
peppercorns
pickling spice
rosemary
sage
tarragon
thyme
turmeric

And, of course, don't forget plenty of **salt and pepper** in plastic bottles or vacuum sealed bags. Salt shakers made of aluminum or open-topped table shakers are useless on a boat. They permit the salt to become damp. Salt shakers with self-closing caps are good for long cruises, and small disposable units are excellent for weekends.

THE PANTRY LIST

almond extract
anchovies
artichoke hearts, marinated in oil
baking powder
beans, canned: kidney, black, chic pea
beans, dried: lentils, split pea, black-eyed
beef, canned, corned, stew
beer
bullion cubes: chicken, beef
bulger wheat (tabbouleh mix)
bread crumbs
bread or muffin mix
capers
cake mix
carbonated water
chili paste
chili peppers, dried
clams, tinned, chopped
clam juice
chocolate
clam juice, bottles

coconut milk, tinned or dried
coffee
consommé: chicken, beef
corn starch
crackers
cream, canned
curry paste: Madras, Punjab
dates
fois gras, small cans
flour, all-purpose, gravy flour
fruit, dried
grains: barley, cracked wheat,
honey
horseradish
jalapeños, jars, chopped
ketchup
kosher salt
marmalade: bitter orange, raspberry, apricot
mayonnaise, jars
milk, sweetened/unsweetened condensed
miso
mushrooms, dried
mustard, Dijon
nuts, whole and sliced: almonds, walnuts, pine nuts, macadamia, walnuts, pecans, peanuts
oils: olive, corn, peanut,
olives
oysters, smoked, in oil
pancake mix
pasta: spaghetti, linguini, macaroni, twists
peanut butter
pepper corns, black, red
pickles
popcorn
rice, assorted
salmon, canned
salsa
steak sauce: A-1, Lea & Perrins
sweet potatoes, tinned
soup: beef, chicken, tomato, creamed mushroom
soy sauce
spirits: Triple Sec, rum, sherry, brandy, port
sugar: white, brown
Tabasco sauce
tahini
tomatoes, Italian, whole
tomatoes, sun-dried
tomato paste, sauce
tuna, canned
vanilla extract
vinegar: white, balsamic, rice
wine
Worcestershire sauce

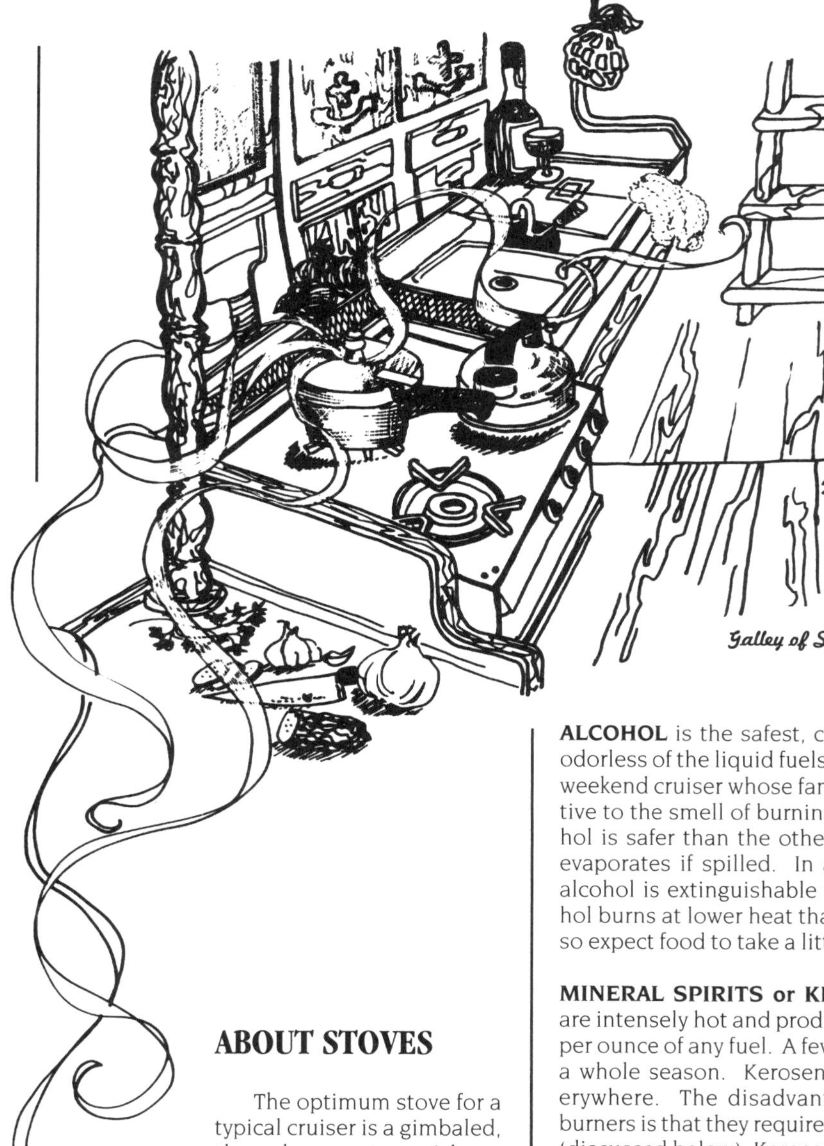

Galley of Sundancer

ABOUT STOVES

The optimum stove for a typical cruiser is a gimbaled, three-burner top with an oven. The galley of smaller vessels may only be big enough for a two burner stove without an oven.

All marine stoves should be gimbaled. **Gimbals** are pivots which keep the stove level when the boat is underway. The stove top should have **fiddles and rails** around it to keep pots from sliding off. Stainless stoves are beautiful but expensive. Camper stoves are cheaper and work just as well but sometimes lack fiddles and rails.

ALCOHOL is the safest, cleanest and most odorless of the liquid fuels. It is ideal for the weekend cruiser whose family may be sensitive to the smell of burning kerosene. Alcohol is safer than the other fuels because it evaporates if spilled. In addition, burning alcohol is extinguishable with water. Alcohol burns at lower heat than the other fuels, so expect food to take a little longer to cook.

MINERAL SPIRITS or KEROSENE stoves are intensely hot and produce the most heat per ounce of any fuel. A few gallons may last a whole season. Kerosene is available everywhere. The disadvantage of kerosene burners is that they require an alcohol primer (discussed below). Kerosene is a smelly fuel which takes some getting used to. Mineral spirits are more expensive than kerosene but burns cleaner and produces less odor.

Preheating: Alcohol and kerosene stoves burn vapor, not liquid. The liquid fuel is converted into vapor when it passes through a tube in the burner head. The tube must be preheated with alcohol. This can be an aggravating and occasionally exciting procedure. The alcohol primer pan must be completely filled or the vapor tube will not get hot enough, with dire results—blazing liquid fuel will spurt out of the burner head, run down the stove onto one's bare feet, enlivening the meal in an unexpected way. It will then be necessary to turn the burner off and fight the galley fire. You can then seek first aid while the burner head cools enough to re-prime.

PROPANE is hot, odorless, easy to use but highly explosive. Leaking propane is heavier than air and runs like water, especially on a cool day. It seeps through flooring and seeks the lowest spot in the boat—the sump under the engine. What a glorious bang it can make when the engine is started! Propane is best tamed by the development of good habits, especially turning it off at the tank with an electric switch in the galley. A propane "sniffer" alarm and a bilge blower provide added safety.

Propane is available almost everywhere in the world, but tank fittings vary from country to country. If you cruise, it is best to carry a spare fitting for your tanks, a few pieces of copper tubing and a flare tool. A local fitting can be used to make an adapter.

In isolated places, propane is often available only in individual tanks. A tank-to-tank adapter can be made and the full tank inverted over the empty one, partially filling it over a period of twenty-four hours. Propane is an excellent fuel if used properly.

LIQUID NATURAL GAS has all of the advantages of propane but it is lighter than air and is therefore less likely to cause an explosion. Unfortunately it is only sporadically available in the United States and is therefore not a cruiser's choice.

ALUMINUM TANKS are much more expensive than steel but are worth the price because they are lighter and do not rust. Store the tanks OUTSIDE, not in a locker or down below or buy a special locker with a vent tube. Small tanks are easier to handle than large ones. Keep in mind you will often be hauling them for miles down the road or beach. Keep the valves covered to avoid corrosion.

BACKUP SYSTEM: No boat is complete without a small backup burner with its own fuel supply, such as a gas camping stove with spare cartridges or a gas grill. Carry a one week reserve fuel supply.

ABOUT REFRIGERATORS AND ICEBOXES

REFRIGERATOR: A good refrigerator is one with plenty of insulation, easy to clean surfaces and a good drain. The bigger the box the better. You can make the space in a box smaller by stuffing a life jacket into it.

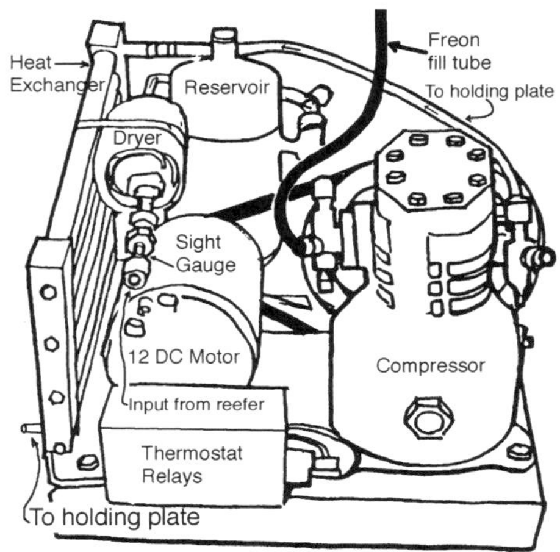

OPERATION: The cold in a marine refrigerator comes from a large tank (holding plate) located in the box. The holding plate contains a liquid which is frozen by a refrigerant gas which is piped through it. A marine freezer operates the same way but contains a liquid which freezes at a lower temperature.

A **compressor** drives the refrigerant gas through a **heat exchanger** which has its own separate water pump. The exchanger cools the gas as it travels to an **expansion valve** near the **holding plate** which allows the gas to expand and cool. The refrigerant then returns to a **reservoir** after passing through a **sight gauge** and a **dryer** which filters out moisture and debris. The sight gauge allows you to actually see the refrigerant while it circulates. Some refrigerant is colored and some is clear. If it is clear the best way to be sure the system is full (rather than empty) is to watch the sight gauge at the moment when the compressor is turned on. The gauge should be nearly full. A thin stream of fluid indicates a recharge is needed.

Small amounts of gas are normally lost at fittings and in the compressor. More refrigerant must be added once or twice per year. More frequent demands indicate an unacceptable leak.

When the refrigerator is started, the compressor must run a long time to freeze the liquid and chill the box. Thereafter a thermostat activates the compressor as needed, preventing the plate from defrosting. If the plate defrosts, considerable energy is needed to refreeze it. Avoid this.

EFFICIENCY: Marine refrigerators are much more efficient than home units but frequent opening of the doors to get drinks causes cold loss. Where ice is readily available carry an ice chest for drinks, reducing cold loss in the box.

During warm weather the compressor should run three or four times every 24-hours. Should yours run more often, examine the holding plate. If the plate fails to freeze the system may need a recharge or there may be ice crystals in the line, requiring a dryer change. Next, inspect the refrigerator's insulation. Feel the outside of the box, search for cold spots, indicating a gap in the insulation.

Sailors have a tendency to pack their refrigerators full. This interferes with the ability of cold air to circulate. Consider installing a small blower inside the box. Packing frozen food against the holding plate will often keep the food frozen but reduces the plate's efficiency. Stacking block ice against the plate has the same effect.

Ice is usually stuffed around the food before a cruise. This keeps it colder and reduces demands on the compressor. Buy blocks of ice and break them into large chunks. Don't buy crushed ice or cubes. They freeze into a cement-like mass.

MAINTENANCE: A holding plate contains some type of antifreeze (called eutectic fluid), which freezes below the temperature of water. As a result, when moist air contacts the holding plate it freezes on the plate, creating a coat of ice which interferes with the plate's efficiency.

This ice must be removed periodically and one is tempted to chip it away, an extremely dangerous procedure because the gas tubes or the holding plate may be damaged. The optimum method is to spray hot sea water on the ice. The plate can also be coated with silicone car polish which inhibits ice buildup.

A wise skipper with a mechanical refrigerator knows a bit about the mechanics of marine refrigeration. This includes a basic understanding of how the system works and how to charge it. Carry spare gas and dryers. Spare dryers to fit your particular 'fridge my be hard to find in foreign lands.

REFRIGERATOR COMPRESSORS and their water pumps require huge amounts of energy to operate, regardless of what the salesman tells you. The three most common energy sources used to drive refrigerator compressors are: (1) the vessel's engine, (2) the battery bank, or (3) AC electricity.

ENGINE-DRIVEN COMPRESSORS use the boat's motor as a power source. The engine will drive a big compressor which will chill the holding plate quickly. The disadvantage is that it will be necessary to run the engine every day as long as the box is in use. This annoyance multiplies over time, especially at the dock. Such a system also means you can't leave the vessel for a few days without shutting down the 'fridge. Some boxes contain a secondary system for use at the dock, but the more systems, the more failures.

BATTERY-DRIVEN COMPRESSORS are powered by a DC motor which runs off the boat's batteries. In port a charger keeps the batteries up. Offshore, the engine is usually run in the morning and everything which requires electrical energy is operated then.

AC COMPRESSORS: Larger vessels often use AC driven compressors. AC compressors are cheaper since they are more common and they are more efficient but they require a generator or big inverter.

ICE has the virtue of simplicity and is particularly useful for short cruises. If you do not plan to make long cruises, do not buy a mechanical refrigerator as they are expensive and maintenance-prone. Regardless of what any table tells you, ice will usually not last more than 4-5 days in summer. Block ice lasts longer than crushed. Jugs of juice or water can be frozen and then drunk when they defrost. Their added advantage is that they do not drip. Read more about ice selection on page 14. Fruit and vegetables set directly on ice are often damaged by the cold.

Pelicans in front of the Key Biscayne Light

3 The Basics

In this chapter you will find recipes for stocks and sauces which will be used as bases for many recipes in this book. Additional sauces, dips and marinades are found in Chapter 19. Take a look at this chapter so you will know where to look when we say *"make a roux"* or *"add to a white sauce"* . . .

BOUQUET GARNI

A collection of herbs used to enhance both the flavor and aroma of many stocks, soups and stews.

The vegetables (sometimes called a *mirepoix*):
a leek (traditional) or large onion halved or chopped
several carrots, chopped
several celery stalks or celery seed

The herbs:
a few peppercorns
1 teaspoon oregano
1 bay leaf
1 teaspoon thyme
1 sprig parsley

Traditionally the herbs in a *bouquet garni* are tied together inside a piece of gauze to keep them from adding debris to a stock or stew. You can also strain the stock or use the technique which is termed "calling the moose" by Arctic guides who use it to settle tea leaves. In this case you sprinkle a little cool consommé or wine from a pop bottle all over the surface of the soup holding the bottle a foot or two above it. The cool liquid sinks, taking the leaves with it.

STOCK

Stocks are the heart of so many recipes in this book, and are therefore very important. A good stock is far removed from canned consommé. We use consommé as the base for a hearty stock, which is a liquid packed with as much meat and vegetable essence as possible. The more meat and vegetables you use the better the stock will taste.

Traditionally a stock is the product of a *pot de feu*, a pot left to steam endlessly on the stove or next to an open fire. Into the pot goes all leftover scraps, bones and vegetable ends and out of it comes—a stock! Alas. One cannot keep a pot endlessly simmering on a boat. The nautical *pot au feu* is the pressure cooker.

If you have a crew of four you are well advised to buy some **consommé** in 1-1/2 quart cans which will be made into soup and some smaller (14-1/2 ounces) cans which can be used for gravy. Canned beef stock is found all over the world but chicken consommé is harder to find. You may therefore want to stock up on it.

You can also use **bouillon powder** as a stock base. The advantage is that the powder takes up little space and, if purchased in small packages and vacuum sealed, lasts a long time. Powdered bullion is extremely **hygroscopic**, which means that it absorbs moisture from the air. If a powdered bouillon container has been opened, be sure it is well sealed. In terms of quality, powdered bullion is a second choice over the canned product. One occasionally finds "gourmet" bouillon and this is preferred over the ordinary cubes found in the supermarkets.

In order to extract every bit of nourishment from the bones and vegetables in your pot, pressure cook for at least thirty minutes. Then remove the solids (which are cooked-out), strain and skim the stock.

When making a stock, NEVER add salt since the canned consommé is already salty and the salt flavor is concentrated as the liquid is reduced by cooking. All of our stocks contain the same basic ingredients:

consommé
a *bouquet garni*
as much meat, chicken or fish scraps and bones as possible

In addition to the standard herbs and vegetables, you can add other left over vegetables or parings.

ADDING WATER TO STOCK: Logic would dictate that if you put stock in a pan under a roast or in a soup, for example, and cooking reduces the volume, all one must do is add water to restore the lost volume. That sure makes sense to me. Unfortunately, when you do so you reduce flavor while restoring volume. I know this defies logic. Add more stock!

CHICKEN STOCK is made from every scrap of the chicken which is not going to be eaten including the backbone, head, feet, wing tips, liver and heart. Start with canned chicken consommé.

PORK STOCK (great for lentil and split pea soup) is made from smoked ham hocks, the ears, feet, other pork scraps and chicken stock. As second choice use salt pork, bacon, ham, canned pork or pork bones.

MEAT STOCK (other than pork) is made from any scraps of beef, veal or lamb and beef stock. We find beef consommé or bullion is too strong for us and must be diluted with wine. Fatty pieces of meat are okay as the stock will be skimmed later.

FISH STOCK: Typically a fish stock is made by boiling fish bones, vegetables and herbs in water or chicken stock for about twenty minutes. We prefer to use a technique called ***sweating***. First, one sautés the vegetables and a *bouquet garni* in a little oil. Use enough vegetables to make a layer about an inch deep in the pot. You can use cooking oil, olive oil, bacon fat or butter, depending on what flavor you wish to achieve.

The vegetables will not only add flavor, they will keep the fish above the liquid so that it will initially steam rather than boil. Sauté until soft. Then add a half glass of dry, white wine and as many fish heads, bones, ribs, etcetera as you have, 2-1/2 to 3 pounds is about right but feel free to stuff the pot full. The more the better and the more stock you get. Cover and simmer over low heat for about twenty minutes. The fish steams on top of the vegetables and this extracts all the juice. If you do not have enough liquid, add a little chicken stock. Pour through a strainer.

FUMET or FUMÉ: When making sauces with fish stock it is often advisable to make a *fumet*, which means you steam or simmer the fish stock to reduce its volume by half. This technique does NOT work for clam juice which is already concentrated and very salty.

COURT-BOUILLON is a light vegetable stock used for poaching fish. To make a flavorful vegetable stock it is necessary to use lots of vegetables—fill your pot full! Add the vegetables and herbs for a *bouquet garni* and sauté in a little oil or butter until soft. Add a glass of dry white wine, a cup or two of water or (better) fish stock. Simmer twenty minutes or pressure cook about eight minutes. Strain. After the fish is cooked, make the Court-Bouillon into a *fumet* for use as a sauce.

MISO STOCK: Mix miso in a chicken stock or beer. This makes a tasty non meat stock which can be pressure cooked with a *bouquet garni*.

SKIMMING STOCKS: The most effective way of skimming is by using a **fat separator** which is a cup with a spout which pours from the bottom of the cup, leaving the fat (and cholesterol) behind. Buy the four cup model. Also see page 75.

BASIC SAUCES

THE ROUX

A *roux* is a thickening paste made from fried flour and oil. It is used in soups, sauces and gravies. Flour is a good thickener, but

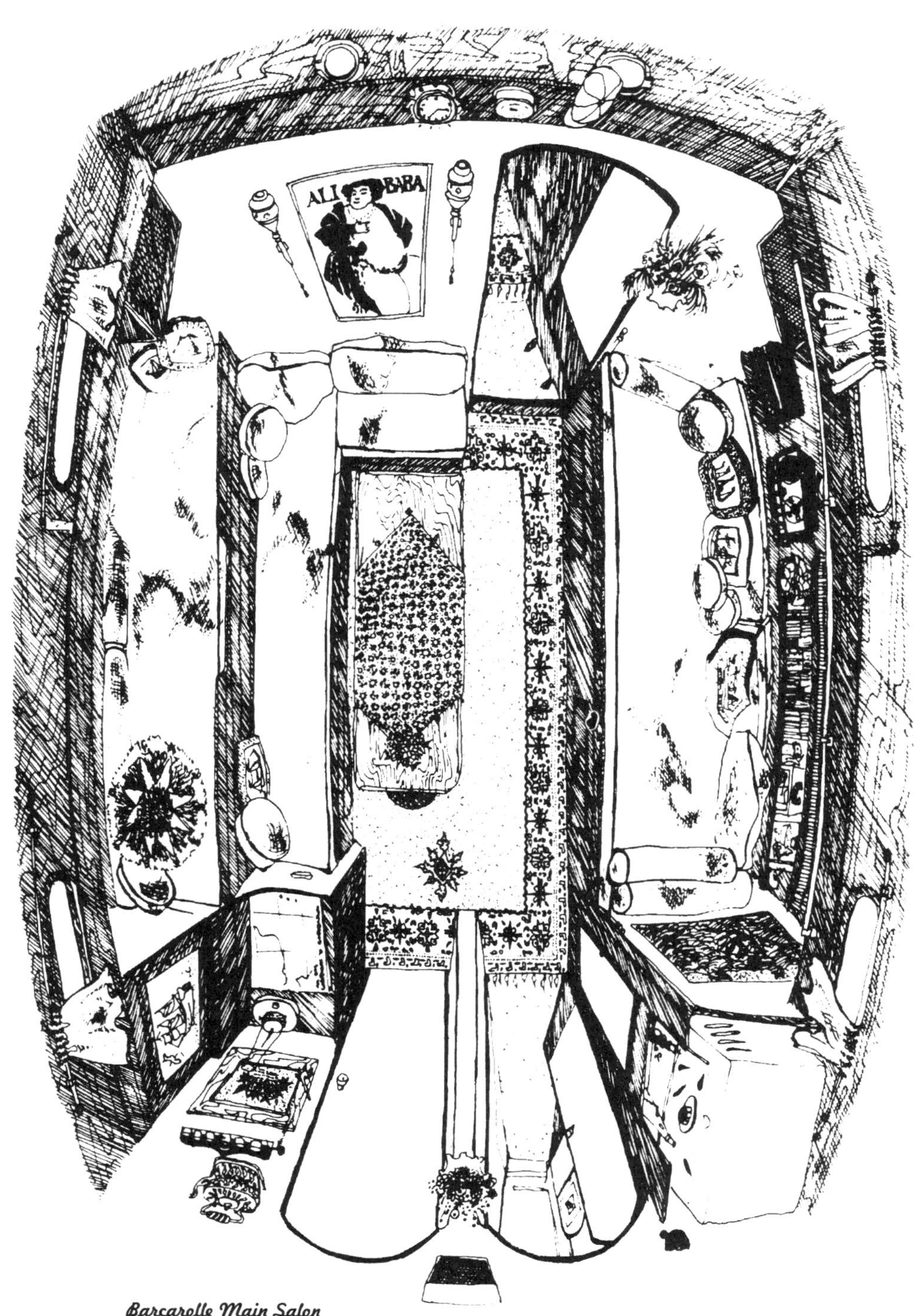

Barcarolle Main Salon

unless it is fried, it contributes a strong starchy taste to the food. **Gravy flour** is a specialized flour product designed to reduce the lumps which occur when flour is added to a hot liquid. When frying food, gravy flour can be lightly and carefully sprinkled on and it fries with the food. When a sauce is added, it bonds with the flour. This technique is called *braising*.

A roux is made from approximately equal amounts of oil and flour. To make a *roux*, fry three teaspoons unbleached, all-purpose flour (or gravy flour) in four tablespoons (a half stick) butter and two teaspoons cooking oil for three or four minutes over medium heat stirring frequently or until the flour is a light golden—NOT BROWN. Cool bottom of pot with a wet sponge to arrest further cooking. If you do not want to use butter, use oil instead. As soon as the flour is adequately fried, milk, stock, wine or some other liquid is added to the pan to make a basic sauce.

CLASSIC ROUX SAUCES

WHITE SAUCE (WHITE BÉCHAMEL): When the *roux* is finished, add 1-1/2 cup hot milk, a pinch of salt and white pepper and stir furiously. The porridge-like goo is a béchamel or white sauce base to which you can add many things.

INDIA SAUCE: Add as much curry powder to a white sauce as you wish. This gives a more delicate curry flavor and aroma than the classic curry sauce.

Moroccan cork grove

CHEESE SAUCE (MORNAY): Add half cup grated cheese to the white sauce and stir furiously. You can add Gruyère, which is classic, but any hard white cheese is OK. Thin with white wine as needed.

BROWN SAUCE OR GRAVY (BROWN BÉCHAMEL): Add a rich stock (which has been simmered until reduced by half) to a *roux* and use as the basis of a gravy, or to thicken stews. If you are making a gravy, cream can be added at the end.

AURORA SAUCE: To a béchamel sauce add tomato puree.

POULET SAUCE: To a béchamel sauce add lemon juice and a glass of white wine with an egg yolk beaten into it. Whisk furiously until thickened. Cool instantly.

FINE HERBS SAUCE: Simmer a variety of herbs, preferably but not necessarily fresh in the stock for a few minutes, add to a *roux* and thin with white wine.

GRAVY (BOREALIS SAUCE): Combine a cup each of dry red (or white wine) and stock, four crushed, chopped garlic cloves, a bay leaf and pepper. Simmer until reduced by half and add to a *roux*, whisking furiously. Add sautéed mushrooms if desired. This is a sauce for meat, chicken or fish and you use the corresponding stock.

MAYONNAISE SAUCES

If you think store-bought mayo is good, you haven't tried making your own. Mayonnaise is a sauce or dressing which evolved over thousands of years and its predecessor, aioli (creamy garlic dressing), predates the ninth century. Europeans make a big deal out of homemade mayo and each bistro takes great pride in their secret recipe. For some reason, the man of the house makes mayonnaise in France. Perhaps it's one of those "man" things, like grilling steaks.

In those pre-blender days of yesteryear a considerable amount of elbow grease was a big part of the mayo recipe. It called for copious whipping which was done on a slab of marble using the flat of a knife to whip up the emulsion. We use a food processor. If you do make fresh mayo, you will discover a light, fluffy sauce which is so delicious. This is NOT an end-of-the-passage sauce as it calls for very fresh eggs.

Mayo is an emulsion of egg yolk and olive oil. The trick is to get the oil into the yolk without breaking the sauce, in which case the oil and egg separate. Here are some things to remember:

- Use fresh eggs at room temperature.
- Never use less than three yolks to make the blender happy and reduce the amount of air whipped into the sauce.
- SLOWLY, SLOWLY dribble the oil into the blenderized yolks.
- Dribble in three or four tablespoons of oil and wait for the mixture to thicken before proceeding.
- If the mixture does not start to thicken within a few seconds the eggs are too old and will not thicken. More about that later.
- If you add the oil too fast or in excess and the mayo breaks, remove it and add another egg, then add the broken sauce a little at a time.

One last word: fresh mayonnaise is a fair weather dish. It simply will not bind together if the barometer is falling.

FRESH BLENDER MAYONNAISE

Add to blender:
3 egg yolks
1 teaspoon dry mustard

Start motor, slowly dribble in 2/3 cups olive oil. Dribble in two teaspoons lemon juice.

Add salt and white pepper to taste

I must confess that on occasion all of my attempts to raise a mayonnaise have failed. When that happens I run the blender until hell freezes over, then refrigerate the mixture, which has been stiffened somewhat with trapped air. This usually makes the mayo gel. You can sometimes make an uncooperative mayo go off by adding a little store bought mayo or a little garlic and lemon juice. If it still won't cooperate you can stiffen it with grated cheese, cottage cheese or stiff egg whites. Fresh mayo is worth the trouble!

MODIFIED MAYO RECIPES:

AIOLI: add and chop as much garlic as you dare and add to the mayo.

AVOCADO DRESSING: add avocado, cream cheese, hot sauce, lemon juice, garlic.

CURRY MAYO: Add two or three teaspoons curry paste (see below) to one cup of mayo (for seafood).

DILL MAYO: add powdered dill and a little more dry mustard.

GREEN GODDESS: Anchovies, Italian parsley, chives, scallions, garlic and equal amount of sour cream.

MUSTARD MAYO: add dry mustard, lemon juice and honey.

NIÇOISE SAUCE: add tomato paste, red pepper, chives and tarragon.

REMOULADE MAYO: add remoulade sauce, capers, anchovy paste, cilantro or parsley and chives.

RUSSIAN DRESSING: add ketchup, horseradish, lemon juice and honey.

TARTAR SAUCE: add relish, capers, chopped egg white, parsley, Dijon mustard and lemon juice.

THOUSAND ISLAND DRESSING: to Russian dressing add sweet relish.

TOMATO SAUCES

MARINARA SAUCE

You can make a great, light tasting marinara sauce from fresh Italian tomatoes which have been lightly steamed—to facilitate skin removal—then thoroughly squeezed to remove the seeds. Makes 3 cups.

1 can (35 ounces) Italian tomatoes, squeezed, chopped
3 teaspoons olive oil
1/2 cup chopped onion
6 cloves garlic, chopped
1/2 cup rich red wine
1/2 cup Italian parsley, chopped
2 teaspoons tomato paste
2 teaspoons each: oregano flakes, basil, thyme
juice of 1/2 lemon
pinch of sugar, salt pepper

Sauté the onions and garlic until onions are soft. Add remaining ingredients and simmer for twenty minutes.

TOMATO CREAM: Liquefy tomato sauce and replace half of the milk in a white sauce with it. This sauce goes well over fish and pasta.

CURRY

Curry powder is a combination of spices which include: coriander, turmeric, chilies, salt, cumin, garlic, ginger, cinnamon, cloves, anise, and mustard. However, curry powder is NOT curry. You may get a bit of curry flavor by just dumping curry powder into something and there are recipes which call for this; but all of the curry recipes in this book call for a beginning from **curry paste**.

Curry paste is made by sauteing curry spices, fresh herbs and vegetables in oil. The result is a intensely flavorful dough-like mixture which is added to cooking meat, vegetables or fish. You can make a curry paste from curry powder as follows:

CURRY PASTE

1 medium onion, finely chopped or grated and squeezed
1 hot pepper, seeded and chopped
4 teaspoons oil
8 cloves garlic, chopped
1/2 cup cilantro
1/2 cup parsley
4 teaspoons curry powder

Sauté onions in oil until soft. Add curry powder. Add more of the individual spices mentioned above as desired. Sauté until strong curry smell disappears, two to four minutes. Add all other ingredients and simmer for twenty minutes. Cool and liquefy as desired with coconut cream, wine, fruit juice—some people use whiskey.

You now have a curry paste. You can save much trouble by purchasing the **prepared curry paste** in a jar. Curry is spicy but does not have to be blazing hot. If you want mild curry, buy Madras curry. If you want hot curry, buy Punjab curry and make it even hotter, if desired by adding chili paste.

THAI CURRY SAUCE

This recipe calls for coconut milk and sweet potato. These are extremely delicious additions. You can use stock or wine to thin.

3 rounds (1/2 inch thick) of a medium sweet potato fresh or canned, peeled and chopped
1 cup coconut cream
1 cup chicken stock
3 teaspoons medium curry paste, or as much as you wish
juice of 1 lemon
3 teaspoons honey
1 teaspoon each ginger, cumin
1/2 cup currants, raisins or other dry fruit (more about this later)
6 cloves garlic, roughly chopped

Simmer ingredients until potato is soft. Mush everything and correct seasoning. Curry without sweeteners is bitter. Honey is added for this purpose and so is dried fruit. You can use any dried fruit and dried cherries, blueberries even chopped apricots are great. You can also withhold the dried fruit, cook the rest until done and liquefy in the blender to give a creamy appearance, then add the fruit and simmer for a few minutes.

When sauce is cooked add whatever you are currying and simmer until done. Vegetable curries do well with turnips, carrots, squash and potato added. If you are currying chicken or meat, grill, cool and slice before adding for additional flavor. You can even drop raw eggs into the bubbling pan and serve curried eggs. You can mix with shredded crab, shrimp or flaked fish and serve cold in an avocado. Also add to split pea soup. Add to mayonnaise and serve on canned tuna or fresh seafood.

BREADING MIX

1 loaf old white bread
3 teaspoons dry thyme
2 teaspoons oregano
2 teaspoons sage
1 teaspoon pepper
olive oil

Brush bread with a mixture of the other ingredients and toast in a pan. Cut into cubes, return to pan and toss until browned and dry. Allow to steam cool in the pan.

Crush. For variety you can also add crushed corn flakes, crackers, or matzo meal.

CHLORINATED WATER MIXTURE

1 cap bleach to two gallons (a bucket) sea water

GLOSSARY OF COOKING TERMS

Al dente: Term mainly used for pasta. Chewy and slightly underdone. Offering some resistance to the teeth.

Blanch: Term mainly used for vegetables. Plunge briefly into boiling water to set color, loosen skins and prepare for additional cooking.

Blenderize: Finely chop, mince or liquefy food in a food processor.

Braise: Term used in pan cookery. To first fry food, then simmer it in a sauce.

Chicken's ass: The area under a chicken's tail.

Contaminate: Introduction of bacteria and/or mould to food by handling and/or cutting. Food is decontaminated by washing it in chlorinated water or, in the case of meat, fish, or fowl, by washing in vinegar. Contamination accelerates the spoiling of food.

Court-Bouillon: A liquid in which to poach fish. Consists of water or stock, wine, vegetables, and herbs. See recipe in this chapter.

Critter: An animal you are going to eat so-named to avoid personalizing it.

Crush: A process usually applied to spices and vegetables. To smash beneath the flat of a knife which is struck by a fist.

Deglaze: Liquefaction of cooking essence (brown stuff stuck to bottom of pan) for use in a sauce. Consists of adding wine, beer or stock to the pan, then rubbing pan briskly with a scraper.

Dredge: To sprinkle flour, bread crumbs or corn meal over food prior to frying. The same effect is achieved by shaking pieces of food in a bag with flour or corn starch.

Drippings: The liquid and goo in the bottom of a roasting pan. Used to make sauces. Very fatty and must be skimmed. Pan is often *deglazed*.

Drizzle: Slowly pour a thin stream of liquid, such as olive oil.

Eviscerate: To gut an animal.

Fillet: A boneless cut of meat or fish.

Flambé: Term mainly used with desserts. To pour hot liquor over food and ignite it.

Gratin (**Gratinée**): a sauce used mainly with seafood or vegetables. Sauce made of grated cheese and bread crumbs, drizzled with butter or oil and usually baked, then briefly broiled, to brown the bread crumbs.

Julienne: Term used mainly for vegetables. To cut into very thin strips.

Marinate: To soak in a **marinade**, a combination of liquids, usually wine, lemon, vinegar or a fruit juice (the acid), olive oil, herbs, and spices for the purpose of tenderizing and/or improving flavor. **Acid Marinade**: a marinade in which acidic juices such as lemon juice dominate. Frequently used to soften food. **Oily Marinade**: A marinade where the oil dominates for the purpose of adding succulence.

Reduce a liquid by simmering it.

Sauté: Term used for fry pan cookery. To simmer in a liquid or a light oil.

Ceviche (Seviche): A dish made by marinating fish in a pickling solution made of lemon and/or lime juice and spices. Process produces a poached effect.

Sweat: Term refers mainly to fish cookery. To steam liquid out of a fish to make a stock.

Zest: The outer, moist, colored part of a citrus fruit skin.

Ziploc: The registered trade name of a closure developed by The Dow Corporation.

Admiralty Head Light

4 Special Cooking Techniques

ABOUT GRILLING

Every boat should have a stainless steel grill which will produce an endless supply of wonderful meals. Grilled food not only tastes delicious, it keeps the cooking heat and odor out of the boat. A grill is also a back-up device, capable of replacing the ship's stove if it should fail. Marine grills are usually connected to the stern rail so that the smoke blows away from the vessel when it is anchored. Grills placed on lifeline stanchions occasionally are damaged when docking.

SELECTING A GRILL

MARINE GRILLS are made of non-corrosive materials and are therefore more expensive than onshore models. In addition marine grills are designed to clamp onto the stern rail, an important feature. Sparks and embers ejected from the grill drop into the sea.

Mild steel land grills rust very quickly in the marine environment and shed quantities of rust flakes which stain whatever they touch. Using a grill which is not clamped to something solid (like the stern rail) is very risky on a boat.

Gas Grills are extremely convenient, clean, ready to use and add less carbon product to the food than charcoal. Light a gas grill, wait a few minutes, then cook. The heat is easily controlled and gas grills require little maintenance. Leave them on for a few minutes after cooking to carbonize remaining juices. Much of the flavor attributed to charcoaled food can be replaced by using aromatic wood chips when cooking with gas.

Most gas grills are fueled from (expensive) canisters and you should maintain a supply of them since they can provide an alternate source of heat if the ship's stove fails. Gas grills can also be adapted to run from larger tanks to reduce cost. When it comes to convenience there's nothing like a gas grill.

Charcoal/Wood Grills: You can't beat charcoal or driftwood for flavor and that is wood fuel's main attribute. One has only to experience the joy of a driftwood-grilled fish to know that! In addition, charcoal grills, are reliable. This is a virtue, since everything else on the vessel is busy falling apart.

Unfortunately, charcoal/wood grills are dirty and fill up with ash. One must wait an endless half-hour to get a good bed of coals. Charcoal is dirty to store, the paper sack it comes in disintegrates. Charcoal absorbs moisture and the dust goes everywhere.

Despite charcoal's many disadvantages I like it. It is available almost everywhere in the world and the beaches are full of driftwood—at the right price. Be sure you have a strong, waterproof sack with a closure and dump your charcoal into it. Let the bag stand open once in awhile to drive off moisture.

COOKING WITH CHARCOAL: Charcoal burns off into glowing coals which provide hot, even heat. In foreign countries charcoal is often sold in chunks, not briquettes. **Chunks** are pieces of carbonized wood. Chunks start slower and burn hotter than briquettes. When using chunk charcoal it is important to break up the bigger pieces so that everything burns evenly. Chunk charcoal also sparks and pops on occasion, so beware. **Briquettes** are made from ground, pressed, carbonized wood. Briquettes provide uniform heat and form a bed of coals faster than chunks since they are honeycombed with air pockets.

Charcoal starters include kerosene, cooking oil, paint thinner, even candle wax. Don't be fussy, this is war. By far the best way to use starter fluid is to impregnate wads of paper, then stack the charcoal over them. The flames then originate at the bottom of the pile. If you just pour on the charcoal starter, you will have to reignite the charcoal several times, an exciting and frequently terrifying process. Starter fluids burn off long before the coals are ready for use and do not flavor the food.

Charcoal usually takes thirty minutes to burn into a bed of coals covered by fine ash. If you start cooking before the coals are ready the long flames from the charcoal produce a sooty flavor which is unpleasant. A single layer of briquette coals will cook most foods and last about an hour. Two layers will cook a large roast. Three layers will incinerate everything.

COOKING WITH DRIFTWOOD (OPEN FLAME COOKERY): Pick driftwood above the high tide line. The ideal thickness is about 1-1/2 inches. Size consistency is important. Dissimilar sizes burn at different rates. Hardwood is best. If you can break a 1-1/2 inch stick without real effort it's soft wood. Try to pick wood that will fit your grill without cutting. Be sure the wood is dry and free from paint and tar. Smell it and reject rotten wood. Bark covered wood should be examined for insect pests.

Kindling: Twigs can be collected to use as kindling. Soft wood, dry coconut fronds and brush make good kindling Dry coconut fronds burn hot as blazes but are resinous and make a smoky start.

Building a Fire: The chef builds a wood fire in three stages: First, the kindling: waded paper is okay but do not use a petroleum chemical starter as the flavor will linger in the wood. A little cooking oil on crumbled newspaper serves as good kindling if twigs are not available. Next, soft wood is laid over the kindling in a steep cone or teepee. Finally, when the softwood is roaring, mash it down and lay on a bed of hardwood which will then cook the meal. Keep mashing everything down into as even a bed as possible.

Controlling the Heat: When the hardwood is roaring, set the lid ajar on the grill to begin gaining control over the raging monster you have created. Driftwood produces an extremely hot fire which needs lots of oxygen, so adjust the lid and draft carefully to avoid extinguishing it. Wood fires in a grill burn directly to ash. The grill lid traps the smoke for flavor but gets really hot. Use a mitt when handling it.

Open Flame Cookery is an art and is quite different from cooking with gas or charcoal. Wood cooking is fast—four or five minutes per side usually does it. Flame-broiled food should be turned several times to avoid scorching. Thicker cuts can be first braised, then grilled for flavor. Quarter to half-inch thick cuts are best. Thinner cuts finish dry. Thicker cuts result in food which is scorched on the outside and raw on the inside. Thicker cuts can also be turned frequently or basted with a marinade to reduce scorching. Stay close to the grill andkeep a good watch. Thin slices of tender steak, firm fish like swordfish and tuna or any meat which can be served rare to medium rare are delicious when cooked over open flames.

GRILLING TOOLS

- Stainless steel **tongs** are ideal for handling coals and turning food—don't make holes in food like a fork. Tie a loop of

line through handle to hang on the grill.
- Wire grill brush in a small cloth bag with drawstrings. Hang bag on the grill.
- Water bottle with a spray nozzle to extinguish grease fires.
- Stainless skewers are better than wooden ones and don't rust.
- Rag impregnated with vegetable oil (kept in a plastic bag) to wipe over the grill. Prevents sticking.
- Also useful: basting brush, suction baster, large flat spatula.

ABOUT GRILLS AND DAVY JONES: Most of the parts of a marine grill are attached to each other to prevent loss. The grate is usually not attached. The last time I saw my grill grate it was sinking to a mucky grave in an alligator infested basin. I could in fact hear the young alligators chirping, presumably in anticipation something more edible to follow—like a leg. The water was just twelve feet deep but my grapple failed to find the elusive grill. My magnet would not attract stainless steel. The little boys hanging around the pier apparently thought their lives were worth more than the ten dollars I was offering for the grill's recovery. There were no volunteers to go play with the alligators.

GRILLING TECHNIQUES

HEAT CONTROL: Most grills have **draft holes** in the bottom and adjustable **vent holes** in the lid. The bottom of the grill should be free of ash to allow air to enter the draft holes. During start-up the lid is left off or just used as a wind shield. When the coals are glowing nicely the lid is clamped on tight a few minutes before the cooking process begins, to bring the grill to a high, even heat. You want the air to enter through the draft holes (not under the lid), pass through the hot coals to the food, then exit by the vent. Air flow is controlled by opening and closing the vent holes in the lid. Partially closing the vent retards the expulsion of exhaust gasses and this reduces the inflow of oxygen. The food cooks slower and the coals last longer. Completely closing the vent kills the fire.

PREVENT SCORCHING-SWEPT COALS-THE PIE PLATE METHODS: Fat from meat or chicken often drips onto the coals and ignites. The resulting grease fire chars the food. You can prevent grease fires by sweeping the coals to one side of the grill, then cooking the food on the other side so that fat does not drip onto live coals.

You can also sweep most of the coals to the edges of the grill, and place a disposable pie plate under the grate. The grease drips onto the plate and boils away, rather than onto the coals, where it will burn. The sloped edge of the pie pan vents heat around the food. Grilled food takes longer to cook this way—up to forty minutes for chicken halves, but is worth the wait! Use this technique. You will always produce delicious, unscorched food.

USE OF A RACK: You can also use a small rack in a shallow pan to catch drippings. Add a little water, wine or stock to the pan. Replenish the liquid as needed, don't let the pan dry out. Use the drippings to baste the meat. Food cooked on a rack does not need to be turned, so this is useful when cooking roasts. If wood is not used to make smoke, the drippings can be made into gravy. Smoke usually (but not always) taints the drippings.

ROASTING on a grill means cooking food in a pan containing a liquid which is replenished as the food cooks. This is a good technique for tough meat or mature birds which are tenderized by slow cooking in a tenderizing liquid. Allow forty minutes. Liquids containing red wine and/or tenderizer help break down the fiber in tough meat. The big advantage of grill roasting is that it is done outside, keeping the boat free from the heat. Use a disposable pan as this method is messy.

The meat or chicken is first seared thoroughly on a hot grill, then dropped into the pan. A typical roast liquid might contain an inch of chicken stock, wine or beer. You can also add tomatoes, zucchini, chopped potato and onions which cook into a thick sauce. After twenty minutes I usually add: carrot chunks, small whole potatoes, celery, garlic, pepper and oregano. As soon as the sauce is bubbling cover with aluminum foil and reduce the heat.

AROMATIC WOOD CHIPS such as **mesquite** or **hickory** may be added to a charcoal fire and the smoke will flavor the food. The wood should be soaked in water, preferably overnight. The water makes the wood smoke, not burn, which is desired. The wood is added when cooking begins. Place chunks at the edge of the fire. Keep spraying them to prevent ignition. You can also place chips in an aluminum pan or foil pouch to keep them from burning. Use the sprayer often. When the wood begins to smoke, peak under the lid. The smoke should not extend down to the coals, smothering them.

MARINADES: A marinade is a liquid mixture in which food is soaked BEFORE cooking. A marinade penetrates the raw food and alters its flavor. Garlic in oil and soy have particularly penetrating qualities and are frequently used in marinades. Powdered mustard, pepper sauces, lemon and honey cling well to food. A papaya tenderizer can be added to soften tough meat. Marinades are frequently used when grilling. Oily marinades are particularly important when cooking seafood to prevent drying. Learn more about marinades in Chapter 19.

BBQ SAUCES

BBQ SAUCE is a thick liquid brushed over food which has already been sealed by heat. It is therefore used late in the cooking process. For example grill sauce is brushed on chicken when the skin is crispy and golden and the chicken is almost done. BBQ sauce brushed on raw chicken results in a stewed chicken with rubbery skin. When cooking with driftwood, sauces should be a little thinner than normal so that they do not interfere with the cooking process, which is brief.

SPICY BACON BBQ SAUCE

1/4 pound bacon, smoked if possible, finely chopped
1 onion, grated and squeezed
8 cloves garlic, chopped
2 tablespoons hot chile pepper sauce
1 tablespoon cumin
1 tablespoon each, pepper, oregano
1 can chicken stock
2 cups ketchup
1/2 cup cilantro, chopped
1/2 cup brown sugar
juice of 1 lemon
2 tablespoons steak sauce

Fry the bacon until golden, drain and blot. Add remaining ingredients and simmer twenty minutes. Pour in a jar while still boiling hot. Cap loosely. When cool, cap and refrigerate for up to a week.

CLASSIC BBQ SAUCE

Use for meat or fowl; makes a lot of sauce so reduce quantities as necessary.

Combine:
14 ounces ketchup
1 onion, finely chopped
4 tablespoons Worcestershire sauce
2 tablespoons brown sugar
1/2 cup vinegar
1 tablespoon Dijon mustard
1 tablespoon each cayenne pepper, cumin, coriander, paprika
1/2 tablespoon ginger
4 cloves garlic, chopped
3 tablespoons vegetable oil

REHEATING GRILLED FOOD: You may reheat grilled food by placing it in a Ziplock and dropping into boiling water. Grilled food also reheats well in a microwave. Pan reheating dries the food, so add a few tablespoons of water to the pan and cover.

GRILLING FOWL

SELECTION: Buy only young chickens, not more than four pounds. Capons (gelded roosters) are larger, up to eight pounds and very tender. Treat like a turkey. Larger chickens are too tough for the grill. Turkeys may be as heavy as eight pounds. If heavier they will not fit in the grill. Ducks should not weigh more than six pounds.

PRE-GRILL: Brush fowl with oil before grilling. You can add hot chilies, chili mix, red pepper, or mustard to the oil. You can make a mush of lemon juice, balsamic vinegar, garlic and an herb like cilantro, cumin, rosemary, thyme or sage and a little sugar. Make pockets under the skin of the bird with your finger and fill with mush. Kneed evenly under the skin. This flavors the birds, makes them more juicy but also slightly increases the cooking time. Very tasty.

ROASTING IN A PAN: Ship grills are small and it is hard to find a pan which fits them. A makeshift pan can be made from layers of aluminium foil. Add chicken stock, beer or wine to the pan and renew it constantly. Add a few carrots and chopped onion to enhance the stock. Never allow the pan to dry out. The juice and drippings make a potent gravy. Use a small rack which keeps the bird from being stewed.

PROTECTING THE SKIN: Grills are much hotter than ovens and care must be taken to protect the skin from scorching. (1) An oiled cloth can be placed over the breast or other parts as they begin to brown. The oil can be renewed or the cloth can be frequently basted with pan juices. (2) Slices of orange are also effective for flat areas. (3) A piece of aluminium foil can be pressed over endangered parts. (4) A sauce or thick marinade can be brushed over the skin.

SAVING THE NUKED BIRD: If you have cooked the bird too fast and the skin is charring you can paint the skin with BBQ sauce or a glaze, such as honey and lemon juice. You can retard further damage to specific areas with slices of orange. The breast can be covered with bacon strips, or a cloth impregnated with oil. Any part of the bird which is cooking too fast can be protected with aluminum foil. If a grease fire has scorched your bird you are better off removing it from the grill, allowing it to cool, skinning and trimming the char, then pan finishing in a rich or hot sauce. A pan finish with grilled peppers, pepper, cumin, garlic and butter is excellent.

WHEN IS IT DONE? If you have not nuked your bird, it is done when its skin is a crisp, golden color. You may also test for doneness with a toothpick or (better) a wooden skewer stuck deep into the drumstick joint. Juice from joints should be yellow, no blood. Don't stab the poor thing to death, make as few holes in the bird as possible. Juice from meat should run clear. If no juice runs, the bird is overcooked. The interior of the breast should be hot but not burning. The toothpick should steam when removed.

CHICKEN

GRILLING WHOLE CHICKEN: Buy whole birds because they stay fresh longer than cut up pieces. Cook them whole for convenience. The best way to cook a whole bird: Open the bird by removing the backbone. Fold legs flat and slip drumstick ends through a flap in the skin, brush all over with

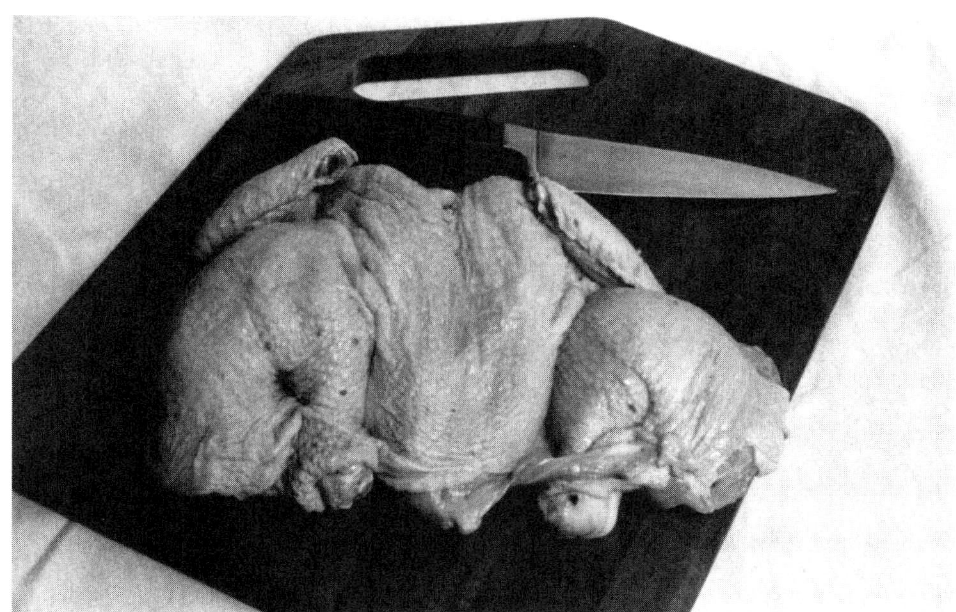

Whole chicken ready for the grill

a little oil or marinade, place it on the grill skin up with the pie pan beneath. Using this technique the thighs, which take longer to cook are closer to the heat and the breasts are near the cooler center. The bird takes thirty to forty minutes to grill and does not need to be turned. This is the best way to grill a chicken. Trust me. It makes the bird easy to handle and reduces the chance of losing it over the side. Fowl can be grilled before the meal until not quite done, then cooled, cut up and pan finished in a variety of sauces. Delicious.

CUTTING UP A WHOLE CHICKEN: The technique illustrated below divides the bird into five pieces, allowing you to debone the breast meat easily before serving. (1) Remove legs (2) Remove wings with portion of breast meat (3) Debone breast

GRILLED CHICKEN PARTS: Cut up pieces take about twenty minutes to cook and should be turned several times to prevent scorching.

FINISHING IN BACON FAT: Notwithstanding our modern horror of bacon fat, a classic technique is to sprinkle bacon fat brought almost to combustion temperature onto the chicken at the last moment, before removing from the grill. This adds a very little fat to the skin and produces a delicious taste.

PREPARING DOMESTIC DUCKS, GEESE AND TURKEYS: A six to eight pound whole, uncut bird will fit inside a shipboard grill but it needs a little help. We usually help it by first wrapping it in a moist towel, then setting something heavy like a tool box on it for a half-hour to flatten. We admit to having just jumped on a bird or two on occasion to achieve this goal. It is extremely unwise to stuff a bird which is to be flattened.

High heat is the enemy of a whole bird. Use two layers of coals and the pie pan deflector. Allow **eight minutes per pound** cooking time unstuffed, twelve stuffed. This is much less than recommended for oven roasting. Aromatic wood is recommended.

GRILLING DUCKS, GEESE AND WILD BIRDS: Domestic ducks and geese are really fatty birds which should be halved or quartered and defatted as much as possible. The best way to defat a duck is to chill it and pull off the lumps of fat. Skinning and trimming is extremely effective for reducing fat, but the grilled skin is delicious. Whole birds must be cooked slowly on a rack with a pan and should be frequently basted. Prick the skin all over before grilling to allow fat to drip out and be sure to use the pie pan to reduce heat and to catch fat. These birds produce an amazing amount of fat The slower you cook them, the more fat drips off.

Duck should never be cooked over open coals as this results in very determined grease fires. Grilled birds can be roasted whole in a pan with a rack and the pan should contain water or stock which should be replenished as it evaporates. The liquid prevents the dripping fat from burning and the steam helps render out the fat.

If the duck is cooked whole, a quartered onion or (better) an apple is usually stuffed into the cavity for aromatic purposes and to draw off bitter flavors. Discard after cooking. To **accelerate cooking time** toss a couple of big, long bolts into the body cavity. The BBQ vents should be partially closed to damp the fire. This reduces the heat, conserves fuel and concentrates the heat toward the top of the bird. If the duck's skin starts to brown after about twenty minutes it is cooking too fast and should be loosely covered with foil. **Slow cooking** is the name of this game. Cooking time should be 60-90 minutes, the slower the better.

GRILLING WILD BIRDS: keep in mind that wild birds are much less fatty than domestic fowl and cook much faster. Protect them from high heat, and baste frequently with an oily marinade. Wild birds taste strange to the unaccustomed palate so they are frequently served in a sauce which dominates them. A spicy grill oil or dry mustard sauce works well. Read more about cooking wild birds in the Chapter 13.

ROASTING WILD BIRDS: Split bird like a chicken. Marinate for a few hours in: oil, salt, pepper, powdered bay leaf, thyme and parsley. Poke finger under skin and force marinade under. Grill using pie pan deflector. Add a few bacon strips over breasts and paint drippings over bird top and bottom as it cooks. Cook until golden. Do not turn.

GRILLING BEEF

HAMBURGERS are possibly the world's most popular grilled food. Hamburger is typically made from ground beef, sometimes with a little pork mixed in. Fatty burgers are succulent and bad for you. Lean meat is less satisfying and better for you. Sirloin and tenderloin make tasty, relatively lean burgers and these cuts are recommended. Tenderloin makes a very lean burger. Flank steak makes a burger which is too lean and some fatty meat should be added to it.

One is always wise to buy a piece of meat and grind it yourself. You will then know exactly what you are eating. In addition, meat which has first been washed, then ground and dropped on the grill is much less likely to be contaminated with ground-in bacteria. Commercial ground meat and the machine which grinds it are of unknown cleanliness and may grind surface bacteria into the meat. And how long has the ground meat been sitting around? Store bought ground meat should be cooked medium.

Commercial ground meat is finely ground so that everything—meat, connective tissue, tendon and often bits of bone are chewable. But the best burgers are coarsely ground and come from trimmed pieces and a little fat. People who dislike adding fat can add olive oil instead, but remember, bad for you is tastier.

We are burger purists and never add anything to ground meat before making it into burgers. After all, if we wanted meat loaf we would make a meat loaf! We prefer to pour sauces over the cooked meat which provides a nice contrast of flavors. In any event NEVER add salt to the meat before cooking as this will dry it. Other chefs add egg or a bit of butter or oil (for moisture), herbs, chilies, garlic or hot sauce. Fold in the seasonings. Handle the meat as little as possible to avoid drying or contaminating it.

The easiest way to make a burger from ground meat is to tightly wrap a quarter pound ball of meat in a Ziplock bag or a cloth and squish it to about three-quarter inches thick. Thinner burgers tend to cook dry. Give the ball of meat a good whack. The meat is compressed a bit after squishing and this is important. Leave in the bag until cooking time. The burger should be brushed with cooking oil before being slipped onto a hot grill to prevent sticking. Slip the burger onto the grill, wait a few seconds, then lift it around the edges with a spatula, being careful to not reposition it. This prevents sticking.

Cooking time for a medium rare burger is about five minutes per side total time. A medium burger takes six to seven minutes per side. Sear the burger on each side for two minutes over a hot flame to seal and color it. Flip after searing, grill an additional minute more on each side. Don't ever squish a burger down with a spatula as this forces out juice. If you are going to add cheese on top, keep an eye on it as melts quickly. The texture of cheese breaks down if it is allowed to overheat.

SKEWERED MEAT is normally cooked quickly. Have your water sprayer handy to arrest grease fires. The meat is usually marinated for flavor and to protect it from the drying effects of the heat. More marinade can be brushed on as the meat cooks. Tough meat with good flavor can be served this way. Meat tenderizer can be added to the marinade or the meat cubes can be beaten until

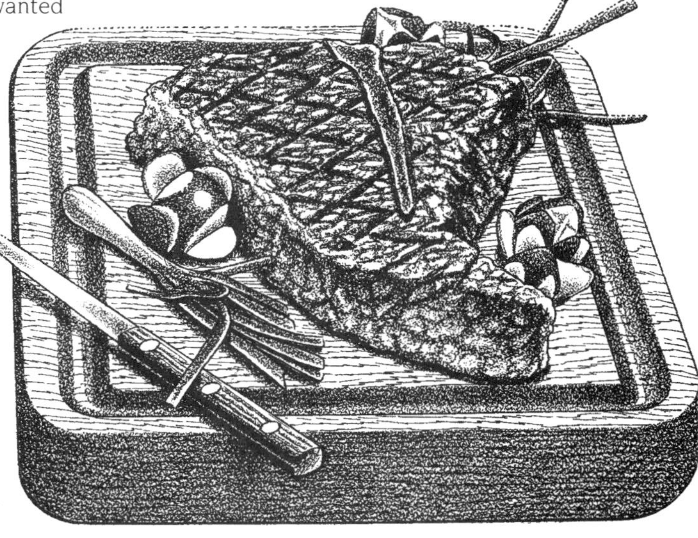

they whimper which is better and helps you work out your tensions.

Meat is cut about 1-1/2 inches square. Smaller pieces cook more quickly. Sugar cube-sized pieces cooked on a wooden skewer are called "**brochettes**." They take about three minutes to cook. Goat and other tough meats are frequently served this way. Traditionally cumin is brushed on the meat in the last few moments of cooking or the meat is marinated in cumin, oil, garlic and pepper.

Meat and vegetables look great together on a skewer but cooking each separately allows more control. If you want some color on the meat skewer, add a few slices of red pepper as this vegetable burns with dignity. Brush vegetables with oil to avoid scorching.

STEAKS AND ROASTS: Steaks should be at least three-quarters inches thick. Larger pieces, such as roasts and legs should be cooked on a rack. Sear each side over high heat for a minute or two, then reduce the heat and allow about three or four minutes more per side for medium rare finish or about five minutes if the pie plate is used. Allow about seven minutes per pound for a medium rare roast. **For Carne asada** and **skirt steaks** (thin cross cuts of tougher meat) allow three minutes per side for medium rare. After meat is cooked it should be allowed to cool a few minutes to allow juices to congeal.

LEAN OR TOUGH MEAT: Fillets of lean or tough meat can be of fine flavor and very good eating but they are usually slow-cooked and become tough(er) and dry when grilled. If you are going to grill a slice of tough meat, beat it with a meat hammer until it begs for mercy, oil it, fling it onto a red hot grill, scorch each side for a minute or two and call it done.

Such meat can be cut into thin strips about one to two inches wide and a quarter inch thick, beaten if desired, soaked overnight or at least a few hours in a spicy marinade (with tenderizer if desired). This tenderizes it. The strips can then be tightly rolled, tied or skewered and grilled like a burger.

The cooked roll is then sliced (rather than unrolled) to make the pieces even finer and easier to chew. The sliced meat is then added to a rich sauce. Some people periodically remove the roll from the flame and trim off the cooked meat. This is a good technique for making meat tacos or fajitas.

GRILLING LAMB

Lamb seems to be specifically made to grill. It is fatty enough to resist drying and sucks up all kinds of marinades. We like the chops and legs for grilling. A deboned leg of lamb can be stuffed with dressing, just like a turkey. Always cook it on a rack with a pan. Grilled leg of lamb kabobs in a spicy marinade or mustard sauce are a delight. Plain old grilled lamb is fine and dandy. You can hardly go wrong. Lamb is slightly more fatty than beef and takes about 15% longer to cook. Grilled lamb loves to associate with garlic, cumin, rosemary and pepper.

LEG OF LAMB: A nicely done lamb leg is the pinnacle of grilled cuisine. The leg may be purchased whole or you can just buy the thigh, which weighs four to six pounds. A five-pound thigh, bone in, serves four with leftovers and takes about thirty-five minutes to grill. Test for doneness by making a deep stab into the meat. A copious upwelling of blood indicates more cooking is needed. Try to get a piece which has been separated at the joint, so that both ends of the bone are uncut. This reduces the chance of contamination and of a sharp bone piercing the bag.

Storage: After purchasing, the leg should be washed in vinegar, salt and water, patted dry, then dropped into a bag containing oil, a few uncrushed cloves of garlic and a few crushed peppercorns. The bag should be squeezed until the air is completely gone, then sealed. Store in the coldest spot. A leg so prepared should last three or more weeks in the refrigerator.

The night before the lamb is to be cooked it should be deboned by slicing the leg open along the bone, then working the bone out with a small knife. It's better if you remove the bone without slitting the flesh.

If you don't want to go to the trouble of deboning the leg you can force garlic into the flesh. Make little stabs into the meat and under the fat. Insert slices of garlic. Marinate the meat overnight in the marinade which follows but omit the nuts.

LAMB MARINADE/STUFFING

Make a thick mixture of garlic, olive oil, parsley, chopped walnuts, chestnuts or macadamia nuts, sage and pepper. Pack into the leg and close with string. Add a little oil to the leftover mush and brush it on the meat. Keep cold until a few hours before dinner.

COOKING: Roast on a rack for thirty minutes and begin to check for doneness every ten minutes thereafter. Combine one cup each red wine and beef stock and two cups orange juice. Place in the pan to catch the drippings. Baste frequently. Keep at least an inch of liquid in the pan by adding more wine or stock. Be generous with the pan juice, it will become gravy later. About fifteen minutes before the lamb is done, brush all over with mustard and do not baste. Keep the mustard out of the drippings. Use the drippings to make a gravy.

When the leg is done, remove the lamb and rack, set aside covered with a towel for fifteen minutes to cool and congeal the juice.

THE GRAVY: Pour the pan juice into a cup and suck off the drippings with a baster, leaving the fat. You may serve the pan drippings as is or thicken them. To thicken, add the stock to a *roux*. **Arrowroot** is a good thickener which should be dissolved in a little water or wine, then added to simmering stock. Do not allow to boil. A little cream may be added at the end.

SHISH KABOB

2 pounds tender lamb, cut into 1-1/2 inch cubes
2 cups Spicy Meat Marinade (See SAUCES)
1 tablespoon each cumin, tumeric, ginger
6 garlic cloves, mashed
3/4 cups oil

Add to taste:
tomatoes, small onions, bell peppers, mushrooms

Marinate the meat for a few hours. Drain. String meat and vegies on skewer. Push vegetables together, give each meat chunk a bit of room. Brush all over with oil and herbs. Grill over high heat, brushing with oil occasionally. Be prepared for grease fires. Leftover kabobs do well in a hot curry sauce.

GRILLING PORK

American pork is much leaner than it used to be. When grilled, it should be treated as lean meat, cooked quickly over high heat (or slow cooked in a pan with a liquid). Brush a pork chop or tenderloin with oil and cook over a very hot grill for a few minutes per side.

Pork ribs and most pork purchased in developing countries is usually fatty. The meat should be chilled and the fat trimmed. Fatty pork can be cooked slowly on the grill with a pie pan beneath it or slow-roasted until extremely tender. Pork should be cooked until white throughout, but that does not mean white and dry. If you roast or cook over a rack, be sure to skim the fat from the drippings before use.

PORK RIBS are really tasty if stood on end in a pan containing a little water and roasted on a medium grill for about 40 minutes, occasionally painting with sauce. The fat drips off the meat, making it much healthier to eat and the meat is absolutely tender.

The fast, delicious, dirty way is to cut the rack into four to six rib "hands." Slit between each rib leaving enough to hold the hand together. Slow grill for about twenty minutes with a drip pan beneath; otherwise you are guaranteed a grease fire. Grilling directly over coals produces scorched, fatty ribs. The slower you grill ribs the happier you will be.

RIB SAUCES: Ribs may also painted with a thick mixture of honey, lemon juice, powdered mustard and pepper. Do this about fifteen minutes before serving. Brush with prepared mustard or steak sauce.

GRILLING FISH

SMALL FISH: The best way to grill small fish is to roughly gut them leaving head and fins on. Skewer them and scorch them quickly over a really hot grill or open flames. Do not use a marinade. This technique sears the skin and burns away most of the scales. The rest are brushed away. Traditionally three cuts are made in the skin on each side. The classic technique calls for cooking over open flames, with sprigs of aromatic herbs thrown onto the coals as the fish cooks. You can brush with a mixture of oil, lemon juice and rosemary after cooking.

MEDIUM FISH up to three pounds or whatever will fit on the grill. They should be scaled, brushed with oil and grilled with the pie pan deflector. Normally the head and tail are left on unless the fish is too large that way. Allow about five minutes per pound. Slip the spatula beneath the fish frequently to prevent sticking. Exercise particular care that the first side does not overcook to reduce the chance of breaking the fish when it is turned. A medium fish or fillets can be roasted on a greased sheet of foil to prevent sticking and breaking or use a shallow pan with stock or wine and vegetables. Use the pie pan deflector to reduce heat. The fish should be basted several times and does not need to be turned again. When almost done, add thin orange rounds splashed with honey.

LARGE FISH should be cut up into 1-1/2 inch thick fillets to allow even cooking. Large pieces can be placed in a greased pan or on a sheet of aluminium foil which slows the cooking and keeps the fish from breaking when it is lifted off the grill.

WHEN IS IT DONE? Fish cooks much faster than meat or fowl. Fish is most effectively tested with a finger poke and with a spoon. Slip the spoon between segments and give a slight twist. The segments should separate easily and the interior should steam. Firm fleshed fish such as swordfish and tuna are a little more resistant than fish like snapper or sea bass. If fluid wells up when the fish is opened, it needs a little more cooking. Fish is done when it is white to the center but still moist. If a fish falls apart when lifted with a spatula it is already overcooked.

A MARINADE is recommended when grilling fish. It is important to grease the fish before grilling to avoid sticking. We bought a big pizza spatula which we slightly sharpened to turn the fish without breaking it. Firm fleshed fish like tuna and swordfish can be marinated, skewered and grilled.

We often marinate fish in soy sauce thinned with a little rice vinegar and beer. Soy sauce penetrates fish flesh with amazing speed. Fish should be marinated until they are golden colored, about twenty minutes. Fish marinated until they are soy colored will be dominated by the soy. You can also mix a pepper sauce into this marinade or add powdered mustard, chili paste, curry paste, powdered herbs such as oregano, sage or thyme. The red chile paste marinade which becomes a sauce is a favorite of ours.

CHILE PASTE RED PEPPER GRILL MARINADE

Makes 2 cups

6 cloves garlic
1/2 cup olive oil
1 tablespoon red chile paste
2 roasted red bell peppers or anjo dried peppers
1 tablespoon each powdered cumin, thyme, oregano, salt, pepper
1 to 3 tomatillos (optional)
3 tablespoons Balsamic vinegar
salt

Blenderize all ingredients. Paint on fish, chicken or meat and refrigerate at least one hour but better overnight. This is a winner brushed an fresh tuna or swordfish steaks for grilling. Makes a thick paste. Stores two to three weeks in fridge.

FOIL STEAMING FISH: Fish and vegetables can be placed in a foil pouch and dropped onto the grill. Meat does not cook well this way and ends up stewed. Do not wrap the fish tightly, leave an air pocket for steam. Grease the foil to keep the fish from sticking. Add a little butter or oil and seasoning as desired (but not salt, which is added at the end) and a tablespoon or two of wine, beer or water. A marinade is frequently used when foil steaming

One can also lay the fish on a bed of cooked rice (and shredded coconut) with a little wine. The rice absorbs the juice of the fish as it cooks. Add thin slices of lemon or sprigs of rosemary for flavor. Avoid sliced mushrooms which end up stewed. You may also

bake fish on a bed of raw vegetables. About twenty minutes is typical for a slice of fish about 1-1/4" thick. Do not open the foil to test for doneness. Push a skewer or toothpick through the foil into the fish. The toothpick should steam when removed.

GRILLING SHRIMPS AND SCALLOPS

Shrimps and scallops can be marinated for a few hours in a spicy marinade. You can also sauté minced onion, parsley, garlic and a pinch of celery seed in olive oil. When finished add lemon juice, then use this as a brushing mixture. Skewer and cook quickly on a very, very hot grill or over open flames. Brush marinade over the cooking seafood frequently. The important thing to remember is DO NOT OVERCOOK. Learn the feel of properly cooked seafood by poking it. Three or four minutes per side is plenty.

GRILLING VEGETABLES

CORN is delicious grilled in the husk. Grilling without the husk results in tough, scorched corn. The husk does a surprisingly good job of insulating the corn from the heat and must be scorched black before the corn is done. To intentionally scorch the corn for flavor, remove it from the husk after cooking and grill briefly. Some people soak the corn in sea water before grilling and this adds a nice flavor.

EGGPLANT: Thin Japanese eggplant can be peeled, cut in half lengthwise, marinated for a half-hour and grilled over medium heat, lifting with tongs occasionally to prevent sticking. Delicious. The larger globe eggplant can be cut into rounds and cooked in the same way. You can also just toss the entire unpeeled eggplant onto the grill and cook until the skin is charred, turning occasionally. This makes the eggplant light and fluffy with a grilled flavor.

MUSHROOMS: We really prefer just throwing oil painted mushrooms on a really hot grill, keeping a bowl of garlic, hot pepper, salt and oil on the side into which each mushroom is occasionally plunged. The top of the mushroom is lightly browned, then it is flipped and the underside is grilled until it stops dripping and becomes firm. Toward the end, sprinkle the underside of each cap several times with soy sauce—or immerse whole mushrooms in oil, then skewer and grill. They get a better finish when cooked individually but are easier to handle skewered.

PEPPERS are a classic grilled vegetable. They can be cut open and grilled flat, skin side down. This method requires no turning. Or you can save grill space, cook them uncut and keep turning them. The pepper is roasted when the skin is mostly charred and the uncharred portion is wrinkled. Fast, hot cooking is best. See Salads for a great pepper salad recipe. Learn more about peppers in Chapter 16.

POTATOES can be foil-baked on a grill but the process takes about forty minutes. If you want baked potato, cut up big potatoes or use small ones to reduce cooking time. Brush pieces with oil. Pierce the foil with a fork. Push nails into large potato ends to speed cooking. Start potatoes well before you begin cooking the main course. Wrapped in a towel they will stay hot for a long time.

POTATOES PARBOILED AND GRILLED WITH ONIONS: Cut up unskinned potatoes into 1-1/2 inch pieces and boil about five minutes until potato is cooked firm. Add potatoes to a mixing bowl containing oil, garlic, salt, chopped or dry parsley and hot peppers to taste. Toss the potatoes in the mixture, skewer and finish on the grill. Baste occasionally. While the potatoes are grilling, slice a big onion or two into thick rounds. Hold the round down with your hand and skewer through the side with toothpicks to keep the rings from separating. Soak in the oil mixture and slip the rounds on a hot grill. Burn a bit. Turn only once, otherwise don't touch. Cook until brown. Serve with the potatoes. Roasted peppers go very well with this dish.

SUMMER SQUASH: Cut up, place in a pan with a little water and butter. Grill (or bake) for twenty to thirty minutes. Occasionally brush with a syrup of water, brown sugar, lemon juice and cinnamon. Dot with butter.

TOMATOES grill well, especially the smaller ones. Gently squeeze out as many seeds as possible. Skewer and brush with a mixture of oil, garlic, lemon juice, oregano and a pinch of sugar. You may also soak bay leaves in warm water for an hour, then place between tomatoes. Add hot sauce to taste. Baste often.

PRESSURE COOKING

As was discussed in Chapter Two, if your ship is big enough for just one pot, make it a pressure cooker! This wonderful tool, used only occasionally in the home, becomes the unvarying pot of choice in the galley. It may be used as an ordinary pot. But if the sea becomes rough, the lid may be clamped on, effectively preventing spills even if the pot departs from the stove on a voyage of its own. The pressure cooker is also a great storage container. If you have made a great cauldron of something delicious, just leave it locked in the pressure cooker.

DANGERS: Many people consider pressure cookers dangerous. Cooking is dangerous and therefore some danger is associated with a pressure cooker, but no more than with other techniques such as frying. The risk of a pressure cooker accident is small compared to the risk of a grease fire.

EXPLOSION is the main worry I hear about. Pressure cookers cannot explode. They have a **safety plug** in the lid which is designed to blow out before the pot explodes. The **pressure valve** is a weight which rests on a vent tube. When pressure inside the pot increases, the steam lifts the valve, allowing steam to escape. If the **vent tube hole** becomes blocked with food pressure can build inside the pot and blow out the safety plug.

If the valve suddenly ceases to jiggle, possibly indicating a blockage, manipulate it with a fork. Slight jiggling with the fork should produce loud snorts of steam. Should this not occur, remove the pot from the flame, allow to cool and clear the hole with a toothpick. DO NOT play with the blocked hole when the pressure cooker is still pressurized.

Pressure cooker manuals written after World War II recommended not cooking items such as split peas and barley because they are thick and might clog the hole. I have pressure cooked these ingredients literally thousands of times without mishap. Read the manual enclosed with your pressure cooker for further advice.

MORE ABOUT VALVE BLOCKAGES: An accident can occur if the valve hole becomes blocked at the end of cooking, such as when the chef takes the pot off the flame to cool. It is possible that moving the pot will cause a little piece of food to jump into the hole. In this case the valve ceases to jiggle, making the chef think the pot is cool. If, at that moment, the chef forces open the pot the pressurized food will burst out. I learned this the hard way once, luckily while wearing an apron which protected me from a scald, but we had a minestrone flavored main salon for a long time afterward.

Obvious indicators tell you that the hole is blocked. First, the safety valve has not dropped down, making an obvious klunk followed by a sucking sound as air rushes into the cooling pot. If in doubt give the safety plug stopper a push to see if it is loose. Second, the lid is extremely tight because pressure is keeping it closed.

Strait of Gibraltar seen from Morocco

DRY COOKING: There is no culinary disaster quite like cooking all of the liquid out of a pot of pressure cooked food. The ghastly smell is usually the first warning, but by that time, it's far too late to save the meal. Just a few minutes after the horrible smell, the safety plug in the pressure lid melts. Contrary to popular belief, this does not cause an explosion, because all of the water and hence all of the pressure has dissipated. However, at this point you have not only ruined the meal, but caused the pressure cooker to become badly encrusted with charred food. DO NOT COOL WITH WATER at this point because the cooker may crack. Wait for it to cool naturally, then soak overnight in a strong bleach solution.

SAFETY HABITS: Develop a few habits which will greatly reduce the possibility of running out of liquid. **Listen to the rhythm of the pressure valve**. If the jiggling of the valve changes, shake the pot and listen for liquid. If in doubt, put the pot in the sink, pour tons of salt water over it until the safety valve sucks air, open the pot and see what's going on. The pot reheats quickly.

TIME SAVINGS: The pressure cooker reduces cooking time by about two-thirds by increasing the boiling temperature of the cooking liquid. Normally, it is impossible to make water boil above 212° F. If you increase the flame, the water boils faster, but the temperature remains the same. When a pressure cooker is pressurized to 15 pounds above normal atmospheric pressure, water in it will boil at 250° F. This greatly accelerates the cooking process.

The time savings for brown rice is typical. Brown rice would take 45 minutes to cook using conventional methods but takes just fifteen minutes in a pressure cooker, a time savings of 66%. Lamb shanks, which would be roasted for an hour in a 375° F. oven take just eighteen minutes in a pressure cooker, a time savings of 70%. Baked beans, which might simmer for three hours, cook in just forty minutes, a time savings of 75%.

FUEL AND LIQUID SAVINGS: A pressure cooker is more of a closed system than a pot. Since very little steam escapes, much less heat escapes. Less liquid is needed to cook the food. The fuel and time savings are increased because the smaller amount of liquid takes less time to heat.

USING THE PRESSURE COOKER

- A pressure cooked meal is always simmered for some few minutes before putting the lid on. Meats and chicken are thoroughly browned in oil or butter. This sears the flesh, seals in juices, gives better color, and helps equalize the cooking time with the vegetables.
- When the liquid is rapidly simmering, the lid is clamped in place and the pressure regulator is added. The flame is reduced. When the pressure regulator gives a loud, definite snort or jiggle, the timing of the meal begins. The flame is reduced to low, or just enough heat to allow a jiggle every half minute.
- If you are cooking something delicate, remove the pot from the flame and cool it with water immediately. Since the temperature in the pot is well above boiling, a boiling temperature exists long after the pot is removed from the flame.

USING THE PRESSURE COOKER IN BAD WEATHER

Most galley chefs instinctively turn to canned food in bad weather. Perhaps the easiest meal is an individual tin of stew or soup that has been heated in the pressure cooker and poured into a mug.

Hard-boiled eggs are popular in bad weather because they are a mild flavored food which can be eaten with crackers and this is a plus for queasy crew. Stock them for a quick snack. Boiled eggs can be made in a pressure cooker, lid on, pressure regulator off. Use two cups of cold water and not more eggs than will cover the bottom of the pot. Cook seven minutes after steam comes from the pressure vent. Soft-boiled eggs take 3-1/2 minutes.

H.M.S. Bark Resolution

IMPORTANT RULES FOR PRESSURE COOKING

- Never fill the pressure cooker more than three-quarters full, and never more than half full when making thick soups or heavy sauces—these sputter and may block the pressure vent.
- Salt food after cooking. There is less liquid to carry the seasoning and added flavors are intensified under pressure. Try to use the cooking liquid as a sauce, since it contains many nutrients.
- Bring the pressure pot up to the first jiggle over high heat, then reduce the flame to the minimum necessary to produce two to three jiggles per minute.
- Timing a pressure cooked meal begins with the first jiggle or heavy snort of steam—not with the steady hiss which begins much sooner.
- When pressure cooking delicate items, stop cooking by internal heat immediately—pour cold water over the pot.
- **Listen to the rhythm of the pot**. Changes in the sound of escaping steam may indicate problems.
- Never force a pressure lid open. The lid is locked by steam pressure, you will be burned should you force it.
- Equalize the cooling time of ingredients by cutting longer cooking items into smaller pieces.

PRESSURE COOKING CHICKEN AND MEAT

PRESSURE COOKING CHICKEN: You can pressure cook a chicken in one cup of liquid or you can add 1-1/2 quarts and make soup from the resulting stock. The question is, where do you want the flavor? If you want it in the stock, add some onions and carrots and pressure cook the critter into mush—twenty or thirty minutes is okay. Then throw away the bird and keep the stock—a good technique for tough old hens and roosters.

If you want to eat the meat, pressure cook a whole bird eighteen minutes or cut up parts twelve minutes. If you brown the cut up pieces first, pressure cook eight minutes. Pressure cooking leaves the bird extremely soft and succulent and is highly recommended.

BRAISING AND PRESSURE COOKING MEAT: Pressure cooking small pieces of tough meat breaks it down but much of the meat's flavor is lost to the sauce. Conversely, pressure cooking a tender, expensive roast toughens it. Tender meat should be grilled, baked or stir-fried.

It is not unusual for a chef to create a pressure cooked meat stew, then throw away the cooked-out meat and add tender, browned meat which has been quickly stir-fried.

Meat should be browned before pressure cooking to seal in flavor. Meat can be sliced and marinated before searing. A cooking time chart follows.

Nesting tern

MEAT (4 Servings)	MINUTES
Pot roast of beef, 3-in. thick, 2 lbs.	22
Short ribs of beef, parboiled 5 min.	20
Hamburger stew, 1 to 1-1/2 lbs.	10
Beef stew, bite-sized chunks	12
Beef or veal shanks	18
Swiss or flank steak	15
Chicken, cut up, add 8 min. for old bird	12
Lamb shoulder, 2-1/2 to 3 lbs.	20
Lamb stew	15
Mutton, trim excess fat, 2-1/2 lbs.	20
Ham shank or shoulder, 3 lbs.	25
Ham, 2-inch slice, uncooked 2 lbs.	15
Oxtails in a stew, trim excess fat	18
Pork shanks	18
Pork shoulder 2 to 3 in., cut, browned	15
Pork chops, in a stew	14
Pork ribs, parboiled first to remove fat	8
Rabbit stew, add 4 minutes for hares	12

PRESSURE COOKING FRESH VEGETABLES

Most vegetables cook quickly in an ordinary pot with a little water and do not require pressure cooking. On the other hand, many chefs tout pressure cooking vegetables because it preserves their food value.

Vegetables can be added to the cooking liquid when pressure cooking meat or fowl. In this case the vegetables become mushy and their flavor is contributed to the liquid. Nevertheless they can be mashed or blended to thicken the sauce.

A second technique is to pressure cook a meal with vegetables, remove and discard them when done and add fresh vegetables which are then simmered in the hot sauce.

COOKING TIME: A few longer cooking vegetables can be pressure cooked to advantage and we have listed them below. Other vegetables can also be pressure cooked but need only a minute or two to cook, so it's hard to time them.

VEGETABLE	MINUTES
Artichokes	6
Beans, lima or fresh soy	3
Beets, large, quartered	5
Beets, small, whole	5
Brussels sprouts	4
Cabbage, wedges	4
Carrots, small or cut up	4
Okra	3
Onions, sliced or chopped	2-1/2
Onions, small whole	5 to 7
Parsnips in 1/2 to 3/4-inch slices	2
Potatoes, sliced or diced	3
Potatoes, small whole	8
Potatoes, yams or sweet, quarters	6
Pumpkin wedges	9 to 12
Turnips, quartered	4
Squash, hard winter, sliced 1-in. thick	10

PRESSURE COOKING DRIED BEANS

Most beans and grains can be pressure cooked from the dry state. Black beans and large limas are best soaked overnight. The table below specifies cooking times from the dry state.

Never add less than two cups of liquid per cup of beans. This will leave very little liquid in the pot, as is desired with rice. We often add three cups and if we want to absorb excess liquid we add broken pasta to the pot when the beans are cooked. The pasta absorbs water as it cooks.

BEAN	MINUTES
Black beans	40
Black eyed peas	15
Northern beans	20
Kidney beans	22
Lentils	10
Lima beans	20
Navy beans	18
Pinto beans	15
Soy beans	30
Split peas	12

LEGUME DISHES

BOSTON-STYLE PORK 'N BEANS

Here's the primal recipe for pressure cooked baked beans. You can make this a one pot meal by adding hot dogs or bits of fried meat <u>after</u> the beans are cooked.

2 cups dried beans
1/2 pound salt pork or a ham hock
3 tablespoons brown sugar
1 teaspoon salt
1 teaspoon dried mustard
2 onions, whole

Ancient look-out tower on Gibraltar Strait

6 stalks celery, whole
4 tablespoons molasses
2 tablespoons Worcestershire sauce
4 tablespoons catsup
1 beer
water

Soak beans overnight in plenty of water. Wash and drain. Chop pork, fry and drain oil. Add all ingredients and enough water to cover. Pressure cook thirty minutes. Cool, open lid, stir, simmer to desired consistency.

DAAL (CURRIED LENTILS OVER RICE): See page 87.

LENTILS WITH SPINACH AND APPLES

2 cups lentils
5 cups chicken stock
1 onion, chopped
1 onion, split
2 stalks celery, finely chopped or grated
3 stalks celery, whole
3 carrots, whole
1 tablespoon cumin
2 teaspoons dry mustard
1 tablespoon powdered ginger
1/2 teaspoon tumeric
juice of 2 lemons
4 cloves garlic
3 tablespoons butter
1/2 pound spinach, washed and chopped
3 apples (Granny Smith or Pippin), peeled, julienned
salt, pepper

Pressure cook everything but the apples, spinach and chopped vegetables for ten minutes. Remove vegetables and discard. Add everything else and simmer until spinach is soft.

ABOUT LEGUME SOUPS

(Also see Chapter 5)

Beans play an important role in the galley since they are cheap and store well but the heart of a good bean soup is a great stock. A bean soup needs four cups of stock or a combination of stock, beer or wine per cup of beans, otherwise it will be too thick.

OTHER PRESSURE COOKED SOUPS

When making pressure cooked soups the cooking time is determined by the time needed to cook the slowest ingredient. Dried beans are the slowest cooking ingredient followed by pasta which takes about four minutes to pressure cook. Vegetables which are to be eaten (rather than cooked into the stock) are added when the soup is done.

Add fresh vegetables such as peas, carrots, or grated cabbage to the pot and close immediately. Leave the pot on the still hot burner. The internal heat of the soup cooks the added vegetables just crisp and the fine flash of color spices the meal.

PRESSURE COOKING DRIED FRUIT

Dried fruit makes a fine dessert and cooks beautifully in a pressure cooker. Fresh fruit may be added, after the pressure cooking is completed. Put the fresh fruit in the pressure cooker with the flame off, the internal heat of the pot will cook it sufficiently.

Dried fruit should be soaked in enough water to cover for an hour prior to cooking. All other ingredients, except fresh fruit, should be added at this time. The recipe below, made with any type of fried fruit, is a favorite "end of the passage" treat.

PRESSURE COOKED FRUIT COMPOTE

Combine:
2 cups dried fruit
4 cups raisins
juice of 1/2 lemon
3 tablespoons brown sugar or honey
1 tablespoon rum
1 teaspoon cinnamon
4 cups water

Pressure cook for two minutes. (If using figs or prunes, cook for six minutes.) Cool slowly.

IT IS BEST NOT TO PRESSURE COOK...

- FISH, which is delicate and easily overcooked.
- MILK PRODUCTS, which tend to scorch. This includes cheese.
- FRESH FRUIT, which requires lower heat.
- EGG PRODUCTS, which become tough when pressure cooked.

STIR FRYING

STIR FRYING is an ancient technique in which food is cooked very quickly by tossing it in a small amount of extremely hot oil. A few simple tools (a slotted spoon and a spatula with rounded blade) and very little fuel are required—perfect for a boat! All stir frying recipes follow the same basic technique, so once you have mastered the concept, you can to design your own meals.

THE PAN: A fry pan can be used but a traditional wok with a rounded bottom is preferred since its sloping sides move the food toward the bottom of the pan which is the hottest part. Traditional woks are well suited for use on a ship stove. Purchase a **ring stand** which stabilizes the wok over the heat.

Cheap woks work just as well as expensive ones but cheap woks are made from mild steel which rusts. Keep them well oiled. Stainless woks with a nonstick surface are better for a boat. The optimal wok is about twelve to fourteen inches in diameter with a lifting handle and an insulated fry-pan type handle. The two handles make it much easier to lift the wok in a seaway.

TEMPERATURE: The entire "secret" of stir frying is **high heat**. Very high heat seals in juices without overcooking the inside. Meat comes out browned on the outside and moist on the inside. Vegetables flash fried in this way come out crisp and delicious, retaining their original bright colors. The entire cooking process takes just a few minutes. In order to maintain high heat, add food to the wok a little at a time.

Traditional Chinese chefs use stoves which produce much more heat than Western stoves. It is not unusual to see flames entirely enveloping the wok! To achieve this high temperature we carry a twelve inch gas burner ring which was originally designed to melt lead. We purchased it in a plumbing store but they are also sold in oriental markets. This burner makes a fine backup stove and is portable. If you don't have enough heat, buy a small wok which will concentrate the heat you do have into a small space.

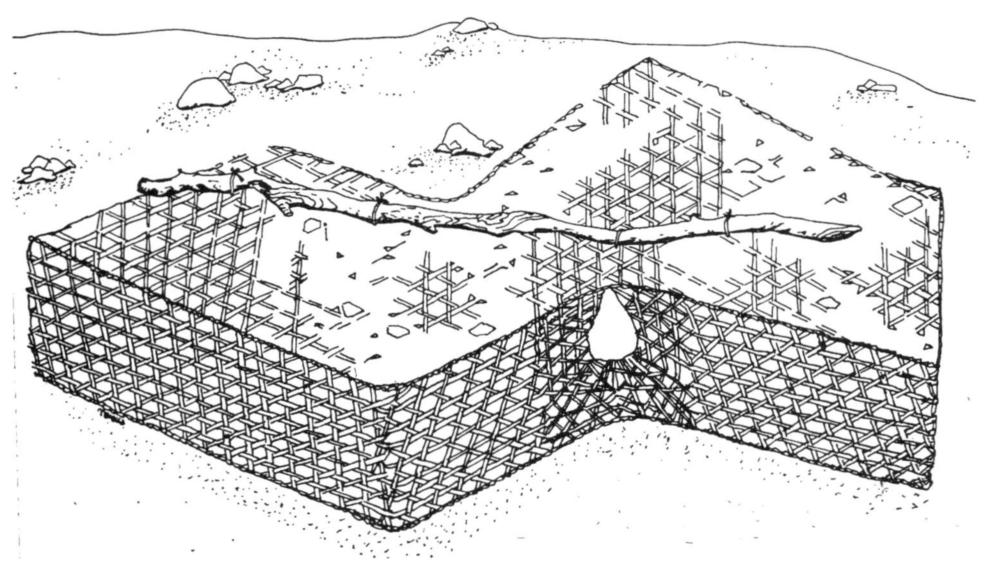

Hatian fish trap

THE OIL: Since high temperatures are typical of wok cookery olive oil and butter are not recommended since they break down and scorch. Traditionally **peanut oil** or **sesame oil** are used as they are resistant to high temperatures.

STIR FRYING TECHNIQUE: PLANNING AND PREPARATION

Stir frying is an extremely rapid process which once started cannot be interrupted. Therefore, preparation is everything. All ingredients must be cut into small pieces, placed in individual dishes, ready for instant action. Sauces, herbs and special ingredients should also be ready for instant use.

PREHEATING THE OIL: The oil is preheated until it is thin, fragrant and shimmering, almost smoking. I frequently hold a large pot lid between myself and the wok when I add ingredients, to avoid burning spatters. Since the cooking food is always concentrated in the bottom of the pan and is constantly tossed just a few tablespoons of oil are required. The scant amount of oil makes it possible to achieve the high temperatures required for this type of cookery.

STIR FRYING MEAT, FISH OR FOWL

Meat, chicken or fish (hereafter called "meat") is cut into small, bite-sized pieces, about a half inch in diameter which are frequently marinated before cooking. They are stir fried with herbs and spices. If vegetables are to be included in the dish, they are usually stir-fried in oil for a few minutes. A little water, stock or beer is then drizzled into the pan to create steam, which finishes the vegetables. They are then reserved. The meat is added next and cooked until done, about five minutes. Sauce is then added and finally the vegetables are reintroduced.

BRAISING WITH THE WOK: Meat can also be dredged in corn starch by shaking the pieces and seasoned corn starch in a plastic bag. The coated meat is added slowly to the wok to maintain high temperature, and browned (two to three minutes). The browned meat can then be *braised*, which means that a sauce can be added to the wok which bonds instantly with the fried corn starch. A favorite sauce I use is a mixture of soy sauce, garlic, ginger, dry mustard and a little beer. Traditional sauces include sweet and sour and lemon ginger. In this case the pan must be *deglazed* of goo with a spatula using a little beer or wine. When the pan crust is liquefied, add vegetables and toss.

WOKING VEGETABLES

The object when woking vegetables is to have them all finish at the same time. Delicate vegetables such as summer squash, onions or peppers are usually just cut into bite sized pieces. Snow pea pods are usually just trimmed. Tougher, longer cooking vegetables such as carrots or turnips can be julienned. Larger pieces of carrot or broccoli, cabbage slices and cauliflower florets can be **blanched** for a few minutes so that their cooking time will match that of the delicate stuff.

BASIC CHICKEN STIR FRY

Everything is going to happen very quickly so have all ingredients next to the stove, ready for use. Serves four.

2 cups chicken meat, skinned, diced
3 tablespoons oil
1 onion, julienned
1 carrot, julienned
1 red pepper, julienned or cut into small squares
2 summer squash, chopped
1/4 cup beer with 1 teaspoon of arrowroot or corn starch
8 dried Oriental or Shitake mushrooms, reconstituted, squeezed dry

The marinade:
1/4 cup soy sauce
2 tablespoons sherry
6 cloves garlic, blenderized
1/2 teaspoon ginger
1 teaspoon dry mustard
1 teaspoon chili sauce (optional)
1 tablespoon peanut oil

Cut up the chicken and marinate it for fifteen minutes, stirring occasionally. Reserve. Cut up the vegetables and reserve. Add two tablespoons of oil to the wok and bring to high heat, shake the wok to distribute the oil, toss in the vegetables, a little at a time and stir furiously to coat everything with oil. Stir-fry until done, about three minutes. Skim off with strainer. Reserve.

Add the chicken and onion and cook five minutes until done.

Add rehydrated mushrooms, sprinkle in remaining marinade a little at a time, allowing it to be absorbed before repeating process. About one minute.

Add the beer/thickener and toss. Add vegetables and toss. Let sit two minutes. Bon Appetite!

SZECHWAN BEEF

This classic recipe calls for Szechwan peppers but any medium hot dried pepper will do. In a scant ten minutes you will create separate meat and vegetable dishes from a single pot which can be combined with rice or pasta to make a complete meal. This recipe is your introduction to beef stir fry. Serves four.

3/4 pounds tenderloin or any prime beef chilled to firm then sliced very thin cross-grained to bite-sized lengths
10-15 dried hot chiles, no seeds
2 large carrots, long julienned strips
4 thin slices of parboiled cabbage
1 cup tender fresh vegetable (red pepper), sliced very thin
cilantro, parsley or fennel, if available
4 garlic cloves, crushed into 1/4 cup oil

Cooking sauce:
1/4 cup soy sauce
3 tablespoons sherry
4 cloves garlic blenderized
1 teaspoon dry mustard
1 teaspoon sugar
juice of 1/2 lemon
1/2 cup beer
1 heaping tablespoon corn starch

Grill the chiles until almost charred and reserve. Marinate the meat for fifteen minutes in the cooking sauce and reserve. Cook the cabbage as described above and reserve. Stir fry remaining vegetables in the chili oil until done, about two minutes and reserve. Add the meat and cook until done. Reserve. Add the cabbage and vegetables and heat. Add the garlic-oil, lemon, salt pepper . Make a hollow in the center of the wok. Add meat and cooking sauce. Toss until thickened. Combine meat and vegetables on plate.

BEEF AND SCALLIONS WITH CABBAGE

4 slices blanched cabbage, dribbled with lemon juice, oil and a pinch of fennel seed
24 scallions, cut into 2-3 pieces each
2 peppers, roasted, cut into strips
4 jalapeño peppers, julienned
4 tablespoons oil
1 pound beef, thinly sliced, marinated in soy sauce, pepper and cognac, dredged with cornstarch
lemon juice
salt

Add oil, bring the wok to high heat and add scallions. Keep pressing them into the oil until slightly burned. Add peppers and heat until bubbling. Sprinkle with lemon juice and salt. Reserve. Add cabbage and heat until bubbling. Reserve. Add beef and brown. Add the sauce and thicken. Serve beef on top of vegetables.

SWEET AND SOUR PORK (OR FISH): THE SWEET AND SOUR CLASSIC

Serves four

1 pound lean pork, diced, tossed in a beaten egg and dredged in corn starch
1 medium onion, julienned
2 medium carrots, long thin slices
1 bell pepper, one inch squares
6 cloves garlic, crushed in a little oil
1 cup pineapple, diced
2 medium tomatoes, peeled seeded and chopped

Sweet and sour sauce:
1/2 cup each apple vinegar, brown sugar, catsup
1/4 cup each cornstarch, pineapple juice
2 tablespoons soy sauce

Wok pork a little at a time until browned and reserve. When finished scrape wok to loosen debris and bring oil to high heat. Add carrots, garlic, onion and cook until onions are golden. Dribble in a little water as needed and add bell pepper. Add pineapple and tomato and heat until bubbling. Add pork and sauce. Thicken. You can also dredge the meat with corn starch and braise it in the sauce in which case thickener is not added to the sauce.

SPICY BRAISED CHICKEN AND PEPPERS

Stir fry onion and mixed vegetables in a

little oil and reserve. Add one pound diced chicken, tossed in egg and dipped in corn starch. Stir fry as above until browned.

The sauce:
1 cup tomato puree
hot sauce to taste
1/2 teaspoon coriander
3 cloves garlic crushed in 3 tablespoons oil
1/2 lemon juice
1 teaspoon sugar

Pour off excess oil and add sauce. Toss. Combine with vegetables

ELABORATE CHICKEN STIR FRY

3 cups chicken meat, in small pieces
18 dry mushrooms, reconstituted

The vegetables:
1 onion, sliced
1 red pepper, julienned
3 stalks celery, pared, cut into thin strips
2 carrots, in pared strips
10 scallions
1 cup snow peas, de-stringed
2 teaspoons ginger, grated
6 garlic cloves, roughly sliced
1-1/2 cups chicken stock
2 cups bok choy (optional)
3 teaspoons hot chili oil
3 teaspoons soy sauce
1/2 cup peanuts
2 teaspoons peanut butter
4 teaspoons peanut oil

This is the kind of meal that can grow out of control, resulting in dinner for eight when you are serving four. To prevent this, envision the mound of food you desire, then cut up everything with this mound in mind.

Blanch the chicken in the stock and reserve. Add the mushrooms to the remaining stock to reconstitute. Heat the pan and two teaspoons oil, one teaspoon chili oil. Add onion and stir fry until golden. Add chicken and stir fry two minutes. Add mushrooms and toss, sprinkling with soy sauce. Reserve.

Deglaze pan with chicken stock from mushrooms. Add vegetables except carrots and ginger. When vegetables are soft add carrots. Reserve vegetables. Add peanuts, more oil, peanut butter and one teaspoon chili oil. Toss. Reintroduce everything and toss a few times to reheat. Easy on the tossing as you don't want to combine flavors.

STEAMING WITH A WOK: In addition to stir frying, a wok is traditionally used as a steamer pot. A little water is added to the wok and brought to a boil. If the food to be steamed cooks at the same rate an aluminium steamer rack is placed over the boiling water and the food is added. If several different dishes are to be prepared, bamboo steamer trays are stacked over the boiling water, so that one pot of steam cooks the entire meal. Complete meals of meat and vegetables can be made this way and sauces made separately can be poured over the food when it is arranged on the plate. The Chinese even steam dumplings filled with spicy pork or shrimp in the trays.

5 Soup

SOUP, MY LOVE?

The morning after, swinging at anchor on a tranquil bay, is always the best time. The sun is always shining then, a high fire in the sky and noon seems always just around the corner. There is a sort of languorous fatigue left over from the night before or the day before; a fatigue that makes us move slowly and awkwardly like slow motion dancers in the sunlight. We see the world with eyes grown young in the night. Colors seem purer then. Fresh coffee is fragrant and overwhelming; the taste of an orange is a new experience.

We are mostly silent together and look at each other like strangers, as though there were some questions to be answered, but we cannot find the words to ask. The sun always seems to be shining the next morning but even if it were to rain, the rain would be a friendly rain, warm and gentle and full of spice smells of damp earth, the browns and greens of life casting their fragrance like confetti to the wind.

The night before may be just as good, those first few minutes of safety and shelter when the anchors are down and the running lights put out. Then there are only the gentlest sounds—the muted creak of a block, water slapping lightly against the hull, and the occasional whisper of the wind. Exhaustion hangs heavily about us, but for a few minutes we are beyond sleep and there is time for a glass of cognac and a last look at the stars. The cockpit is quiet then, in the darkness, almost a temple with the big oak tiller pointing silently at the stars, the compass a glowing pool of red and the cockpit seats like pews, deserted in the moonlight.

Those few minutes, the first minutes of rest and safety, with the sails furled and the anchors down, are as strong and mellow in their intensity as the taste of liquor. The anchor light shines far above us from the masthead. It sways gently in the darkness when all other lights are out. Even then, in the darkness, behind closed eyes, there is the sound of the waves. Perhaps it is only in the mind. That sound is always with us when we are at sea and the night is rough. The whitecaps cast themselves upon us, muttering as they pass in a welter of foam. They seem almost to stalk us like wild beasts.

Leaving them this time at the mouth of the bay as we sailed away into tranquil water, we heard them yammering behind us like voices calling from far away. We heard that sound afterwards, in the darkness, when the anchors were down and the lights out, behind closed eyes when sleep first comes. But perhaps it was only the blood against our eardrums like the sound of the sea in a shell.

We never leave port in bad weather, preferring to sit at one of the many little bistros by the quay, watching the sea gulls patrol the shore, drinking coffee, listening to the waves, far away, thinking of how mussels in wine would taste for lunch. We sat thus once in Port Sollar (Majorca) watching the wind move the almond trees high up on the hill. The hills are very sparse. Only a few goats can live there among the almond trees. The trees seem to be cast from the same gnarled rock from which they grow—heavy, twisted, black trunks in fields of stone. We watched the wind move the almond trees and sat drinking coffee, talking intensely with a stranger about God, paradise, pollution, the Fiji Islands where he had lived, and the quality of young breasts in Ibiza. We left when the storm blew itself out and sailed off in the sunrise.

But I sometimes think of the sea as the girl with green eyes. There is often a surprise behind her smile. A day of sunshine, a night of stars: but by first light the wind was blowing hard from the North and it was time to shorten sail. That is a job of which we are never fond. We always wait too long, hoping that it is merely a vagrant breeze and soon will pass. Sometimes it does.

We talked about that, too, with the stranger in the cafe and asked him if he were ever afraid at sea, knowing the answer in advance but wanting to see how he would phrase it. "Well," he said, "sometimes all I want to do is get into some port and give peace a chance." Then he laughed and we all had another round of cognac. The sunlight was so good then and the almond trees swayed in the wind.

Setting the storm jib is the worst part of the job. It is absolutely necessary to work in the bow, on the very front part of the bow, the part that rises majestically up into the air on the crest of the waves; then comes down heavily, burying itself beneath the sea. It is like cresting the hill in a roller coaster about every thirty seconds, feeling that funny feeling in the pit of your stomach as the seat drops away and the rush of the wind, then the leaden weight of arms and legs as you, coming down, meet the bow, going up.

The only difference between the bow and the roller coaster, aside from the water and the bashing that you are taking from the rigging and lifelines is the fact that when the bow goes up on the crest of a wave flinging you into the air, it also moves sideways, so that unless you are somewhat careful you will find upon descending that there is only green water waiting to break your fall. As a consequence, your arms and legs find it very busy work looking for a place to attach themselves. This makes the job of snapping the 15 or 20 piston hanks of the jib to the stay a trying experience. We set the jib, then double reefed the mainsail, water running like sweat from our red foul-weather suits.

The stranger in the cafe, whose name was Fred, has lived for three years on one of the small Melanesian Islands in the Fiji group south of Suva. Rebecca, John, Fred, and I sat around one of those little cafe tables hardly bigger than a dinner plate, littered with empty cups and glasses. Sunlight danced upon us through the tree leaves and the air was warm and filled with the smells of summer. We talked of the people who lived in the Fijis, about attempts to "civilize" them—give them television sets and jobs—and how that had failed so miserably and how they seemed to find everything humorous that Fred thought was serious and relevant. Then we talked about Gauguin—the kind of life that his paintings portrayed and whether some remnant of that society existed. Then we swam in the sea.

Nightfall in rough weather, when land is somewhere just over the horizon is a time for decisions. The sea sinks fewer boats than the land, for the land is silent and unforgiving. A Polaris shot at dusk tells us that we are 18 miles north of our projected landfall in a comfortable upwind position. The seas have gotten very steep and are now breaking regularly. The chart shows that we will have to pass between several small, unlighted rocks of undetermined height, with positions that seem to wander from one chart to another and which, in fact, have the PA (position approximate) symbol next to them. One of them is decorated with a wreck which is supposed to be awash.

We had already hit a wreck several years back and are not particularly interested in them as they tumbled beneath us with a phosphorescent glow. But we never actually saw the sea, though we were closer to it then than when we stood among the trees, listening to goat bells and watching the sunset. We could have reached from the deck and touched the sea but we did not. It was not a friend that night and although we knew it was there and could have touched it, we did not, but looked instead into the night toward the land, trying to touch it with our minds.

At last there was a light. We thought at first that it was a star on the horizon. Then, as it grew brighter we thought that it might be a ship on the rim of the sea which would come toward us, unfolding itself from a point of light and go rushing past, leaving us a little sad as though at the parting of a friend. But the light did not move and we finally knew that it was not a ship.

We thought then that perhaps it might be a fishing boat working with lights, rolling in the heavy seas. But finally we knew that it was a beacon, though far away, and we counted the flashes and the seconds of darkness before the light. We watched the beacon for a long time as though to be sure that it was the particular beacon we wanted. But we continued to look hungrily at the light after we knew what it was, as though we could taste it and it somehow satisfied a craving. We watched the light with the darkness all around us and it seemed that we were stationary on a carousel with the boat going up and down and it was really the light that was moving toward us. And we watched for the rocks and the submerged wreck that would kill us in the darkness. We stared ahead into the night but it was hard and cold like a stone, so we looked at the beacon which bloomed like a flower far away, and we watched it through the binoculars, hoping somehow to bring it nearer.

And then through the glasses we could see a glimmer of foam at the tower's base, the sea lacing its fingers through the fingers of the shore and we could hear the dull boom of breakers, not from the shore but from abeam of us. We knew then the location of the wreck and that we had passed it. Something was gone from our minds, a weight which we had not known was there. But it was gone and we knew then that it was fear.

Then we passed the light and in our human way cared no more about it but looked instead ahead, into the night, searching for some deep pool of silence in which to drop the hook. As we passed into calm water, the hatch was thrown back and Rebecca popped her head out. "Care for a cup of soup, my love?"

ABOUT SOUP

What does a good cruising chef do when a long passage lies ahead? Make soup—a hearty, nourishing soup that will last for days. A big mug of it, handed up to the man at the helm, seems, at times, like an offering from the gods. And what better food is there for the beleaguered sailor who must have one hand for his boat and is left with only one to feed himself? Soup—it seems to nourish the very soul.

We care nothing for the stocks and bouillons (which we use as bases for *real* soup), the consommés variously garnished, which sharpen the appetite, but do not stick to the ribs. These pottages have their place in the world and we love them, but not on a boat. Every recipe in this section has been included with the idea of providing a hearty meal-in-a-bowl that is both satisfying and relatively easy to make.

Soup making on our boat revolves around pressure cooking. You will see that almost every recipe in this chapter calls for fish, chicken or beef stock, wine or beer, consommé, broth or bouillon—not water. Learn more about pressure cooked soups and stocks on page 58.

FROZEN SOUPS: It makes no sense to buy a frozen soup that is only as good as canned. The canned variety will last longer, especially if the refrigerator fails. Lean toward frozen creamed seafood soups, bisques, chowders, vichyssoise and rich, fresh vegetable soups, such as fresh pea and minestrone. These frozen soups are far superior to the canned variety because they more nearly preserve the delicate flavor and texture of the fresh soup.

CANNED SOUPS: Some tinned soups are quite tasty. There ease of preparation and long shelf life make them an essential for the cruiser. Know the comfort of a food locker filled with hearty, tinned soups that can be made as a hot snack or as the basis of a square meal. The best canned soups are those that, when made fresh, require considerable boiling and contain ingredients that do not readily break down when cooked. The best among these are the legume soups, split pea, black bean, and lentil. Also quite good are some of the tougher vegetable soups, such as corn and tomato. We don't like canned soups such as vegetable or asparagus containing delicate vegetables which have been cooked to mush, then canned.

DILUTING: In addition, diluting condensed soups with either milk, stock, or wine is better than using water. Generally, we have discovered that most tinned, condensed soups call for more diluting than we like. Therefore, dilute slowly, adding half of the liquid first, and the rest after checking the consistency and taste of the soup.

IMPROVING: The flavor lost when soup is canned is caused by the breakdown of important fruit and vegetable acids that are sensitive to heat. Some of these can be replaced by the introduction of lemon juice, a little minced onion, or even vinegar. If a soup tastes a little bland, draw a little from the pot and try experimenting with it. If the result is a failure, the whole pot will not be a loss.

FREEZE-DRIED SOUPS vary greatly in quality but none of them are truly excellent. The classic variety, contained in foil packets, sold in supermarkets are usually rather disgusting, with a poor aroma and a gluey consistency indicating that corn starch or whey has been added to replace missing body.

On the other hand, "gourmet" freeze dried soups, frequently sold in cups have become more common as the demand for quick snacks and light lunches has increased. Most of these products are designed to be mircowaved after adding water. This results in a low calorie dish bordering on the verge of being tasty. These soups make a fine addition to the reserve cache and are also useful in bad weather.

HEAVY-WEATHER SOUPS: People who don't get seasick like hearty soups in bad weather. Heat up hearty canned soups in the pressure cooker with the lid locked on to prevent spills. Seasick crew aren't interested in hearty soups. They are interested in death, preferably immediately. Get some liquid into a seasick crewman, even if he doesn't want it. Seasickness is caused by an inner ear disturbance, not an upset stomach.

Each time a person is sick he/she loses body fluids and soluble ions. He gets weaker and weaker without soup. Even death can occur but most of the time the person only wishes that death would occur.

Chicken broth is best for such ailments, just like your mother told you. It should be served warm during that brief moment of wellness which precedes another bout of seasickness. A gut full of soup is a benefit even if it is thrown back up because without it the body will flood the empty stomach with soluble ions and some liquid which is better off remaining in the blood.

THICKENERS

There are two ways to make a soup more substantial: by adding starch to the liquid, thereby thickening it, or by adding other foods such as grated hard-boiled egg white, pasta, chopped or minced vegetables or rice, giving the soup more body

It is impossible to guess how much of a thickener you will need so an excessive amount of thickener is mixed with a liquid to dissolve it in a separate container. The thickening liquid is then added to the soup a little at a time. The classic three thickeners are: arrowroot, corn starch and flour.

ARROWROOT is the first choice as a thickener because it has the lightest taste, works the fastest and is the most effective per spoonful. Unfortunately, it is **sensitive to heat** and suddenly becomes gummy if boiled. Arrowroot and corn starch are added as a thickener after the food is cooked. The heat is then reduced to low and the thickener liquid is added a little at a time, stirring furiously. The process continues over a period of several minutes until the desired consistency is reached.

CORN STARCH is cheaper and more available than arrowroot and does not clump or break if boiled. It has a slightly more pronounced flavor than arrowroot.

FLOUR'S main virtue is its availability but its starchy taste is the most noticeable of the three. The starch taste is eliminated by first making a ***roux*** , which is flour sautéed in butter or oil. After a *roux* is made, a liquid such as stock or wine is added to create a porridge-like liquid thickener which mixes with cooking food and does not clump.

RICE AND PASTA THICKENERS: Quick-cooking rice or pasta can be added to a soup or sauce to absorb water and add body but these thickeners add a starchy taste to soup unless thoroughly cooked. If you are going to use rice or pasta as a thickener, use a fast cooking rice or small pasta and pressure cook it with beans so that it cooks to mush. This also applies to other starchy vegetables like potatoes. Rice and pasta can be cooked separately and added to the soup when it is done.

DEGREASING SOUP

Pour the liquid into a tall, small-diameter container like a juice pitcher. Wait a few minutes for the fat to rise. Gently lower a drinking glass into the liquid with a bit of the glass rim just below the liquid surface. Draw off as much fat as possible. Using a baster, suck the soup in the bottom of the glass from beneath the fat and return it to the pot. Repeat several times until the soup is fat free.

ABOUT ADDING CHICKEN OR SEAFOOD TO THE SOUP

The flavor of most soups and chowders is enhanced if appropriate pieces of fish or fowl are added to the pot. If this meat is to be eaten, it is usually best to separate it from the soup before it is cooked out. Serve it on the side with a rich sauce or horseradish that will enhance the somewhat depleted flavor.

You can also make a separate batch of meat or fowl which is sautéed and added to the soup near the end of the cooking process. This protects the meat's flavor. Listed below are some good sauces for soup fish, meat, or fowl.

- Horseradish sauce for boiled or corned beef
- Mustard sauce for meat and fish
- Garlic sauce for beef
- Hollandaise for fish
- White wine sauce for fish
- Curry sauce for chicken

Barcarolle main salon

CHICKEN SOUPS AND STEWS

CURRIED GREEN BANANAS AND CHICKEN IN THE BUCKET

A soup from the Blue Mountains of Jamaica! One fine morning we were swinging on the hook just outside the yacht club in Montego Bay, Jamaica, when we saw a small ketch working its way into the anchorage. She was a lovely sight from a distance, with everything hung out to catch the last gusts of the dying morning breeze, but as she approached, we could see that she was much more beautiful—from a distance.

Her sails were made mostly from old bed sheets held together with grommets, assorted pieces of blue jeans, and flour sacks. The largest and, undoubtedly, strongest pieces were the flour sacks. She did have a fine looking main halyard that might once have anchored a brig. She has been many colors in her life; they all showed somewhere or other. Her predominant colors were red and white, and she flew an absolutely huge American flag that the crew used as a sun awning. Her name was *Felicidad* and she had a sunburst covering her stern.

The wind died before she approached the dock. The motor was apparently inoperative, so the crew broke out oars and bits of wood to row, looking for all the world like a bunch of ants towing a crumb of bread. The dock master was very British—all crisp Bermuda shorts and knee socks. He was in no way interested in the current addition to his yacht club and plainly told them so, even though they showed him the classic salmon-colored U.S. Yacht Document that plainly stated the vessel was classified (or had at one time been classified) as a yacht.

The dock master finally agreed to let them take on water if they would leave immediately thereafter. The crew was a jolly lot of American hippies with a huge black Jamaican cook named Jesus. We agreed to tow them across the bay with our dinghy, and Jesus invited us to lunch aboard the *Felicidad*.

Things were a bit chaotic below; the color scheme was approximately the same as the exterior. The "galley" was the inevitable single burner Primus with a bucket that doubled as a pot. Since there was no head room, Jesus had to stand in the main salon and cook on the coach roof with his top half sticking out of the midships hatch.

In the bucket that day was chicken curry with green bananas and pieces of coconut in a soup, which just covered the other ingredients. The green bananas were quite starchy, similar in flavor to potatoes and surprisingly filling. It was a really fine, completely satisfying meal, which, to that stoned crew, and with a cook named Jesus, must have seemed like a gift from God.

1 chicken, skinned and cut into small pieces
4 teaspoons curry paste
4 slices bacon
1 cup green pepper, chopped
5 carrots, sliced
1 apple, chopped
coconut chunks (optional)
6 cups chicken stock
1 cup coconut milk
1/2 cup cooked rice
1/4 cup parsley, chopped
4 cloves
1 tablespoon each salt and pepper
6 green bananas (or plantains), quartered
1/2 cup each almonds and raisins

In a large pot or bucket, fry bacon; reserve. Brown the chicken in bacon grease for about fifteen minutes, drain. Reserve chicken. Add remaining ingredients except apple and green pepper; continue to cook about twenty minutes until bananas are tender like boiled potato. Add apples and green peppers; simmer until peppers are tender. Pour over chicken and bacon. Serve with sliced fruit, such as peaches and apples sprinkled with lemon juice.

CHICKEN VEGETABLE SOUP

1-1/2 quarts chicken stock
1 cup diced, parboiled potatoes or pasta
2-3 cups cut up vegetables
1 teaspoon each oregano, thyme
1/2 teaspoon celery seed
2 onions, chopped
6 cloves garlic, chopped
2 cups chicken bits (no skin)
1/2 cup red beans

Make a pressure cooked stock with all of the chicken scraps. Cool soup, degrease, strain, add pasta and boil five minutes. Add all other ingredients and simmer until vegetables are crisp. Sprinkle a little grated Parmesan cheese over all.

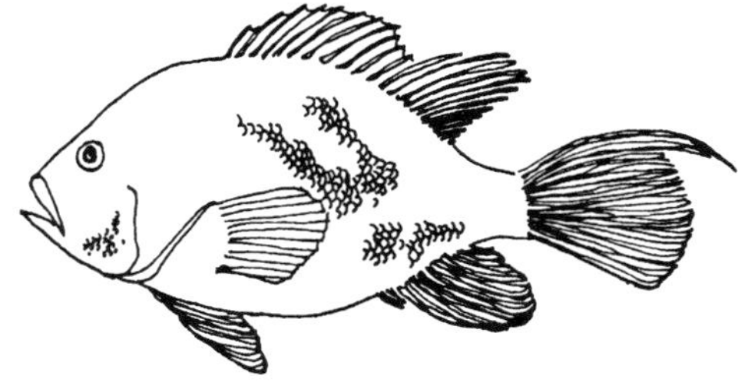

FISH SOUPS AND STEWS

The heart of any seafood soup or stew is a good fish stock. Fish bones, tails, fins, and heads, crab shells, lobster bodies and shells, shrimp shells and tails, even conch scraps are made into a fish stock (see Chapter 3). If you want still more flavor, after the stock is made it can be reduced by simmering until half its volume is gone, producing a *fumet* . A *fumet*, in addition to its delightful flavor is somewhat thicker than a stock and adds body.

BOUILLABAISSE: SOUP FROM THE ANGELS

Bouillabaisse, rumored in legend to have been brought directly from heaven by angels, merely tastes heavenly. It certainly originated in some very humble French fishing villages centuries ago. It is sold today in some very fancy places at some very fancy prices but one is just as likely to find it knocking around on some very smelly fish boats in some very isolated ports.

The French are very fond of saying that the real bouillabaisse is found only in southern France. It is true that some of the fish used in classic French bouillabaisse, rascasse, rouget and sea ravens come from French waters and cannot be easily found in other places. Nevertheless, the heart of a great bouillabaisse is a variety of fresh fish. It is the wonderful taste that counts. So if you have invited some culinary impresario to taste your fine fish stew and he pokes around suspiciously with his spoon hunting for the rascasse that is not there, we suggest you further insult him by telling him the origins of the recipe which follows!

Our bouillabaisse recipe comes from a fish trapper named Sam, a shrewd Nassau fisherman who single-handed a thirty-four foot live well smack to the vast stretch of reefs and shoals called the Yellow Banks. Sam was a well-equipped sailing businessman. The fish were trapped in reed cages, then transferred to a huge bait well that took up the entire 'midship section of his smack. When Sam couldn't sell his entire catch (which was rare), he smoked what was left in his on-board smoke house, and sold smoked fish at a higher price the next day.

Like most fishermen who service Nassau, Sam tied his smack, the *Miss Jane*, 'longshore near the Paradise Island Bridge, and sold his wares directly from the bait well to the shoppers passing by. What a delightful way to buy fish! The small conch boats, loaded high with hundreds of brightly colored shells, were tied by the quay. The tap, tap, tap of the conchmen's hammers punctuated the air. The huge mollusks were slipped from their shells and eaten on the spot with a dash of lime. A big wire basket full of scuttling, rustling crabs stood near the curb. Little boys were selling turban shells, piled high like walnuts in the shadow of the bridge. Near them a fat lady in a big straw hat had hung five huge green moray eels by their heads and was preparing to skin them. She sharpened her knife on the cobble stones.

Sam stood with his long knife, knee deep in the cockpit of *Miss Jane*. The sail, a coat of many colors, hung loosely in lazy jacks and afforded some protection from the sun. The live well was a living reef with sunlight brightly dancing. There were blue angels, rockfish, a big grouper motionless on the bottom of the tank, and a bright snapper dashing about nervously. We picked a fat grouper; and after a short discussion, a bargain was struck. Sam went after the fish with a net, following a brief chase around the tank, much splashing and an occasional oath, the big grouper was gleaming and flopping on the carving block. Ah, what joy! Fresher fish could not be found.

When a greenhorn tourist came to make a purchase, Sam generously offered to fillet the fish free of charge. He had a quick tongue and ready smile; his customers seldom noticed the few pieces of meat "accidentally" left on the head, tail, fins, and backbone that were flung into a garbage can. The greenhorn paid for the fish by the pound, but got only the fillets laced on a palm frond.

Sam was a master at the game and was

Sam

seldom caught, but when he was his look of astonished disdain clearly said, "Who would want this trash?" That night the contents of the "garbage can" miraculously became the ingredients for some of the finest soups and chowders we have ever tasted and whatever was left uncooked was smoked, hung in the rigging and sold the next day—at fancy prices.

When the market closed at sundown, all the other fishermen would "come along" the *Miss Jane* with a cup or bowl, smoke their pipes, and wait for Sam to "finish the pot." About eight o'clock, when the dishes were washed and the pipes smoked out, Sam would go home a contented man.

Since most of the following recipes were created "on the hook," they are useful to the cruising chef. Since Sam's galley had only a two-gallon bucket, which doubled as a bailer, you may be assured that these are all one-pot meals. The secret of success for all fish stews, chowders, and soups is to add the edible fish pieces last, cooking them just long enough to be tender. If the fish is overcooked, it loses all of its flavor to the soup and becomes mushy and tasteless.

The secret of fine bouillabaisse is a mixture of fresh fish, the kind that a bunch of hungry divers might take from a reef on a windless Sunday afternoon. And since those divers can't always spear exactly what they want, the hodgepodge of mixed ingredients is just what the galley needs for a fine bouillabaisse. This recipe over-feeds six. Don't worry about making too much, bouillabaisse tastes even better the next day.

SAM'S SUNDAY SPECIAL BOUILLABAISSE

Serves six

3 cups hot fumet
2 cups chicken stock
1 pound canned Italian tomatoes, coarsely chopped (or fresh) and well drained
2 large onions, coarsely chopped
1/2 cup celery, diced
1 teaspoon saffron
1 slice orange peel
4 garlic cloves, roughly crushed
2 teaspoons each: fennel (important), thyme
2 teaspoons salt and pepper
1/2 cup olive oil
3 bay leaves, broken up

And the fish, any or all:

Florida lobster, sliced into 5 sections, shell on
grouper, cut into 1-1/2 inch squares
snapper, cut into 1-1/2 inch squares
moray eel, small, skinned and sliced into 1/2 inch pieces (extra delicious here!)
shrimp, shelled and deveined
clams, mussels, or cockles

Sauté the onions, garlic, orange peel and herbs in olive oil 'til the onion is soft. Add *fumet* and bring to simmer. Add tomatoes and bring to rolling boil.

Add all seafood and enough chicken stock to make seafood awash. Bring to a furious boil, immediately turn off and remove from heat. Let stand five minutes.

Pour liquid over slices of good bread which has first been fried in oil, thyme, oregano and sprinkled with Parmesan cheese. Arrange fish on top. Serve as a stew with chunks of toasted garlic bread. Your crew will sign on for another voyage.

SAM'S ONE-BUCKET CREAMY FISH STEW

This recipe uses fish fillets. Any delicately flavored fish may be used—the more varied the fish, the better tasting the dish. Note that the ingredients to make the fish stock are not included here and that the vegetables used to make the stock are discarded. The vegetables in the recipe are sautéed quickly and the fish is cooked quickly to preserve flavor. If you don't like pork oil, use olive oil.

3 medium potatoes, diced
2 onions, quartered
1/2 cup celery with leaves, chopped
8 slices bacon, or 1 cup salt pork, chopped, fried reserved. Use fat to make stock.
4 cups fish stock. Use bacon fat to sauté the stock vegetables
1 teaspoon each thyme, marjoram
2 cups half and half or condensed milk
6 peppercorns
1-1/2 to 2 pounds fish fillets whole
dash of dry sherry
salt and pepper

Fry bacon or salt pork and reserve. Sauté onions, celery, herbs in oil until soft and reserve. Drain oil for use in stock. Make a fish stock using the drained pork oil to sauté the vegetables. Strain. Bring stock to rolling boil.

Add potatoes and cook two minutes. Add sautéed vegetables and boil furiously for one minute. Add fish and immediately turn off heat. Let stand five minutes. Add half and half, sherry. Salt and pepper to taste. Sprinkle bacon on top of the fish.

MATELOTE (FISH STEW)

Make this simple, two-pot, one-burner recipe with any firm fleshed, delicate flavored fish. Matelote is an unusual fish stew in that red wine instead of white is used. Do not use mullet, mackerel, or hake.

The stew:
1-1/2 pounds fish, varieties may be mixed
1 large onion (small boilers are better) blanched
4 carrots, diced and blanched
2 tablespoons tomato paste, or 2 fresh tomatoes, skinned, seeded and chopped
1 hot pepper or a dash or red pepper
A *roux* sufficient for liquid, or use corn starch in water
a *bouquet garnis*
liquid to cover fish, 50:50 reduced fish stock (a *fume*), or clam juice (not reduced) and good red wine

The garnish:
precooked shrimp
smoked oysters

Blanch (parboil) onions and carrots for five minutes and reserve. Make a *roux* to thicken the stock in a small pot.

Simmer enough wine and fish stock to cover fish. Add a *bouquet garnis* and simmer fifteen minutes. Add fish and bring to simmer. Add the precooked vegetables and simmer until fish is done. Pour off liquid into saucer. Reserve and cover fish to keep warm. Strain stock, add a pinch of pepper if desired. Reheat *roux* until it bubbles.

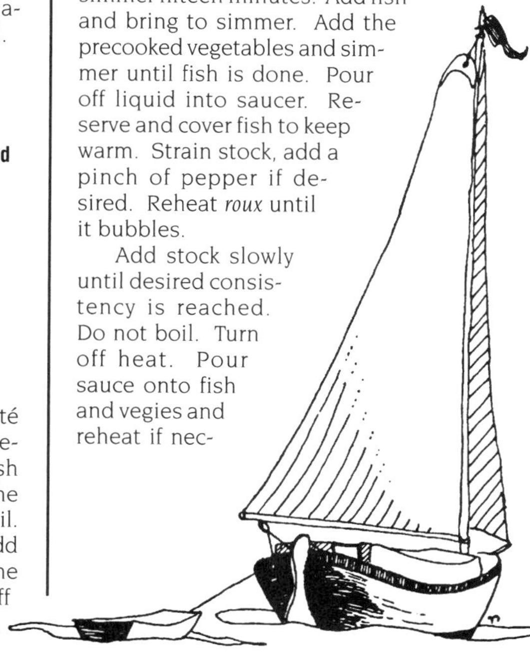

Add stock slowly until desired consistency is reached. Do not boil. Turn off heat. Pour sauce onto fish and vegies and reheat if necessary. Don't overcook, the fish will crumble.

CRUSTACEAN SOUPS AND STEWS

ITALIAN CLAM SOUP (Zuppa de Vongola)

The Italians are inordinately fond of little clams. They call them all vongola, though a number of different species are sold under this name. Perhaps for culinary purposes the Italians have the right idea; any little clam will taste quite similar when cooked into a soup. Should you have no small clams and plenty of big ones, grind them up. Use fresh or tinned clams.

1 medium onion, diced
1 bay leaf
3 large garlic cloves, finely chopped
1 large onion, chopped
1/2 cup olive oil
3 cups tomato juice
2 large carrots, chopped into slivers
1/4 cup parsley, chopped
3 cups tomatoes, chopped, peeled, seeded and roughly blenderized
2 quarts vongola, or 1 pint chopped clams and their juice
salt and pepper to taste

Sauté in olive oil until onion is golden: onion, garlic, parsley, bay leaf. Remove bay leaf, add tomatoes and juice; ... until thick. Liquefy. Add tomato juice, carrots, and clams. Bring to a boil, simmer ten minutes. Garnish with chopped parsley and Parmesan cheese.

Tinned clams are also acceptable, although their flavor is slightly damaged. Add them and a little clam juice at the end. Simmer just two minutes. In either case, serve individual portions in bowls or heavy weather plates and sprinkle with fresh parsley. Buon Appetito!

MUSSEL BROTH SOUP

2 pounds mussels, de-bearded and well scrubbed
2 sprigs parsley, chopped
1-1/2 cups dry white wine
2 shallots, coarsely chopped (optional)
1 large onion, diced
2 tablespoons butter
1 bay leaf
1 teaspoon thyme
2 egg yolks, well beaten into cream
2 cups heavy cream or unsweetened, evaporated milk
salt and pepper to taste

Put all ingredients, except cream and egg yolks, into the pot; simmer fifteen minutes. Pour soup through sieve and liquefy. Return liquid to the pot; add cream and eggs. Do not boil.

Simmer over very low heat, stirring constantly until soup just begins to thicken.

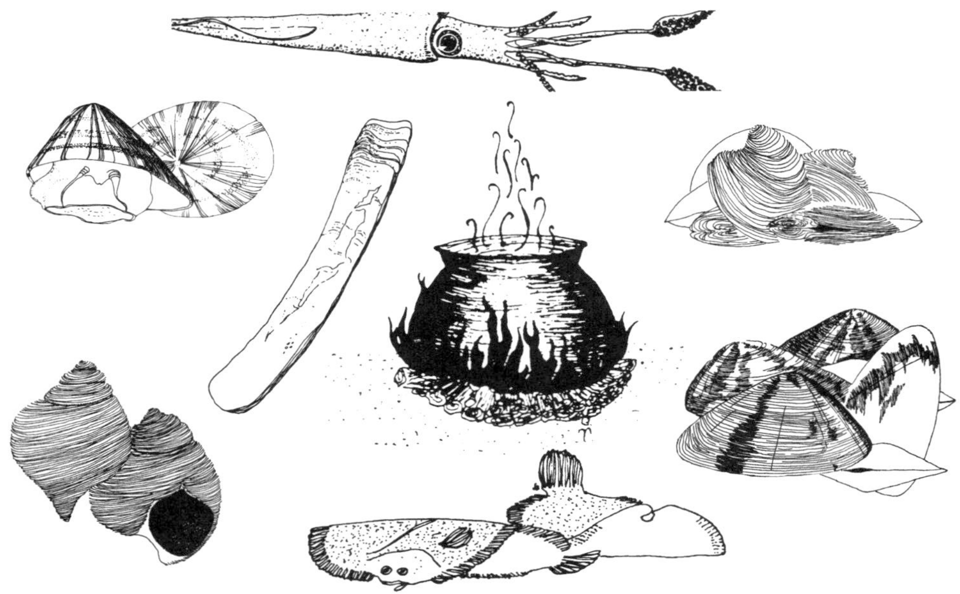

hot, without shells, on buttered toast, garnished with finely chopped celery. Or serve floating in the soup.

SHRIMP BISQUE OR SOUP

A bisque is thick, like porridge. A bisque can be thinned with milk or cream, making it into a soup. The recipe below is for a bisque.

4 tablespoons butter
1/2 grated onion
1/2 teaspoon celery salt
2 tablespoons parsley, finely chopped
1/2 cup dry white wine
1-1/2 pints seafood, shelled, deveined, and coarsely chopped
2 cups milk
1/2 cup cream, or condensed milk
1/4 cup hard cheese, grated
pinch of salt and pepper
pinch of paprika

This bisque can also be made from or in combination with, lobster or oysters, fresh or tinned. Combine the butter, onion and celery salt in a double boiler or in a sauce pan over very low heat. Sauté lightly, stirring constantly for five minutes. Add the seafood, milk, cream, or two cups condensed milk, pinch of salt and pepper, pinch of paprika

Sauté and stir until milk steams. Add: parsley, dry white wine. Sauté another two to three minutes. Serve over fried, buttered toast.

IMPROVED CANNED MANHATTAN CLAM CHOWDER

Use clam juice instead of water to dilute; add a few drops of lemon. Add more clams, conch, limpets prepared as for previous recipe. Sauté a half carrot, diced and parboiled, with a half onion in a little butter. Cook until the onion is golden. Add to soup.

MANHATTAN CLAM CHOWDER

Small, tender clams of any sort may be used; but if these are unavailable, larger clams, beaten, then ground can be used. Bahama conch chowder may be made using the same recipe by substituting thoroughly beaten and ground conch or whelk for clams. Limpets may also be used. They should be removed from their shells, eviscerated and beaten, then chopped or ground.

If live clams are used, they should be steamed open and the liquid used in the

chowder. The clams should be eviscerated and washed to remove intestinal grit. Serves four.

3/4 pint shelled mollusk meat
4 slices bacon, chopped
1 medium onion, chopped
1 cup clam juice
2 cups potatoes, diced
2 cups Italian tomatoes, drained and chopped
1 cup carrots, sliced
1 bay leaf
salt and pepper

Fry the bacon and onion until onion is golden. Add everything but the clams. Simmer for ten minutes until carrots are crisp. Add clams and simmer five minutes. Salt and pepper to taste; serve with fried toast or crackers.

PORTUGUESE COCKLE SOUP

Prepare as for Manhattan clam chowder; but leave bivalves, always small and tender, in their shells and add to pot. When finished add:

1 cup tomato sauce
2 tablespoons port or sweet sherry
1 teaspoon marjoram

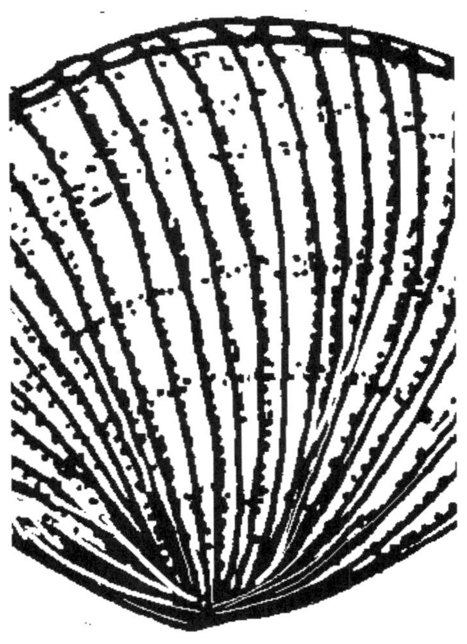

NEW ENGLAND CLAM CHOWDER

New Englanders have as definite an opinion about the best version of clam chowder as they do about which is the best anchor. They consider Manhattan chowder an "infernal invention." We, fortunately, are not from Manhattan. Serves six.

1-2 pints mollusk meat, chopped, or small clams
4 slices bacon, chopped
1 large onion, chopped
3 tablespoons flour
2 cups water including the liquid from mollusks
1 bay leaf
3 cups milk or half and half
2 potatoes, cubed
salt and pepper

Steam open and treat mollusks as in Manhattan Chowder. Fry bacon and onions in large pot. Remove, reserve solids, drain. Add all other ingredients except milk and flour; simmer ten minutes. Add milk and flour, pre-mixed to avoid lumps. Simmer until soup thickens but do not boil.

CONCH INN CONCH CHOWDER

This is such an outstanding recipe for conch chowder from the Conch Inn at Marsh Harbor, Abaco Island. Try it if you have a few conch lying about. You can also throw in green tomatoes, bananas and tomatillos.

1/2 pound salt pork
1 ham bone or smoked hock
1 bay leaf
1-1/2 quarts chicken stock
bouquet garni with plenty of vegetables
hot dried chiles or chile paste
1 cup Italian tomatoes, canned or two fresh, peeled, seeded
2 tablespoon tomato paste
2 potatoes, diced
2-3 conch, pounded and ground or finely chopped

Slice salt pork and fry until crisp. Reserve pork as garnish. Pour off excess fat leaving three teaspoons. Pressure cook ham hock, herbs in stock for fifteen minutes. Strain. Add three ground conch. Pressure cook twenty minutes.

Cool, open pot and add canned tomatoes and diced potatoes. Simmer until potatoes are done. Add additional beer, stock or wine as desired. Thicken with a *roux* as desired. Do not salt as salt pork will add enough.

CRUISING CREAMED SCALLOP SOUP ST. JAQUES

2 cups chicken stock
1/2 pound potatoes (2 medium), chopped
1 egg yolk
3/4 cup scallops, pen shells, surf clam muscles, or ray wings
1/4 cup heavy cream or evaporated milk
1/2 cup dry vermouth
1/2 bay leaf
1/4 teaspoon thyme
1 clove garlic, minced
1-1/2 pints seafood, shelled, deveined, and coarsely chopped
2 cups milk
1/2 cup cream, or 2 cups condensed milk with 1/2 cup water
pinch of salt and pepper
pinch of paprika

Pressure cook potatoes, onions, bay leaf, thyme, stock, salt and pepper for five minutes, or simmer in pot eighteen minutes until soft. Add scallops and garlic; simmer gently for five minutes. Remove and reserve scallops, bay leaf and liquefy vegetables adding a little stock if too thick.

Return puree to pot over medium heat. Turn off heat when pot simmers and add beaten egg yolks and cream. Stir continuously until soup thickens, returning briefly to flame if it does not. Do not let soup boil. Chop scallops and return to pot.

VEGETABLE SOUPS

RUSSIAN BORSCHT

Borscht is a thick beet and cabbage soup or stew. Water or stock may be used as the liquid. Borscht is supposed to have a pronounced sweet and sour flavor, so balance with lemon juice and sugar to taste.

2 tablespoons butter
2 chopped onions
2 thinly sliced potatoes
1 cup julienned beets
4 cups chopped cabbage
4 cups chicken stock
2 teaspoons salt
1 teaspoon each dried dill, caraway seed
2 tablespoons apple vinegar
1 tablespoon sugar
1 cup tomato purée
lemon juice to taste

Simmer potatoes and beets in stock in large pot until tender. Reserve. Return stock to pot. Cook onions and caraway seed until onions are golden. Add remaining ingredients and simmer in stock until tender. Add potatoes and beets, simmer twenty minutes. Borscht is traditionally served cold with a dollop of sour cream on top.

FRESH PEA SOUP

Serves four

6 cups peas
1 onion, chopped
3 tablespoons dried mint
1 quart chicken stock
1 teaspoon curry powder
1 cup cream
1 teaspoon salt
dash pepper

Sauté the onion in a pot until soft. Add everything but the cream. Simmer five minutes until peas are tender. Blenderize. Add cream. Serve hot or cold. Delicious.

MINESTRONE

Serves six

1/2 cup each garbanzos and red beans, canned
1 teaspoon each: thyme, oregano, marjoram, sage
3 cloves garlic, coarsely chopped
1/4 cup parsley, or 2 tablespoons parsley flakes
1 leak, sliced
1 cup tomatoes, chopped, drained, deseeded and skinned if fresh
3 stalks celery, chopped
1 cup macaroni
1 tablespoon olive oil
2 ounces salt pork or bacon, diced small
1 teaspoon each: basil, oregano, marjoram
2 tablespoons tomato paste
1/4 small cabbage, shredded
1-1/2 quarts chicken stock
1/2 cup grated Parmesan cheese

Fry the meat bits until golden and drain. Add all ingredients except cheese; simmer for twenty minutes. Vegetables should be crisp. Correct seasoning. Mix in Parmesan cheese and serve.

MINESTRONE—THE EASY WAY

Add to 28-ounce can minestrone soup:
1/2 onion
carrot parings
handful of cabbage, grated
any available fresh vegetables
1/4 cup dry white wine
1 teaspoon wine vinegar
1/2 cup Parmesan cheese, grated

CANNED TOMATO AND SWEET PEPPER SOUP

Canned cream of tomato soup is one of those few meals that we really like and it is the basis for several other soups, such as gazpacho. You can enhance canned tomato soup by adding a roasted red bell pepper and liquefying, then adding some chopped red pepper on top.

PASTA FRAJOLE

1 pound pinto beans
bouquet garni
1 ham hock
1/4 cup olive oil
2 cups chopped onions
6 cloves garlic, roughly chopped
1 tablespoon each oregano, basil
2 bay leaves

1 can (28 ounce) Italian tomatoes, drained, squeezed, chopped
1-1/2 quarts chicken stock
1 cup pasta twists
1 cup Italian parsley
1 teaspoon each salt and pepper
1/2 cup Parmesan cheese

Sauté the onions, garlic and herbs in all of the oil until onions are soft. Reserve. Pressure cook the *bouquet garni*, beans and ham hock in a good stock for twenty minutes.

Remove ham hock and *bouquet garni*. Remove about a half-cup of the beans and a little broth and liquefy. Return liquid to pot. Add the pasta and simmer until done. Add the other ingredients except the cheese and simmer for ten minutes. Serve and sprinkle the cheese on top.

MISO SOUP

Miso is a fermented, concentrated soy product which comes fresh as a paste and must be refrigerated. Normally, I have religious objections to anything knowingly billed as healthy, but in this case I am willing to say that miso soup is healthy and nutritious—in addition to being delicious! If you had a Jewish Japanese mother or grand mother she would undoubtedly tell you that miso chicken noodle soup is the equivalent of Judeo-asiatic penicillin—curing all ills—and also very tasty. And, after all that, it's easy to make. Oy vey! Such a deal! Try this basic soup and after that your eyes will be opened to the powerful flavor of miso.

6 scallions, cut lengthwise in 2-inch slices
1/2 carrot, in peelings
4 dried mushrooms, reconstituted, sliced
1/2 cup cooked pasta twists or macaroni
4 cups chicken stock
2 tablespoons heaping miso
pinch of chopped parsley for garnish

Heat and mix miso in stock. Add pasta and simmer. Add scallions and serve immediately. Garnish with parsley.

FRENCH ONION SOUP

Hearty onion soup, the way the French make it, is a serious affair. Long afternoons, sometimes even days are spent simmering a small mountain of beef bones and scraps, carrot ends, celery leaves and fine herbs into a rich stock—the heart of the soup. The second stage of straining, chilling, skimming, and restraining the bone-laden pot is equally time consuming; but that rich, sparkling stock gives real French onion soup its unbeatable flavor.

This approach is quite impossible on a boat but you can (and should) still make a rich, pressure cooked stock, jamming as many bones and scraps into your pressure pot as possible. By adding a few little extra touches, some wine and a bit of brandy, you can produce a delicious soup.

1-1/2 quarts rich beef stock
2 cups dry red wine
1 big *bouquet garni*
6 onions, in rings
1 tablespoon flour
2 tablespoons oil
6 slices French bread (toasted)
1 tablespoon marjoram
1-1/2 cups Parmesan cheese
butter

Sauté the onions in the soup pot until golden, then sprinkle in the flour and lightly brown. Reserve. Add a little stock and deglaze the pan. Add all of the stock, the herbs and heat. Add the bread and sprinkle with cheese, cover and allow to melt. Dot with butter and glaze under broiler.

POTATO SOUP

1-1/2 quarts chicken consummé
4 medium baking potatoes
2 medium leeks (white parts), chopped
2 medium onions, chopped

Sauté the leeks and onions until soft, add all other ingredients and simmer until potatoes are soft.

VICHYSSOISE

Liquefy the soup described above and strain. Add two to three cups heavy cream; chill. Serve garnished with chopped chives or green onion ends finely chopped.

FROZEN SPINACH AND PEA SOUP

This recipe calls for a pack of frozen spinach and a pack of frozen peas. So simple yet it is absolutely delicious.

2 can chicken stock
1 package each frozen peas and spinach
1 cup cream
1 tablespoon curry powder
3 tablespoons mint flakes

Sauté the vegetables and curry in the chicken stock. Add all other ingredients and liquefy. Good hot or cold.

LEGUME SOUPS

MUSHROOM-BARLEY SOUP

Mushroom-barley soup is another of those wonderful, hearty meals-in-a-bowl that is just as good at the dock as underway. It can be made with those beautiful black Chinese (or any variety) mushrooms, sautéed for a few minutes in a little oil.

I first came to know this fine dish when I was working as a laborer in Les Halles, the Paris fruit and vegetable market of days gone by. What a marvelous place! During the day traffic was normal; but at night trucks would arrive from all over France with fantastic things to eat. There were no stalls; the farmers would park by the curb and sell direct. Laborers (including myself) would haul the meat and produce to waiting vans.

When the nights grew cold the farmers would make trash can fires from broken crates. In the Fall chestnut vendors would roast their nuts in big pans over the flames. The rich smell of wood smoke and roasting chestnuts drifted through the market place. When the leaves began to fall the trucks came in full of barrels of cider surrounded by golden oak leaves which had blown up from the road.

These were good times for me, a very young man just out of school, the proud owner of a BMW motorcycle, living with a Norwegian girlfriend on the fifth floor of a five story walk-up with a view of the Sein. My girlfriend, Nicole, studied jewelry metallurgy at the Ecole Polytechnique in the morning and we slept in a big, creaking bed in the afternoon. The world of food, wine, love and Paris revealed itself to my boggled eyes. There was no chance of ever returning to the Real World. I had tasted adventure and it was sweet. Life would never be the same.

I would get up at 6 p.m. and work until 4 a.m., at which time the local restaurants would lower their prices so that the laborers could afford to eat. At 4 a.m. everyone ate like kings, including the two of us.

One hardly needed a menu to know what was being served that night. Boxes of produce, bags of bread and sacks of fresh seafood had been dropped off on the sidewalks during the night. Burlap bags of periwinkles, oysters and cockles still dripped with sea water. Whole tuna lay on the cobblestones, awaiting the chef's boy. Channel fish seemed to stare from their beds of ice and mesh sacks of crabs writhed unnervingly in the dim light.

You can be sure that many a crock of onion and mushroom-barley soup and many a fresh grilled fish disappeared down our famished gullets. After all, hauling fruit all night and making love all day is hard work! Then we would walk to the local bistro and rub elbows with laborers, students, revolutionaries, poets, absinth drinkers, and fools. After a few aperitifs we would take the bike to the river and watch the sunrise. There is no experience quite like being young and in love in Paris.

When dawn touched the roof tops, the farmers began to depart. When the first commuters rushed along these streets an hour later, they found them silent and deserted. All that remained were a few pigeons patrolling the curb, the scattered ashes from the chestnut vendors' fires, and an occasional fractured box. The fantasy world of night was gone.

Mushroom-barley soup was a favorite of the French farmers and laborers who worked in Les Halles. Considering how thoroughly they were surrounded by fine food, mushroom-barley soup had some tough competition! This is another one of those hearty meals that keep well. Pork scraps and carrot ends, mutton bones and parboiled barley can always be added—a virtually immortal, bottomless pit of fine flavors.

MUSHROOM-BARLEY SOUP

1 large onion, diced
3 tablespoons olive oil
2 carrots chopped
1-1/2 cups chopped mushrooms
1-1/2 pounds pigs feet or ham hocks (you can substitute miso here)
1 cup raw barley
8 cups chicken stock
1 teaspoon caraway seed
4 cloves garlic
2 teaspoons salt
4 tablespoons sherry

Fry onions and carrots over high heat in large pot until onions are golden. If you are

Author in France 1964

using fresh mushrooms add them here. If they are diced or canned, add them just before serving. Add more oil as needed to avoid scorching. Sauté until the onions are golden, sprinkling once or twice with soy sauce. When done reserve.

Add all other ingredients except the sherry. Bring to boil and simmer until barley is tender, about thirty minutes or twelve minutes pressure cooked. If you are using a pot rather than a pressure cooker, keep adding a little water to prevent barley from drying. Add reserved vegetables to pot.

Soup should be thick, more like porridge. Add three tablespoons sherry. Serve with a cold, white wine. You can also mix yogurt and a little cream and add this to the soup.

DEEP SEA SPLIT PEA SOUP

The heart of any good soup is a great stock. A pork and chicken stock makes the best split pea soup base, so start by making a great stock. You can add tinned shredded ham to this soup as a garnish.

1 pound dried split peas
1-1/2 quarts chicken stock
2 tablespoons curry powder
4 garlic cloves, whole
1/2 pound of salt pork, or (better) 1 ham hock
1 onion, chopped
1 bay leaf
1 teaspoon thyme
1 cup cream
5 peppercorns
2 tablespoons sherry (optional)
2 carrots, chopped

In pressure cooker fry meat, herbs, carrots and onion until onion is golden. Add stock and herbs and pressure cook fifteen minutes. Strain and discard solids.

Add peas, celery, bay leaf, curry, and bouillon; pressure cook for fifteen minutes. The soup should be about the consistency of porridge at this point. Thin with milk as desired. Add sherry, salt and pepper to taste; reheat and serve with croutons or grilled cheese sandwiches.

Split pea soup is just as good the next day, perhaps better. Since the split peas will absorb more water, it may be necessary to add water as you reheat. Add it slowly and avoid diluting the soup; split pea soup is traditionally served thick and hearty. You can also use the cold, paste-like mixture "as is" as a sandwich spread, with bacon, tomato, tuna, onion.

IMPROVED CANNED SPLIT PEA SOUP

Thin with milk instead of water. Add pork meat and onion; follow recipe above. Add two carrots, well chopped, one-half teaspoon celery salt; simmer until carrots are soft. Add two teaspoons sherry. Six Servings

BLACK BEAN SOUP

Black beans, like split peas and lentils, make a number of hearty soups. They also are the basis for a traditional Cuban dish, black beans and yellow rice, surrounded by little pieces of pork, cooked in a savory oil. To make that dish, just add less stock and use the pork recipe below.

Unlike most legumes, black beans really should be soaked at least four hours or better overnight in double their volume of water. Starting dried, they take forty minutes to pressure cook. We once cooked a pot of black beans for four hours without success. The beans were almost as hard after four hours as when we began. The only thing I ever met tougher than that was an old rooster.

Start off with a slam-dunk **pork stock**. This traditionally begins with a can of chicken consommé pressure cooked forty minutes or more with as many pigs feet and ears as possible. The other seasonings will then be cooked with the beans. Black bean soup, like lentil and split pea soup, tastes even better the next day.

Fry in pressure cooker until the onion is golden:
1 large onion, diced and chopped
1 hot pepper

Add:
1 bay leaf
1-1/2 quarts stock
1 hot pepper
1/2 teaspoon lemon juice
1 cup celery with leaves, uncut
2 cups black beans, soaked
1 cup white rice
1 teaspoon each: cumin, oregano, sage
1 bulb garlic, whole

Pressure cook for fifteen minutes. Simmer thereafter until beans are tender and soup is thick. To further thicken, make a *roux*, add a little soup to it and then put the mixture into the pot.

You can also add to the soup, Greek olive slices, hot peppers, chopped roasted red peppers, hot pickled carrots. Serve in a bowl with handful of well-chopped onions on top.

The sautéed pork:
1-1/2 pound pork cubes, cut in one-inch squares
1 tablespoon cumin
1 bay leaf
1 hot pepper or a pepper sauce
3 tablespoons olive oil
1/2 cup brandy
1 cup beer

Brown pork sprinkled with cumin in oil in a small pot. Add all other ingredients. Half-cover with liquid and simmer over low heat about one hour or until tender. This meat is traditionally served on the side with black beans and rice

IMPROVED CANNED BLACK BEAN SOUP

Since black beans are such tough customers they usually hold their flavor when canned. The canned product may be improved in any of the following ways.

In a pot fry:
6 strips bacon <u>or</u> chopped ham
1 large onion, diced
1 carrot, finely chopped

When onion is golden add the canned soup.

LENTIL SOUP AND DAAL

Lentil soup is one of those hearty meals-in-a-bowl that are inexpensive and, therefore, excellent for large groups. All of the ingredients are long-lasting and the soup is even better the next day. For this reason we have made the recipe for six. After all, if it was so good at dinner, why not have a cup of it for lunch the next day?

Daal is the curried lentil portion of the classic lentils and rice. The recipe for it is the same as for the soup but less stock is used. The finished product is the consistency of mush. Daal is traditionally a vegetarian dish. If you prefer, you can omit the pork.

1 large onion, diced
2 carrots, chopped

2 tablespoons soy sauce
1 cup mushrooms (or add dried reconstituted mushrooms at end)
1 ham hock, pigs foot or piece of salt pork (or 3 tablespoons miso)
1-1/2 quart chicken stock
1 bay leaf
2 cups lentils
2 tablespoons curry paste
1 tablespoon each: cumin, ginger, oregano
1 cup coconut milk
1 bulb garlic, whole

Fry onions in pressure cooker, sprinkling once or twice at end with soy sauce. Reserve. Add remaining ingredients and pressure cook ten minutes. Open, simmer until soft, adding stock as needed.

LENTIL BURGERS

A good way to get two different meals from one pot is to first make a big pressure cooker pot of lentil soup, followed the next day by lentil burgers which make a great lunch. Lentil burgers are high in protein and low in fat. Makes eight patties.

3 cups cooked lentils, (or mix with cooked soy beans)
3 cups onion, grated and sauteed in butter until golden
3 cups cracker crumbs or crushed corn flakes
3 eggs, beaten
1 teaspoon vinegar
salt and pepper

Mix together all ingredients; make into patties. Flour the patties all over; fry over high heat, five minutes per side.

CREAM OF NAVY BEAN SOUP

1-1/2 cups navy beans washed and soaked for 4 hours
1/4 pound ham in large piece
1 onion, chopped
1 cup cream
6 cups stock
3 carrots, diced
1 bay leaf
2 teaspoons each salt and pepper

Add all ingredients (reserve half the ham) and pressure cook for twenty minutes. Remove ham, bay leaf, liquefy. Add cream and warm. Grate remaining ham and sprinkle on top as a garnish.

GAZSPACHO

Gazpacho is the wonderful cold vegetable soup from Spain. It is a hot weather delight with its tangy taste, and is a lot of fun to eat. There are actually more than thirty different varieties of Gazpacho, each a regional specialty. Gazpacho Malagueno, for example, is made with grapes and sliced almonds, while Gazpacho Andalusia has more to do with onions, tomatoes, and green peppers—not a grape in sight. Our Gazpacho recipe does not come from Spain at all, but from the Spanish island of Mallorca.

One sunny day, we sailed into the snug little harbor of Port Sollar on the north side of Majorca. The harbor is entered through a narrow break in the cliffs. The sheer rock face opens grudgingly to give access to the bay. We approached this formidable channel in the early hours of morning, with sea mist swirling around us, wetting our foul weather gear, surrounded by the silent brooding of the high, dark cliffs.

We had no motor (as usual) and reached the mouth of the cut on the last vagrant morning breeze. We drifted in utter silence on the dark water—the black rock sheer and shining in the early light. The lighthouse, far above us, was staring blindly with its extinguished eye. Finally, rowing in the dinghy and towing our yacht *Fire Witch*, we passed between high rock into the lovely bay.

Completely surrounded by soft, green mountains the bay was just a basin, like the hollow of a hand—full of sunlight, light breezes and clear water. Protected by the mountains and the narrow entrance, Port Sollar is one of the loveliest harbors in the Mediterranean. A wide, tree-lined promenade, dotted with little shops and restaurants, runs completely around the bay

By the time we had worked the *Fire Witch* to her berth by the quay, it was time for lunch. We had this wonderful Gazpacho Andaluz—just right on a hot summer day—followed by *caricolles con salsa*, which turned out to be garden snails in a fresh garlic mayonnaise. It was the perfect tribute to a perfect day.

This recipe for Gazpacho Andaluz has been slightly modified to suit the convenience of the cruising chef, and to satisfy the stomachs of the crew. As described it is a two-pot meal that serves six. Gazpacho Andaluz is invariably served cold, or at least cool.

GAZPACHO ANDALUZ

Serves six

3 large, fresh tomatoes, peeled, seeded, and chopped
1 can tomato soup (condensed)
2 cans water (not stock)
2 green peppers, seeded and chopped
1/3 cup olive oil
5 cloves garlic, minced
3 tablespoons lemon juice
1 teaspoon sugar
1/2 cucumber, chopped and seeded
2 cups of mixed vegetables: cauliflower, radishes, celery hearts and leaves, turnips, palm heart
salt and pepper to taste

Add all the above ingredients to a stainless pot and let stand in a cool place overnight. Add enough of any or all of the vegetables, finely chopped.

Season with heaping teaspoon of one or more of the following herbs. Use fresh herbs, or soaked dried herbs for an hour in water: chives, tarragon, basil, dill, celery seed (well crushed). Chill in refrigerator, or cool place for three or four hours minimum; overnight is better.

Just before serving, add:
2 large potatoes, diced and boiled; or croutons

The potato adds body to the soup, and makes it a hearty, robust meal. The Spaniards omit the potato, adding, instead, a generous handful of croutons.

6 Eggs

ABOUT CRUISING EGGS

SELECTION: **Free ranging chickens** lay superior eggs. The shells are thicker and the membranes beneath are tougher. The egg is more resistant to contamination and also more flavorful, with a richer yolk than hatchery eggs. In addition, The best eggs for a long voyage are those which have **never been refrigerated**.

Supermarket eggs come from hatchery chickens. They are less flavorful and more fragile than hatchery eggs. They are of undetermined age but are stamped with an expiration date which usually gives them a month of shelf life. Refrigerated eggs will last up to six months. Store with small end down. If purchased refrigerated keep refrigerated.

PREPARATION: Wash eggs in chlorinated water and sun dry. Eggs which float in the dip water are rotten.

INCREASING SHELF LIFE OF UNREFRIGERATED EGGS: Physiological changes occur in eggs over time. The whites lose their firmness and their ability to keep the yolk in suspension. The membrane surrounding the yolk becomes less resistant to mould. The yolk becomes pale and slowly settles to the bottom of the egg where it spoils. The settling process may be postponed for up to six weeks simply by **turning the egg container over** every two or three days. This is the simplest most reliable method of making eggs last longer.

Some sailors coat eggs with **Vaseline** to extend their shelf life. The vaseline does create a protective barrier against mold but there is nothing quite so sporting as trying to handle greased eggs in a seaway. Eggs can also be **varnished**, dipped in **paraffin wax**, or packed in a solution of **waterglass** (sodium silicate, one quart per two gallons water) or in salt. Water glass is an ancient, effective way to preserve raw eggs without refrigeration.

STORAGE: The cardboard cartons in which eggs are sold in supermarkets can be used for storage but plastic containers which may be purchased at camping stores are better because they can be sterilized in chlorinated water.

BAD EGGS: There is absolutely no difficulty recognizing a bad egg. It is discolored and has a bad odor. After you have discovered a few rotten eggs break those remaining into a glass one at a time, rather than opening them directly over the food. In this way the occasional bad one can be eliminated without ruining the meal.

When you begin to find many rotten eggs, hard boil the rest. After hard-boiling your only alternative is to pickle the eggs (see page 99). Pickling makes them virtually immortal, but seriously reduces their food value. Don't forget, the best egg is a fresh one.

SEPARATING OLD YOLKS: As the weeks pass, yolk membranes degenerate to the point where the yolks always break when the eggs are opened. The yolk itself becomes pale and thin. These eggs, though of disappointing appearance, are perfectly edible.

SEPARATING THE YOLK FROM THE WHITE OF OLD EGGS: Separating the yolks of older eggs should definitely be classified as a sport. Egg yolks three or more weeks old usually break upon opening, no matter how careful you are. The method we recommend (having plucked a few old yolks in our time) is the Greenwald Shot Glass Technique, modestly named after the author.

The shot glass is first used as originally intended. This gives the wrist a fluidity that might otherwise not exist. Break the egg as close as possible to the bottom of a flat fry pan. We assume, from our own experience, that the yolk breaks immediately. The shot glass is placed immediately over the yolk while the white is poured quickly into another dish.

BEATING EGGS: Whole eggs are combined, not beaten, for use in omelets or scrambled eggs. This means whipping them with a few strokes of a whisk or fork, just long enough to incompletely combine the white and yolk—ten or fifteen seconds. More and they will be thin and tough. A little cream helps restore a thick, rich quality to old eggs.

Egg whites must be fresh and free of all traces of yolk if they are to stand when beaten. The mixing bowl must be free of all fat and oil and should be dry. Egg whites will beat to three or four times their original volume; they can be stiffened by adding a half teaspoon lemon juice per three egg whites when they are frothy.

EGGS AS THICKENERS AND BINDERS: Eggs make good thickeners as is evident in famous sauces such as hollandaise and mayonnaise, in custards and as binders in all sorts of cakes and pastries. Hard-boiled egg whites can be grated and added to oil and vinegar to add body and reduce the amount of cheese in a salad dressing. The yolk can be sprinkled on the salad.

COOKING EGGS

Many approaches to cooking eggs follow. You will notice the frequent use of the term "butter/oil." Oil considerably raises the scorching temperature of butter which is used for flavor.

HARD AND SOFT-SIMMERED EGGS

The best way to hard or soft-boil an egg is to simmer it. Boiling cooks the egg too rapidly, resulting in toughness and uneven texture and the egg shell often cracks.

Place eggs in cold water and cover. Don't overcrowd them. Bring to a boil. Remove from heat. Let stand:

- 3 minutes: very soft, yolks runny and whites jellylike
- 4 minutes: yolk still runny, white set
- 6 minutes: yolk soft, white set
- 9 minutes: white set, yolk just beginning to set
- 15 minutes: hard-boiled

Plunge into cold water to stop further cooking.

POACHED EGGS: Poached eggs are delicate and a few tricks are needed to ensure good results. There are two methods of poaching an egg. The traditional way is to drop the egg into a buttered poaching tray or a cup which is placed in gently simmering water. Another technique is to drop the egg into buttered, simmering water acidified with vinegar, which keeps the white from dissolving.

Poaching liquid: White wine or champagne is a good poaching liquid to which vinegar need not be added.

POACHED EGGS AND BAKED BEANS ON TOAST

We think this may be one of those recipes only certain people can love, like a peanut butter and banana sandwich or watermelon with vinegar. Nevertheless, we seem to have this craving, especially when the first light of dawn is just upon us, the morning fix is in the book, and the decks are still wet with dew.

Eggs riding triumphantly on a righteous portion of baked beans and generously buttered toast taste like the sun feels when it pops its yolk above the horizon. With the eggs gone, the sun shining and the bight of the morning breeze in the sails, our watch is finished. We lie back in total contentment and watch the sky turn blue.

EGGS BENEDICT

Eggs Benedict consists of a toasted, buttered English muffin covered with a few slices of hot Canadian bacon and a poached egg on top covered with Hollandaise sauce. Forget about cholesterol, full steam ahead!

GOURMET FRIED EGGS

This recipe produces a soft, evenly textured fried egg. Heat a little butter over high heat in a small pot: When the butter bubbles add two eggs and cover. Keep on high heat until you can hear the eggs bubbling-about a minute. Turn off the heat. Wait five minutes. Resist the temptation to peek as this releases steam. Cook from three to five minutes. The slower the egg cooks, the softer and more delicate its texture.

HUEVOS RANCHEROS

This recipe consists of a slightly toasted corn tortilla with two poached eggs on top covered with a spicy marinana sauce which has been zipped up by adding chopped hot chili pepper or sauce. A sprinkle of Monteray Jack or American cheese goes over all.

BULL'S EYE TOAST

Tear a hole about two inches in diameter out of a piece of bread. The bread is toasted in a greased pan with a lid. When toasted on the first side the bread is flipped, allowed to toast for a minute, then a raw egg is dropped into the hole. After a minute the toast is flipped again. Sprinkle cheese on top. Cook one minute. Turn off flame and let sit two minutes. Serve as is or pour syrup over all. You can dip the bread in egg/milk and make a **French Bulls Eye Toast**.

SCRAMBLED EGGS

All kinds of tidbits can be added to scrambled eggs . You can add precooked vegetables, ham, prosciutto, smoked fish, asparagus tips, *fois gras*, chopped liver or hot peppers. Vegetables are usually precooked and added at the end of the cooking process. This keeps them from being coated with egg and preserves their appearance.

You can make a **scrambled egg island** in a pool of sauce such as marinara, guacamole, curry or sour cream dill. You can add grated cheese or cream cheese during the cooking in which case the eggs are cheese flavored throughout, or you can add little dices of several different cheeses toward the end, which result in little globs of cheese flavor or you can sprinkle cheese on top. Smoked cheese does very well this way.

You can also serve scrambled eggs on top of things such as slices of avocado and prosciutto, sliced browned potatoes or toast.

CREAMY SCRAMBLED EGGS

Combine two or three eggs per person plus three tablespoons of cream and a little salt and pepper. Have about a handful of grated sharp cheddar per two servings ready for use. Add the eggs to a preheated pan, reduce heat and stir continuously. Add cheese as eggs begin to gel. Remove from heat just before the eggs are done to your taste as the heat of the pan will finish them.

LUMPY SCRAMBLED EGGS

Combine two or three eggs per person and one tablespoon of cream or milk . Salt and pepper to taste Beat for fifteen seconds. Add eggs to sizzling hot oil and butter and reduce heat. When eggs begin to set, sweep them toward the side of the pan with a spatula in long, even strokes. Tilt and shake pan to help uncooked eggs spread. Scrambled eggs are finished when just set, yielding to the touch, and shiny in appearance. Remove from pan and serve. Eggs left to sit in the pan will continue to cook and will become dry.

THE CAPTAIN'S BLUE WATER SCRAMBLED EGGS

Always a favorite with the crew, this recipe combines the flavors of mushrooms, onions and cheese.

4 tablespoons butter
1 cup small to medium mushrooms, sliced in half
1/2 cup onion, chopped
3/4 cup mushrooms, chopped
1 teaspoon marjoram
3 egg omelet mixture
salt and pepper

Sauté mushrooms and onions in butter over high heat until onions are golden and reserve. Add basic omelet mix to pan. Cook for twenty seconds without disturbing eggs. Sprinkle a generous handful of grated mild cheese. When cheese begins to melt, scramble the eggs.

When eggs are almost done, still shiny and yielding to the touch, turn off heat and sprinkle on mushrooms and onions. Cover the pan with a lid for 30 seconds to warm everything evenly and serve.

Borabesh, Morocco

AN UNUSUAL APPROACH TO SCRAMBLED EGGS— SCOTCHMAN'S DELIGHT

This unique recipe calls for the egg mixture to be cooked in a double boiler, producing a rich, sauce-like scrambled egg that is then poured over a special toast. Serves Two.

2 slices bread
4 tablespoons Parmesan cheese
3 egg basic omelet mix
shot of sherry
1/2 teaspoon of any or all: tarragon, rosemary, dill
2 tablespoons minced anchovy
1 teaspoon minced garlic
3 tablespoons olive oil
paprika

Add all ingredients to a double-boiler and stir constantly until eggs thicken to heavy porridge consistency. If they are too thick, add more cream. Reserve. Add anchovies, garlic and oil. Bring to a simmer. Stir and rub pan. Rub mixture on both sides of bread and fry until bread is golden. Pour eggs over the toast, sprinkle with a dash of paprika and serve.

PIPERADE

1/2 cup each red and green bell peppers, peeled, blended
olive oil
1 cup fresh tomatoes, peeled, finely chopped, seeded, slightly blended
3 eggs
2 garlic cloves, blenderized

Place all the vegetables in a blender and chop as finely as possible. Add to pan with oil and simmer over low heat until soft. Reliquify in blender and return to pan. Reheat vegetable mush and drop in whole, unbeaten eggs, stirring them briskly in the pan.

SCRAMBLED EGGS RANCHERO: hot peppers, bell peppers, sausage, corn and salsa over all.

ITALIAN SCRAMBLED EGGS: oregano, Italian salami bits, sliced olives sprinkled with Parmesan cheese.

CURRIED SCRAMBLED EGGS: curry paste and raisins.

AH, THE OMELET

The omelet is the sailor's friend and its mastery is well worth the effort. If you do not know how to make a basic omelet, now is the time to learn. Don't worry about ruining the first few. Like riding a bicycle, once you have the technique, it's yours forever. Omelets are frequently stuffed with a filling which is added last. The pan is of some importance. A sailor's omelet pan must have sloped sides and a non-slip surface. The bigger the pan, the thinner the omelet. Use a twelve-inch pan if you have room. A ten inch pan is okay for a three-egg omelet.

THE BASIC (FLAT) OMELET

Unstuffed omelette serves one. If stuffed, serves two. This is a dish that takes not more than a few minutes to make and it requires your full attention. Do not over-oil the pan or the eggs will end up fried.

3 eggs
2 teaspoons butter
1 teaspoon oil
2 tablespoons cream
pinch salt and pepper

Combine all ingredients in a mixing bowl just before use and beat for ten seconds with fork.

Heat the fry pan until butter and cooking oil sizzle. Pour in egg mixture, swirl it around. Reduce to low heat. Add grated cheese if desired.

Prevent sticking: As soon as the eggs begin to set keep pan frequently in motion with short, deft movements. The movement is a combination of a push and a twist. This process prevents eggs from sticking to the bottom of pan.

Timing: An omelet takes about three minutes on the first side and one minute or less on the other.

Turning the omelet: First, be sure the omelet slides freely in the pan. Our turning technique is to put a plate on top of the eggs, then invert the pan. The eggs drop onto the plate cooked side up. The omelet is then slid back into the pan and finished.

Folding: When the omelet is done add whatever goes in it on one side. Remove the pan from the flame and tilt the stuffed side toward a plate, helping the omelet along with a spatula and by shaking. When most of the stuffed side is on the plate, use the spatula to flip the other side on top.

THE THICK, FLUFFY OMELET (MOUSSELINE)

A thick pancake-sized omelet with a thin, browned, slightly tough exterior and a thick, moist, fluffy interior, similar to a soufflé.

4 eggs
dash water
1 teaspoon lemon juice
3 tablespoons cream
3 tablespoons butter/oil
salt and pepper

Beat the whites of two eggs stiff, adding lemon juice and water. Reserve. Mix the two yolks with two more eggs, cream, salt and pepper. Combine with egg whites using a few quick strokes.

Heat three tablespoons oil with a teaspoon of butter in a fry pan. Bring to very high heat. Pour mixture in pan and reduce heat. Handle thereafter like a basic omelet. Many chefs bake this mixture in the oven at 325 F. for fifteen minutes.

MUSHROOM OMELET

Sauté chopped **fresh mushrooms** in butter until golden. If you are using **dried mushrooms** cut them up with a scissors or break them apart, reconstitute and add them at the last moment to the omelette. Sprinkle on some of the water which is full of flavor.

Sauté in pan over medium heat:
2 cups mushrooms, chopped

Add:
1 medium onion, chopped
pinch celery seed
1 tablespoon fresh parsley, chopped
pinch of salt and pepper

Remove contents of pan and reserve. Make a basic three egg omelet. When the eggs are almost set pour vegetables in a broad band across one half of omelet. Fold.

FRUIT STUFFED OMELETS

The quickest stuffing for a breakfast or dessert omelet is a high-quality fruit marmalade mixed with a little lemon juice. Read more about these omelettes in Chapter 18.

TWO DELIGHTFUL LOBSTER OMELETS

If you love steamed lobster as much as we do, you may wonder why we bother with a lobster omelet. The reason is because there are times when one lovely lobster must feed three or four people. This first recipe was a favorite of King Edward VII. It's easy to see why.

LOBSTER OMELET BARON DE BARANTE

Three pots, two burners, feeds three

1 cup mushrooms, sliced
2 tablespoons butter
2 pinches each salt and pepper
2 tablespoons flour
3 tablespoons oil
1 cup ruby port or sherry
4 teaspoons lemon juice
1 cup heavy cream or unsweetened condensed milk
1/2 cup grated sharp cheddar cheese.
1-1/2 cups cooked lobster meat or fresh crawfish, sliced
pinch of nutmeg (optional)
soy sauce

Sauté mushrooms in butter and oil over high heat, stirring constantly. When mushrooms are golden, sprinkle with a few drops of soy sauce and pepper sauce. Reserve. Add all other ingredients except cream and simmer a few minutes. Return mushrooms to the pan and warm.

Make a *roux*. Add the cream to make a white sauce. Add filling ingredients and mix. Add milk to thin if needed. Simmer until hot.

Make the basic three-egg omelet. Put lobster filling in center; fold and pour a little sauce on top. Sprinkle with a few drops of sherry.

LOBSTER OMELET II

This second lobster omelet fares equally well with shrimp, mussels or scallops.

3 tablespoons butter/oil
1/4 pound lobster meat in small chunks
1/2 green bell pepper, chopped
1 small onion, chopped
1/2 cup tomato puree
1 teaspoon each: lemon juice, sugar, oregano
pinch of salt and pepper

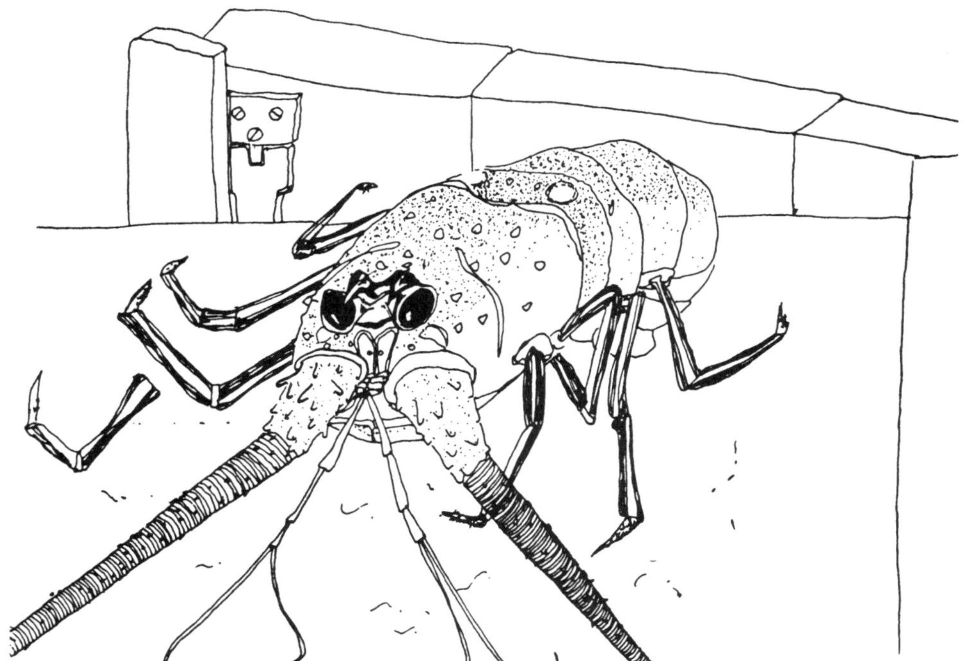

Sauté pepper and onion in sauce pan over high heat until onions are golden. When onions turn golden, reduce heat; add all other ingredients except egg mixture and lobster. Simmer for five minutes, stirring occasionally. Add one cup sliced, cooked lobster. Simmer lobster over low heat to warm; set aside.

Make the basic three-egg omelet. Pour in the filling, reserving some of the sauce to pour on top.

CREAMED CRAB OR MIXED SEAFOOD OMELET

We have a small but dependable crab trap, which automatically goes over the side when we are in a clean anchorage. It has provided many delightful meals, and on occasion, has come up almost groaning from the weight of crabs. But there are those moments when we have taken our luck for granted, invited guests for lunch, then pulled up our trap to find, alas, only two crabs.

That may not be enough to have cracked crab for lunch, but the meat of two crabs is most adequate for creamed crab omelets that are a real delight. One of our favorite combinations is crab, shrimp, and crawfish tail in whatever proportions are at hand.

2 cups seafood cooked and flaked
1 generous tablespoon butter
4 tablespoons heavy cream mixed with a teaspoon flour (no lumps!)
2 tablespoons sherry or Madeira
finely chopped chile pepper (as much as you dare)
pinch of salt, pepper, nutmeg

Sauté in a small pot all ingredients except crab and egg mixture over moderate heat: Add crab, simmer until hot, stirring constantly. Make a basic omelet for two. Pour in seafood and fold.

DEEP SEA TUNA OMELET

An end-of-the-passage delight made with long-lasting ingredients.

1 small onion, chopped
1/2 cup grated Swiss cheese
4 tablespoons butter and oil
1/4 cup cream or mayo
1 tin (7 ounces) tuna, drained and flaked
4 tablespoons heavy cream or unsweetened condensed milk
1/2 teaspoon each salt, pepper

Sauté onion in sauce pan over high heat until golden. Reduce heat and add tuna, salt, pepper, and cream. Simmer lightly for five minutes, stirring regularly to heat fish. Add cream or mayo, combine, turn off heat. Do not let simmer.

Make a basic omelet, sprinkle with cheese, pour tuna into a broad band in center of omelet while eggs are still quite runny. Fold omelet as soon as you can lift edges.

HAM AND SWISS CHEESE OMELET

4 tablespoons oil/butter
3 Italian tomatoes, skinned, chopped and seeded
1 teaspoon parsley
3 teaspoons white wine
1/2 cup chopped ham
1/2 cup grated Swiss cheese
generous pinch of salt and pepper

Sauté ham and onion for approximately five minutes in pan. When onions begin to turn golden add to all other ingredients except egg mixture. Cook until mixture is steaming. Make basic omelet with cheese. When omelet begins to set, add filling and fold.

EGG FOO YUNG

1 large onion, blenderized
3 scallions, blenderized
3 cloves garlic, blenderized
3 tablespoons oil
6 eggs, lightly beaten
1/2 cup green pepper, finely chopped
1/2 cup reconstituted mushrooms
salt and pepper

Brown onion and garlic in oil. Add remaining vegetables, sauté five minutes. Add eggs, stir once or twice and serve with sauce.

Sauce:
1 cup chicken stock
2 teaspoons soy sauce
2 tablespoons corn starch

Mix all ingredients, simmer until thick. Do not boil. Pour over eggs.

MEDITERRANEAN FRITTATAS

The Italian frittata (called a **tortilla** in Spain) is one of the most popular slow-cooked flat omelets in the Mediterranean and is usually served at room temperature, cut like a pie. This is a somewhat dry, fluffy omelet which gets its zing from the additions. It can be sprinkled with lemon and butter after it has set if you want more moisture.

Traditionally the frittata is finished under the broiler. You can also turn the omelet over and pan-finish it. Put a lid on the pan as soon as the eggs are poured; wait about ten minutes without lifting the lid. Place a large plate on top of the eggs and turn.

PROSCIUTTO AND MUSHROOM FRITTATA

Prosciutto, salami and dry sausage are standard stock items on a cruise and so are dried mushrooms. This is therefore a perfect recipe for the cruiser.

1 tablespoon butter
1 tablespoon oil
1/2 cup onions or shallots, chopped
1/2 cup prosciutto or salami, slivered
3/4 cup mushrooms, dried, reconstituted
1-1/2 cups potato, cooked, diced
6 egg basic omelet mix

Heat butter and oil. Sauté potato and onion until onion is golden. Add mushrooms and cook one minute. Add eggs and cook over low heat until bottom is done, about six minutes. Broil or turn and finish. Sprinkle on prosciutto and serve.

PEASANT FRITTATA

We learned this recipe from a Frenchman who tied up alongside in St. Tropez. He fed us this lovely omelet, helped along the road with large glasses of robust Algerian wine, Camembert cheese, black Spanish olives, and crusty, home-baked French bread.

A peasant frittata is a dish of opportunity whose ingredients vary, depending on what's available. Leftovers play an important roll. Cottage cheese, or a mixture of Ricotta and cottage cheese is frequently added for a custard-like finish.

In any event, the finished product looks more like an egg cake than a delicate French omelet. It can be made using either the basic or thick omelet mixture.

THE OMELET: A six-egg omelet mix is poured into the pan and the precooked ingredients are arranged on it. The mixture is cooked with a lid over very low heat for about fifteen minutes. The heat is turned off and the pan is allowed to stand with the lid on for another five minutes.

For Thicker Variation: Separate whites and beat them stiff. Add yolks with a few strokes. Arrange the cooked or blanched ingredients in a very hot pan sizzling with oil/ butter and pour the foamy omelet mixture over it. The bottom is fried, then the top is grilled under the broiler. This makes for an omelet with a nice brown finish, a leathery exterior and a moist, fluffy inside.

The filling:
1/2 cup each parboiled carrots and potatoes, diced
1 medium onion, diced
6 bacon slices
1 green pepper, diced
2 cloves garlic, finely chopped
1 teaspoon marjoram
1 cup precooked vegetables, such as corn, zucchini, yellow squash, or green beans
6-egg omelet mix

Fry bacon slices until brown and reserve. Sauté all other ingredients except egg mixture until onions are golden. Pour on whipped egg mixture. Granish with bacon.

ARTICHOKE, ROASTED PEPPER AND POTATO FRITTATA

1 cup jarred artichokes marinated in oil, slightly chopped
4 tablespoons oil and butter (2 tablespoons for pan, 2 tablespoons for finish)
1 teaspoon rosemary
1 cup home-fried potatoes, parboiled and sliced
1/2 cup grated hard cheese
1 roasted red pepper (you can also skin the pepper with a peeler and fry in oil)
8 large black olives, sliced
6-egg omelet mix
salt and pepper

Home fry the parboiled potatoes in oil/ butter with rosemary, salt and pepper. Add the artichokes and omelet mixture. Cook and turn. Sprinkle on cheese. Arrange all other ingredients, turn off and cover until cheese melts. Sprinkle with butter and lemon.

MISCELLANEOUS EGGS

CHINESE SALTED EGGS

We are not exactly certain whether this is a recipe, or a storage technique, or a blend of both. Salted eggs are made by boiling them in a saturated salt solution. Salted eggs last four to six months. Hard or soft boiled, salted eggs look and taste great.

Handle eggs carefully; don't crack them. Store in wide-mouthed quart jars that have good lids. Add enough eggs to fill the jar. Pour saturated salt water into jar to fill. Store in cool, dark place. The egg is not greatly affected by the salt for a month. After thirty days, take one egg out and taste. If you wish to arrest the process, pour off the salty water and add an equal quantity of fresh, boiled water. Let cool and reseal for another three or four months.

PICKLED EGGS

Hard-boil all eggs, allow to cool, then shell and discard the bad ones. Pack all the others in a scalded jar and pour over them a steaming hot mixture of the following, enough to cover:

vinegar and water (50:50)
mustard seed
salt
hot sauce to taste

Allow to stand at least three or four days before eating. Does not require refrigeration .

DEVILED EGGS

Hard-boil six eggs, then let them stand for a few minutes in cold water and shell. With a very sharp knife slice them in half, lengthwise, and carefully remove the yolks.

Combine thoroughly:
1/4 cup mayonnaise
2 teaspoons Dijon mustard
1 teaspoon white vinegar
1/2 teaspoon each salt, pepper
6 hard-boiled egg yolks

Combine the mixture quickly. Stuff whites with the yolk mixture; sprinkle with paprika and serve.

Sundancer departing San Diego for Zihuatanejo, Mexico, December, 1993

7 The Sarasota Shuffle and Other Dances

When people think of clams they usually have in mind cherrystones, little necks, or quahogs and, indeed, these are probably the best-known clams in the United States. But any experienced clam digger worth his salt knows that literally hundreds of other varieties of edible clams exist, many even more succulent and delicious than the commercially available varieties. They range in size from the tiny, wedge clams that are usually less than half an inch in length, to the huge surf clam, more than six inches long or the gooyduck—as long as a man's arm!

I first learned clamming, not as an amateur, but as an honest-to-god professional. It happened one summer during high school vacation when I was hitchhiking through the South looking for some adventure and a little work. A friend named Beau and I chanced to be in Sarasota, Florida where we learned that a commercial clam supply house was in need of a few hands to harvest quahogs.

Being a bit broke, the idea of work actually intrigued us. We could dig clams for a month, and, in the critical few days before payday, we could eat and trade the smaller ones for supplies. Quahogs like somewhat sheltered waters and a bottom consisting of mud and sand. Some people hunt quahog with a stout clam rake which is used to turn back the sand, exposing them. The clamming procedure in Sarasota Bay consisted of walking along the shallow water, pushing a little runabout, "feeling" for clams in stocking feet.

It is amazing how well educated the toes become if given a chance. After all, it's almost a snap to tell the difference between a half-buried clam and, say, a sunken beer can or an old tire. After a short time, we developed the Sarasota Shuffle, a dance akin to a cow trying to throw a stone from its hoof.

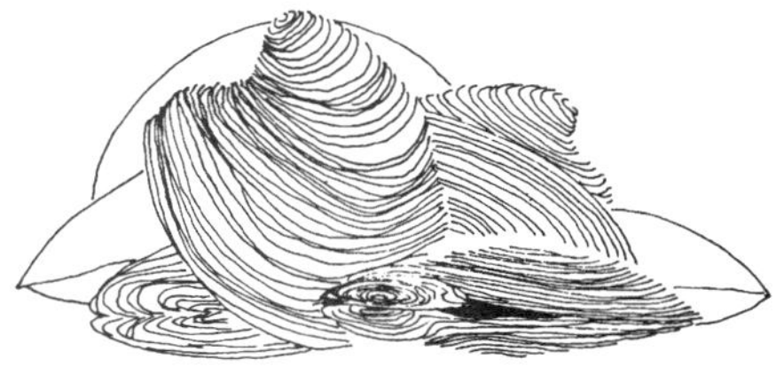

Quahogs

It consisted of standing on one foot while probing ahead in a half-circle with the toes of the other. A sort of half-step terminated our dance. One moved a little forward, a bit sideways, then repeated the whole act with the other foot while humming Muskrat Ramble in three-quarter time. Cut feet or "turtle toe" as we called it, although very infrequent, was always a worry. The old timers at the clam house always warned us, with straight faces, to be sure to get shark insurance from Blue Cross.

With these stories always somewhere in the back of my mind you can imagine my reaction one day, while doing the Sarasota Shuffle, when I felt something grab my big toe. I let out a scream and vaulted over the transom into the skiff, landing on my chest with genuine indignity in a pile of clams. Quickly examining the injured part, fully expecting to find it half-gone, I discovered my toe squarely in the open jaws of a big scallop. I ate him in revenge.

Unlike clams, scallops don't clam up, even when you haul them from the water. Mess with them and they'll snap right back at you. But in the process, they lose all their water and quickly die. Fishermen therefore cut out the huge abductor muscle and throw away the rest. Many of the world's scallop lovers think a scallop is a little solid circular creature without a shell!

Few mollusks are superior in flavor to the fresh scallop. The entire creature is delicious. Thus alerted to the delicacy just a toe's length away, Beau and I borrowed diving gear and, in clear patches of bay, chased scallops. Scallops have primitive eyes. They're mainly good for telling day from night but are also good enough to spot toes doing the Sarasota Shuffle. The scallop gets away by forcefully snapping its shells together to expel water and move backward six or eight inches at a time. So scallops know where they have been but not where they are going, reminiscent of some sailors we know.

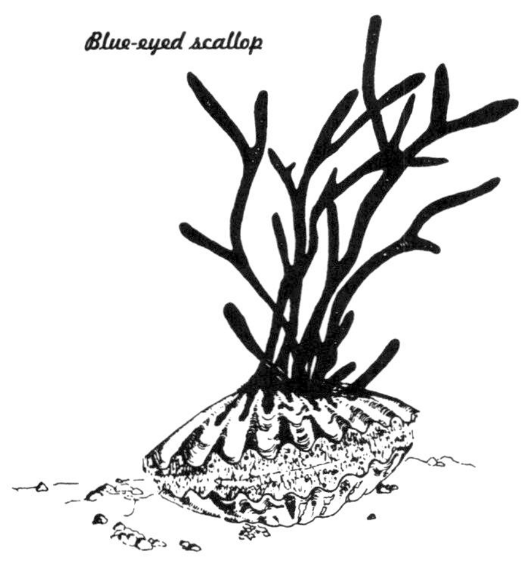

The Clam Corporation paid us three cents per pound for our labors. This might sound like a losing proposition but the clams were mostly large ones intended for use in canned soups. About fourteen clams weighed ten pounds. Beau and I would dig nearly two thousand clams daily to make twenty dollars each, but that was really a lot of money for a couple of high school kids in those days, and we didn't mind the work. In addition, there was an abundance of clams, and we usually had made our "twenty" by nightfall.

But we started hard. After the second day of reaching down and grabbing clams with our hands, we completely wore off our fingerprints. A bit discouraged, we had already gone through a good set of calluses as well, and the weekend wasn't even in sight. Then, a fellow clammer took us down to the local blacksmith and had him make us a pair of clam forks. A clam fork looks exactly like a huge meat carving fork cut off about three inches from the tines. The tines are usually made from quarter-inch rod about four inches long and terminate in dull points. At the other end, a length of three quarters-inch tubing, long enough to act as a handle, is welded. After a clam was located with the Sarasota Shuffle, we would reach down and, in one motion, slip the fork under it and pry him out of the sand.

The kindly landlady who rented us a room knew many different ways to cook clams but Beau and I soon yearned for—anything else!

PEN SHELLS

Pen shells are scientifically closer to oysters than clams. There were plenty of them in Sarasota Bay, and the sharp lips of their shells were one of the chief reasons we wore heavy socks. Beau and I soon discovered them, then cut our hands getting them out of the mud and broke the delicate shells trying to get at the insides. Finally, we were repulsed by the unappetizing-looking creature inside. Since we weren't exactly hurting for shellfish, we promptly thought no more of them. It's probably a good example of how an animal comes to be known as inedible.

It wasn't until fifteen years later that this creature probed the culinary lobes of my mind. It happened when I was anchored in a place the Miami Marine Patrol deemed unsuitable. The police urged us to move into the marina (which was full) or haul in our hook and quietly steal away. They threatened to fine us for rowing our six-foot dinghy at night without running lights, and I guess they would have been pretty mad about us stealing pen shells from the bay bottom. Then a little Tahiti ketch with a Martha's Vineyard registry worked its way under sail into the anchorage near us and dropped the hook.

The mud hadn't even settled before the police were there telling the captain to move to the city marina. The skipper said he wouldn't mind moving there "atall" but "seein as how (he) didn't have a motor an' it bein' illegal to sail under a draw bridge (he) wouldn't mind "atall" if they'd give a tow.

It was about ten miles to city marina and the police had other things to do that day, so our two little boats were soon alone on the hook. With both my admiration and attention fully aroused, I watched somewhat in amazement as the skipper proceeded to dive up a big bucket full of pen shells.

Knowing that pen shells do not grow in northern waters, I rowed over in the dinghy to kindly tell this Yankee about how inedible they were.

"You going to eat those pen shells, Mister?" I asked.

"Ah yep," he replied.

"Not many folks around here eat them," I said.

He looked at his overflowing bucket and said "Ah yep."

"Most folks think they're kind of tough and gritty," I said.

"Mostly," he replied.

I was beginning to realize that he was a man of few words, but while his jaw was a little slow his hands weren't. He was opening the pen shells with a knife, cutting out the huge abductor muscle and throwing the rest back into the bay, thus explaining the "mostly" in answer number three. Since our conversation seemed to have run aground, I rowed off to do a little pen shell fishing on my own.

There are different species of pen shells in different parts of the world but they are very similar in shape and all taste about the same. They can be found from Cape Hatteras to Florida, including the Gulf Coast, throughout the Bahamas, the upper Caribbean, and on the west coast of Mexico around the Yucatan. There are also several species of pen shell in the "Med."

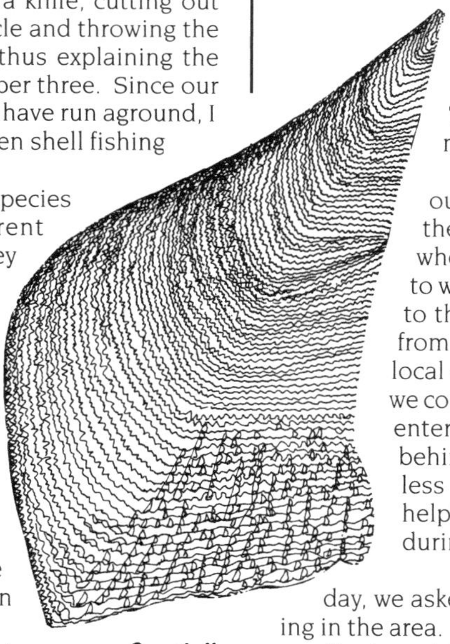

Pen shell

The largest are the noble pen, or Nero's pen shell, which refers to the days when they were the pinnacle of fine cuisine. We first discovered the Nero's pen shell in the clear, shallow waters of Western Sardinia. We had not planned to stop there but a vicious Norther sent us running under storm sails for the nearest port of opportunity.

This turned out to be the Gulf of Oristano—a huge bay with a relatively small opening. It was quite an experience. One moment we were taking aboard green water; then, as we entered, the bay water had just the slightest ripple—not even the hint of a wave. The wind instantly moderated and we were able to hoist the working jib and mainsail to pass in ghostly fashion along our course.

The hills looked as though they were made of living steel in the bright moonlight. We could still hear the angry sea yammering behind us. With the full moon, with the clear sky and stars, with the hills stretching before us like mountains of the moon and the moonlight blending with the phosphorescence of our wake, we came in silence to an anchorage at the foot of a hill covered with ruins.

Greek columns, beautifully preserved, glowed whitely in the moonlight as they marched toward the sea. A Punic tower, misshapen and silent, seemed to watch darkly from the crest of the hill. A short distance away there was a village with houses made from reeds. The embers of their fires made reflections on the walls.

In the morning, we found ourselves swinging at anchor in the midst of a tiny fishing port whose inhabitants used gill nets to work the fertile bay. We rowed to the bistro, a little place made from cement block and reed. The local dialect was Sardinian, which we could not understand, but as we entered the bistro, a young lady behind the bar greeted us in flawless English. She was a student helping her parents run the bar during summer.

During the course of the day, we asked if there was any good diving in the area. The fish in the bay were a bit small, she said, but there were some "big shells" at the foot of the ruins. We went there that afternoon and found, among the shards of pottery and ruined columns, the largest bed of noble pen shells we have ever seen.

There were literally hundreds of them so big that their shells were later to serve as plates big enough to hold a full course meal. The shells themselves were a translucent white, covered on the outside with a brownish green periostracum. After we worked a patch of these shells free from the bottom, we opened them with a thin fillet knife.

The mollusk within was the most awful looking thing we have ever seen. Coils of intestines were woven in unpleasant colors of orange, black, and brown. No wonder the local population disdained them! But the abductor muscle was absolutely huge. It was slightly bigger than a silver dollar and about 1-1/2-inches thick. We ate a number of them right on the spot, flavored with nothing more than sea water in which they lived and a little lemon juice.

Later that day we would sprinkle them with celery salt and a little flour and fry them lightly in butter. What a delight! The next day we steamed them for five minutes in dry, white wine and served them with fresh mayonnaise to which we had added a little mustard. Could this have been what drove Nero mad? Thus we spent our days, walking the countryside with our friend, Maria, and eating nature's wonderful gifts from the sea.

Pen shells live in gritty, sandy mud with just the edge of their lips protruding. They do not have any sort of escape locomotion, so once you have found them with either the Sarasota Shuffle technique or flippers and mask, simply pull them up. The huge, single abductor muscle is found near the base, or pointed, end of the shell and is easily severed by slipping a knife between the pen's imperfectly closed lips.

The curious thing about pen shells is their interior. It is frequently inhabited by a little, red crustacean which looks so much like an American lobster we thought we had discovered something new.

This little beast is, in fact, a shrimp which lives inside the pen shell for protection. It gets its food from debris in the water sucked in by the pen shell's siphons. These little shrimp are hermits and, with the exception of cohabitation for breeding, will readily attack each other. We have tried, on several occasions to save these shrimp when we shuck pen shells. There are usually three or four in a pail after we are through, but in the morning there is inevitability just one and a few other bits and pieces.

WEDGE SHELLS

Wedge shells are tiny clams not much larger than a penny. They come in all sorts of colors, so many in fact that trying to identify a wedge shell by color would be a futile job. Wedge shells, wherever they are found, look like tiny, smooth, brightly colored cherrystones. Should you turn over a shovel full of wet sand and find it full of shiny little clams, you have probably found wedge shells. Species live from Massachusetts to Florida, throughout the Caribbean and Central America, the Mediterranean, and in great numbers along the west coast of the United States. What these delicious gems lack in size is more than compensated for by number. Quite frequently, you can find them filling the bottom of tidal pools and puddles. Empty shells at the tide line display their presence.

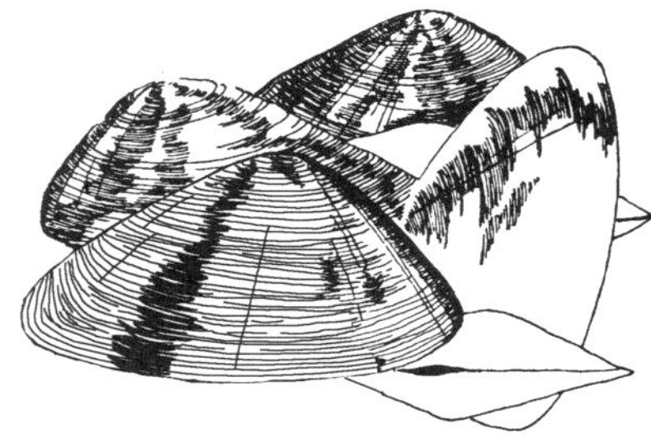

They are so small that Americans just don't consider them food, other than for an occasional use in broth. But the Spanish, French, Portuguese and others take these clams quite seriously, and I am certain that literally thousands of tons are sold annually. For example, wedge shells, called Vongola in Italy, are widely esteemed for the making of clam sauce for spaghetti. A handful of these little beauties in wine and garlic sauce, over spaghetti is a great treat. Many restaurants serve big plates of wedge shells for customers. Wedge shells are so delicious that we ate them three or four times per week when we cruised the coast of Italy.

Rinse wedges free of sand. They are then left for the rest of the day in a bucket of sea water sprinkled with a little corn meal which they will eat, ejecting intestinal grit. By dinner they will be ready to eat.

Because wedge shells are so small, it is a bit tedious to shell them by hand. There is an easier way. Steam them open in one cup of dry, white wine. Let the broth cool, then pour half the shells and all of the liquid into a jar. Tightly cap the jar and shake the whole thing hard for a few minutes. This will free quite a few of the clams from their shells. To remove the shells, give the mixture in the jar a vigorous shake. This will cause the free clam meat to swirl up at which point you can pour it off.

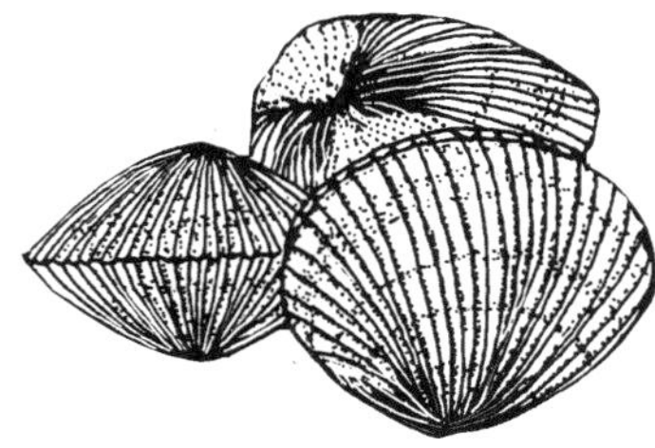

COCKLES

Cockles of various sizes and species are found all over the east coast of the United States from Maine to Florida, throughout the Gulf Coast, along the shores of the British Isles, in the Med, and along the west coast of Africa. The word cockle actually refers to a relatively large number of different species, and in many areas, various bivalves are called cockles when in fact they are not. Most small bivalves are edible and it is only a question of how they get from the sea to your stomach. For simplicity and our culinary purposes, it is merely necessary to classify cockles as large or small, and treat them accordingly. The smaller ones can be eaten whole while larger ones are usually better when ground. Cockles seem to prefer estuaries or protected bays where the surf is light and the sand not too compact. They have no siphons and are usually found lying about the sand at low tide.

We spent several weeks on the hook in Portimão, Portugal, a lovely little town on the Algarve coast, not far from Cape Sagres. A river broadens as it runs past the town. This grand river continues southward, across numerous sand banks and spits, until it broadens into a small estuary whose mouth is protected by a breakwater. The river current is accentuated by ten-foot tides which, when on the ebb, run with a vengeance. It is essential to drop an upstream and downstream anchor and be clear of the port's fifty fishing boats when the tide turns.

Being a Miami boy, where a big tide is three feet, I was not attuned to all of the problems big tides can cause. After a few hours ashore we returned to the quay to find our dinghy apparently stolen. Upon looking closer I discovered the painter line turned around the cleat just where I left it.

Peering down into the murky depths I could just see my dinghy, oars and all, lying on a platform, looking just like a ceramic wreck in a fishbowl. I then vividly remembered that the dock had two platforms, separated by a set of steps. I was now on the upper platform, looking down at the submerged lower one.

It was September. The leaves had fallen and cold winds promised Winter. The tide was ripping along. No thought about swimming out to the boat. We finally decided to wait out the tide in a cinema and saw Tony Curtis in *The Gladiators* dubbed in Portuguese three times. We then returned to the dinghy and bailed it out.

Despite the natural barrier caused by the current, the sand banks and bars of the river were covered with common cockles as much as three miles inland. How they got there against the current is a mystery to me—finding their way into the mouth of the breakwater against this outward flow.

Nevertheless, when the tide is out and miles of sandy beach are exposed, literally thousands of small cockles are to be found. The townspeople gather them when the tide is out, but despite their determined efforts, the supply never seems to diminish, averaging about sixty pounds of cockles per square yard.

These little cockles are about 1-1/2 to 2-1/2 inches long and their meat has a fine clam flavor. They are numerous enough on some parts of the European coast, mostly south of Biscay, to be gathered commercially and canned. Canning does damage their flavor but they but they are still quite tasty.

Since our visit to Portimão, I have seen numerous cockle shells on beaches all over the world. Don't let their drab, unassuming shells fool you; the contents within make really fine eating and can be used in any of the recipes for wedge shells or fried clams. Or, you can also just steam them in a little white wine .

LARGE COCKLES

Considering the unassuming size of the common cockle, the Atlantic cockle, found all over the southeast coast, Bahamas, Caribbean and throughout the Gulf of Mexico, is a real giant. It grows as large as six inches, though the median size would be closer to four. It is particularly abundant in Florida and the lower Gulf states, and from the Yucatan channel as far south as Belize.

In some parts of Florida, such as around Marco and Sanibel Islands, giant cockles and scallops were particularly abundant in pre Colombian times. Primitive man came from miles around to eat them. These islands are several miles long and solid enough to build houses upon, are actually huge kitchen middens made entirely from the discarded shells of ancient feasts. There are still areas in South Florida where giant cockles can be found in great abundance.

As with their smaller brothers, Atlantic cockles are usually found in protected bays or estuaries where there is relatively light surf. They are not deep burrowers and are usually found either on the sand or just below it.

Large cockles are very popular in Europe. They are a pronounced flavored clam which make wonderful broths and fritters. The shells of the bigger ones are nicely hollowed. People have a natural tendency to save them for use as containers or ashtrays.

LIMPETS

Limpets are algae-eating sea snails which look, behave and taste like small abalone. Many limpet lovers, including myself, think they are even better. Limpets have a single cone shaped shell and a large fleshy foot used for clinging to rocks. They rarely move far from a customized depression in the rock created by the constant grinding of their shell.

A limpet colony may have dozens of creatures clinging to a single rock but each knows exactly where its own personalized depression lies. If you touch them or bump the rock alerting them to your presence, they will adhere with 300-400 pounds of resistance and can be incredibly tenacious. If you are not swift enough to catch them off guard you can drive a screwdriver beneath their shell with a hammer.

Limpets come in all sizes but the largest is the Owl limpet (about three inches in diameter), found on wave-swept rocks in the intertidal zone along the Pacific coast from Canada to Southern Mexico. Other species are found throughout the world. I ate some mighty fine ones in the Azores. Hunt them by wading around in tidal pools at low tide, armed with a stout butter knife, putty knife or screwdriver. Where there is one there are hundreds and your dinner is assured.

Limpets can be scraped from their shell with a spoon and cooked like abalone. They can be ground and made into fritters or cakes. They can be pounded, floured and fried. You can also cook them in the shell. This is accomplished by scrunching up a sheet of aluminium foil and pressing them into it upside down. A mixture of garlic, butter, lemon juice and hot sauce is squirted on top and the whole affair is broiled for five to ten minutes until the sauce sizzles. Bon appetite!.

An ancient way to prepare limpets is to place them foot down on a cookie sheet, allowing the critter to attach itself. Then shredded coconut fronds or light kindling is placed over all and fired off. This cooks them in their shells. After ten minutes, brush them off and swish them in butter and wine.

MUSSELS

Mussels thrive on rocky shores where the water is cold and surf not too great. Mussles grow from the high tide line to ten or fifteen feet below mean water. They attach themselves to rocks and each other with

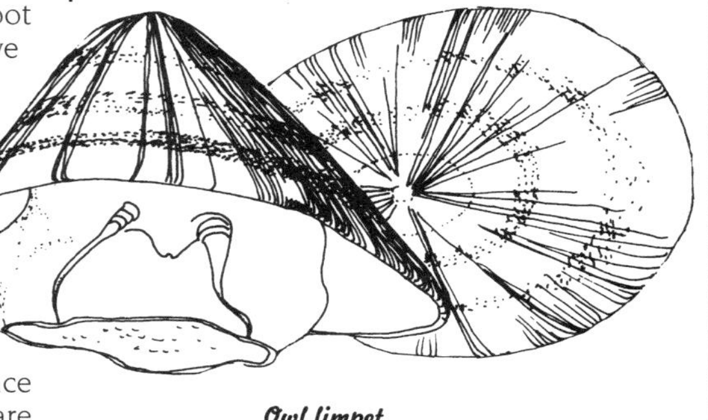

Owl Limpet

fine, very tough threads. Where there is one there are usually thousands. Bon appetite!

Select only the largest. Wear gloves to protect yourself against their sharp lips. Use a small pry bar or heavy screwdriver to pry them free. Mussles will last a long time stored in a mesh sack which, when underway can be tossed on deck, covered with a wet towel and bucketed down two or three times.

CATCHING THE WILY CRAB

Crabs are found in every ocean and estuary. Some species live in the abysmal depths while their cousins are found in brackish inlets miles from the sea. Land crabs live on land but even they need access to water to refresh their gills and breed. All crabs are edible, even land crabs. The most delicious crab I ever ate was the coconut (land) crab, found in Polynesia. Hermit crabs, which occasionally grow to astonishing size, are also very delicious. Crabs are scavengers and should never be taken where the water is not clean.

Soft-shell crabs are ordinary crabs which have just molted. They are harvested and packed in ice before the new shell hardens. They are often breaded, fried and served on toast. The entire crab, including the shell is eaten.

It is astonishing how easy it is to catch crabs and how frequently they are found. Saltwater crabs are usually caught in baited traps. The **best bait** is some sort of seafood product, such as chum, chopped trash fish, fish guts, crushed mollusks such as whelks or even crushed crab! The bait should be put into a holder to prevent the crabs from devouring it.

Wire mesh holders allow the distribution of the scent and permit visual inspection of the bait by the crab, but the mesh reduces the critter's ability to eat the bait. A tin can may also be used as a holder. The bait is placed inside and the lid pushed back into place. A few holes are punched in the can to allow distribution of the scent.

Bamboo crab trap with can entry

Star traps fold flat and stow well. They lay flat on the bay bottom when open and close when hauled up. Any crab on the bait at this moment is caught but others which have come and gone escape.

Box traps look like lobster traps and some are collapsible. They are much larger and harder to store than star traps but the crab once inside cannot escape, so the trap can be tended less frequently.

Traps are typically deployed by dropping them overboard, weighted with a brick or diving weight. A line with sufficient scope to allow for the vessel's movements is connected from the trap to the boat. In tropic waters it is sometimes better to drop the trap in deeper, cooler water, sixty to one hundred feet deep. In this case the line is connected to a float. Be sure to add five to ten pounds of weight to the trap to prevent currents from moving it. Haul up with the windless.

Storage: Crabs, once caught, can be left

in the trap if it is a box trap or in a mesh sack if you get underway. Wet the sack down hourly and protect it from the sun. Crabs left on the anchorage bottom in a mesh sack are frequently attacked by rays, octopi or sharks.

COLLECTING URCHINS

It's hard to believe that something which looks as unappetizing and formidable as an urchin could be delicious, but delicious is the only way to describe this specialty. Urchins are usually collected by diving, using tongs, or spearing them with a long gig from a boat. It normally takes a big bag full and some time and effort to get a dinner for two, but it's worth it!

The first and apparently biggest question, in view of the urchins' formidable spines, is how to get at the good part inside. This trick is actually easily accomplished since the spines are very sharp but quite brittle. I usually start by dropping the urchin bag on cement six or eight times to get the spine removal process underway. After that I dump the bag on cement or a wet beach and push the urchins about with a deck brush for awhile. Then put on heavy gloves and rub the urchin like an apple. This leaves them suitable for handling with gloves.

Nestle the urchin bottom up in a wet towel to stabilize it. Do not hold directly in the hand. Use a spoon or a putty knife to punch out the entire bottom of the shell. Rinse the shell in sea water and remove all loose guts and debris.

The edible part of the urchin is its eggs. Attached inside the top of the shell are five radial arms of **orange roe** which may be scooped out and served raw as sushi (uni) or cooked with herbs and bread crumbs (see Chapter 10). Each urchin has about two tablespoons of roe and a portion is about three-quarters cup. Look closely at the roe to be sure you see tiny eggs. Reject the smooth looking sacks of milt found in male urchins. Entire colonies of urchins eject eggs and milt into the surrounding water at the same time leaving fertilization to chance. So, if you open a few urchins and find no roe, wait a few weeks and try again.

NOOSING THE MANTIS SHRIMP

The Mantis shrimp looks somewhat like a shrimp but is not related. It has two razor sharp-toothed arms which it holds folded like the arms of a praying mantis, hence its name. The appendages are blindingly quick and lash out to catch prey. Wear a glove to handle these critters!

Mantis shrimp live in holes in calm tidal flats which are not quite uncovered at low tide. Where there is one there are thousands. The holes are about as big around as a quarter and about a foot deep. The main tunnel connects to lateral escape tunnels, so forget about digging them out.

You can easily determine if you have a Mantis hole by delicately brushing a straw near the hole, making the creature think something good to eat is nearby. It will peek out to investigate. Do not think your problem of catching the Mantis is solved. They are lightning fast and are not easily caught.

Mantis shrimp are five to ten inches long, so you can see that there is some good eating to be had—if you can catch them! The only question is how to get the Mantis out of its hole. An old trick is to bait them out. Securely attach a piece of seafood like a whelk foot or a clam muscle to a piece of stiff wire. Place the open tines of a pair of spaghetti tongs on either side of the hole. Keep them immobile. Gently slide the bait down the hole and when the shrimp hits it, slowly draw it out. The shrimp will follow and when he is out far enough, grab him with the tongs. Natives often use a loop of string attached to a stick. The loop goes around the hole. The bitter end is tied to a finger. It is pulled taught when the shrimp emerges. Boil them whole and eat the tail. Delicious.

BEACH COMBING

Another fine technique is to idle along the low tide line of a rocky shore turning over rocks. Your labor is greatly eased if you employ a boat hook or short gaff, which will eliminate much bending over. Wear heavy gloves and boots because small, extremely short tempered, extraordinarily aggressive,

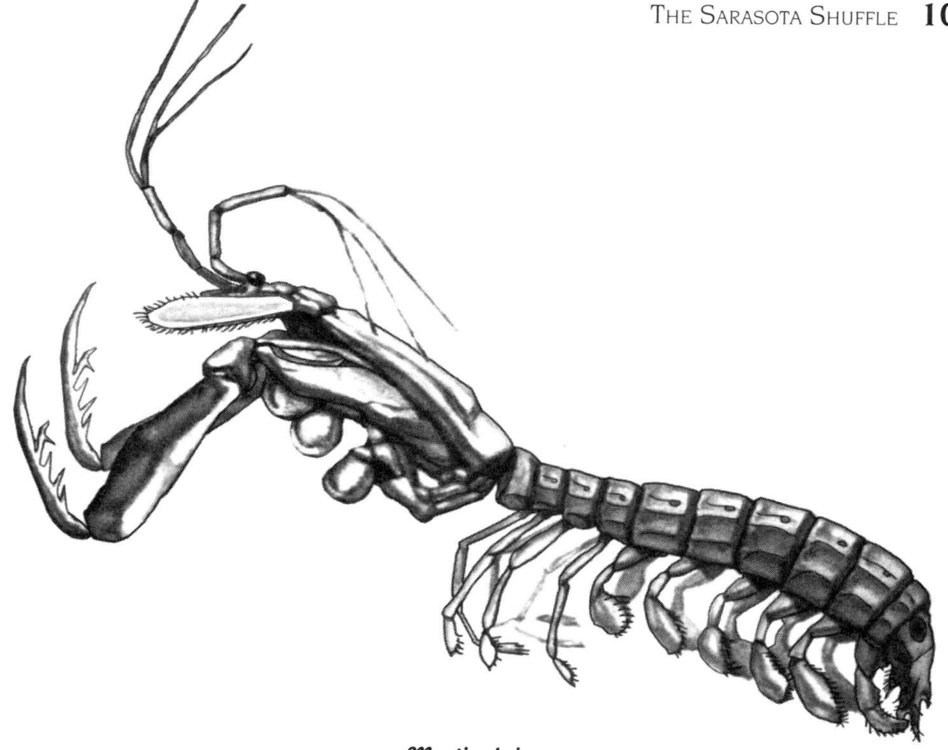

Mantis shrimp

but fortunately very small brown moray eels hide under these rocks—a fact my bare feet discovered the hard way! These critters may bite but they are also extremely succulent and tasty.

Stand between the rock and the water so that you can cut off the escape of any fast moving critter which darts out. As soon as the rock is turned over, plunge your gloved hand into the cavity and feel around for crabs, small octopus or eels. Grab them fast and fling them high onto the beach with a quick flip. If you find an eel too big to handle, flip it on the beach with the boat hook. Hold it down with the boat hook, put your foot behind its head and cut it off.

Feel the cavity where the rock was laying for shellfish such as clams or scallops. Their lips will just protrude from the sand. Examine the rock for clinging mollusks such as oysters which are usually well disguised and overgrown with vegetation. Use a screwdriver or abalone knife to pry them free.

If a rock is too big to turn over, examine it and see if it has a protruding lip. If so, feel under it for shellfish. By the time you have gotten tired of beach combing you should have a fine nice mixture of mixed seafood which will make a fine bouillabaisse.

There are many different types of wonderful and delicious sea creatures in the world and we do not claim to know them all. We do know that wandering around with a few tools and a bucket—and an active curiosity—has put many a dinner on our plate.

With your sailboat and dinghy it is possible to visit deserted islands and sand flats that the landlubber can never reach. These are hunting grounds that can yield rich harvests of food and fun.

Clamming, crabbing and beachcombing not only stretch your budget, they are fine ways to idle away a sunny day and, to my mind, sure beat sunbathing. Even the complete novice can be an immediate success as a clam hunter and beachcomber. Returning to the ship with the makings of a fine meal gives one a great sense of independence

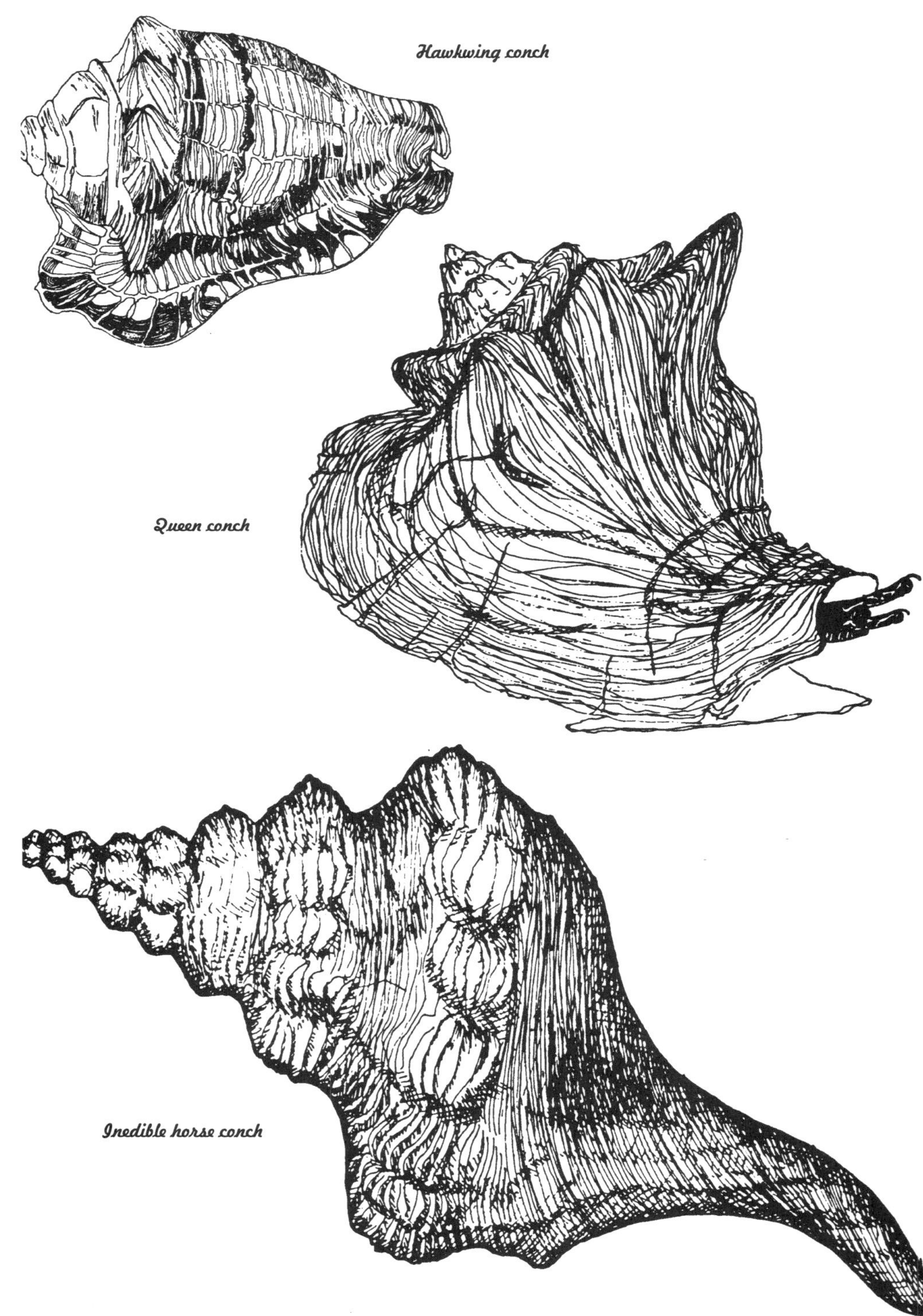
Hawkwing conch
Queen conch
Inedible horse conch

8 Mollusks

ABOUT SHELLFISH

SELECTING: Shellfish sold in developed countries are usually *cultured* (grown commercially) and are therefore safe to eat whenever they are sold. Wild shellfish are traditionally eaten raw during the cold months (those months with an "r"), although there is in fact no particular time of year when a mollusk becomes poisonous. The "r" rule derives from the fear of shellfish poisoning, caused by warm water shellfish ingesting organisms during warm months which are harmless to the shellfish but toxic to humans, a very rare phenomena. The number of people who have died from shellfish poisoning is extremely small, less than from bee stings.

Since shellfish obtain their food by filtering debris from water, they should only be taken from areas where the water is quite clean. When shellfish are taken close to populated areas there is some risk of infection from cholera during the summer and from hepatitis. Cholera is killed by cooking. Hepatitis infection from shellfish is exceedingly rare but the virus is killed only by pressure cooking. Some people eviscerate mollusks and wash away their dark intestinal material which is the location of harmful bacteria if any are present.

Bivalves which "clam up" should be purchased closed or they should close quickly when handled. Those which do not close are dead. Do not let the fishmonger tell you they are "breathing." I assure you, they have breathed their last. Fresh shellfish should be bursting with juice. Tap one against the other and reject any which sound hollow. Avoid any which have big cracks or broken shells.

CLEANING: All bivalves should be scrubbed and made as clean as possible with a stiff brush prior to cooking. Mussels should be bearded by pulling the beard toward the front of the shell. The "beard" is a web of fine golden-brown threads which the mussel uses to anchor itself to rocks.

DEGRITTING: All bivalves taste better if allowed to sit six hours or preferably overnight in a generous amount of sea water onto which has been sprinkled a half a cup of corn meal. The mollusks will consume the cornmeal and eject their intestinal grit. This is important when preparing surf clams, quahogs, and steamers because their intestines are particularly gritty. If you don't have the time to feed them corn meal, the soft stomach portion of larger mollusks can be cut open and the grit washed away.

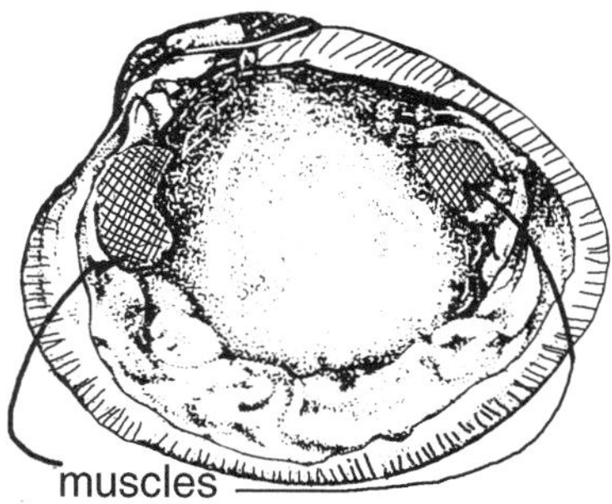

OPENING CLAMS: To open fresh clams, use a clam or butter knife, place it on the shell lips and tap with a hammer until the knife blade forces a slight opening. Slip in with a thin, sharp knife and cut the incredibly tough abductor muscles. Clam abductor muscles are located on either side of the shell toward the rear, so don't go hewing around inside the shell with your knife. Never try to break away the lips of a clam or cockle as the shell usually fractures leaving shell fragments in the meat. Open over a bowl to catch the juice. Chill before opening.

A little stealth may save you much trouble. Place the shells, with lips up, in a pan of sea water. After an hour or so, the shells will begin to open. Very carefully, so as not to disturb the others, slip a small nail into the opening. The shell cannot close and you will be able to proceed with the cutting of the abductor muscle.

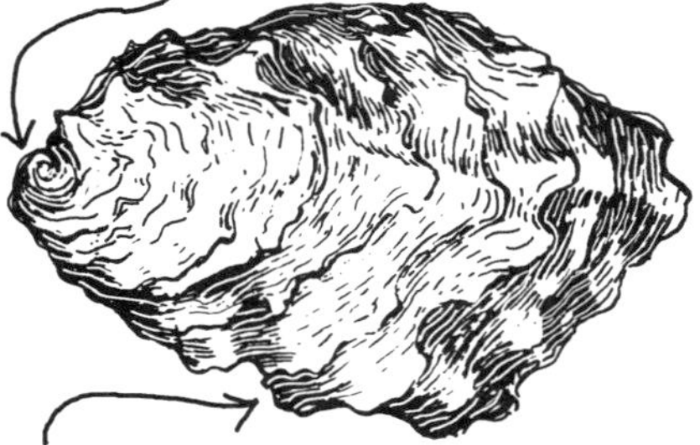

Opening an oyster

OPENING OYSTERS: Prior to opening scrub the shell briskly with a brush. Position oyster with rounded side down on a chopping block so that as much juice, called "liquor" as possible is retained. Use a cloth or oven mit to protect your hand. Use an oyster knife which has a little, diamond shaped blade. The point does the initial opening job. Buy a good knife as cheap ones bend. You can also use a small, good quality screwdriver. Insert the point into the hinge of the shell and twist until the hinge disarticulates. A thin knife is then slipped into the shell, and the single abductor muscle, toward the front of the shell, is cut.

If the oyster does not want to open by twisting with an oyster knife at the valve, break off a piece of the oyster's shell at the lips big enough for the entry of a thin knife. Wash away the broken shell fragments. Slip in the knife pressing toward the top of the flat shell and cut the single muscle that holds the oyster together. Remove the flat shell and cut the muscle where it is attached to the lower shell. Be careful not to lose too much of the liquor. Examine the meat for debris caused by your forced entry.

CLEANING MUSSELS: Mussels secrete a fine thread called byssus which helps anchor them to the surrounding rocks and other mussels. This golden thread, although fine, is remarkably tough. The byssus can be grasped, pulled forward toward the front of the shell and torn free. The shell should be scrubbed with a brush.

Mussels can be eaten on the half shell with a little lemon juice. A knife is easily slipped between the lips and drawn toward the muscle which is approximately opposite the beard. Note muscle location in diagram.

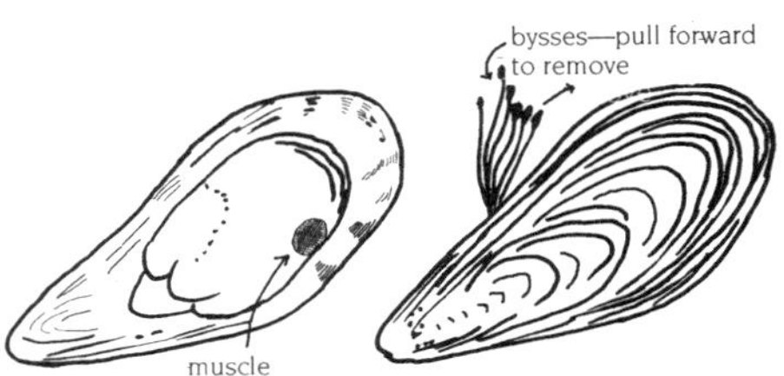

Opening a mussel

Some mussel bodies are white, some are orange. Both are perfectly edible. Mussels are very tender and full of flavor. They are excellent just steamed open and dipped in butter or sauce. Mussel soup and stews are also a delight and the fine meat is a good addition to seafood Newburg.

STORAGE: Live bivalves will last a long time if placed in a bucket and hung in the sea. Do not put them in a cloth or mesh sack and hang the sack over the side since shellfish-eating rays and sharks will make short work of them.

Shellfish can be kept refrigerated at about 50° F. Do not store mollusks in a closed plastic bag because they will smother. Do not store them directly on ice as this kills them. They do best lips up in an open tray covered by a towel soaked in salt water.

REFRIGERATED MOLLUSK MEAT: Fresh, shelled mollusks that come in refrigerator tins or jars (such as oysters). They may be stored directly on the ice or in a refrigerator at 35° to 40° F. for about four days. No more. The important thing to remember is that you store the meat in its own liquor or, in any event, never wash it until you are ready to use them. Regarding the danger of spoilage, let your nose be the guide. If they smell rank, don't eat them.

Regardless of how the mollusk is prepared, whether it is tough or delicate, the liquor inside its shell is tasty and should not be discarded. It can be used to make fish sauces.

CANNED SHELLFISH

SMOKED SHELLFISH PACKED IN OIL such as oysters and mussels are the pinnacle of canned cuisine, if there is such a thing. They are loaded with flavor and have a quite acceptable consistency. They do wonderfully as hors d'oeuvres and can also be scrambled into eggs, or be tossed on a pizza. Get some.

PACKED IN NATURAL JUICE: Shellfish suffer from the cooking necessary to sterilize them. They are already wounded in flavor, so treat them gently. Never wash canned shellfish since this reduces the flavor. They are used most successfully in recipes where they do not have to be cooked at all or where they can be introduced when the food is cooked. A little lemon juice often will improve their flavor. Canned or bottled clam juice, by contrast, holds up well and can be added without hesitation wherever clam juice is called for.

INTERCHANGING SHELLFISH

Recipes for mussels, oysters, and clams are somewhat interchangeable as are recipes for scallops, surf clams, and pen shell mussels. In addition, excellent variety can be achieved by mixing one or more different species together. Almost invariably each complements the other and everyone compliments the cook.

MUSSEL RECIPES

STEAMED MUSSELS WITH WHITE WINE AND HERBS

2 pounds live mussels
6 garlic cloves, chopped
1 can Italian tomatoes, drained and chopped
1/4 cup parsley, chopped
2 tablespoons oregano
1 bunch scallions or 1 medium onion, chopped
2 tablespoons lemon rind, chopped
1-1/2 cups white wine
2 tablespoons lemon juice
a *roux*
pepper

Place cleaned, bearded mussels in a pot. Add all other ingredients and steam fifteen minutes. Pour off broth and strain. Thicken juice with arrowroot or a *roux*. Pour sauce over all.

MUSSELS ON TOAST

2 pounds mussels
toast
Hollandaise sauce

Steam open mussels, remove from shell. Make a Hollandaise sauce. Make buttered toast. Place mussels on toast and pour sauce over all.

MUSSELS IN A SALAD

2 pounds mussels
3 tablespoons olive oil
6 garlic cloves, mashed
1 red pepper
1/2 cup cilantro or parsley, chopped
2 dashes hot sauce
juice from 1/2 lemon
2 avocados
3 tomatoes, sliced, seeded
1 cup vinagrette dressing

Steam open mussels and marinate in oil and herbs for an hour until cool. Serve over avocados and tomatoes. Pour vinagrette over all.

BROILED MUSSELS WITH CHEESE

2 pounds mussels, steamed and shelled
2 tablespoons olive oil
3 tablespoons butter
1 onion, slivered
1 red pepper, slivered
1/2 cup cilantro or parsley, chopped
8 garlic cloves, mashed
1 egg mixed in 1 cup of milk
1 cup grated cheese (in the milk)
1 cup cracker crumbs
1 cup celery, chopped

Sauté oil, garlic, onion in oil for a few minutes. Add mussels to milk mixture and toss. Place mussels in oven casserole (usually served in individual ramekins). Dot with butter, melt under broiler. Sprinkle with bread crumbs and broil under low heat until crumbs brown. Serve with toast.

MUSSEL BISQUE

3 pounds mussels
2 cups each white wine and water
1 medium onion, blenderized
2 stalks celery, blenderized
1-1/2 cups cream
salt, pepper, nutmeg

Add all ingredients and steam until mussels open. Strain broth. Remove mussels from shell and reserve both separately. Add cream to pot and scald. Add broth and mussels and heat. Garnish with chopped parsley and pinch of cayenne.

CLAM RECIPES

Little clams are tender and just need a little steaming. Big clams may need to be ground or they can be eviscerated and pounded. Use the little clams or tenderized big ones in soups and chowders, tougher ones in Mrs. Kelly's Clam Pancakes (page 115), or grind, add hot peppers and onion, batter and fry. You can also just cut them into thin strips, dip in egg and milk, double bread and fry.

STEAMERS, LONG-NECK OR SOFT-SHELLED CLAMS

Longneck clams are found in Atlantic waters as far south as Cape Hattaras. The leathery "neck" contains both of the clam's siphons.

Longnecks live just below the sand surface in the intertidal zone. They are gathered commercially by the millions while many more are collected by amateurs for home consumption. Nevertheless, the demand is greater than the natural supply; for this reason commercial farms raise them by the ton.

Longnecks are hunted at low tide by watching for the telltale squirt as the clam, detecting your advance, hastily withdraws his siphon. When a relatively larger number of squirts indicate a concentration of clams, the sand is turned back and the mollusks collected. When plentiful, they may be collected by the quart or the bushel basket; the largest, four to five inches long, is just as sweet and delicious as the smallest.

Longnecks are sandy clams, and should be washed several times in a bucket. Change the water a few times, and agitate the clams to loosen clinging sand. They should then be soaked for a day in the sea water/corn meal mixture. Last but not least, a small cup of clam juice should be served with each portion of long necks. The diner may then swirl each clam in the juice to free it of the last bits of sand.

Longnecks may be eaten raw, by slitting the rubbery "skin" along the edge of the shell, shucking off the tough neck, and dipping in cocktail sauce. We have always preferred them steamed, allowing about one quart or more per person. Serve them with a cup of clam nectar, some melted butter, a few seafood fritters on the side, and cold beer or a big jug of lemonade. After long necks have been degritted, they may be used in all of the recipes for sweet, tender clams. Long necks are great for clambakes.

STEAMED CLAMS

Any clam can be served steamed, but the guide to good eating is to use only the smallest ones, such as cherrystones, or the most tender species, such as razor clams and grind the rest. If your steamed clams do turn out to be made of old golf balls, don't throw them out. Grind and use them for fritters.

STEAMING

Place one-half inch of water or wine in the bottom of the pot and dump in the clams. Close the lid and steam for about fifteen minutes, or until all of the clams are open. Do not overcook since this toughens the meat. Serve with hot melted butter.

CHOWDERS: See Chapter 5

CLAM HASH KNICKERBOCKER

2 cups chopped clams, fresh or canned
1 cup clam juice
2 cups potatoes, boiled and well chopped
2 teaspoons each parsley and chives, blenderized
1/2 onion, chopped
1 cup mushroom, chopped
3 tablespoons butter and oil
2 tablespoons sherry
3 eggs, beaten
1 teaspoon each salt and pepper

Combine everything but clams. Melt the butter and oil in a skillet; sauté the mixture over low heat for twenty minutes, stirring two or three times, to keep from burning. Add fresh or tinned clams and fold into mixture. Press flat. Brown hash for about ten minutes using medium heat; be careful not to burn. Serve steaming hot with a side dish of fried bacon.

MRS. KELLY'S CLAM PANCAKES

The landlady from my Sarasota clamming days (see Chapter 7) called these clam fritters, but they resemble the potato pancake.

Combine:
3 medium potatoes, grated and squeezed
2 eggs, lightly beaten
1 large onion, grated and squeezed
1 cup breading mix or cracker meal
1 teaspoon each salt, pepper
2 tablespoons baking powder
2 cups clams, ground or well chopped

Make into patties about two inches in diameter and no more than half-inch thick. Fry in vegetable oil until potatoes are quite brown. Drain or blot excess oil and serve immediately.

CLAMBAKE

Some of the best seafood we have eaten was cooked at a clambake. All you really need for a clambake are lots of clams and potatoes but all sorts of delicious things can be added. Traditionally, a pit about eighteen inches deep is dug in the sand and lined with flat rocks or bricks. The pit requires eight to ten pounds of rocks per square foot. A big fire is built and allowed to burn for at least an hour, adding fuel steadily to make a good bed of coals. When the coals are ready, sweep them toward the edges of the pit to expose the hot rocks. A six-inch layer of seaweed or chopped lettuce is added.

Food is added to the pit in a single layer. Brush small or medium potatoes with oil or butter, wrap in foil, pierce many times with a fork and place on the stones, close to the coals. Corn in the husk also goes here.

Fish is usually cut into individual portions and wrapped in foil (see Foil-Baked Fish, page 153). Chopped vegetables such as summer squash and tomatoes are often enclosed with the fish.

If pork is included, it is usually cut into individual portions and wrapped loosely in foil. Traditionally the pork is roasted separately while the pit steams.

If live crabs are on the menu they should be contained in a mesh sack. Place whole fish which have been gutted and scaled directly on the clams or crabs. Traditionally the fish are wrapped in banana leaves to make handling easier. You can use foil but leaves are much better.

After you have added food, cover with a four-inch layer of seaweed. The briney steam from seaweed enhances the flavor of the food. Clean wet burlap sacks are placed on top of the seaweed to close the pit and contain the steam and heat. Allow at least three hours for steaming. Resist the temptation to take a peak.

As soon as the pit is opened and the food removed, turn the sea weed back, sweep the coals over all and throw on more wood. You will need heat to toast those marshmallows and to burn the used plates. When everything is cooked, sit down and enjoy the feast. Be sure to have a big pot of melted butter, coleslaw, and lots of cold drinks on hand.

SHELLFISH FRITTERS

Any type of shellfish can be used for fritters including surf clams, whelks, periwinkles, conch, and limpets. Other seafoods, such as chopped shrimp, little pieces of fish, crab meat, or even vegetables, may be added. This helps to stretch a short supply of clams.

Mollusks may be steamed or grilled open. They must be chopped or ground for fritters. The tougher they are, the finer the pieces should be chopped.

The chopped or ground seafood should be drained and patted dry otherwise the batter will not cling. Add just enough batter to bind the seafood, about equal portions of batter and seafood. If using a variety of seafood, mix it roughly before adding to the batter. Keep stirring to a minimum to avoid breaking up the meat.

In the South, seafood fritters are extremely popular and often served on the side with lobster and steamed crab. They are also tasty as a main course.

OYSTER RECIPES

GRILLED OYSTERS

Grill oysters open and squirt in chili sauce, salsa or a few drops of lemon, butter and hot sauce. Use grilled oysters in other recipes such as Oysters Rockefeller (see next column).

FRIED OYSTERS

Pat oysters dry and double dip in egg and bread crumbs and fry a minute or two in hot oil. Pat dry.

SAUTÉED OYSTERS

A *roux*
1 cup hot chicken stock
1 cup hot cream
1/2 cup dry sherry
1 cup cooked, chopped ham
2 cups oysters
salt and pepper

Make a *roux* in a pan and add all liquids. Stir until creamy. Add oysters and ham. Bring to simmer and turn off. Serve on toast.

OYSTERS ROCKEFELLER

Oysters Rockefeller are traditionally made by first grilling (or steaming) the oysters open. The meat is then lifted and a bed of hot spinach is slipped beneath. The oyster is then breaded and grilled. You can also make this dish by using jarred fresh oysters and make the dish in an oven casserole.

12 oysters
1 package frozen spinach, or 2 pounds fresh spinach, thoroughly washed
1/4 cup butter
1/2 cup bread crumbs
1/2 cup slivered almonds
1/2 lemon juice
1 cup sour cream
3 tablespoons horseradish
salt and pepper

Steam open oysters and reserve. Boil a large pot of water and parboil fresh spinach for one minute. Drain, chop, squeeze and reserve. If using frozen spinach, defrost, drain and warm. Sauté almonds in butter until golden, add almonds to spinach; add a sprinkle of lemon, salt and pepper. Make a bed of spinach and slip on oysters.

Brush oysters with butter. Grill until oysters are just sizzling, but do not let edges curl. Sprinkle on bread crumbs and brown. The object is to slightly dry and toughen the oyster, but not much.

The sauce: Mix horseradish, lemon juice, sour cream, salt and pepper, and warm. Just warm, do not simmer. Pour sauce over all and serve.

OYSTER RABBIT

1 cup oysters, patted dry
3 cups grated cheddar cheese
3 tablespoons butter
2 teaspoons dry mustard
1 teaspoon paprika
1 cup beer, hot

Warm cheese, mustard, butter, paprika until melted. Slowly stir in hot beer. Add oysters and sauté over low heat two minutes. Serve over toast or rice.

SEA SNAILS

ABOUT CONCH (pronounced "konk"): There are a number of different varieties of this huge, snaillike mollusk, most of whom are found in the warm Atlantic and Pacific waters and in the Indian Ocean. All are edible except the huge horse conch, really a giant whelk, which may exceed eighteen inches in length. Conch are slow moving bottom feeders that live in shallow water on sand or grass. Their huge shells are easily spotted when snorkeling and there is no trick to finding them. When there is one there are a million and where there are none you may not see them for days.

Most conch are timid and immediately retreat into their shells when handled. But there are several small (three to four inch) varieties called fighting conch that don't know this and will attack you aggressively when you pick them up. You may well wonder how an overgrown snail can move to the attack, and it is best that we tell you before you find out the hard way.

All conch have a horny covering on their foot called an operculum. It is pointed at one end, rather sharp, and covered with mucus. The conch will take one look at your hand and spear you with its operculum so severely (though fortunately not with lightning speed) that you will immediately forget all about conch fritters and begin thinking about first aid. The best defense is hold the creature in its shell by placing your thumb over the flat part of the operculum.

Your next problem is getting the damn thing out of its shell—no easy task for the uninitiated. There is no way to pull the conch from its shell; it is a better puller than you and always wins this game. Breaking the shell with a rock is also a loser's game unless you don't mind dropping a boulder on your dinner and picking the pieces of shell from the mess.

There is, in fact, only one reasonable way to separate the conch from his home: Grab the operculum and attach a vise grip to it. This will prevent the conch from pulling far back into its shell when you begin the opening process and make removal from the shell much easier. Hold the shell in the left hand, with the opening downward and the spiral toward you. It is better to work away from the boat as the shell and slime tends to fly everywhere. Using the claw of a hammer, make a slit in the shell (see illustration) between the third and fourth spiral. Rinse the slit and using a small knife with a narrow blade, cut the tendon which holds the conch in its shell. The tendon is beneath the meat. It is a broad flat sheet which lies against the pink center column, extending several inches into the shell. Slip a knife into the slit beneath the meat and cut the tendon completely. The conch can be removed from the shell with a slight pull. If it will not come out, the tendon is not completely cut. Resist the temptation to force the conch free by pulling with the vise grips. The operculum is brittle and easily broken.

Kill the conch with a scooping cut which removes the eye stalks and snout. Do not delay as the conch is now thoroughly aggravated and can secrete an amazing amount of slime. Cut away the guts and the colorful orange-yellow mantle. Feel the mantle for conch pearls before discarding it. Some people save the mantle for fritters but eating it raw is an acquired taste. The clear rubbery "style," of unknown function, looking like a piece of spaghetti, may be eaten raw but doesn't have much flavor. A short digestive tract runs from the snout to the center of the body. Cut it open and wash the meat.

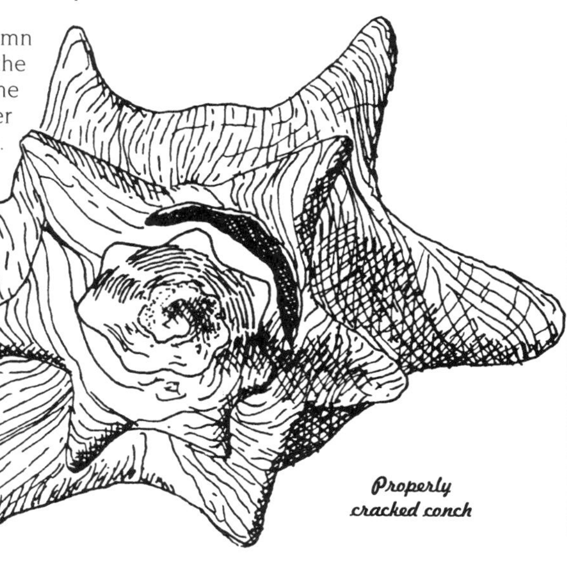
Properly cracked conch

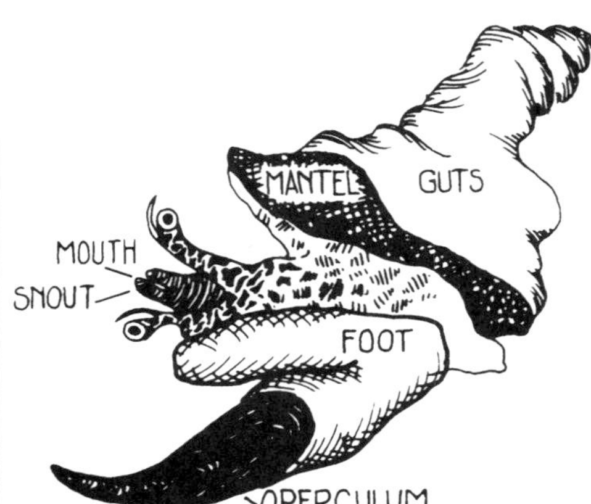

The dark, tough skin must now be removed, a difficult job as it is slimy and doesn't want to come off. Absorb the slime with corn meal. Make a series of slits through the skin radiating away from the operculum. Pull the skin off with a butter knife or pliers. Conch meat is extremely tough—but tasty. You will have to either beat it with a tenderizing hammer or grind it. Put the meat into a plastic bag so it won't spatter and pound with a meat hammer until it begs for mercy. Wash the meat and your tools in vinegar. The conch is now ready for use.

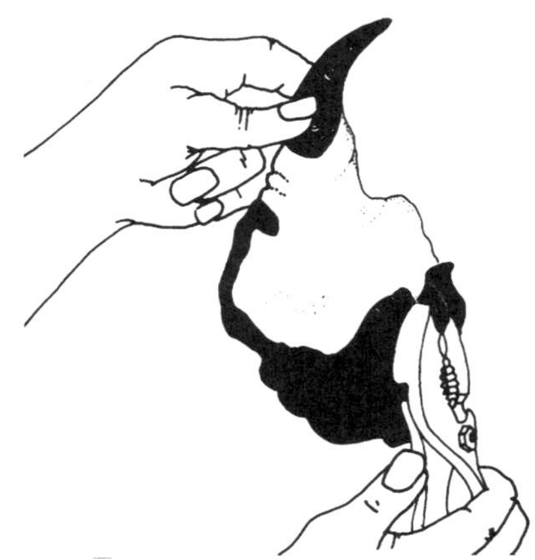

STORING LIVE CONCH: Live conch will last all day out of water if kept in cool, wet sea water. The natives collect a bunch of conch, tap a hole in the lip of each shell, tie them together, and throw them over the side at night. The conch all try to go in different directions (like some sailors we know) and therefore go nowhere.

CRACKED CONCH: This popular Bahamian recipe is the West Indies' answer to the hamburger. When one fried conch is served on a hamburger bun, it's called a conchburger. When two fried conchs are served on a plate they are called "cracked conch." Call it what you like, the taste is great!

Thoroughly pound a cleaned conch until tender. Rinse conch in salt water and sprinkle all over with lemon juice. Dust conch thoroughly with flour. Pan fry in a half-inch vegetable oil until golden. Serve as hamburger with some garnishes or on a plate with a side dish of potato salad.

CONCH CHOWDER: See SOUP.

CONCH SALAD

Conch salad is similar to Gazpacho with less liquid and a lot of chopped or ground conch. It is made spicy with hot sauce after all the ingredients are in the pot. Add the hot sauce slowly and stir. It is better to add a bit less hot sauce and allow each person to season to taste. The hot sauce does not appear in the recipe below.

3 cleaned conch, beaten and chopped or coarsely ground
1/2 large onion, chopped
1/2 cup celery, chopped
6 cloves garlic, chopped
3 tomatoes, peeled, seeded, chopped
1 teaspoon each: salt, pepper, sugar
1 green pepper, chopped
1/2 cup whole scallions chopped
2 tablespoons garlic, chopped
1 hot pepper, chopped
1/2 cup oil

Add everything to the pot. Stir well and allow to stand several hours before serving. Even better the next day.

PERIWINKLES AND TURBAN SHELLS

Periwinkles are another of those animals that are not popular in the United States, but are eagerly consumed elsewhere. There are about a dozen different varieties of winkles, the largest two inches long, about twice the bulk of a land snail. These are very tasty but tough little devils and need some cooking to arrive at the chewy but pleasant consistency needed for eating. Since they are usually free for the taking along any rocky shore, the price is certainly right!

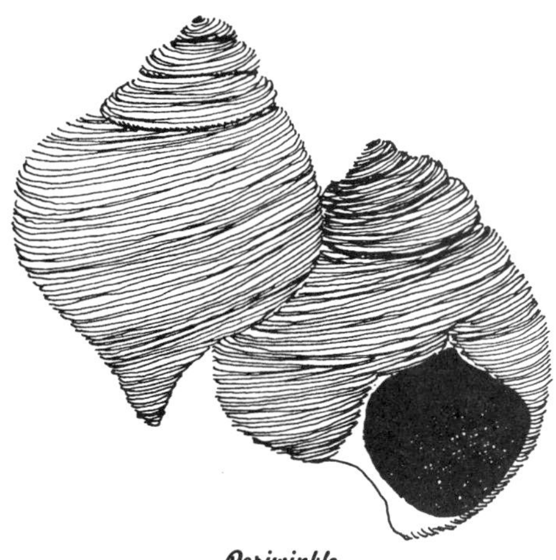

Periwinkle

Rinse and simmer winkles in their shells for twenty minutes in salted water (about two tablespoon per quart with a generous pinch of *bouquet garni*). The salt helps shrivel the meat to improve texture and facilitate its removal from the shell. Remove and trim away the gut end.

Turban shell

Pressure-cook the winks in a little (two-thirds cup) simmering broth for twenty minutes. Sprinkle in a little finely chopped green onion, carrot shavings and a shot of sherry, strain the solids and reserve. Thicken the broth with a *roux* or by adding an arrowroot or corn starch liquid to the broth. Serve over rice with the winks.

LAND SNAILS

French vineyard snails pay for their gluttony when they become the dinner rather than the diner in the Fall during the grape harvest. In France, wild snails are seasonal. Traditionally wild snails are first starved for a few days to rid them of plant material which is harmless to them but toxic to people. The snails **operculate** or "clam up" by withdrawing into their shells and sealing themselves in with a mucus which dries into a translucent membrane. This sealed state indicates that they are safe to eat. The snails are ready to eat just about the time the Beaujolais Nouveau is ready to drink. Snail eating is therefore associated with the harvest.

But no one, certainly not those gastropod lovers the French, would be satisfied to eat snails just once a year. Farm raised snails are available year round. Farm snails are fed lettuce and vegetables to fatten them, then fresh herbs, after which they are whisked off to market, their guts full of oregano and basil. They are often sold in mesh sacks which allows them to breathe and be hosed down. These are lively little devils. Do not give a bag of them a chance to get away. You will probably find all of them but the last few will probably be found by smell. Oh yes—be sure the lively snails you buy really are farm fed and not "just out of the woods." Ask.

Sea snails do not operculate but should be withdrawn into their shells and withdraw even further when handled. Snails which hang out of their shells and do not withdraw vigorously when handled should be avoided.

PREPARATION: Wash in lukewarm water and soak them for several hours in salty water with vinegar and a pinch of flour. Then blanch them for five minutes in heavily salted water. Allow to cool and remove from shells. Simmer in a sauce pan containing white wine and stock to cover with a big *bouquet garni*, several cloves of garlic, some carrots and onions. Add one teaspoon salt. Simmer three hours or pressure cook eighteen minutes. Slow cooking is better. Allow to cool. Remove the black end of the guts.

In the classic recipe the shells are cleaned, herb butter is pushed in followed by the snails. This is a huge pain in the transom. They can also be served very elegantly on toast.

SNAILS ON TOAST

4 slices bread
3 tablespoons oil
3 tablespoons anchovies mashed in 3 tablespoons olive oil plus a clove of garlic
4 tablespoons butter
1/4 pound grated cheese
a garnish-any combination: roasted peppers, asparagus, sliced olives, artichoke caps, etc.
3 cups cooked snails
1 small onion, finely chopped
1 egg
1 cup cream
garlic to taste

Lightly fry the toast in a little oil and butter. Scrape on a light layer of anchovy paste. Add a light layer of grated cheese like Parmesan and melt. Add toppings. Sauté in snail pot (without snails) ten minutes: butter, finely chopped onion, oregano, pepper and as much garlic as you dare. Add snails. Turn down heat and add one egg mixed in a half cup of cream and a little lemon juice. Stir furiously, until thick. Serve over toast. Sprinkle sherry over all.

OCTOPUS

The octopus found at fish shops inhabit shallow water and never exceed a few feet from tentacle to tentacle. Sailors' fables tell about huge monsters of the deep who attack whole ships, grappling them with their vicious tentacles, and pulling them down to Davy Jones. The famous giant octopus episode in Jules Verne's *Twenty Thousand Leagues Under the Sea* makes even the most sensible of us wonder if the sea harbors these fantastic creatures.

Late one night, alone on deck and deep into the dog watch, I heard a commotion in the sea nearby. I switched on our cockpit torch, a powerful light, to see what was about. Suddenly the water just astern seemed to boil, a huge octopus rose from the sea and seemed to float just above the waves; its arms splayed wildly. It glared balefully into the torch beam, then, with a splash was gone. My hair stood right up on my head as I reached down the companionway for a pistol, but then there was only the moonlight, the gentle swell, and the sparkle of the sea. In the morning I realized that the monster I had seen was certainly a deep water octopus, surely not more than four to six feet from tentacle to tentacle, not big enough to suck even a dinghy under. We greatly respect these strange creatures and have spent many an hour watching them beneath the sea—and also enjoy their delicious flavor.

DANGER: A small, blue speckled Pacific octopus usually found around the coasts of Australia is venomous and very deadly but not poisonous to eat.

KILLING, CLEANING: Most fishermen pick the beast up by its tentacles, being careful not to get close to the beak (which is sharp and often venomous but usually not deadly) and beat it a few times on the gunwale. Others hit them with a hammer between the eyes. Do not let them linger on the spear or in the dinghy; they may escape and, in any event, get very tough if allowed to live wounded.

When the octopus is dead, slit the hood, remove the viscera, and pop off the beak. Chill, cut the tentacles into very thin rounds and beat each one lightly. If not beaten, the octopus provides the toughest meat you have ever tasted. The meat can be further tenderized by marinating in an acid marinade for a few hours. After tenderizing but before cooking trim away the tough skin and tentacles. Poach for two or three minutes in enough water to cover, plus one-half cup vinegar. The octopus is now ready for use. You can also boil the whole tentacle for twenty ,minutes, cool, chill and slice paper thin. These wafers may be served with a horseradish sauce.

USES OF OCTOPUS: Octopus is mollusk-like in flavor and when ground (raw) may be substituted for tender mollusks in any recipe including chowder, fritters, Newburgs, or casseroles. But our favorite recipe is the Mediterranean *Fruite del Mare*, fruit of the sea, a combination of whatever tender mollusks you may find, especially mussels, clams, cockles, and squid. All are simmered in **crab boil** for an additional five minutes, then drained. They are then allowed to marinate in the same onion, vinegar, spice combination described for pickled shrimp. Absolutely delicious.

OCTOBURGERS: Cut oblique one inch slices of the tentacle near its base. Beat with a meat hammer until the thickness is reduced by half. Soak in wine and vinegar and garlic for an hour. Pat dry. Flour or batter and fry. You can also fry them as is in butter and oil over low heat.

OCTOSTEW

1-1/2 pounds tentacles, beaten, poached, cut into bite size pieces
1 large onion, julienned (long slivers)
2 tablespoons olive oil
6 cloves garlic, chopped
1 cup white wine
1 cup chicken consommé
1/4 cup parsley, chopped
3 tomatoes, peeled, seeded, chopped
1 fennel root (fresh) if available, if not 1 teaspoon fennel seed
1 potato, peeled, diced, parboiled

Fry potatoes in oil a few minutes. Add garlic, fennel, tomatoes, sauté ten minutes. Add all other ingredients, simmer fifteen minutes.

SQUID

The mysterious squid is a mollusk that carries its vestigial shell in the shape of a small spear-shaped plate inside its body. One species, called a "cuttlefish" has a thick, pronounced plate but is otherwise just as tasty as other varieties. The plate is usually the only part of the cuttlefish that most Americans ever see. Even then they do not realize that the "cuttle bone" sold in pet shops for parakeets is from this animal.

Squid are usually not encountered by the individual in sufficient numbers to make their capture worthwhile; they are usually netted by trawlers. Once, however, when we were in mid-Atlantic, we heard a huge rain squall approaching, yet the sky was clear. Suddenly, with a dull roar, the water churned all around us and hundreds of tiny shapes shot into the air. Some even hit the sail.

We found, to our astonishment, that they were little squid, so intensely engrossed in mating that they did not resist even when picked up and slipped into a bucket of water. In the mating ritual the pair faced each other and locked their many legs with much petting, rubbing, and changing of color. The male had an extra leg-like appendage which, in human fashion, he offered to the female. She not only accepted it but kept it! One would think such behavior would encourage celibacy in male squid.

Becalmed one evening in the middle of a transatlantic passage, I sat in the cockpit watching the stars, occasionally disturbed by an elusive noise. I finally realized that it was the occasional "click" of my fishing reel. I had neglected to reel in the trolling line—the lure was hanging several hundred feet beneath the glowing stern light.

The line had some sort of dead weight on it. It offered no struggle as I reeled it in, making me think I had hooked a big plastic bag. To my amazement out of the water came an unusual squid, a brilliant, angry red in color, perhaps three feet long, thicker than a man's leg and weighing perhaps thirty pounds.

As I attempted to pull it over the transom by the leader, it took one look at me with enormous eyes and squirted me in the face and chest with a powerful acid, quick as lightening wrapped a tentacle around my hand and pulled with amazing force, nearly taking me over the side. I screamed in pain from the acid, struggled free and rushed to the sink to wash my face. By the time the pain was gone my woolen sweater had burned away where the acid had hit it. I returned to the deck and cut the line. That squid was the winner, not the dinner!

Squid vary tremendously in size. Tiny but delicious sepia fit comfortably in a tablespoon. But the giant, deep sea squid is the favorite food of sperm whales. We have seen tentacle marks on dead whales that measured twenty feet long. Imagine how large the whole beast must have been! We once saw a squid taken from a whale's stomach that weighed over three hundred pounds. The most commonly found squid, usually found frozen in the United States, is sold as fish bait. They are six to eight inches long.

Squid, in our opinion, ranks right up at the top of the list of fine seafoods and it is usually the cheapest; it is easy to prepare, is pure protein, and is worthy of consideration by any cruising gourmet. The Europeans, who treat squid with much reverence, have a variety of fancy recipes, including cooking the squid in its own ink. In Thai cooking, squid is first scored with a sharp knife. Scoring makes the squid roll up when cooked. The scored meat is then cut into pieces an inch long, poached and served in a spicy sauce and the rolled pieces tend to hold the sauce.

We love squid and clams poached in a pan with the squid thrown on top of the clams. The squid and the clams still in their shells are mixed with a white sauce made with their juice or spicy marinara and tossed onto pasta. Squid is also excellent dipped in milk, then cracker crumbs and deep fried.

CLEANING SQUID: Pull off the semitransparent membrane that serves as the skin. Separate the head and legs from the body. Separate the legs from the head by cutting just below the eyes. Pop off the beak at the center of the tentacles and save the tentacles. Squeeze out the intestines. Pull out the cuttle bone and rinse everything. If the squid is bigger than twelve inches, it should be beaten to make it tender.

FRIED SQUID (CALIMARI FRITE)

Slice the hood-like body into rings. Pat dry and shake rings and tentacles in a bag with seasoned flour. Sauté in vegetable oil for about five minutes or until golden. Do not overcook as it toughens the meat.

STUFFED SQUID

The squid tube just screams for a stuffing and a sauce. The mind runs riot. I have even stuffed them with left over turkey stuffing, sautéed them in oil, with brandy spooned over all at the end and served in—turkey gravy! Delicious. Whatever you use, pan finish the stuffed tube by sautéing in oil over low heat. Stuffing suggestions:

- Grated fried onion and herbs, capers, sliced olives, feta cheese, hot peppers;
- Spinach, Ricotta cheese, lemon juice, sautéed, slivered almonds and their butter all served with marinara sauce I;
- A paste of liquefied cooked carrots, leaks, garlic and oil with slivers of mushroom;
- Mashed or home fried potatoes, cheese and sliced hot peppers;
- Chicken meat, soy sauce, ginger, garlic
- Sautéed almonds, onions and celery with sliced mushrooms and a dash of sherry;
- Cooked mushrooms, bread cubes, parsley, oregano, olive oil.

Squid sauces:
- any of the mayos
- hollandaise
- marinara
- any of the white sauces
- tomato or tomatillo salsa

SEAFOOD FRITTERS

Remember, the secret of a successful seafood fritter is to go heavy on the seafood and light on the batter. The batter is simply used to bind the pieces of fish together and to cover them with a pleasing, crispy coat.

Make two to three cups of prepared seafood into sixteen little mounds. The mounds must cling together; a small amount of flour may be dusted over seafood to assist in this process. Learn more about fritters in Chapter 17. Immerse seafood in batter, coating thoroughly. In one smooth motion, transfer coated seafood to small skillet containing one-half inch of very hot vegetable oil. Let the excess batter on the spoon or your fingers run onto the fritter. Fry until golden brown, turning occasionally. Do not permit the fritter to stick to the bottom. Fry until golden.

ABALONE

Abalone is a cold water one-shelled mollusk similar to limpets. It clings with its huge foot to a rock. It lives in water which varies from waist deep to several hundred feet and is found in California, Mexico, Japan, Australia and the islands around Malaysia. The Pacific coast of Baja, Mexico is also the home of a large concentration of abalone, but it is being rapidly depleted by commercial divers. Abalone is extremely popular and sells at fancy prices and is generally overfished—everywhere, making adults hard to find.

CATCHING: The abalone shell is covered

with a dark perisotracum which is usually completely encrusted with barnacles and other marine life. Experienced divers detect it by its shape and by the series of vent holes which are not encrusted. The creature is pried from the rock to which it clings with a short pry bar or "Ab-Iron." A swift, decisive levering effort deprives the animal of time to tighten its grip on the rock.

CLEANING: Pry the meat out of its shell by slipping a spoon between the body and shell and severing the adductor muscle, no easy job. Use a rough scrubber to grind off the tough black skin. Attempting to slice this cover away results in loss of meat. Slice the meat across the grain, about a quarter-inch thick, resulting in a pancake-shaped slice. Place it in a plastic bag and beat hell out of it with a meat hammer, being careful to not beat it to pieces. The beaten slice should be about an eighth-inch thick.

COOKING: Abalone is traditionally dipped in egg, then floured and fried. It can be treated like any other mollusk, particularly conch, and substituted in any mollusk recipe.

SCALLOPS

Only the abductor muscles of scallops are sold commercially, although the entire scallop is edible. The reason is that the scallop can't "clam up." It quickly loses its internal water and dies. You can keep them alive in a bucket of sea water. When we talk about cooking scallops we are talking about the abductor muscle only. Little scallops are shallow water "bay" creatures. Big scallops are from deep waters. Big scallops are more tender, can be eaten raw safely and cook very quickly. Scallops make a wonderful Ceviche. Both types are extremely delicate and are best poached in a little wine and served with a sauce. They can also be grilled very quickly on a very hot grill.

SCALLOP SUGGESTIONS

Serve on a bed of rice with a dollop of any of the fresh mayos (see Basic Stuff), cheese sauce, hollandaise, any of the white sauces, or in tomato sauce.

SCALLOPS GRILLED WITH BACON

Boil the bacon to defat and partially cook. Wrap a piece around each scallop and skewer, one serving per skewer. Brush with lemon, oil salt, and pepper. Grill briefly over very high heat.

COQUILLE ST. JAQUES

This is frequently served in a scallop shell as an appetizer but we have made it more hearty to serve as an entrée.

2 pounds scallops
3 potatoes, sliced thin and blanched 2 minutes
2 cups dried mushrooms, reconstituted
1/2 cup fish *fumet* or a little clam juice in wine
1 cup white wine
2 stalks celery, peeled and sliced
1/4 cup cream
2 tablespoons butter
3 tomatoes, peeled, seeded, chopped fine
1 cup bread crumbs
1 cup hard white cheese, grated
a *roux*

Add scallops, wine and *fumet* to pot and steam scallops until done, basting frequently. Chop scallops and combine with everything but the potato and butter. Butter an oven pot and line with potatoes. Add mixture and bake in a 350° F. for ten minutes. Remove from oven, drain off juice and thicken. Sprinkle with cheese, then bread crumbs and brown in oven. Don't let cheese burn.

SCALLOPS AND MUSHROOMS IN CHEESE (MORNAY) SAUCE

1 pound scallops poached two minutes in wine
2 cups cheese sauce
dash hot sauce
1 cup sliced reconstituted mushrooms with a dash of soy sauce
juice from 1/2 lemon
salt and pepper

Combine all ingredients except mushrooms. Pour over pasta. Add mushrooms as a garnish.

URCHINS

Read about catching and preparing urchin on page 116.

URCHINS SERVED IN THEIR SHELL

Urchins are Echinoderms like starfish, not mollusks, but where does one put a recipe for an Echinoderm? Here. Clean enough urchins to provide one cup of eggs. Wash and parboil them in salted water, then drain and chop.

Fry until browned:
1 onion, chopped
3 slices bacon, chopped (drained after cooking)

Add:
1 cup bread crumbs
1/2 cup celery and/or green pepper, chopped
1 cup cooked rice (optional)
1/2 teaspoon pepper
salt to taste
1 cup urchin roe

Sauté until the bread browns slightly. If too dry, add butter and little chicken stock. Stuff into the urchin shell and serve.

Shrimping at Dinner Key Marina

Coconut Grove, Florida, 1969 where my lifelong love/hate affair with the sea began: Shrimp came in with the tide and were attracted to the lights on the dock. The air was cool and balmy and full of the pungent smell of the sea. The tide made delicate sucking sounds around the pilings. Sailors would fire up their gas lanterns and hang them on oars suspended over the water to attract the shrimp. Soon the dock looked like a Japanese garden party, twinkling with lights and alive with laughter. Someone always remembered to bring a bottle of rum and a bag of limes. In the festivities many a shrimp escaped.

9 Crabs, Lobster & Shrimp

ABOUT SHRIMP

BUYING SHRIMP: Shrimp abound in coastal areas near brackish estuaries or mangrove swamps which provide a place for their larval development. Where there is one shrimp there are millions—and a well developed commercial fleet to harvest them. Shrimp have become a commodity like oil or auto parts. There is a world price for them which varies little from place to place and "bargains" should be considered suspect. The local shrimper with his hand made net is getting hard to find and so are fresh local shrimp, which are the pinnacle of fine cuisine. When you find them, buy them.

Fresh or recently defrosted shrimp should be heavy, firm and translucent; freshly caught shrimp are about as translucent as ice. Their shells are shiny and have no mold spots. Old frozen and defrosted shrimp are limp, opaque, the shells are dry and their tail, when extended does not retract. They have a "fishy" smell.

SELECTION: Shrimp can be purchased "**green**" (whole), "**headless**" or "**peeled**." The head segment contains the guts which are full of flavor and are used in sauces. The head is also the most perishable part of the creature. Try to avoid buying peeled shrimp; they lose moisture in the shelling process.

Try to buy shrimp which are still frozen rather than those which have been defrosted since defrosting results in loss of juice. Cook shrimp directly from the frozen state if possible. If a recipe requires them to be peeled before cooking, just dip them in hot water for a few seconds to thaw the shell, which can then be removed.

Prawns are freshwater shrimp which are less flavorful than ocean shrimp. Wild, or river prawns are delicious but more delicate in flavor than ocean shrimp. Cultured or pond-raised prawns are downright bland. Buy them at a really good price or not at all and dominate them with a spicy sauce.

SIZE: The bigger the size, the higher the cost. Do not buy big, expensive shrimp if your recipe calls for cut up shrimp or cleaned shrimp in a sauce. Buy the cheaper, smaller variety and save, save, save. Big shrimp should be served whole as the centerpiece of your meal. You can also buy just one or two giant shrimp per person as a centerpiece and complete the entree with smaller shrimp.

CULTURED, FARM OR POND RAISED SHRIMP: Wild shrimp eat plankton which flavors their flesh with that strong "shrimpy" taste. Farmed shrimp eat commercial "shrimp chow" purchased by the bag which results in their indifferent flavor. They aren't worth the price. The most common farmed shrimp is the tiger, with black bands and spots, grown in the Philippines, Ecuador and Thailand. Shrimp from these countries are usually cultured. Other countries are developing this industry and culturing other varieties. Alas, once these critters have been removed from the package, there is no way to tell what you are getting until you taste them.

HOW MUCH SHOULD I BUY? The cleaning operation reduces the weight of the shrimp by half. **One pound uncleaned (green), yields a half-pound of meat**. Shelling shrimp reduces their weight by about a third. Six to eight medium cooked shrimp per person are a main course portion.

CLEANING: To clean shrimp, twist off heads, pull off legs, then remove shell, prying from underside with your fingers. Larger shrimp are sometimes shelled by cutting the shell on the dorsal side and slipping it and the legs off in one piece.

DEVEINING: We usually devein only jumbo shrimp but if yours have a pronounced dark gut, slit them along the top with a sharp knife and rinse.

BUTTERFLY SHRIMP: Make a deep dorsal cut from head to tail, leaving a bit of meat to keep the halves together. Press between plates to flatten.

CANNED SHRIMP: Canned shrimp require no cooking, but should be lightly rinsed in cold water to reduce saltiness. Soaking will reduce their flavor and make them soggy.

SHRIMP COOKING TECHNIQUES

BAKED SHRIMP: Shellfish are usually baked with thinly sliced or precooked ingredients which reduce oven time and prevent the shrimp from overcooking.

SHRIMP AND POTATO LASAGNA

You can use a mixture of crab, scallops or other seafood in this simple, delicious dish.

3 large potatoes, peeled, thinly sliced lengthwise
2-1/2 cups raw seafood, chopped
1 cup onions, finely chopped, sautéed
1/2 cup scallion ends, chopped
1-1/2 cups white cheese, grated
1/2 cup butter/oil
1 cup heavy cream
2 egg yolks
salt and pepper

The sauce:
1-1/2 cup béarnaise sauce
3/4 cup dried mushrooms, reconstituted

Layer a buttered and oiled baking dish with potatoes. Add a layer of seafood and sprinkle with cheese and onions. Repeat until the ingredients are used. Mix the eggs and cream, pinch of salt and pepper. Pour mixture over all. Use a fork and also shake the pan to get some of the mixture down into the potatoes. Bake in a 375° F. oven until everything is bubbling. Cut into squares and serve with béarnaise sauce over all. Garnish with scallions

BOILED SHRIMP: Shrimp are delicate little beasts, and great care must be exercised to not overcook them. Use plenty of water, stock, or shrimp boil (water with prepared spices) to prevent a significant drop in water temperature when shrimp are added. Bring water to a rolling boil; add shrimp, bring to a rolling boil again and remove from the heat. Let stand for a few minutes, drain and allow to cool to room temperature.

PICKLED SHRIMP WITH ONIONS

This is one of the most delightful shrimp appetizers I've ever tasted. It's so good that it brings pangs of sweet remembrance, even as I write these words. The shrimp should be cooked in the shells. Squid, scallops, octopus, and other shellfish may be added. You can add flavor to this dish by including the shrimp shells with the shrimp boil.

1 pound small or medium shrimp, shelled
1 onion, chopped
2 cups rice vinegar
2 cloves garlic, finely chopped
1/2 teaspoon celery seed
1 cup celery, peeled and chopped
1 cup corn oil
1-1/2 ounces of crab and shrimp boil
1 teaspoon salt

Wrap shrimp boil mixture in two pieces of cloth to confine it in the pot. Boil one pack for twenty minutes in one cup vinegar plus enough water to cover. Add shrimp. Remove from flame; drain let stand for twenty minutes covered. Remove boil spices; shell shrimp, drain; place shrimp shells in a gauze and add to the mixture. Add other ingredients and remaining pack of shrimp boil. Place in Ziplock bag, refrigerate and let stand for at least one day before eating. Longer marinating is better. Toss occasionally. Serve with crackers. Pickled shrimp keep in the refrigerator for about a week. They will last longer but their taste deteriorates.

BRAISING: Breaded fried shrimp can be dropped into a pan of simmering sauce, such as soy, beer, garlic or a BBQ sauce and tossed for a few minutes until the sauce bonds with the breading.

FRIED SHRIMP

The secret of tasty fried shrimp is to plunge them into oil which is almost smoking hot. Fried shrimp are usually battered or dipped in a milk/egg mixture and then bread crumbs. A batter can be made lighter and more crispy by adding a bit of soda water or shaved ice. The gas in the soda and the vaporized water from the ice virtually explode in the oil, making the batter crisp and fluffy.

1 pound raw shrimp, shelled
1 tablespoon cognac
3 teaspoons Worcestershire sauce
1/2 cup seasoned flour
2 eggs, beaten
2 tablespoons butter, melted
1/2 cup beer

Toss shrimp in cognac and Worcestershire sauce or soy sauce. Combine all remaining ingredients to make batter. It should be thick and sticky. Move along quickly as the bubbles in the beer burst upon contact with the hot oil, making the crust fluffy and crisp. Dip shrimp in batter; deep fry in a generous amount of hot peanut oil. Get the oil as hot as possible to start with. Cook until batter browns, two to three minutes. Drain and blot. Serve with sweet and sour sauce.

SHRIMP ACAPULCO

In this recipe the shrimp are partially cooked by marinating overnight in lime juice.

24 to 30 large shrimp, shelled, with left tails on
1/2 cup lime juice
1/2 cup vegetable oil (coconut oil is best)
6 cloves garlic, finely chopped
1/4 cup parsley, chopped
4 chilies, sliced finely
salt, pepper, butter

Combine all ingredients; let stand over night. Toss occasionally. Drain ingredients thoroughly; pan broil over high heat for four minutes, tossing constantly. Brush with butter and sprinkle with fresh chopped parsley.

GRILLING: See page 57.

SAUTÉING in this case means simmering very gently in a sauce. The cooking time for shrimp should be very brief, not more than ten minutes. Finish the sauce and have it simmering when the shrimp are added. Outstanding sautéing sauces include: marinara, curry, butter and the *roux*.

SHRIMP IN DILL SAUCE

Serves two

5 tablespoons butter
3 tablespoons onion, chopped
3/4 pound raw shrimp
1 cup dry white wine
3 tablespoons flour
1 cup milk
2 tablespoons fresh dill
1/4 cup parsley, chopped
a *roux*

Sauté shelled shrimp, butter, onions and dill five minutes. Reserve shrimp. Make *roux* in same pan without cleaning, by sprinkling in gravy flour, stirring constantly. When the *roux* turns golden, add wine to thin as desired, stirring constantly. Return shrimp to pan; simmer until hot and serve. Garnish with parsley.

SHRIMP WITH TOMATO CHILI

1/2 stick (4 tablespoons) butter
6 cloves garlic, minced
1-1/2 pounds shrimp, peeled, deveined
1 red pepper, julienned
2 hot peppers, cooked, seeded, chopped
1 teaspoon each: cumin, oregano, salt
1/2 cup chili powder
1 cup tomatillos, peeled, diced
1/4 cup sun-dried tomatoes, chopped
1 cup tomatoes, peeled, seeded, diced
1/2 cup white wine
pinch black pepper

Sauté garlic, shrimp, pepper, chilies, herbs in butter until shrimp is white Add other ingredients and sauté over low heat until sauce thickens.

WOKED SHRIMP

This is a true gourmet one pot main

course which can be served over plain rice. Like most wok recipes this dish moves right along, so have everything ready for instant use in piles on the counter.

12 shrimp, thinly sliced lengthwise
1 cup dried mushrooms, reconstituted
3 tablespoons butter
2 carrots, sliced thin and long
1 cup vegetable of opportunity
1 onion (or 3 shallots), julienned
1/4 cup oil
1 chicken bullion cube
1 tablespoon miso (optional)
2 hot peppers, thinly sliced
6 garlic cloves, crushed
1/4 cup cilantro, chopped
1/4 cup soy sauce
corn starch
1 cup beer

Make a mixture of beer, soy sauce and a chicken bullion cube. Use miso instead of soy if desired. You will use only part of this mixture to thicken. Get oil very hot in a wok and add the onion and carrots. Stir fry until carrots get soft. Add butter and additional vegetable, fry one minute Add beer in dribbles to make steam. Stir frequently until done.

Skim vegetables onto a bed of hot rice. Add oil, hot peppers and garlic to wok. Stir fry over high heat for two minutes. Add shrimp and stir fry for two minutes. Add mushrooms and stir fry until everything is bubbling. Add corn starch thickener dissolved in water a little at a time and allow to thicken. Do not boil. Pour over vegetables.

SHRIMP STOCK is usually made from the shells, particularly the heads which are full of flavor. Simmer them for a half-hour in white wine with a *bouquet garni* and vegetables in a small pot. Drain and reduce by simmering. Use in sauces or just thicken into a *roux* or cool and add to fresh mayonnaise.

SHRIMP PATÉ

This delicate, tasty little nothing is actually quite rich and filling. Mounded into a hollowed tomato or avocado, it makes an exotic and easy dockside appetizer. Underway, served on crackers with pieces of cheese, it makes a fine warm weather lunch.

3/4 pound fresh boiled or canned shrimp, drained
1 onion, minced and squeezed
1/2 cup mayonnaise
1/4 cup canned black or Greek olives, sliced
2 teaspoons lemon juice
1/4 cup parsley
3 teaspoons condensed milk
salt, if needed

Finely chop shrimp; fold in other ingredients. Let stand for a few hours. Serve chilled, if possible, or at room temperature; sprinkle with parsley or chives.

MISCELLANEOUS SHRIMP DISHES

SHRIMP BISQUE OR SOUP

This bisque can also be made from, or in combination with, lobster or oysters, fresh or tinned. A bisque is thick like porridge. It can be thinned with milk or cream, making it into a soup. The recipe below is for a bisque.

1-1/2 pints seafood, shelled, deveined, and coarsely chopped
4 tablespoons butter
1/2 onion, grated
1/2 teaspoon celery salt
2 tablespoons parsley, finely chopped
1/2 cup dry white wine
2 cups milk
1/2 cup cream or condensed milk
1/4 cup hard cheese, grated
pinch of salt and pepper
pinch of paprika

Combine the butter, onion and celery salt in double-boiler or over very low heat. Sauté lightly, stirring constantly for five minutes. Add seafood, milk, cream (or two cups condensed milk), pinch of salt and pepper, pinch of paprika. Sauté and stir until milk steams. Add parsley and dry white wine. Sauté another two to three minutes. Serve over fried, buttered toast.

SEAFOOD NEWBURG

This recipe, popular with lobster, shrimp, or crab, is also excellent with any mild flavored fish. Seafood leftovers, except those cooked in a strong sauce, blend well in a Newburg. Combined seafood is particularly good. Small, succulent shellfish, steamed open and drained, make a nice addition.

1/4 cup cream sherry
1 teaspoon paprika

3 egg yolks
1/2 cup condensed milk

Melt in pan and sauté for three minutes:
3 cups seafood
2 tablespoons butter
corn starch

Sauté cream sherry two minutes. Add paprika. Combine and add egg yolks and condensed milk. Lightly simmer until thickened, do not boil. Add seafood and cook five minutes or until done. If consistency needs improving, thicken with corn flour or arrowroot mixed in a little milk. Serve over toast or rice. For variety, try adding celery seed, or sprinkling a mild cheese over all.

KEDGEREE OF SHRIMP—NEW ORLEANS STYLE

1 pound medium shrimp, shelled (do not remove tail)
2 cups Italian tomatoes, drained, chopped
1 onion, chopped
2 cups cooked rice
2 hard-boiled eggs, grated
1/4 teaspoon celery seed
4 slices bacon
salt and pepper

Fry bacon and reserve. Brown onion in bacon drippings. Drain. Blot. Add tomatoes; simmer five minutes. Add shrimp; simmer another three minutes, covered. Add all remaining ingredients including bacon, crumbled; simmer another three minutes, stirring frequently.

SHRIMP COCKTAIL SAUCE

Combine:
1 cup catsup
2 tablespoons horseradish, or 1 teaspoon powdered mustard or wasubi powder
juice of 1 lemon
pinch of salt
pinch of sugar, if desired

ABOUT CRABS

Every crab I ever met I "et" and it was delicious! Whether it is a crab from land or from the sea, the fine textured flesh and delicate flavor make it an esteemed culinary delicacy. In my opinion, every crab is delicious,

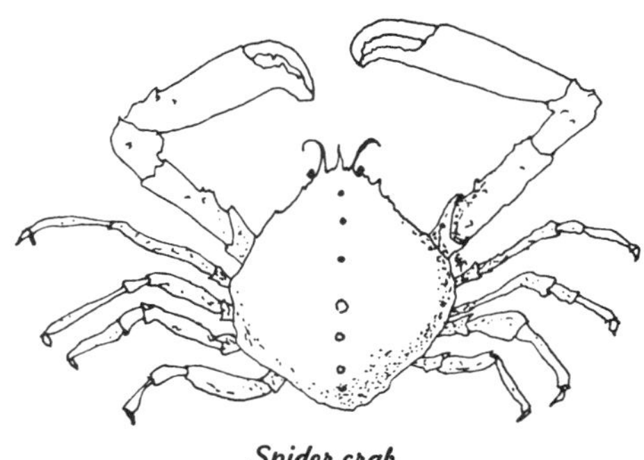

Spider crab

the only question is whether they are large enough to be worth the trouble of cooking and cleaning.

Generally speaking, when it comes to saltwater crabs, the colder and deeper the water, the larger the crab. The huge Alaskan king crab, which may exceed eight feet from leg tip to leg tip is hauled from ever deeper waters and is typically taken at the 100-150 fathom line. Blue crabs which weigh less than a pound inhabit shallow bays.

Tiny crabs may be too small to clean but they can be chopped up and cooked with vegetables in a little wine and water. Bring the liquid to a boil and allow to cool. Pour into a narrow bottle and give it a good shake. Loose crab meat will swirl up into the liquid and the shells will fall to the bottom. Quickly pour off the liquid. The resulting rich broth can be thickened and used as a soup.

BUYING CRAB: Except for "softies," crabs should be purchased cooked or alive and not merely "breathing." They should start moving as soon as you pick them up or be too dangerous to pick up by hand. If not they are "dead crab," not a good sign. Dead crabs spoil very quickly.

COOKING: Crabs cooked alive often break off their own legs and claws as the temperature rises, so kill them before cooking. The easiest way to kill crabs is to force a screwdriver between their eyes and "pith" them by wiggling the screwdriver around, destroying the brain.

Crabs may be steamed for fifteen minutes in a large covered pot with a half-inch of sea water, or they may be put in cold sea water, brought to a boil for five to ten minutes depending on size. After cooking, drain and let the crab cool in the sink.

HOW MUCH SHOULD I BUY? One pound of King Crab legs will feed two. A two pound whole Dungeness crab or a pound of Dungeness crab legs or two cups of cleaned crab meat will serve two.

CLEANING COOKED CRABS: Some crabs have considerable body meat. Other species have most of their meat in the legs and claws; but, even these crabs have a large lump of meat where the leg joins the body. Therefore DO NOT break the legs away from the body. The only way to get the meat is to clean the cooked crab as follows:

1. Remove the upper shell. If you pry the shell forward from the rear, it will lift like the hood of a sports car. Don't be discouraged by your first glimpse of the insides; remember, it's well worth the trouble for that superb flavor.
2. Scrape the crab butter from inside the shell. Crab butter is a yellow paste that adheres to the upper shell inside the "points." It is delicious and may be made into all kinds of patés or sauces. Some people mix the fat with butter as a dip for the meat. Delicious.
3. Tear off the "tail" and remove internal spongy material. This includes the thin cover tissue, the gills, and all viscera.
4. If the crab is a female with eggs under the tail, carefully snip off the tail and save; crab roe is delicious raw or steamed. Most crabs sold commercially are males. Pickling the eggs in salt for a few days, then rinsing improves their texture.
5. Break the crab in half along its midline.
6. Separate by breaking the body and legs into sections. The legs and claws may be cracked with a lobster cracker. Meat can be freed from the body segment by tapping it sharply against a bowl.

All of this is a messy, delicious job, and if you are serving cooked crab legs, we recommend that only good friends be invited to the orgy as shell tends to fly everywhere. Put a roll of paper towels on the table. Cover the table with newspaper. Cleaned crab meat may also be used in all mixed seafood recipes, Newburg dishes, fritters, devil sauces or just chilled and eaten with cocktail sauce.

CANNED CRAB MEAT: **Fresh crab** in cans must be kept refrigerated. The meat has been cooked but not sterilized. There is usually a refrigeration warning on the lid. Canned crab which requires refrigeration may be used the same as fresh crab; it is quite delicious.

Crab in **unrefrigerated tins** has been cooked until sterile and is immortal. The texture of the meat is damaged but some good flavor remains. Treat canned crab with great love and tenderness. Use it in recipes where other ingredients dominate the flavor, or where other fresh seafood is added. Always add the crab at the last minute to prevent further flavor loss.

HERMIT CRABS: Marine hermit crabs often grow to great size and inhabit conch or other large shells. These large crabs are extremely delicious and taste more like lobster than crab. They may be steamed in the shell with the opening toward the top of the pot. As the heat penetrates the shell the beast will usually abandon it, making your work easier. If the crab remains inside the shell pull it out gently as the meat is in the tail. Large hermit crabs (in their shell) should be steamed in a small amount of water for about fifteen minutes. The cooking time varies depending on the size of the shell but it is better to initially undercook the crab which can then be removed from its shell and steamed to completion.

CRAB DELIGHT ON TOAST

As is true with most of our crab recipes, fresh, precooked shrimp, lobster, or fish may be added either to expand the crab, or to create a mixed seafood delight. In this recipe all ingredients are either precooked or don't need cooking, so the object is to just thicken and heat.

1/2 pound crab meat, fresh or frozen; or 2 cans (approximately 6 ounces each) crab
2 teaspoons butter
2 tablespoons flour
1 cup milk
2 slices stale bread, cubed
1 cup mushrooms, sliced
1/2 teaspoon crushed celery seed or celery salt
1 teaspoon lemon juice
1/2 cup dry white wine
1/2 cup Gruyère or Swiss cheese, grated
paprika, salt, pepper

Make a béchamel sauce (a *roux*, thinned with milk). Add all other ingredients except crab, cheese, and paprika. Simmer for five minutes over low heat, stirring frequently. Do not boil. Reduce heat until liquid just steams. Add crab; stir, sprinkle with cheese, then paprika. Warm until cheese melts. Serve on toast spread with anchovy butter (anchovy paste and butter).

CRAB WONTON

A wonton is a thin wheat flour noodle. Wontons are usually "stuffed" which, in this case, means two wontons are glued together around something tasty using flour and water as a paste. Frequently the "something" is fried pork in a spicy sauce. In this case the "something" is a delightful combination of crab, sautéed vegetables and cheese. Makes eight wontons, serves two. Keep in mind that each wonton requires only one tablespoon of stuffing. Estimate how much this will look like before making the mixture.

16 wontons shells, about 4 inches
1 cup cooked crab meat
1/2 red pepper, peeled, julienned
1 small onion, julienned
2 Serano chiles, finely julienned
8 cloves garlic, blenderized
1/2 cup white wine
4 tablespoons oil/butter
2 tablespoons sherry
1/4 pound sharp cheddar cheese, grated
capers
salt and pepper

Sauté the vegetables in butter and oil for a few minutes until soft. Add the wine and simmer five minutes. Pour into a mixing bowl. Add the crab, capers and cheese. Toss lightly. Place about one heaping tablespoon of mixture in center of a wonton. Brush wonton edges with flour paste. Cover with another wonton and press closed. Boil in salted water until wonton becomes translucent and floats.

Sauces: (1) canned cream of tomato soup with a dash of sherry and lemon juice; (2) a sauce béchamel blenderized with a roasted red pepper, Parmesan cheese, lemon juice, thinned with milk; or, (3) soy sauce, garlic, ginger, mustard powder and beer thickened with a little corn starch and garnished with scallion ends.

The delicious hermit crab

CRAB ENCHILADAS IN GREEN SAUCE

Tomatillos look like little green tomatoes in a leaf wrapper but they are actually related to the gooseberry.

1 pound tomatillos, chopped, drained
1/4 cup cooking oil
3 hot chiles, seeded, chopped
6 garlic cloves, chopped
1/2 cup cilantro
2 cup crab meat
juice of 1/2 lemon
8 tortillas
1/2 cup sour cream
1/2 cup hard white cheese, grated

Boil tomatillos until just soft. Liquefy. Drain. Sauté chilies, garlic and cilantro in a little oil. Add tomatillos, lemon juice, and simmer twenty minutes. Add crab and toss. Roll in tortillas. Warm tortillas in a pan, rotating them several times. Sprinkle with cheese, melt and serve.

QUICK CRAB OVER RICE

2-3 cups crab meat or assorted seafood, cooked
1 green pepper, chopped
3 tablespoons onion, chopped
2 tablespoons flour
1 teaspoon Worcestershire sauce
1-1/2 cups milk
1/2 cup condensed tomato soup
1 cup Gruyère or Swiss cheese, grated

Melt butter in pan; sauté onions and pepper until onions are translucent.

Add flour, dissolved in milk; stir until mixture thickens. Add Worcestershire sauce and soup; heat until steaming. Fold crab in lightly; sprinkle with cheese. Simmer over low heat for five to eight minutes. Serve over white rice.

SPICY CRAB CAKES

In this recipe, we use about a half-cup of jerk sauce, which is a Jamaican spice. You can use chili pepper paste, hot sauce, pepper sauce or whatever you like. Add to mixture slowly until you get what you want.

3/4 pound of crab, cleaned and cooked
1 cup bread or cracker crumbs
1 tablespoon baking powder
juice of 1 lime
2 tablespoons honey
2 eggs, beaten
1 large onion, grated, thoroughly squeezed
1 cup red or green pepper, finely chopped
1/2 cup Jamaican jerk sauce, or 2 teaspoons chile paste
1 teaspoon salt

Combine ingredients which should be almost as thick as hamburger. Make into balls about 1-1/2 inches in diameter. Flatten into cakes in the pan. Sauté over medium heat in a little olive oil/butter. Remove when browned and blot. Serve with cocktail sauce, tartar sauce, or mustard and honey.

SEAFOOD AU GRATIN

Seafood Au Gratin is traditionally baked and served in individual crocks, but it can be quickly cooked in a pan over low heat and served over toast. Goes well with lobster, shrimp, crab and scallops.

1/4 cup butter
1 pound cooked seafood, shelled
2 tablespoons flour
1/2 cup white wine
1 cup cream or condensed milk
2 tablespoons sherry

Dungeness Crab

1 cup mild cheese, grated
salt, pepper, paprika

Melt butter in large pan; stir in flour. Let flour bubble for a minute; stir constantly to remove lumps. Add cream and wine; stir over medium heat until thickened. Add seafood and cheese; cook over low heat; stir constantly until cheese melts. Serve on toast; sprinkle with salt, pepper and paprika.

THE NOBLE LOBSTER

ABOUT LOBSTERS: Lobster species differ greatly in appearance and some are not closely related to others but they all taste great! The so-called **American lobster** has claws. It varies in color from green to dark blue. A meaner, more voracious critter is hard to find. They fight each other to the death for territory, and the winner usually consumes the looser! They eat their own young and give no quarter. They would probably be glad to eat you as well if they could, so shed no tears when you consume them! In the Northeast American lobsters are hatchery raised until they are about three quarters of an inch long, then released. Large numbers of male lobsters are caught during the summer months and stored in ponds for sale during the winter.

The **mole lobster**, a clawless relative of the American lobster, looks more like a crab with a fat abdomen. It is a cold water species found on or around weed beds, usually near isolated islands. Many are found in the Azores, while some have been netted off the Shetlands, Greenland, and Iceland. Mole lobsters seem almost as broad as they are long since up to sixty percent of the creature's weight is a huge hunk of tail meat.

There are several species of clawless, warm-water **spiny or rock lobsters**, also called **crawfish**. Do not confuse crawfish with **crayfish**, (sometimes called "**crawdads**") which are a smaller, less delicious fresh water species. Another freshwater river shrimp which may run up to eight ounces is called a **langoustine**. It is also tasty but more bland in flavor than saltwater shrimp.

Unlike the aggressive American lobster, spiny lobsters are usually timid and retiring. During the breeding season they seem to lose their instinctive fear, often crossing shallow grass beds in great numbers—boldly

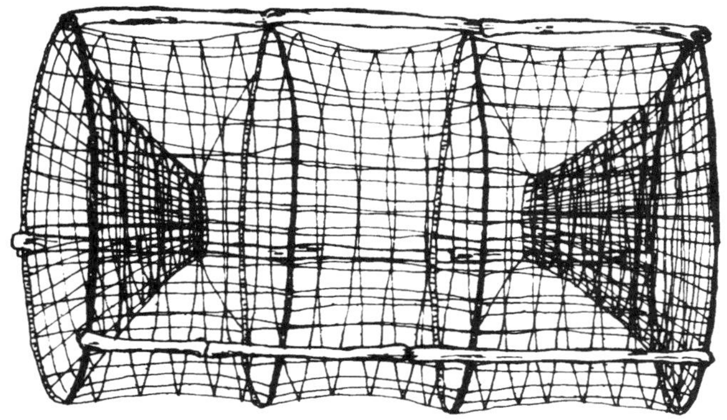

Azorian lobster trap

advancing en masse, antennae waving. In days gone by, when their numbers were greater, so many would migrate at the same time that some were pushed onto the land by the press of the multitude. Spiny lobsters grow about the same size as American lobsters. They can be found in tropic seas all over the world. Fresh spiny lobsters are just as delicious as fresh American Lobsters.

The Mediterranean Sea and the Indian Ocean are home to several species of clawed, shrimp-like crustaceans. Their size, however, never exceeds one-half pound; normally they are only four to six ounces. Their claws are long, thin and of equal size. They are tasty like shrimp, but do not share the absolute gastronomic pinnacle with American and spiny lobster.

SELECTING FRESH LOBSTER: A fresh lobster must be alive and still have at least a little fight left in him, otherwise he is what the fishmonger calls "still breathing." If the fishmonger sees you looking at a lobster for signs of life, he will take it and give it a shake, knowing that its primitive nervous system will still react, even though the lobster is dead. Dead is unacceptable because it begs the next question: how long dead?

SEXING LOBSTERS: Female lobsters are more succulent than the males and may contain delicious roe. The females are at their peak just before the egg-laying season when they contain roe. Lobster connoisseurs know this and often ask for females when they dine out. As a result most of the females go to the better restaurants. It is rare indeed to find a female lobster for sale but lobster aficionados always search for them.

Lobsters may be sexed by examining their **swimmerets**, small finlike appendages on the underside of the tail. The males have narrow swimmerets. The first set are modified so that, when they are pressed together, they form a sexual organ with a duct to convey sperm. The females carry their eggs attached to the swimmerets which are larger and more rounded than the males.

Normally American lobsters reach the market with pegs in their claws, not only to prevent mayhem in the fish shop, but also to keep them from destroying each other. Should you chance to meet an unplugged lobster, grab and close the claws. They close easily. Wrap a rubber band around them.

Keep in mind that the thin claw is for feeding and the fat claw is for crushing. You really, really don't want to find out how hard the fat claw can crush. Lobsters sold with one claw missing are called "shorts," not to be confused with illegal, undersized lobsters which are also called "shorts." You can get real bargains by purchasing shorts with just one claw. We are of the general opinion that when it comes to buying lobster bigger is better. You get more meat proportionally because the meat in the legs becomes accessible. The meat in a large lobster is just as tender and delicious as in small ones.

SELECTING PRECOOKED LOBSTER: Make sure the meat has the briny odor of the sea. Pull the tails back; they should recurl when released. If they do not the critter was dead when it was cooked, not a good sign.

FROZEN SPINY LOBSTERS: Frozen spiny lobsters are sometimes tough and often have an iodine taste if the tail is over ten ounces. It's expensive and generally has little of its distinctive fresh flavor. Who needs it, especially when frozen shrimp taste better and are cheaper.

HOW MUCH SHOULD I BUY? The American lobster, most commonly found commercially in the three quarters to 2-1/2 pound range, makes a fine meal. A one pound lobster feeds one and a 2-1/2 pound lobster

feeds three—or it can feed one. While these sizes are typical market weights it is not unusual to find fifteen or twenty pound monsters on occasion. Large lobsters are just as tasty as small ones. The largest spiny crawfish I ever caught was fourteen pounds and it was delicious!

STORAGE: Live lobsters will keep for a day if refrigerated at 45 to 50° F. Placing them in a thick sack surrounded by ice has similar effect. American lobsters may be kept alive indefinitely in a mesh sack or pen if stored in their native water. Warm water quickly kills American lobsters, so don't keep them in tropic seas.

KILLING AND COOKING: Lobsters are usually cooked whole without any preparation. The most humane way to kill a lobster is to pierce it between the eyes with an ice pick or screwdriver. This kills it instantly. You can also add an inch of sea water to a large pot, add the lobster and bring slowly to a boil. The lobster just keels over. Plunging them into boiling water causes a violent reaction indicating that the lobster objects to this technique. It is also dangerous for the chef.

A common practice, when a spiny lobster is too big for the pot, is to twist off the tails. Kill the lobster first by pithing between the eyes or just chop the body in half lengthwise if you are broiling. Once the lobster is dead the tail muscle relaxes and pulls free with the help of a spoon inserted to free the muscle at its insertion. In addition, if the lobster exceeds about 1-3/4 pounds, meat can be found at the base of the antennae and the base of the legs. These joints may be twisted off and cooked with the tail. Larger lobsters have edible meat in the legs.

STEAMED LOBSTER: Add about three quarters of an inch of sea water to large pot. Add lobster. Cover; bring water to fast boil. When steam begins escaping from under lid, reduce flame and cook for fifteen minutes. No more. **Boiled lobster** are similarly cooked, but in boiling water it takes longer to heat the water and is not fuel efficient.

BROILED LOBSTER: Split lobster in half from head to tail; discard the dark stomach, a hard sack near the head. Squeeze lemon all over and dot with butter; let stand for a few minutes. Brush with melted butter; slip under broiler for seven minutes, checking frequently and basting with more butter to prevent drying.

DEEP-FRIED TAIL

We disdained this Caribbean specialty until we tried it. However, it requires close to a quart of very hot oil. Kill lobster and sever tail nerve by slipping a small knife between body and tail joint. Tail should relax. Slip a butter knife up inside the body cavity against shell and separate the tail meat. Remove tail. Dip exposed meat into a fritter batter (see page 266) Drop in very hot oil. Watch out for spatters.

The oil does not penetrate the lobster because the steam from inside the shell blocks its entry. Fry half-pound lobster tails for four minutes.

GUTTING: After cooking, a four to six-inch piece of antenna is usually broken off, and the broken end is slipped into the anal vent. With a good jerk the antenna is pulled out, effectively eviscerating the beast.

OPENING:

1. Work should be done in the sink. Use a heavy scissors or a pair of cooking shears. Work with a towel and be careful of hot splatters.
2. Cut the underside of the shell from the anal vent to the tip of the head. Just cut through the shell.
3. Lay in the sink, let drain.
4. Now cut the lobster from the end of its tail along the top to its head.
5. Finally, cut through the front of the head, giving you two body halves.
6. Separate. You can divide the tail later.
7. Crack the claws and joints with a cracker.
8. Allow to drain.
9. Remove the head sack. Be careful to retain the green liver which is delicious. If there is any black, gooey material inside, remove it.
10. Twist off the claws at body.
11. Crack each arm segment with a cracker. Allow to drain.
12. Lever the lower part of the claw from side to side, not up and down and pull it free. If done properly the meat will remain with the claw and not be lost.
13. Break legs the same way and pull each segment free, taking the cartilage with it. If the meat doesn't pull free, squeeze it out with your teeth.
14. Discard the spongy gills and suck the meat in the body cavity free. Serve with hot melted butter.

LOBSTER THERMADORE

meat from 1 lobster
2 tablespoons butter
3/4 cup white wine
1 teaspoon dry mustard
3/4 cup cream

Kill lobster and remove as much meat as possible from it. Thinly slice the meat and sauté for a few minutes and reserve. Add other ingredients and simmer over low heat to reduce until thick. Place cooked lobster on herb toast and pour sauce over all.

LOBSTER À L' AMÉRICAINE

We call fried potatoes French fries and the French call them *potato frites*. Correspondingly, this dish, named "Lobster in the American Style" is French. Serves two.

2 lobsters
1 teaspoons each olive oil, butter
1/2 cup brandy
2 cloves garlic, minced
1/2 small onion, grated
1/2 cup white wine
4 tablespoons (1/2 stick) butter
1/4 cup scallion ends, chopped
1/2 lemon
salt, cayenne pepper

Split the lobster, remove sack, devein, chop off and discard head. Quarter lobster. Retain tomale and eggs if any and add to pan with lobster. Blanch the claws three minutes, cool and remove meat. Add to pan. Get oil very hot. Sauté lobster in oil ten minutes, turning all pieces until color changes.

Add a dash of white wine, cover and steam five minutes. Remove lid and simmer until liquid is reduced and thick. Add brandy and ignite. Remove lobster. Reduce liquid to a half cup. Add butter, scallion ends, onion, garlic and simmer until thick Arrange lobster on plate and pour sauce over all. Lobster can be served on top of julienned squash and pasta. Add salt, pepper, and lemon.

AMERICAN LOBSTER STUFFING

Lobster stuffing is usually made from the green liver and red coral, or premature roe, mixed with a tablespoon fried bread crumbs, a little lemon juice and a teaspoon cream sherry. We personally prefer the lobster au natural. If you decide to make the stuffing, have the ingredients mixed and ready for instant use; this way there will be no delay in getting the lobster to the table.

LOBSTER OMELET: See Omelets

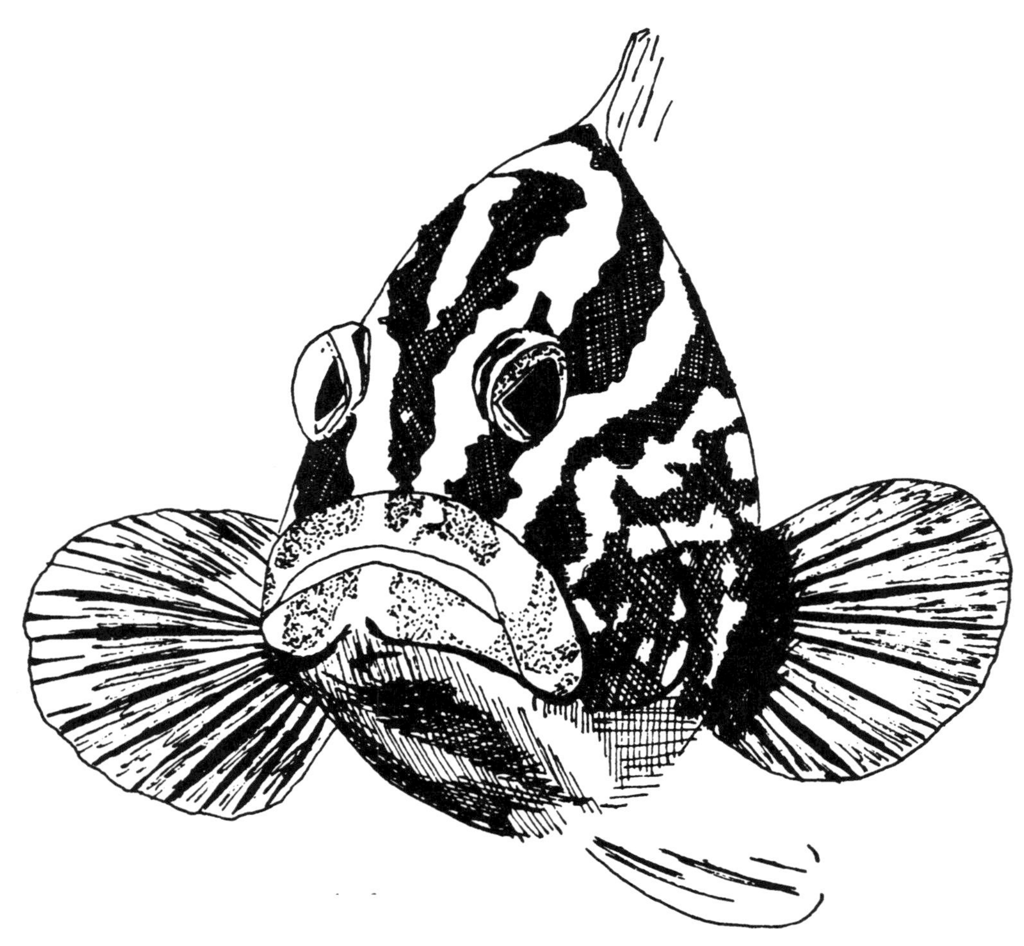

Nassau Grouper

10 Fish

FISHING

I am not what could be called a sport fisherman. Whereas sport fishermen envision their catch leaping above a sparkling sea, I envision mine surrounded by onions and carrots. When the fish leaps, I begin to salivate. I may not be a sportsman but I know how to put fish on the table.

My idea of a fishing rod is a twelve ton sloop with a large two-speed ocean reel hose-clamped to the stern rail. My idea of light line is sixty-pound monofilament with a heavy leader. I haul fish in and make them into fillets.

If a fish is too big to reel in I turn on the engine and tow it for a few miles until it drowns. If that doesn't work I get it as close as possible, then sit on the stern and pot shot at it with an automatic rifle until the matter is resolved one way or the other. If it still wants to fight after being shot, I beat it with an oar. If it's too big to bring aboard, I gaff it and use a machete to whack off the biggest piece I can get.

I learned this useful technique one morning while single-handing across the Atlantic. As is my habit when single handing, I slept at dawn and awoke to a gorgeous day with a very light wind and no swell and the dark outline of Flores, the most Western island of the Azores in sight.

I then stepped to the rail to answer nature's call. While so engaged I kept getting the feeling that something was amiss. At last I realized—the bubbles were going the wrong way! The boat was slightly heeled, the bow was going up and down but our progress was in reverse. This of course was inconceivable and monstrous as it is a well known fact that sailboats do not sail backwards. At last I discovered that the fishing line was bar tight and that something very, very large was towing me back toward the United States at a slow but steady pace.

Normally I would just cut the line but I was close to land and had visions of giving away the fillets of whatever was out there to my friends. Reeling in was out of the question. I had never towed a fish to death but it was time to give it a try. It was time for the engine. After towing whatever was on the line for about an hour, resistance ceased. I now reeled in a very dead monster tuna, weighing perhaps three hundred pounds. Its eye was as big around as a tea cup.

There was of course no chance of hauling it aboard by brute force. I gaffed it, tied the gaff to a halyard and threw the halyard on a winch. The fish started to come up but the small, cheap gaff started to straighten out. I could also hear the block at the masthead squealing in protest. Something was going to give. At that point I ran a line through its gills, secured the line to a shroud and got to work with a machete and saw. I eventually ended up with about a hundred and thirty-five pounds of very fresh tuna, which might not have been the lion's share but it was nevertheless a very good piece.

I am always on the lookout for circling or diving birds, weed patches or jumping fish. If these areas are not too far off course I like to troll around them. In areas of current such as the Gulf Stream, a big swirl of debris often indicates an eddy whose edges are packed with fish.

The entire secret of being a good trolling fisherman is hauling in your lure and checking it frequently. Every hour is not too much. The more often you do so, the more fish you will catch. This is because seaweed and debris get caught on the lure, rendering it ineffective.

Trolling lures fall into two categories for a sailor: lures for a speed of five knots or more and lures for lower speed. When a boat is moving above five knots, the lure goes by the fish like a shot and only the creature's instinct causes a reaction. This is why feather and plastic lures looking only slightly like a fish do well. If the lure goes slower, the fish are able to swim up to it and have a better look. When they see a feather jig going three knots they seem to say "what in Hell is that??" In this case, the lure needs to look more authentic and have much more action, like a big freshwater bass lure.

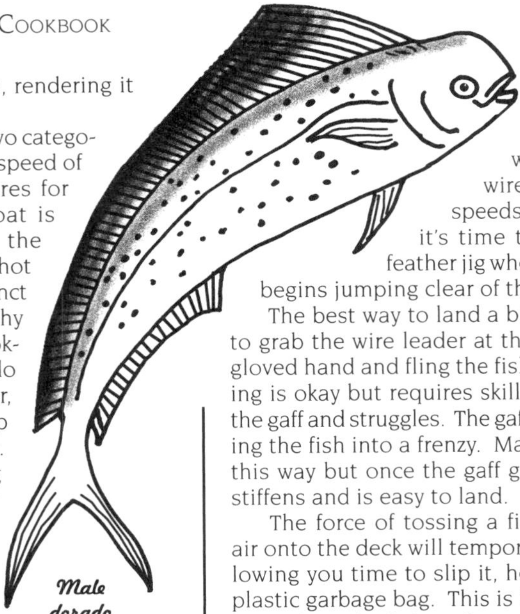

Male dorado

LURES I HAVE USED: Feather jigs, squid jigs, yarn jigs, can lids, spoons, coins, long shank hooks wound with rag and wrapped with Christmas tree tinsel. Light colored lures with a flash of red, blue or green work well on bright, sunny days. Darker lures do better in an overcast.

I prefer a #7 Owner hook with a five-foot 175 pound wire leader. This is an expensive hook which is short shanked, extremely sharp and of the highest quality. Expensive hooks should not be stored in your tackle box, mixed in a rich stew of dissimilar metals and sea salt. They are better off living with your sewing needles. I also use #9 stainless double hooks on a wire leader attached to a heavy swivel. These hooks are not as good as the Owners and can straighten out but they don't rust so they outlast the Owners.

I maintain a supply of six inch feather jigs in a variety of colors and eight plastic squids for moonlit nights. I usually do not troll on dark nights because the critters I have caught bit me, scared me and damn near drowned me and I don't like messing with vicious animals at close quarters on a pitching deck in poor light.

I use six to eight-inch bass-type lures for low speed and prefer mackerel imitators. These lures look just like little fish. I usually replace the light-weight freshwater treble hooks with larger double-stainless hooks by cutting the trebles off and slipping on the doubles, which are then moused with stainless wire. As the boat speeds up you can tell it's time to change to a feather jig when the bass lure begins jumping clear of the water.

The best way to land a bluewater fish is to grab the wire leader at the swivel with a gloved hand and fling the fish aboard. Gaffing is okay but requires skill. The fish sees the gaff and struggles. The gaff can miss, driving the fish into a frenzy. Many fish are lost this way but once the gaff goes in, the fish stiffens and is easy to land.

The force of tossing a fish through the air onto the deck will temporarily stun it, allowing you time to slip it, head first, into a plastic garbage bag. This is important. The bag calms the fish and contains the blood and mess which follows. Send sensitive crew below. Beat the critter on the head with a winch handle three or four times. Don't be shy. Meaner is kinder. If you are just *too kind* to be so brutal, toss a **shot of rum** into the critter's gills. This kills it instantly—and what better way to enter the Pearly Gates than stoned on rum.

Immediately take a chisel, broad blade screwdriver or short, heavy knife and sever its spine just behind the head. Once the spine is cut the fish stops jumping around. Work right through the garbage bag. Use a hammer if necessary. Work a knife around in the wound to make the fish bleed. Close the bag. Allow the fish to bleed a few minutes.

Ninety percent of the fish I have taken by trolling in deep water were **tuna**, and **dorado** (called **mahi mahi** in the West or **dolphin fish** in the East), with an occasional **wahoo** thrown in. Closer inshore, I often get bonito and mackerel which I am not fond of eating. If I keep a mackerel it will probably become bait. Sharks rarely take lures. The fish just mentioned make very reliable eating and clean up similarly. They are big boned and easy to clean.

Almost invariably I steak tuna. This means I gut the critter and save the roe, then cut the fish into about 1-1/2 inch thick slices, like slicing a salami. Tuna have very small scales which I ignore if grilling or wipe away with a scouring pad if pan cooking. The skin is usually left on as it is rich in fat.

Cleaning mahi mahi and wahoo: cut the garbage bag open and work inside it, to reduce mess or lay the fish on a surface which can easily be cleaned up. Have a bucket of sea water standing by to rinse your hands. Periodically rinse and dry your hands. If you get fish blood on your clothes wash it with salt in salt water.

Gut the fish and save the roe. Male mahi mahi have a bold, blunt head. The "roe" they produce is **milt** and is not tasty. Leave the guts in the bag. Cut the fillets from the spine.

Purists will save the skeleton for soup stock but you now have a large amount of fish, so I usually dump the skeleton. Hold the garbage bag over the side and shake out as much debris as possible. Reach inside the bag, grab the bottom and plunge into the sea, allowing the current to reverse and rinse it. Hang the bag on the stern for a few minutes, then store for disposal.

Soak the fillets in several changes of sea water to remove the blood. Trim away the lateral lines which are the color of dark, raw beef. This usually leaves you with four long fillets. Trim away the ribs. Bon appetite!

Catching bait fish: Small bait fish can be caught with lures consisting of really small hooks (#22) with a few pieces of yarn attached. The fish should first be chummed with ground fish, dampened oat or corn meal or tinned sardines.

Bottom fishing: At anchor I use cod sets which consist of a dozen or more baited round hooks on two foot leads set at four foot intervals with a three ounce sinker at the end. I keep a bag of wine corks handy and push the hooks into the corks as I bring them aboard. I usually bait with pieces of small fish.

I drop the set after dark, preferably into water deeper than thirty feet. If the set is to be dropped near the boat, I frequently chum by grinding up whole bait fish and periodically tossing the mess over the side. This brings in the small fish and they bring in the big fish.

If the set is not attached to the boat, it should be attached to something heavy like a small anchor (with a float) so the fish don't swim off with the set. Pick up the set at dawn because the hooked fish are vulnerable to sharks. You get rock cod, sea bass and ugly fish like sculpens which are very tasty. You also get the occasional ray or skate whose wings are very, very tasty. Many a ray wing, with the assistance of a cookie cutter, has become scallops. I also love to use collapsible crab pots but it's getting harder and harder to find clean waters to fish for

Bluefin tuna

The pinnacle of fine cuisine, this fish weighs up to 1,100 pounds and can reach ten feet in length. Sport fish them until one of you dies or tow them until they drown.

crabs and you don't want to eat crabs taken from a harbor unless you like the taste of oil.

Shark fishing is not my favorite sport. I like shark meat on a limited basis but it is not at the top of my culinary list. The tastiest ones, threshers and makos, usually are at least three or four feet long and can be extremely dangerous. Hit them over the head several times with a stout club before landing and immediately jam a paddle or chunk of wood into their mouths to prevent them from biting you. Shark fishing begins with the acquisition of a great deal of **chum**. Ground whole fish do well as chum but many enthusiasts buy animal blood and offal for this purpose. Chumming is done over a period of hours. Once you have succeeded in attracting sharks do not think about swimming in the same place as they will cruise around the area for days. Sharks are caught on a #1 or #0 hook with a heavy wire or light chain leader. It is truly unwise to fish for sharks in a rubber boat.

WHAT TO DO WITH THE FISH...

1. Fried fish roe is one of my breakfast favorites. I just toss the roe sacks in with the bacon. Roe is very tasty but a little dry and gluey, so bacon fat, mayonnaise or a sauce from canned creamed mushroom soup helps the roe along. It can also be removed from the sack and scrambled in a mixture of eggs, milk, fried onions and cheese.
2. Make a ceviche as soon as the fish is filleted which is consumed within a few hours for lunch or as a snack.
3. Try the pickling and curing recipes (page 159) which are truly delicious and which also preserve the fish for weeks or a month.
4. Try scrambled eggs with poached fish or fried fish for breakfast.
5. After I am about sick of fish, the rest is made into chowder which is eaten the third night.
6. Since even a small pelagic fish makes the reefer groan, I usually dump the skeleton. You can *sweat* it with chicken stock, producing a fish stock, which the French call a *fumet*. Make a chowder or use for sauce.
7. If you have a freezer, cut the fillets into individual portions, rinse in sea water and freeze in a Ziplock. When cooking frozen fish, do not defrost as juice is lost this way. Just drop the frozen pieces into a hot pan or onto a hot grill. Poaching frozen fish is also a good way of cooking them with minimizing further loss of flavor.

HOW LONG WILL IT LAST?

A little planning will reduce waste and allow you to enjoy all of your fish.

Day 1-2: Make ceviche, pickled fish and cured fish. Serve roe and fillet.
Day 2-3: Eat fillets, ceviche.
Day 3-4: Eat fillets, ceviche. Make leftover fillets into a chowder.
Day 5-6: Eat chowder. Serve cured fish.
Day 6-7: Eat something else. Serve ceviche snack.
Day 8-9: Make cured fish sandwiches. Eat chowder.
Day 10-14: Make cured fish sandwiches and poached eggs for breakfast, or scramble with eggs.

ABOUT FISH

For seafood soups and stews, see Chapter 5.

VISITING THE FISH MARKET: One of the great joys of cruising is dropping the hook in a fishing port, rowing ashore, and touring the local markets. Throughout the world, fish markets are a gourmet's candy store, so richly stocked with varied wonders from the sea: sharks and swordfish stacked like logs; eels thrown across a counter, their vicious mouths agape; squid of every size from the tiny sepia to deep reef monsters eight feet long; baskets of urchins; mussels; snails; rays; tuna; shrimp; limpets; and oysters, all are there, each with its culinary contribution to make.

SELECTING: Regardless of the temptations, look at everything before buying. I always say "the best fish calls out to me" because the freshest fish looks the best. Most of the sea creatures you find in the market are fresh from the sea, still gleaming and supple. At the end of the day however, the unsold seafood gets a little ice thrown on it and it is left to fend for itself. The rule, as everywhere, is "let the buyer beware." When you look at fish ask yourself a few questions:

1. Does it smell right, especially the gills and body cavity?
2 Are the eyes bulging, glistening, and supple?
3. Are the scales glistening and slippery?

If the fish passes all three tests, especially the nose test, it is a buy. If not, don't let the assurances of the fishmonger sway you. Don't be embarrassed. It's okay. You will impress him and his respect for you will increase. Maybe his second offering will be something better.

CIGUTERRA: When in tropic waters do not let the fishmonger convince you to buy reef fish, which are a potential source of a malady called **ciguterra**, something you really don't want. Ciguterra is a **neurological disorder**. It is caused by consuming reef fish which in turn have eaten smaller fish which contain toxins. The toxins are concentrated in the flesh of the larger fish.

Ciguterra is a mysterious malady which may be present in many different species of reef fish. It may be present on one part of a reef but absent elsewhere. It may be absent for years then reappear. Its precise cause is unknown. The reason for its presence is unknown. There is no quick test for it, no sign of its presence in the fish, cooking does not destroy it. The onset can occur twelve hours after consuming the infected fish or it may not appear for weeks. It can reappear mysteriously months or years later. Nasty.

It is believed that ciguterra originated in the Caribbean. Captain Bligh is thought to have brought it to Tahiti hidden in the barnacles on his ship. The disease decimated the population there.

Islanders live with ciguterra like South American Indians live with malaria. In some island groups, such as Polynesia it is estimated that 100% of all natives have had ciguterra at one time or another. It usually makes one very ill. Occasionally it causes paralysis or death.

Because of this danger, when in tropic waters I tend to buy **pelagic** (deep water) fish which are the same as the ones I usually catch offshore, mahi mahi, wahoo, and tuna. When it comes to culinary adventures in tropic seas, I concentrate my explorations in the realm of crustaceans and mollusks.

BEST BUYS: The best fish to buy is always the local common offshore catch and if that happens to be flying fish, eat them. This also applies if the catch is a very small fish like sardines, which can be spitted and grilled. Check out some additional comments about grilling fish in the Chapter 4.

MARINATING, soaking fish in various mixtures of wine, garlic, vinegar, and onions for a few hours prior to cooking accomplishes several purposes. It helps reduce the fishy odor and taste of dark fleshed species such as mackerel. If marinated in lemon juice and salt, a marinade makes a delicately fleshed fish more firm, reducing its tendency to disintegrate. A good marinade also imparts some of its flavor to the fish. Read more about marinades on page 281.

REMOVING FISH SMELL from pots, utensils, and counter tops, is accomplished by scrubbing them with baking soda or a mixture of salt, lemon juice, and water. Lemon juice also removes the fish smell from the cook's hands.

FREEZING: Frozen fish is a second choice but is usually cheaper than fresh fish and much less perishable. Frozen fish are best poached or cooked in a sauce from a frozen state. When freezing fish, rinse in salt water, pat dry, store in a freezer bag. Suck out air before sealing.

FISH FINGERS: When pan cooking fish, be sure the pieces are not more than three-quarter of an inch thick. If thicker the fish gets overcooked on the outside and undercooked on the inside. Fish fingers are best held together with a strip of skin. They may be rolled in crumbs and fried. You can also bake a fat fish over low heat.

HOW MUCH SHOULD I BUY? Although fish is less fatty than meat it is solid protein and quite rich. One half pound per serving is adequate.

WHEN IS IT DONE? Fish cooks much faster than meat or fowl. Fish is most effectively tested with a finger poke or a spoon. For poached, baked or grilled fish, slip a spoon between segments and give a slight twist. The segments should separate easily and the interior should steam. The flesh should be opaque, not translucent. If fluid wells up when the fish is opened, it needs a little more cooking. Fish is done when it is white to the center but still moist. If a fish falls apart when lifted with a spatula it is overcooked. Firm fleshed fish such as swordfish and tuna never become as tender as snapper or sea bass.

CLEANING FISH

CLEANING FLAT FISH: Members of the very tasty halibut family begin life like other fish with an eye on each side of the head, but as they develop, the eye on one side migrates

Eel fishermen near Puerto Ercole, Italy

to the other side so that the fish, instead of having a right and left side has an up and a down side.

1. With a sharp knife trim away the fins which run around the edge of the fish.
2. Slip a small sharp knife under the skin at the tail and cut through both sides from tail to head.
3. Connect the cuts.
4. Pull the skin free by pulling it off from tail to head. Keep your hand close to the body so that you pull forward, not upward. Use a small sharp knife to assist.
5. Cut away the guts and run your finger along the backbone to remove any dark red clots.

The fish is now ready for cooking. If it is large and will not fit in the pan cut off the head.

SCALING ROUND FISH

It is easier when the fish is wet; it is helpful to have a crewman stand by with a bucket of sea water to assist you. Scaling should be done before gutting, filleting, or steaking the fish, because the guts fill out the abdominal cavity and make the job easier. Hold the fish down by its tail and slide the knife or scaler in short strokes, toward the head. A scaler really works much better than a knife. Be sure to get the base of the tail, around the fins, and under the head. Wash thoroughly in sea water. Feel all over to be sure all the scales are removed.

STEAKING A ROUND FISH

Tuna and swordfish have short, very heavy bones and are therefore often steaked, which is very easy.

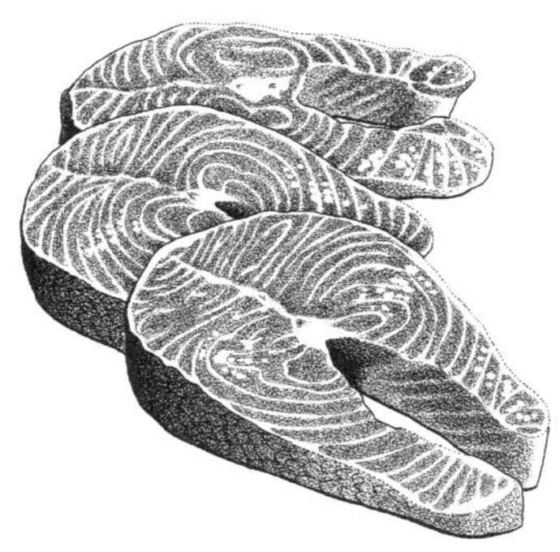

1. First, scrape the fish to remove excess tiny scales and slime.
2. Gut the fish and trim away the fatty belly strip.
3. Wipe the skin with a paper towel.
4. Chop the rear section of the fish free, at the anal vent. This portion will be filleted.
5. Then, just lay the fish on a cutting board and slice like a salami, creating steaks which are about 3/4 inch thick.

FILLETING LARGE ROUND FISH

See illustration on page 148.

A round fish is the kind that has all of its parts in the usual places such as dorado (Mahi-mahi) and wahoo. Normally we steak tuna. The best place to dress the fish is on the cockpit seat so that you can kneel in the cockpit and not have to work bent over. Make bold, decisive cuts so that you don't have many ragged edges and flaps of meat.

1. Cut from anal vent to pelvic fins. Gut the fish and save the roe. Male Mahi have a bold, blunt head. The "roe°" they produce is milt and is not tasty. Leave the guts in the bag.
2. Make a deep cut to the backbone from head to tail, bumping the knife point along the backbone.
3. Make a deep cut behind pectoral fins to connect dorsal and ventral cuts.
4. Separate the fillet from the body, cutting through the ribs.
5. Trim away the ribs.
6. Skinning. Rinse the fillet and pat dry. Place it on some newspaper which has been spread on the cockpit seat. Place the fillet next to the edge of the seat so that the knife handle (and your hand) will be clear of the seat. Hold the tail end of the fillet and slip your knife between the skin and flesh. A large carving knife is better than a filleting knife for this purpose. Hold the tail end of the fillet and make a cut between meat and skin large enough to grab the skin.
7. Grab the skin and saw forward with the knife, angling it slightly downward. A crewman can assist by slightly lifting the fillet as you work so that you can see what you are doing.
8. Soak the fillets in several changes of sea water to remove the blood.

THE LATERAL LINES: Some fish, including mahi mahi and tuna have lateral lines, the color of dark, raw beef, which run the length of the fillet. It is unpleasant and strong tasting. Trim it away. This usually leaves you with four long fillets.

Purists will save the skeleton for soup stock but you now have a large amount of fish, so I usually dump the skeleton. You can

When young they have a right side and a left side but as adults one eye migrates to the othjer side and they have only a top and bottom!

also break it up and make a fine stock (see Basic Stuff) before dumping.

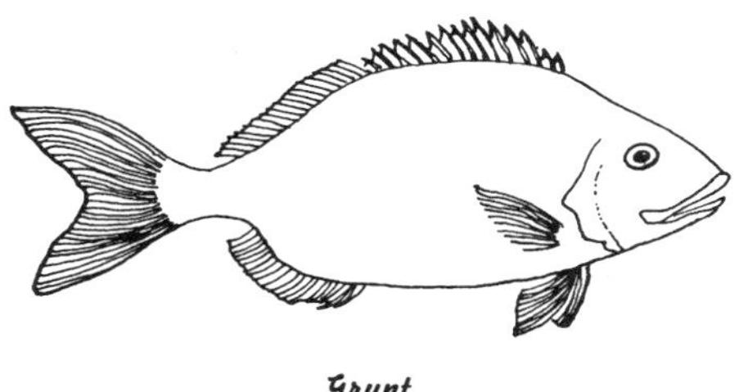

Grunt

A small tropic fish found under piers or on shallow reefs. Grunts loudly when caught.

PREPARING SMALL FISH

The recommended way of cooking small fish such as pilchards or smelts is to roughly gut and spit them, make two oblique cuts through the skin on each side and toss them on the grill over very high heat or open flame for a few minutes. This cooks them and scorches off the scales.

GUT small fish by slipping a very sharp knife into the anal vent, then sliding the blade toward the head until it is stopped by the pelvic (fin) bones. Cut the pelvic fin bones away by sliding the knife under them. Tear the guts from the abdominal cavity with a quick pull. The fish is then simultaneously gutted and decapitated by bending the head back and twisting it off after the backbone snaps. Remove any clinging viscera, and be sure to remove the blood lines under the backbone by gouging them out with a fingernail. Rinse.

ABOUT FISH SAUCES

The base of many fish sauces is a ***fumet***, which is a fish stock that has been simmered until it is half evaporated. Read more about *fumets* on page 38. Some sauces which are not specifically for fish but go well with them include: pesto, marinara, curry, mayonnaise and sweet and sour sauce. Below you will find a few classic fish sauces which are not made from a *fumet*.

WHITE BUTTER SAUCE

4 tablespoons shallots or onions, grated, squeezed
2 tablespoons white vinegar
4 tablespoons dry vermouth
2 tablespoons lemon juice
1 tablespoon powdered dill
1/2 cup cream
1/4 pound melted butter (thin as desired with oil)
salt and pepper

Simmer shallots, dill, vinegar, vermouth and lemon juice in a sauce pan over high heat for a minute or two and reduce. Add the cream and reduce the flame to lowest. Cream should steam. Heat until mixture thickens. Set aside until ready for use, then reheat to steaming. Add butter salt and pepper and whisk until butter melts. Use immediately.

LEMON PARSLEY BUTTER SAUCE

This is similar in flavor but less of an artery-clogger than white butter.

1 tablespoon corn starch
1/2 cup white wine or vermouth
1 teaspoon lemon zest
1 teaspoon lemon juice
1/2 teaspoon sugar
1 tablespoon parsley, chopped
2 tablespoons butter
dash of cream

Add everything but parsley and heat until thickened. Add parsley and serve.

BLACK BUTTER

4 tablespoons butter
2 tablespoons white vinegar
2 tablespoons white wine
1 tablespoon lemon juice
3 tablespoons capers
3 tablespoons Italian parsley, chopped

Lightly brown the butter in a small sauce pot and cool quickly to avoid scorching. Reserve. Add everything else to a small pot except parsley and simmer until almost dry. Add butter, melt, add parsley, stir, serve. If you want to be really exotic you can use these butter sauces as the butter in a hollandaise sauce.

NUT BUTTER SAUCE

Sauté a handful of slivered or chopped almonds, walnuts, pecans or Brazil nuts and

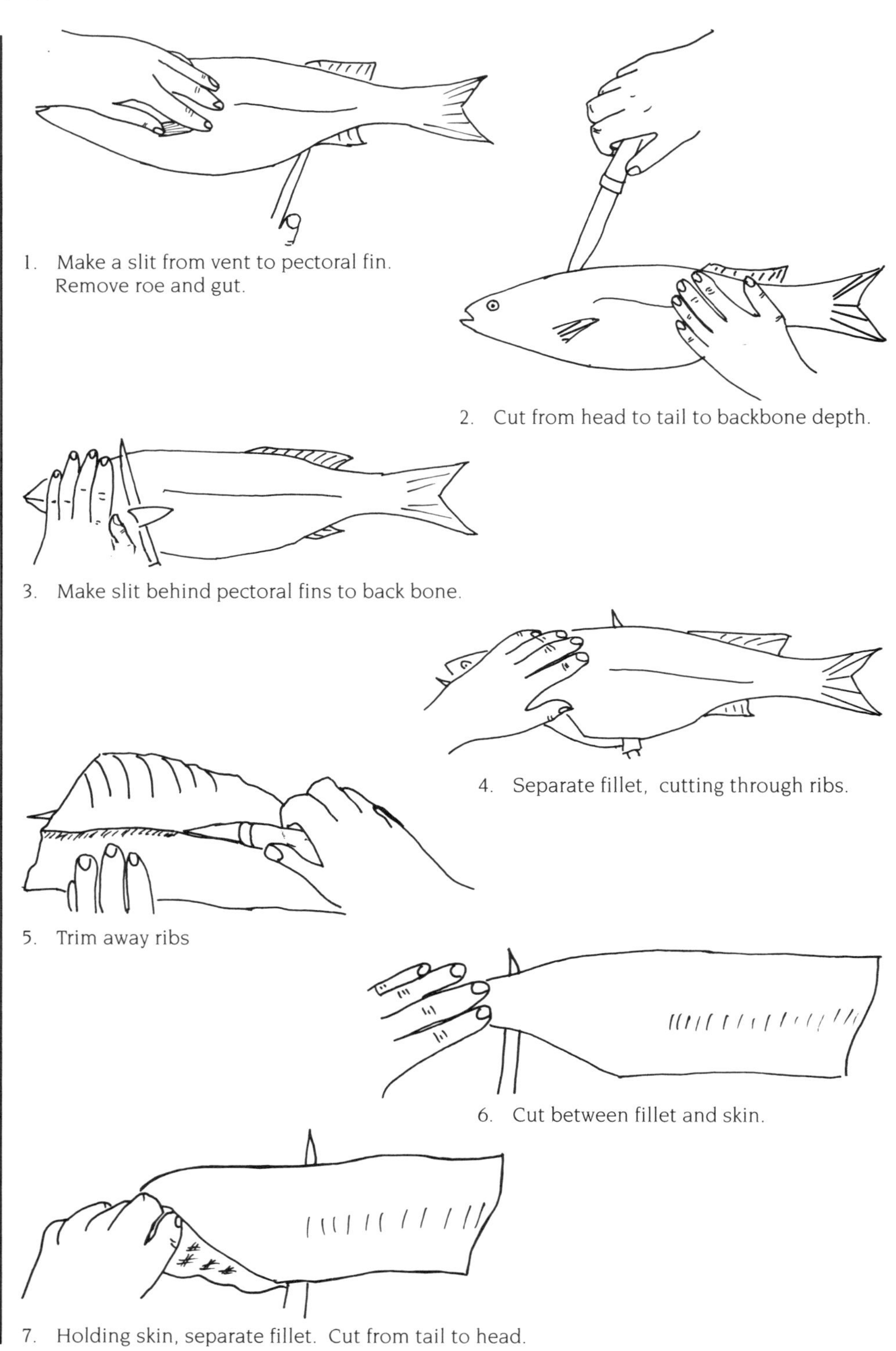

1. Make a slit from vent to pectoral fin. Remove roe and gut.

2. Cut from head to tail to backbone depth.

3. Make slit behind pectoral fins to back bone.

4. Separate fillet, cutting through ribs.

5. Trim away ribs

6. Cut between fillet and skin.

7. Holding skin, separate fillet. Cut from tail to head.

some grated onion in butter over low heat until the nuts are toasted. Pour on fish and sprinkle with lemon and fresh parsley.

SOUR CREAM DILL SAUCE

This is a terrific, quick, reliable sauce which you will probably want to use frequently.

3/4 cup sour cream or yogurt
juice of 1/2 lemon
3 tablespoons dry dill
3 tablespoons horseradish (or dry mustard)
1/4 cup capers (optional)
salt and pepper

Combine and allow to reach room temperature before serving.

MUSHROOM-SOUR CREAM SAUCE

2 cups mushrooms, chopped, sautéed in butter
1/2 cup onion, finely chopped, squeezed
1 tablespoon gravy flour
1/2 cup milk
1/2 cup sour cream
2 tablespoons Dijon mustard
1 tablespoon vermouth or white wine
salt and pepper

Sauté the mushrooms in butter, sprinkle in the flour, salt and pepper. Blend in milk, wine and allow to thicken. Remove from heat, allow to slightly cool, add everything else and stir.

MUSTARD SAUCE

1 tablespoon chopped, squeezed onion
2 tablespoons butter
1 tablespoon gravy flour
1 cup milk
2 tablespoons Dijon mustard
salt and pepper

Sauté onion a few minutes. Sprinkle in flour and pepper to make a *roux*. Add milk and mustard, whisking furiously.

OTHER GOOD FISH SAUCES

- Tomato salsa
- Rarebit sauce
- Chile paste red pepper grill marinade
- Assorted mayonnaises
- Curry sauce or India sauce
- Pesto
- Marinara

FISH COOKING TECHNIQUES

Also see GRILLING.

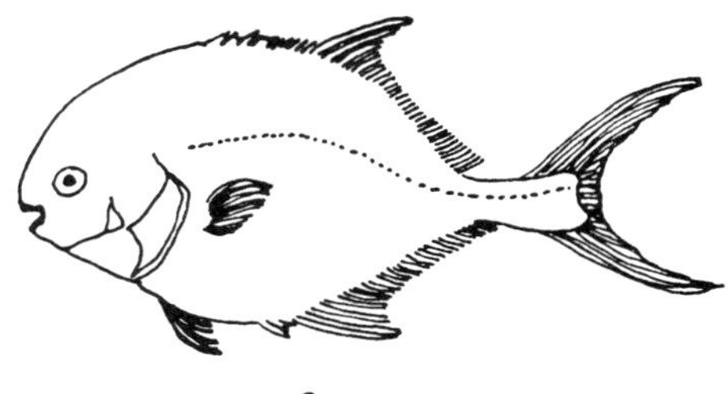

Pompano

Supremely delicious Atlantic fish often caught in the Gulf Stream. Poaching creamy fillets which melt in the mouth. Often served with mustard mayonnaise or hollandaise sauce.

POACHING is an excellent cooking method for fish. It leaves the fish succulent and moist, and is very forgiving of overcooking. When poaching, be sure the fish is not too thick. Poached fish is usually not turned over because it will fall apart. If the portions are more than three-quarters of an inch thick, it is better to divide the fish to make it thinner.

The poaching liquid: Fish can be poached in plain water, but a combination of wine, herbs, onions, leeks and wine is preferable. The liquid should simmer but never boil while the fish is in it. The poaching liquid may be thickened into a *fumet* or further thickened with a *roux*..

Another approach is to remove the fish, then mix a bit of the poaching liquid with a big dollop of **aioli mayonnaise** or one of the other mayos. Heat and stir for a few minutes. Pour back over the fish and vegetables.

Poached fish is never completely covered by the poaching liquid. A good description of how much liquid to use comes straight from the nautical chart: "uncovers and is awash at low tide." We almost always use a slope sided frying pan with a lid rather than a skillet for poaching. Pour the liquid off and slide the fish onto a plate.

BASIC POACHING TECHNIQUE

Butter bottom of large fry pan. Add poaching liquid and boil. Add fish, reduce heat. Simmer until done. Cook five to twelve minutes depending on thickness.

POACHING IN SAUCE: Fish may be poached in any sauce which does not break when simmered such as tomato sauce. Fish marinara is hard to beat. Seafood can be poached in a curry sauce which is delicious. But poaching in a sauce which has been thickened breaks the sauce.

BACON AND POACHED FISH ON TOAST

fried bacon (four slices per serving)
1 cup milk
3 tablespoons cooking oil
2 tablespoons bacon fat
2 serrano chilies, seeded, chopped
juice of 1/2 lemon
1/4 cup Parmesan cheese
1/2 cup white wine
1/2 pound fish fillets (per serving)

Fry bacon, reserve fat, wipe pan slightly. Make toast in pan, wipe clean for poaching. Make a béchamel (white) sauce (page 41) in a small pot using a little bacon fat plus cooking oil. When the flour for the *roux* begins to fry, throw in the hot pepper. Poach the fish in a little water and white wine. Crumble the bacon onto buttered toast, add fish and pour sauce over all. Sprinkle with cheese.

SHERRY SWEAT-POACHED SALMON OR MAHI MAHI

1 cup sherry
1 cup fish *fumet* or chicken stock
3 stalks celery
3 carrots, quartered lengthwise
bouquet garni
4 fish steaks, with skin
1/2 cup mild cheese, grated
1/4 cup parsley, chopped

Lay the vegetables in a crisscross in a skillet to make a platform for the steaks and add herbs. Bring to a simmer, reduce to steaming and add fish and cook about fifteen minutes, until done. Remove fish and keep warm. Strain liquid and simmer to reduce by 50%.

Make a *roux*, then pour in about a cup of the liquid, whisking furiously. As an alternative, mix one tablespoon of arrowroot with a little white wine, simmer some of the sauce in a sauce pan and add the thickener. This makes a clearer sauce. Pour sauce on plate. Place fish in center, sprinkle with a mild cheese and parsley.

PAN FRYING IN OIL AND BUTTER: Butter burns at low temperature and is therefore a poor choice as a frying liquid. Fry fish in peanut oil and add a little butter for flavor. Always use fresh oil. To test the temperature of the oil, drop a pinch of flour into the pan. If it skips on the surface and sizzles the oil is ready. Add fish and brown quickly on one side, turn and reduce heat.

SIZE OF PIECES: If the fish or filet is more than two-inches thick, it must be cut up, steaked, or in some way made thinner. Thick, meaty fish may also be partially pan fried on both sides until slightly brown, then baked in a 350° F. oven for five minutes per pound.

BREADING AND COATING: Fish to be fried may be first dusted with flour, corn meal, corn flakes or matzo meal before cooking. Pat a fish dry, dip it in egg and milk and then shake in a plastic bag with flour or breading mix.

BREADING MIXES FOR FRIED FISH

These combos can also be coated with melted butter and poured over a fish which is to be baked.

- **Oriental:** Three cups chow mein noodles, crushed
- **Almond:** one cup cracker crumbs, one-half cup blenderized almonds
- **Potato Chip:** one bag (4 ounces) potato chips, one cup crushed corn flakes
- **Tortilla Chip:** one cup spicy tortilla chips, one cup cracker crumbs, chopped hot pepper to taste.

FISH TACOS

Pieces of fish are battered and fried.

Batter ingredients:
1 cup flour
1 tablespoon paprika
1 tablespoon cornstarch
1 cup beer
salt and pepper

Chill batter in the refrigerator for an hour. Cut fish into small pieces, sprinkle with flour then dip in batter and fry in very, very hot peanut oil until golden.

Taco ingredients:
warmed corn tortillas

shredded cabbage
mayonnaise
tomato salsa

Add the cabbage to the tortilla, then the mayo, then the fish and finally the salsa.

FRIED FISH ROE, TWO RECIPES

Fresh roe is one of my favorites. I love its gluey taste and I am delighted to see big roe sacks in a fish I've caught. Here are two quick recipes for fresh fish roe: one simple, one elegant. You can also fry the roe, slice it thinly lengthwise and slip it inside an omelet. The well-known gourmet James Beard says that the only way to cook roe is simmered in butter for exactly seven minutes on each side.

2 roe sacks
6 strips bacon
lemon juice
maple syrup

Fry bacon until done and reserve. Fry roe in a little bacon fat and cooking oil (be generous) until golden on outside. Split roe sack and flip. Remove and blot. Crumble bacon strips and sprinkle inside roe; add a few drops of lemon juice and maple syrup and serve.

FRIED ROE WITH FINE HERB SAUCE

1/2 pound fish roe
3 tablespoons butter
1 small onion, finely chopped.
1 teaspoon each: parsley, tarragon, wine vinegar
juice of 1/2 lemon

Fry roe sacks in oil until golden. Remove roe, blot and set aside; add all other ingredients except lemon juice. Simmer for two to three minutes until onion turns golden. Remove from flame; sprinkle with lemon juice and pour over roe.

FRIED EELS MARINATED IN COGNAC

The best way we know to skin an eel is to tie a string around its neck and hang it from the mast. The skin is then cut below the string and pulled off in one piece with the help of pliers. The meat is best filleted below the ribs thus avoiding tiny bones. Eel meat is succulent and has a fine texture.

3 pounds of eel (4 medium, freshwater eels)
2 cups water
2 tablespoons lemon juice
2 cups flour
4 tablespoons cognac
1 teaspoon baking powder
2 eggs, beaten
2 cups milk, fresh or tinned
2 teaspoons each salt and pepper

Skin and gut eels; cut into three or four pieces each. Marinate four to six hours in lemon, cognac, salt, pepper and water. Turn about every two hours. Mix flour, baking powder, pepper and salt. Beat egg and milk together, then blend with dry ingredients. Dip eels in batter; pan fry in peanut oil until browned.

FISH CAKES

1-1/2 pounds fish, chopped
2 eggs, beaten
1/2 cup evaporated milk or cream
1-1/2 cups bread crumbs
1/2 teaspoon paprika
1 small onion, grated and squeezed dry
1/4 cup scallion ends, chopped
juice of 1/2 lemon
pinch celery salt or celery seed
several dashes hot sauce
1 teaspoon baking powder
2 tablespoons flour

Combine the all the ingredients and shape into balls, squeezing out excess liquid. Pan fry in oil, crushing balls into patties as they cook. Serve with horseradish mayonnaise sauce.

FRIED FISH CROQUETTES

1 cup leftover fish
1 cup boiled potatoes, same amount as fish
2 tablespoons butter
1/2 onion, grated, squeezed dry
pinch each: nutmeg, salt, pepper
cream to thin
1 egg yolk
flour
oil

Mash fish and potatoes together. Add remaining ingredients. Roll into cakes, flour and fry in oil until browned.

BRAISING: Braising fish involves frying in a breading or batter until golden, then adding a little sauce and sautéing. The sauce bonds to the breading. You could just sprinkle on a little beer, soy, parsley and garlic.

BROILING: Fish is usually broiled by just brushing it with a little oil and placing it under the broiler. Sauces or coatings are usually added at the last minute, otherwise they burn. If you want to oven cook a fish with a sauce or coating, it is usually baked, then broiled for a minute to give the top some color. Extremely delicate, thin fillets can be coated with a breading mix and cooked using the technique which follows.

BROILED FISH FILLETS AMANDINE

Dover sole is often served this way as the grand entrée of fine restaurants; yet the recipe is quite simple, and any fine flavored fish fillet may be used. The classic technique uses a simple trick—first the pan is covered with oil/butter and broiled until extremely hot. The floured fish is slipped onto the hot pan and the upside is grilled while the down side sautés.

1 cup milk
1/2 cup seasoned flour or breading mix
1/2 stick butter or butter/oil mixture
1/2 cup slivered almonds

Dip fillets in milk. Dust with seasoned flour. Pan fry both sides until golden brown in oil/butter. Remove fish and reserve. Add butter. When butter is melted add almonds. Sauté over low heat until light brown, occasionally rubbing bottom of pan with a spatula. The nuts should take just a few minutes, not enough time for the fish to cool off. Pour butter and nuts over fish, sprinkle with lemon juice.

FOIL BAKING

FOIL BAKED GROUPER OF THE MARSH HARBOR CONCH INN

Serves two per pound of fish.

1-1/2 pounds grouper fillets, approx. 3 x 3 x 1/2"
juice of 3 lemons
1/2 cup milk
2 eggs
salt and pepper
cracker crumbs
hot peppers, finely chopped, mixed with milk
butter/oil

Soak fillets in lemon juice for one hour. Pat dry; dip in milk and egg, hot pepper, then in cracker crumbs. Fry in butter and oil over high heat until slightly browned on both sides, about two minutes each side.

Wrap in buttered aluminum foil, bake for ten minutes at 325° F. or pan bake, covered, for seven minutes over low heat Fantastic!

BAKED OR ROASTED FISH: Oven baking fish is a great cooking technique but it heats up the boat. Baking or roasting on a grill eliminates this problem. Fish can be roasted on the grill but must be kept moist by laying them in an oily liquid and basting them frequently. Fish bake in a 400° F. oven until opaque. Use the spoon to test for doneness. Bake about ten minutes for every inch of thickness measured at the thickest spot.

If you do not have an oven, these same recipes can be cooked in a heavy casserole dish on a burner flame diffuser at medium heat for the same period of time. A fork should be frequently slipped around and beneath the fish, covering the bottom of the pan with liquid to prevent burning.

QUICK BAKED FISH IN MUSHROOM SOUP SAUCE

This is a fast recipe using cream of mushroom soup as a base. Canned tuna may be used to stretch the fish fillets.

3 tablespoons butter/oil
1 cup cream of mushroom soup
1 cup condensed milk
4 tablespoons dry white wine
1 teaspoon celery salt
1 teaspoon pepper

Heavily butter bottom and sides of casserole dish. In a separate pot, heat everything except the fish and stir until combined. Pour thin layer of sauce in casserole. Add layer of fish and cover with more sauce. Bake uncovered at 400° for twenty minutes.

BAKED FISH IN CAPER SAUCE

3 pounds fish
4 tablespoons butter
1-1/2 teaspoons celery seed, crushed
1 cup fish stock or chicken consommé or wine
4 tablespoons butter
2 teaspoons each: capers, lemon juice, chopped chives or green onion ends
salt and pepper
salsa

Brush seasoned, clarified butter over both sides and body cavity. Place fish on platter; add liquid, cover with mixture of butter, celery seed, capers and lemon juice. Bake until done, brushing with liquid once or twice. Sprinkle with more lemon juice. Add chives, salt and pepper. Serve with a salsa.

LEFTOVER FISH RECIPES

FISH PATÉ

Regardless of how the fish was originally cooked, the leftovers, scraped free of sauce, will make a fine paté. In addition, the head, tail, and skeleton left from a filleted fish contain meat that can make a paté. Simply poach these leftover parts in a little chicken bouillon for fifteen minutes. The meat will slip easily from the bones.

Don't throw the cooking liquid away; it makes a good stock. Breaded, fried fish may be used in this recipe without removing the breading. Fish pâté may be used as a sandwich spread, or stuffed into cold artichokes, avocados, or tomatoes.

Mix and refrigerate:

2 cups fish (no bones)
4 tablespoons mayonnaise
11/2 teaspoons Dijon mustard
1/2 cup celery, finely chopped
1/4 cup onion, finely diced
1/4 teaspoon dill
1/2 cup rice vinegar
2 cups toasted cracker crumbs (if the fish has not been previously breaded)
salt and pepper to taste

CANNED SARDINE PATÉS

"Sardine" actually refers to a number of different species of small fish, which are similar in size, such as **pilchards** or **anchovies**. The smallest ones usually have a better texture. In addition to the size of the sardine, the **packing liquid** is also important. Olive oil is best. After olive oil, several different kinds of vegetable oil, including peanut oil are good. Last, and least tempting, are several non-oily sauces. These may be good on other fish, but their use on the sardine usually indicates poor quality.

SARDINE SANDWICH SPREAD

1 cup sardines, packed in oil, mashed into paste
1 tablespoon lemon juice
1/2 teaspoon dry mustard
pinch pepper
1/2 medium onion, chopped, squeezed

Mix all ingredients together and spread on buttered toast.

SARDINE PATÉ

Combine:

1 tablespoon white vinegar
3 dashes Tabasco sauce, or 1 teaspoon prepared mustard
1 tablespoon sugar
1 teaspoon salt

Pour mixture over three pieces dried Melba toast.

Combine:

1 can sardines, drained
2 hard-boiled eggs, chopped
1 onion, chopped
1 tablespoon mayonnaise
3 tablespoons parsley, chopped

Combine melba toast with fish mixture, let stand overnight, if possible. Serve in avocado halves as a cold salad.

FISH PASTA SALAD

A good way to make a fish salad is to make the salad with an oil vinegar herb dressing, then slip the flakes of fish, which have been tossed in a mayonnaise, on top. The recipe that follows is typical. You can also make a fish lettuce or watercress salad.

1/2 pound poached white fish, flaked
2 cups macaroni or twists, cooked
3/4 cup honey mustard dressing
1 bell pepper, roasted
3 hard-boiled eggs, whites grated, yolks reserved
1 small jar marinated artichoke hearts
1/4 cup olive slices
1/2 cup olive oil
4 garlic cloves, finely chopped
1 tablespoon dry mustard
1 pinch pepper
4 tablespoons white vinegar

Toss fish in mustard mayonaise dressing (page 42) and reserve. Crush garlic and combine with oil and vinegar. Stir furiously until exhausted. Add other ingredients except red pepper and toss. Serve fish on top of pasta. Garnish with red pepper.

FISH BURGERS

This was originally a salmon recipe but any whitefish will be just as tasty. Makes 1-1/4 pounds.

2 cups fish meat, flaked
2 tablespoons all purpose flour
1 teaspoon sugar
1 egg, beaten
1/2 cup bread crumbs or mix
2 tablespoons oil
1/2 cup onion, grated and squeezed
1/4 cup parsley, chopped
2 tablespoons soy sauce
1 tablespoon Worcestershire sauce
1 teaspoon each: powdered rosemary, oregano, sage
juice of 1/2 lemon

Combine ingredients and chill. Shape into patties. Brush with oil before grilling.

SHARKS

CATCHING: Sharks, even small ones, don't like being caught and have difficulty with the concept of being dead. A blow on the top of their head kills them but does not eliminate the possibility that a "dead" shark won't suddenly lunge out and ruin your day. Their incredibly durable nervous system makes them dangerous for a long time. Jam an oar down their throat so they can't bite you.

PREPARATION: makos, threshers, leopards are the most commonly consumed species and dogfish are usually the ingredient in fish 'n chips. The flesh should be soaked overnight in vinegar and water to eliminate the slight ammonia smell. Shark meat is always skinned as the skin shrinks during cooking and breaks the meat.

USE OF A MARINADE: Shark meat is very lean and contains ammonia. It should be soaked in an oily acid marinade. It grills well, just like swordfish and can be coated with the red pepper marinade while cooking, but not soy based marinades which are too salty. Serve with mayo, pesto, white sauces, hollandaise, cheese sauce, mushrooms in butter, marinara or salsa.

SHARK 'N CHIPS

This is not the best recipe for a yacht since it calls for deep frying, and since the oil, once used for shark 'n chips, can only be used for future generations of shark 'n chips. Nevertheless, we believe English and certain other Commonwealth nation sailors require occasional doses of this dish or they go into withdrawal and require medical attention. We therefore present this recipe in case of emergency.

This is particularly good with dogfish. Use the fillets from around the spine. The other parts can be used for shark bait. If you

Cape Trionto light

are making french fries (chips) cook them first otherwise they will taste of shark.

In a large pot, bring one inch of peanut oil to high heat. Dip bite-sized pieces of shark fillet in beaten egg, then bread crumbs. Fry shark to golden brown in extremely hot oil. Serves two to three per pound of fish.

SHARK CAKES

Cook shark according to the previous recipe for hash patties. A small shark, about four pounds, provides more meat than is needed for the hash. Use four cups of hashed meat to make these delicious cakes.

Simmer in oil until golden:
1 medium onion, minced and squeezed
1 cup bread crumbs

Remove from heat, combine and add:
3 cups shark meat, cooked, dried, hashed
2 eggs, well beaten
1 small can condensed milk
1/2 cup carrots, finely minced
2 teaspoons lemon juice
1 teaspoon salt
1 teaspoon paprika

Shape into cakes; dip in bread crumbs, crushed corn flakes, or flour. Fry in vegetable oil at high heat until browned on both sides. Continue frying at low heat for eight minutes.

SHARK SALAD

If your shark is over ten pounds use only the body meat close to the spine. The belly meat on larger sharks is tough and requires longer cooking.

1-1/2 pounds shark meat
1 medium onion, grated
2 hot peppers, seeded, finely chopped (optional)
1 bell pepper, diced (optional)
1/2 cup vegetable oil
1/2 cup croutons
1 tablespoon thyme
1 tablespoon parsley
salt and pepper to taste

Fillet and boil body meat in a large pot of water until it is tender and flakes easily, about thirty minutes. Drain the meat and dry in a towel. The finished product should be light and fluffy; drying is important. Hash meat thoroughly with a fork. Blend together all other ingredients. Toss with pasta and serve or mix with a little mayonnaise to make a sandwich spread.

KEDGEREE OF SHARK

Combine and serve hot:
2 cups cooked rice
1 pound shark meat, cooked, dried, hashed
4 hard-boiled eggs, forced through a sieve or grate
1/2 cup white cheese, grated
1/2 cup butter or margarine
1 cup canned condensed milk
1 tablespoon lemon juice
1 teaspoon paprika
1/2 cup cooked celery, finely chopped (optional)
1/2 cup cooked carrots, finely diced

TERIYAKI SHARK

1-1/2 pounds shark, cubed
3/4 cup teriyaki sauce
2 teaspoons dry sherry
1 teaspoon dry mustard
1 tablespoon dry ginger
3 cloves garlic, chopped

Marinate shark thirty minutes. Pat dry. Stir fry or skewer, brush with oil and grill.

RAYS AND SKATES

The cruising yachtsman has the advantage of frequently finding these creatures on sand and grass flats, especially at night. They offer an easy target for a spear fisherman as they lie on the bottom, half covered with sand. Once you have eaten them you will want more.

DANGER: Rays, once landed, should be killed with a blow between the eyes. This is more than just a humane act; rays have a **sharp spine** in the base, not the end, of their tails which should be broken off immediately with a pliers. Although the spine is not poisonous, it is covered with a mucous membrane that causes great pain and infection. The ray's sting is much worse than its bite since rays have no teeth. Skates have neither teeth nor sting.

CLEANING: The edible portion of skates and rays is in the wings, which should be cut away close to the body. The wings may be skinned and used as any fine flavored fish, but they are also quite delicious as a substitute for scallops. They may, therefore, be cut into bite-sized pieces and used in any of the scal-

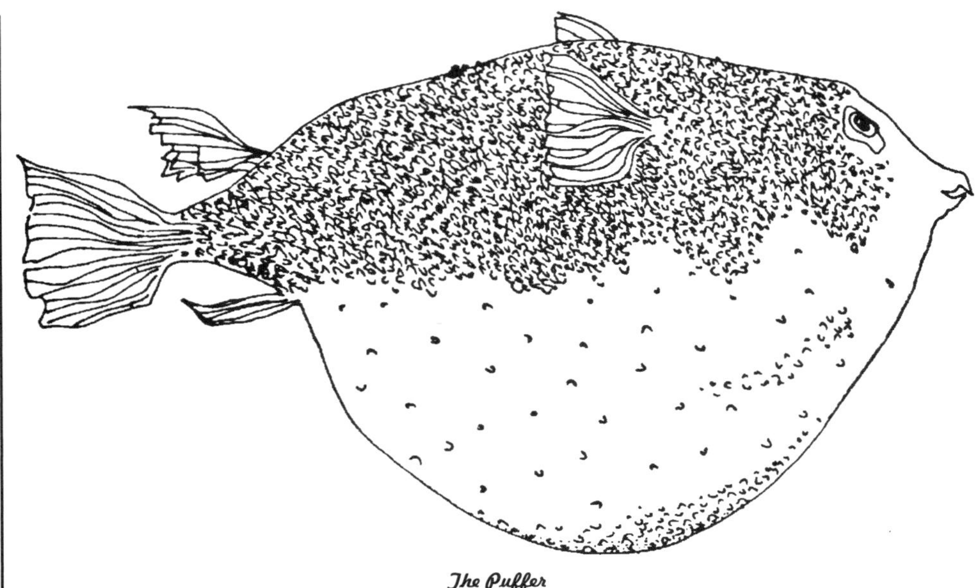

The Puffer

lop recipes in this book. Finally, rays are excellent for stretching a thin supply of crab, shrimp, or lobster meat in recipes where the flaked meat is mixed together, such as fritters and pates.

SKATE WITH TARRAGON VINAGRETTE

Poach until wings are done:
2 skate wings
1 onion, peeled and thinly sliced
A *fumet* or chicken consommé (poaching liquid)
bouquet garni

The tarragon vinaigrette (it's better to make this the night before to marinate the flavors together):
2 teaspoons tarragon
2 tablespoons white vinegar
1 tablespoon parsley, chopped
4 tablespoons olive oil

Warm vinaigrette in a pan for a minute but do not simmer. Pour vinagrette over hot fish and serve with vegetables on the side.

THE PUFFER, THE WORLD'S DEADLIEST DELIGHT

The puffer is a blowfish fish which, when inflated, looks like a grapefruit with fins. They discourage predators by looking much larger when inflated than their original size. The spines also stand our menacingly when the body is inflated.

Catching blowfish is definitely not the angler's idea of high drama. Considering their tiny fins and comical vestige of a tail, it's easy to understand why they don't put up much of a fight. I sometimes wonder how they manage to swim at all. The blowfish's idea of resistance is to take water or air into its body until it looks just like a balloon. When inflated, they offer about as much sport as hauling in a soggy tennis ball. But more frequently than not, they get so excited when hooked, they forget to inflate until they are landed. Then they are more comical than ever, puffing away, getting larger and larger in your hand.

Anglers hate blowfish. They have tiny mouths that nibble away the bait. This tactic drives most sportsmen away, but if they knew how delicious blowfish are, they might decide to stay. Since they have tiny mouths, blowfish require a very small hook with appropriately sized bait. They bite with vigor, and you can pull them in one after another since they seem to travel in schools. Blowfish will take any bait, but seem to enjoy shrimp tails or tiny beach crabs most of all.

The **Pacific puffer,** in addition to inflating itself, further discourages its enemies by poisoning them. The gall bladder of some Pacific varieties contains a toxin twenty-five times more deadly than curare, enough to poison forty to fifty people! The Pacific puffer is so poisonous that the Japanese government licenses puffer chefs to prevent mass poisoning. Nevertheless many a puffer gourmet has died, fork in hand.

One might logically ask why a fish so deadly is consumed with so much delight by so many. The answer is simple; the puffer is exceedingly delicious. Served raw in thin, translucent strips as sushi it is sweet, gelatinous and delicately flavored. Steamed it melts in the mouth. It is a joy in any stew and a cut above poached Pompano which is a fish not to be sniffed at. Perhaps the puffer's flavor is further enhanced by the risk one takes.

Fortunately the **North Atlantic puffer** is not poisonous and is commonly sold in markets as "**sea squab**." The fish is nearly boneless and the drumstick-like fillets contain only the backbone. They may be cooked like any delicate white fish. A more delicious critter is hard to find.

FRESH TUNA AND SWORDFISH

Fresh tuna and swordfish have very firm flesh and therefore cook similarly. Fresh tuna and swordfish taste surprisingly similar to lean veal and can be treated as such. These fish beg to be marinated and grilled. They can be braised, or roasted with tomatoes, onion, and paprika; or served in a stew with potatoes, carrots, and chicken stock; or pan fried in butter and served with a white sauce.

The firm flesh resists the spoon test, so when you use the spoon, look for liquid welling up in the separation. This indicates the fish is not quite done.

Note dangerous spine ➤

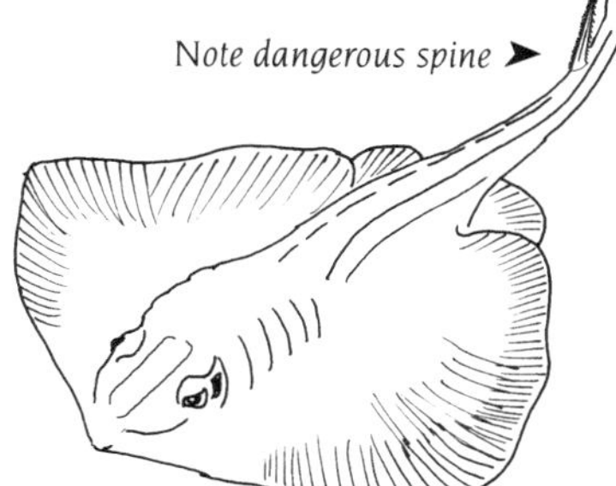

TUNA OR SWORDFISH WITH TWO SAUCES

You will just love this! Grill or poach a fillet brushing with a little oil to prevent scorching. Allow to cool. Chill. Pour steak sauce on a plate and make a little pool. Lay the fish in it and cover with a sour cream dill sauce (see page 149).

CANNED TUNA AND SALMON

Canned tuna comes in several different colors, juices, and cuts. The most flavorful **packaging liquid** is olive, corn, or peanut oil and natural juices, rather than water. The **best cut** is called "**solid**" or "**fillet**" as opposed to "**flaked**" which tends to be mushy. Lighter tuna is usually more tasty than the darker variety. The body meat usually comes in squat cans, the tail meat in tall cans.

Canned fish can be prepared in any number of ways, as though it were freshly poached. It makes a fine tuna salad for sandwiches, or a hot casserole when mixed with a white cream, tomato, or mayonnaise sauce and some peas. Canned tuna does just fine in tuna fritters, and can be mixed with other fresh fish for use in fish cakes. Last, but certainly not least, canned tuna makes a warm weather meal when added to a salad topped with a few sliced, hard-boiled eggs.

MID-OCEAN TUNA CASSEROLE

This favorite recipe is a stove top casserole, handy when the fresh stores are gone.

12 ounces tuna, thoroughly drained
3 cups mayonnaise
1 cup canned peas
1 cup celery, diced, or 1/2 teaspoon celery seed
1/2 teaspoon pepper
1 medium onion, chopped
2 tablespoons oil
cooked pasta

Fry onion until golden. Add tuna, peas, celery, garlic salt and pepper. Cook for fifteen minutes over low heat. Toss onto noodles. Add dollop of mayo per portion.

SERENITY TUNA SALAD

We rafted next to the *Yacht Serenity* one night in Lisbon and were invited for a drink. As the dinner hour approached we prepared to leave; but Julia Wheeler, *Serenity's* first mate, was never one to panic in the face of numbers. She whipped up this tasty, infor-

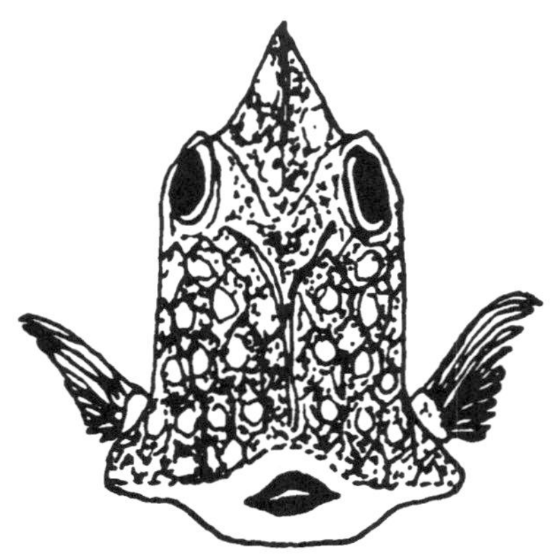

mal dish in no time at all, and made it in generous enough portions to feed about twenty guests. Three cheers for the chef!

6 ounces macaroni, boiled, drained
1 can cream of mushroom soup
1 onion, chopped
1 green pepper, chopped
1 large can tuna (12 ounces or more), thoroughly drained
2 tablespoons lemon juice
2 tablespoons Worcestershire sauce
3 tablespoons dry sherry (optional)
salt and pepper to taste

Sauté onions and pepper in oil until just soft. Add other ingredients; mix thoroughly. That's all! Serve with bowls of fruit salad.

ONE POT TUNA KEDGEREE

Fast, easy, and really delicious, this recipe may also be used for other seafood, such as lobster, crab, or delicately flavored, flaked fish. The beauty of this fine tasting dish is it requires one pot for the total operation.

3 eggs
1 cup white rice
1 cup green peas
6 to 8 ounces (1 can) tuna, drained; and/or other seafood, cooked
2 tablespoons butter
2 teaspoons lemon juice
1/2 cup condensed milk
salt and pepper to taste

To one quart of boiling water add eggs, rice Remove hard-boiled eggs, after ten minutes. Chop them. If you plan to use fresh peas, add them now. Cook rice and peas until the rice is just done; drain. Add all other ingredients, mix lightly. Serve over toast.

TUNA FRITTERS

Combine:
1 can tuna, drained, flaked
2 eggs, beaten
6 tablespoons flour
1 teaspoon baking powder
1 small onion, chopped
pinch salt and pepper

Shape Into patties about three inches wide and a half inch thick; dust with flour. Drop patties into hot oiled pan, fry over high heat until a brown crust forms, about two to three minutes per side.

MARINATED FISH

CEVICHE (SEVICHE, POISSON CRU)

Ceviche is raw fish which has been cooked by marinating in lime juice. It makes a delicious, high protein, low-cal snack, served on or with bread or crackers. Make this from a very fresh fillet of delicate white fish such as mahi mahi or wahoo, not swordfish or tuna. Lasts a week or more in the refrigerator.

The exact amount of lime juice and/or vinegar is difficult to estimate. As a rule I add about three-quarter to one cup of lime juice to one pound of fish, then taste the liquid an hour later. If the tartness of the lime juice has disappeared I add more.

1 pound white fish fillets, cut into small pieces, grape to walnut size
1/2 medium onion, rings
1 green pepper, julienned
1-2 serrano peppers, blenderized with 3 cloves garlic
lime juice and/or vinegar to cover
1/2 cup coconut cream (optional but good)

Combine all ingredients except coconut cream in a bowl and toss. Seal in refrigerator container. Marinate overnight. Will last up to a week. Add coconut cream with a few quick strokes before serving.

PICKLED, SMOKED, SALTED OR CURED FISH

These recipes are not only very tasty, they are good ways to extend the life of fresh fish, something which is important when twenty or thirty pounds of mahi mahi suddenly comes aboard. Make these recipes for consumption later, eat some of the remaining fish over the next two days and make chowder from the rest. About this time the recipes below will be ready to eat.

PICKLED FISH

Cut raw fish fillets into cracker-sized pieces. Place in a saturated pickling salt solution and refrigerate overnight. Regular salt is okay but discolors the fish. Cover with white vinegar and refrigerate twelve hours. You can add hot peppers, carrots, onions, olives at this time. Make a pickling solution:

1/2 cup brown sugar
1/2 cup distilled, high acid (5% or more) white vinegar
2 teaspoons pickling spices (sold in stores for pickling cucumbers)
3 cloves

Boil fifteen minutes, then strain and cool. Discard vinegar, pour on pickling liquid and cap. Store in sealed jar and refrigerate for at least five days before eating. Lasts six weeks.

SALT-CURED FISH: GRAVLAX

Salt curing is a way of preserving fish by using salt to draw out moisture. A Scandinavian gravlax will keep for up to two weeks in the refrigerator. It is usually made from a big fillet of salmon but can be made from the tail fillet of any ocean white fish such as mahi mahi, but is not as good with tuna or swordfish whose texture is too tough for this dish.

The consistency of gravlax is half between smoked fish and sushi. Do not let the unlikely ingredients keep you from trying this dish.

2 fillets, skin on, as big as is convenient for your refrigerator
1/2 cup salt
1/4 cup sugar
2 tablespoons dill
2 tablespoons black pepper

Combine salt and spices, brush thickly on meat side of both fillets Place both fillets flesh side together in a Ziplock bag and rubber band the package so the fillets do not slip apart.

Place in refrigerator with a weight like a book or two on them to press the fillets together. Drain and turn a few times in twenty-four hours. Open the bag and scrape the fillets clean. Pat dry. Serve sliced thinly and add to an open face sandwich with cream cheese for breakfast or as an appetizer.

SALTED FISH: In the days before refrigeration, salted fish commanded higher prices than fresh fish of the same species. Since it stores well without refrigeration, is resistant to mold, and provides tasty everyday fare, salted fish should be considered by yachtsmen for cruises where provisions are hard to find. The only negative aspect is that salt fish must be soaked, skin side down, in at least three changes of water for six to twelve hours before cooking.

BLUE WATER SALT COD IN TOMATO SAUCE

This end-of-the passage dish uses salted cod and other long lasting ingredients for a one pot, one-burner meal.

1-1/2 pounds de-salted cod, chopped small
1/2 cup olive oil
1 large onion, chopped
6 cups basic tomato sauce
4 cloves garlic, finely chopped
hot chili paste, as much as you dare!

Shake small cod pieces in plastic bag with flour and pepper. Sauté onions in oil until browned. Add fish and brown. Add tomato sauce and simmer twenty minutes.

SMOKED FISH: The smoked fish sold in various supermarkets and delicatessens is usually cooked and ready to eat. It does, however require some degree of refrigeration or coolness since smoking fish does not preserve it as well as salting does. Vacuum packing and refrigeration greatly extends its life. Some smoked fish is available canned and is quite good. Within this category are smoked herring and smoked salmon. Buy one can and taste before buying in quantity.

Beza

11 Tapdance on the Lifelines

It isn't the taste of fear that we mind, it's not knowing the cause. Fear is a part of the ship's equipment, like the lifelines or the standing rigging, an essential ingredient that keeps you alive and brings you safely through the storm. You thump the standing rigging with your hand to test its tension—like kicking the tires of a car. The clean, stainless wire gleams as it quivers, muttering to itself. The fine strands within it, strung so gracefully, twist upward, away from you, humming a bit from your blow but mostly keeping their own counsel. The wire is silent and terribly strong. Our lives depend on it. Our rigging has withstood many storms, moaning occasionally in high wind with a voice both anguished and confused. It is strong and silent but fails without warning, and when it fails there is a pop, almost like the breaking of a light bulb; an unusual sound, so gentle for such a disastrous event.

We test the strength of our lifelines by dancing upon them as we danced one sunny, windless day in Port Sollar, Majorca. The turquoise of the sea and the green of the hills ran in our blood and we felt very grand standing on the thin wire in the sunshine. The lifeline stanchions, rising like fingers from the deck, did not seem to notice us. They were silent and did not move, concealing their strength and we were not sure that we had found their measure.

Perhaps the fear which we felt that same night, pounding along beside the high dark cliffs of Majorca with the salt spray staining our faces and running like blood from our red foul weather suits—perhaps that fear was as blind and mindless as the moans of the standing rigging in high wind or fear of the hollow sound of crab's feet, scuttling along through the sand of a silent, deserted beach. We could taste it but not understand. It tasted like a cool, green wine but was hard and unapproachable.

There have been other times when we were afraid, beating toward safety in the fading light, the wind howling down the dark canyon between the Azorian Islands of Pico and Fayal like blood pulsing from an open wound, the black rocks around us silent, waiting. We were afraid then and our fear rasped like the wind off the high black cliffs that surrounded us. Our course was good but our chart small and the time soon approaching to decide whether to run or risk, in the growing darkness, a last tack past the rocks to safety. The fear which we felt then and that which we experienced beneath the friendly Majorcan moon were strangely the same, bonded by something deeper and more complex which we could not understand. The wind was light and the Majorcan sea calm, but in the silence we could hear the wind on high rock and the moans of the standing rigging which gleamed in the moonlight, a luminous thread connecting us with our past. Yes, perhaps it was just the standing rigging.

We had been waiting in Port Sollar for days, waiting for wind, watching the sunsets bloom from the windows of old men in shirt sleeves whose eyes were as bright and gleaming as the sunset in their window panes. We had seen women throw pans of water into the morning heat where it vanished while running down the cobblestones. We reached out and tried to touch the heat; it felt like a kitten but also like a snake and we did not know whether to caress it or withdraw. We watched the flags in the harbor hang limply and whistled for wind, threw pennies for the I *Ching* and occasionally looked at the sad remnants of our long dead motor.

Our crewman John, tall and bearded, had met a girl the other day. Justine was a fine girl, very clever and lithe as a young animal with her Levis on. Her long, dark hair hanging in braids and upturned nose made her look like a little girl, but her fine breasts, loose beneath a green blouse danced when she laughed. The sharp contrasts in her, like the different tastes in a good wine, blended delightfully. She and John had spent the night together on the foredeck, wrapped in a sail with the stars blazing down upon them. They looked good together, two shapes in the darkness and I was sure that if there was no wind for several days, they would not mind.

We walked the *paseo maritemo* at the setting of the sun, the trees casting long shadows on the cobblestones and the leaves crunching beneath our feet. The little tram from Palma clanged in the distance and the first smells of evening were in the air. Then, on a whim we turned inland, into the growing dusk and stopped at a small cafe beneath the trees and drank a bottle of Monopole. It was so good and cold, woody and tart, tasting like the sea feels on a fine day when the rail is down, the rigging quivering and the sun lapping at your brain. We drank the wine, ate little dishes of peppery snails and watched the pigeons patrol the door.

The gas lights of the octopus fishermen dotted the bay as we walked the cobbled streets. It was the hour of evening when old men in black berets play dominoes by the light of street lamps or in the corners of small cafes whose smoky light oozed across the sidewalks. The slap of the cubes upon the table and the smack of their lips as they drank sharp red wine gave rhythm to the night. The fine smell of garlic and tomato sauce threaded with laughter slid from half-shut windows on ribbons of light. We pushed through fallen leaves toward the bay, thinking about dinner and thinking about wind.

We found the restaurant full of sardine fishermen eating huge slabs of bread covered with tomato paste and anchovies, drinking strong brandy and wine. Their voices and the fine smell of roast lamb pushed back the night. We ate bread with garlic and oil, drank rich red wine and waited for the lamb. The little boats of the octopus fishermen had reached the mouth of the bay and solemnly, in single file, they disappeared from sight.

The moon cast its whiteness into the air. The diesel heart of a fishing boat pulsed somewhere in the darkness. Here we were, surrounded by friends in the most beautiful sheltered bay, eating and drinking, warmed by the liquid passion of love, a scene, a place—for this frozen moment most men would gladly sell their souls. Yet we, in our silent madness, waited only for wind.

The wind came that night, tumbling down the mountainside. We stood, high on the hill and watched the moon fracture the sea into a sheet of sparkling white. Rebecca and I, Justine and John stood in the breeze, smelled the pureness of the sea and knew that our frozen moment had passed.

With a fond good-bye to Justine we cast off at once. The high rock walls as we passed the mouth of the bay looked like living steel in the moonlight. We glided between them with only the mainsail drawing, hardly breaking the tranquillity of this dark, silent, sheltered place with the murmur of our wake. The lighthouse swung its bright arms high above us. We looked at it again as we stood away from the bay. It was red and white like a candy stripe—our last sweet taste of the land as we seeped our fingers with the cold fingers of the sea.

We passed the octopus fishermen as we worked our small sloop, Fire Witch, out of the channel. We passed them, one by one—small, dark men, unshaven and in old clothes with spears in one hand, nets in the other. They were trapped in pools of light, their downcast eyes did not notice us, their minds were lost in the endless depths. We set the working jib, sheeted the mainsail ramrod tight, and set our course into the darkness. The wind was light, the moon huge and white. We waited for the joy of the moment to overwhelm us, rushing into our brains like the first taste of a cold white wine.

But the wind was against us and the rush did not come. Soon we were pounding along, close hauled, with the working jib occasionally flapping in protest. John was at the helm, dressed for foul weather, woolen cap, safety line and rubber boots. He played a Dylan tune on his harmonica, and made happy noises. We hated him for leaving so easily when he and Justine could have slept together once more wrapped in a sail, whispering the secret things that lovers say to each other late at night when the flags are dipped in sleep.

Rebecca and I were below, lying on the bunk, watching the moon race back and forth across the companionway. We were afraid but could not explain it, could not understand it. We savored the taste of our fear like wine, trying to find its component parts but it was green and hard and impenetrable, like a stone, and we could not probe its darkness. We lay in each other's arms and talked of our fear, smiled at each other as we listened to John making his happy noises and playing the blues. We hear the rigging muttering its quiet melody of stress and know that somehow this night is connected to other nights spent clawing off a yammering lee shore or sailing by high rock looking at a lighthouse far above us, distant and unreal, with the wind, as on this night, howling against us as though down a canyon mouth. Perhaps the wind, the rigging, and the moon make us think back to all those other nights when we felt fragile and alone, listening to the wind moan among broken rocks and the waves smashing on the shore. We thought, at those times, of human flesh with its miles of nerves strung so incredibly; about how it quivers, sometimes to the touch of love and of how different it is when it is not alive.

In the end we turned back, as much because of the wind as the fear. We ghosted beneath the lighthouse just as the sun touched the hill, dropped the hook in Port Sollar and watched the waiters sweep the empty streets. We thought that day of our fear, of how simple life had been ages ago when we had nothing to do but drink cold Majorcan wine and dance upon the lifelines. We sat at a little cafe beneath the trees, watched the sun climb higher, drank coffee and double cognacs and laughed with the breeze. The sea, fickle mistress, had reminded us of the courage she demands, her ticket of admission to the world's many green islands that lie beneath the wind. How much courage must we pay? Do we have the means to pay it? We think of courage as part of the ship's equipment, like the standing rigging, water shimmering down the slim steel wire which is ramrod tight and humming a bit in the wind. Will it fail us as it has on occasion in the past? We patch our rigging with curses and bulldog clips, our courage with cognac and laughter.

Cape Hattaras Light

12 Meat

SELECTION: Selecting meat for a cruise is different than buying it for home use. Alongshore, when one buys a piece of meat it is usually purchased with a specific recipe in mind. On a boat one or several pieces may have to serve in a variety of different dishes. At home waste is not a serious consideration, so one may buy cuts which require trimming or contain a bone. On a boat space in the refrigerator is much more important than saving a few cents on food. At home the meat goes into the fridge and is quickly consumed. On a boat it may be stored for weeks or months.

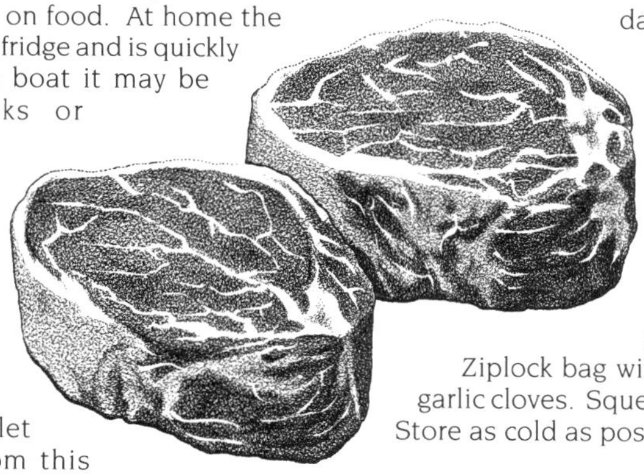

THE BEST CUT is the **fillet** (**tenderloin**) of a young animal. Famous beef recipes such as Chateaubriand, tournedos and filet mignon come from this cut. There are several reasons for our choice. The most important is that the fillet is the tenderest (and most expensive) cut and will reliably come out tasting great if not overcooked. There are other important reasons to select this cut.

THE TENDERLOIN is usually removed from the carcass intact. It has a tough white membrane surrounding it which **protects the meat from bacteria**. In many butcher shops you can get the butcher to whack off whatever size piece you want from a virgin loin, further reducing the possibility of contamination. If you can get the end piece it will be completely surrounded by membrane except for where it has been cut. Last but not least, a loin is smooth and regular, making it easier to wash and sterilize.

SELECTING A TENDERLOIN: Tenderloins from young animals have a little marbled fat, are fine grained, light red in color (note illustration in center of page). Beef loins are up to four inches in diameter. The loins from old critters are coarse grained, dark, almost brown and up to eight inches in diameter. Pork and lamb loins are equally delicious. Wash the meat and quickly heat the surface all over with a blowtorch or scorch lightly in a very hot pan. Drop into a Ziplock bag with oil and a few whole garlic cloves. Squeeze out all air and seal. Store as cold as possible.

OTHER GOOD SELECTIONS: If going on a long cruise try to buy pieces without bones, which do not keep well. Therefore **sirloins, rib eyes** or any high quality cut which is surrounded by fat or white tissue and free from tears or flaps are good choices.

HOW MUCH SHOULD I BUY? The answer depends on your attitude about meat. Hungry crews who are working hard can eat a one pound steak with no problem. The more modern attitude toward meat is that it should play an important but not dominant roll in the meal. The chef would therefore place a portion about the size of a bar of soap, about quarter pound, on each plate and fill out the meal with a sauce, vegetables and a starch.

WHEN IS IT DONE? Most experienced chefs, knowing that meat becomes harder and less resilient as it cooks, test by giving the piece a poke with their finger. It is amazing how educated the finger gets and this is the best technique. When you think meat is done to your taste, make a small slice in the top and examine it. Keep checking until it is cooked the way you like it, then give it a poke to learn the feel.

MEAT COOKING TECHNIQUES

FRYING: The whole secret of frying meat is to have a very hot pan and not cut meat more than three-quarters of an inch thick. The object is to sear the meat in order to seal in juices. The meat should be browned on the outside and pink inside, not gray throughout. Always use fresh oil. To test the oil temperature, drop a pinch of flour into the pan. If it skips on the surface and sizzles the oil is ready. Some galley stoves can't put out high heat. If that is the case, cut the meat into very small cubes and quickly sear it in a small pan.

STIR FRYING is a fast method of cooking meat rarely taking more than eight to ten minutes. Stir frying can be done in any pan but a wok is the pan of choice. The meat is cut into small pieces and stir fried over high heat with savory spices like chili peppers, ginger, crushed garlic or cumin, stirring frequently. The meat can be battered or breaded before frying. Learn more about stir frying meat in Chapter 4.

BRAISING is frying followed by sautéing. For meat this means frying in oil over high heat followed by adding a liquid and simmering. Meat can also be breaded prior to frying or be sprinkled with flour as it fries. The flour will act as a thickener. When the sauce is added it will bond to the flour.

It you are cooking a very tender, high-quality cut you should brown it quickly, sprinkling on flour toward the end, then add a thin sauce and cook just enough to thicken it. If you are dealing with a tough cut, it should be sliced thin and simmered long and slow in an acidic sauce like red wine or tomato sauce to tenderize. Read more about grilling tough cuts at the end of this chapter.

GRILLING AND PRESSURE COOKING: See Chapter 4.

LIVER

SELECTION: Chicken, duck, goose, pig, rabbit, and calves livers are particularly tender. We think rabbit liver is the best of all. Look for more liver recipes in CHICKEN. **Baby calves liver** is on the top of the list, too. Buy them small and light in color. **Baby beef liver**, as opposed to calves liver comes from a weaned animal, while **beef liver**, from the adult, is tough and best used as chopped liver.

Pork and **sheep** livers, if from young animals, are also excellent. Larger livers make a good paté, but avoid them for sautéing. All liver regardless of type, should have any surface membranes and adhering fat removed. **Other livers**, chicken, pork, duck, goose and especially rabbit are all delicious.

PREPARATION: Liver should be soaked and agitated in water for about twenty minutes to free it from any clotted blood. Larger livers, such as baby beef, should be sliced and soaked for a half hour in milk, then patted dry before cooking. Large veins should be cut out with a small, sharp knife.

COOKING: Liver can be pan fried in a small amount of extremely hot oil, so that it is browned on the outside and pink inside. A little soy sauce can be sprinkled on at the end for color and flavor. The pan drippings from larger livers should not be used for a sauce. The pans should not be deglazed. The juice is bitter.

QUANTITY: One pound serves four.

BRAISED LIVER AND ONIONS LYONNAISE

In this recipe the liver is first fried, then soy or Worcestershire sauce is added to the pan. The sauce bonds with the fried flour and the liver is removed from the pan to keep the sauce from drying out. A daub of butter can be added when serving to make the liver more succulent.

1/4 cup oil or butter
1 cup flour
2 cups liver (any type), soaked, marinated
2 medium onions, cut thickly in rounds
2 teaspoons Worcestershire sauce
1 teaspoon pepper

Pat the liver dry and flour it. In a large pan fry the onion rounds on each side in very hot oil until browned. Keep heat on high. Break rounds into rings, push to side of pan.

Add liver and fry for just a minute on each side, until browned. Sprinkle on Worcestershire sauce and cook for a few more seconds until the sauce is bonded to the flour Meat should be pink throughout. You can also dribble on a little butter before serving. Do not pour the pan oil on the liver as it is sometimes slightly bitter

SKEWERED LIVER WITH ROASTED PEPPERS AND OLIVES

3/4 pound liver, cut into one-inch cubes; or whole chicken livers
2 medium onions
6 strips bacon
2 roasted red peppers, one-inch strips
12 green olives, sliced off the pit

Fry the bacon strips in a pan until cooked but not crisp. Reserve the fat. Wrap a slice of red pepper around each piece of liver and a slice of the pan fried bacon around all. Skewer.

Grill or broil for a few minutes over very high heat. While the liver is cooking add the olives to three teaspoons of bacon fat and heat. When the liver is done, spoon off the olives and sprinkle over the liver when it is on the plate.

SWEETBREADS

Sweetbreads usually refer to the **pancreas** but **brains** can be cooked in the same manner. Brains have the advantage that they are invariably tender while the pancreas from large animals have a tough membrane. A veal pancreas larger than the palm is too large and comes from a mature animal. Rabbit and veal pancreata are the most esteemed because they are tender. Like all organs, sweetbreads are very perishable and also high in cholesterol. On the other hand, they are extremely delicious.

All sweetbreads should be soaked in several changes of cold water to rid them of clotted blood, then blanched by putting them in a skillet and just covering with cold water and vinegar, about three to one. The liquid is brought to a boil for about two minutes, then the cooking is arrested by plunging the sweetbreads into cold water.

Sweetbreads tend to curl, so I put them in a plastic bag after blanching and place my tool box on them for an hour to let them cool and to press them flat. After that they should be trimmed and the membrane removed. If the sweetbread is large enough I usually just slice the surface off with a very sharp knife. The prepared sweetbread can be poached, braised or broiled. Grilling makes them dry. Sweetbreads can also be parboiled and added to meat pies.

BRAISED PANCREAS IN MADEIRA OR SHERRY

2 prepared pancreas'
flour
1/4 cup butter/oil
juice of 1/2 lemon
3/4 cup Madeira or dry sherry (you can also add a little chicken stock)
1 cup dried mushrooms, reconstituted
1/2 cup walnuts or almonds, toasted
1 roasted red pepper for garnish (optional)

Flour and fry the sweetbreads in butter/oil. When browned sprinkle on the lemon juice and wine. Cook another minute and serve. Garnish with mushrooms, nuts and pepper. Pour pan juice over all.

GROUND MEAT

One is always wise to buy a piece of meat and grind it yourself. You will then know exactly what you are eating. In addition, meat which has first been washed, then ground and dropped on the grill is much less likely to be contaminated.

Commercially ground meat and the machine which grinds it are of unknown cleanliness and grind surface bacteria into the meat. It is also not unusual for a small amount of meat to remain in the grinder, caught in the mechanism, which may remain there for several hours before it is sold. And how long has the ground meat been sitting around? Store bought ground meat should be cooked until not pink inside.

Lean and tough cuts of meat can be ground and added to a little fatty meat or bacon or you can add oil. Fatty meat can be used in sauces and stews. The meat is chopped with a spatula and pan fried. The fat is then drained off.

ABOUT HAMBURGER

Commercial ground meat is finely ground so that everything—meat, connective tissue, tendon and often bits of bone are chewable. But the best burgers are coarsely ground and come from trimmed pieces of meat and a little fat. People who dislike adding fat can add olive oil instead, but remember, fat is tastier.

We are burger purists and never add anything to ground meat before making it into burgers. After all, if we wanted meat loaf we would make a meat loaf! We prefer to pour sauces over the cooked meat which provides a nice contrast of flavors. Never add salt to the meat before cooking as this will dry it.

Other chefs add egg or a bit of butter or oil (for moisture), herbs, chilies, garlic, hot sauce, etc. Fold in the seasonings. Handle meat as little as possible to avoid drying.

The easiest way to make a burger from ground meat is to tightly wrap a quarter pound ball of meat in a cloth and squash it to about three-quarter inches thick. The squashed meat is compressed a bit by the squishing and this helps keep the burger together. Burgers thinner than three-quarters of an inch tend to be dry.

The burger should be brushed with cooking oil before being slipped onto a hot grill to reduce sticking. A minute after dropping the burger on the grill, carefully lift it in several places to free it from the grate, but do not move or reposition it. This technique will keep the burger from sticking to the grill and breaking when you attempt to lift it.

Cooking time for a medium rare burger is about five minutes per side. A medium burger takes six to seven minutes per side. Sear the burger on each side for two minutes over a hot flame to seal and color it. Flip after searing, grill an additional minute more on each side. Don't ever squish a burger down with a spatula as this forces out juice. If you are going to add cheese on top, keep an eye on it as melts quickly. The texture of cheese breaks if it is overheated.

GROUND MEAT RECIPES

ITALIAN MEAT SAUCE (FOR PASTA)

Slowly simmer ground meat over medium heat, stirring frequently until gray. Drain juice. Add marinara sauce (see page 42) and simmer fifteen minutes. Let stand for one hour.

YACHT ATRIA SPICY BEEF CASSEROLE

This easy-to-make delight is an especially good way to prepare an interesting meal from canned ground beef; however, it is much better with fresh meat. All the ingredients, including the noodles, are pressure cooked together in the same pot at the same time. This recipe is easy to make, always turns out well, and brings compliments to the chef.

1 pound ground beef
1 green pepper, chopped (optional)
5 cloves garlic, chopped
2 cups broad noodles or macaroni
1 large onion, thinly sliced
3 teaspoons Worcestershire sauce
2 teaspoons dry mustard (more, if desired)
3 teaspoons catsup (more, if desired)
1 can (10 ounces) tomato sauce

Add all ingredients to pressure cooker, but do not stir. Mix thoroughly; pressure cook for five minutes after jiggle.

QUICK MEATBALLS AND THREE SAUCES

1 pound ground beef, fresh or frozen
12 crackers, crushed into crumbs
1 large onion, well chopped
1/2 teaspoon pepper
2 eggs, beaten
4 cloves garlic, chopped
3 teaspoons vegetable oil
3 teaspoons steak sauce
1/2 cup flour

The meatballs: Combine meat, cracker crumbs, onion, pepper, garlic salt, and steak sauce. Make into small meat balls, one to 1-1/2 inches in diameter. Roll in flour. Sauté in vegetable oil over high heat until brown, three to five minutes.

SOUR CREAM MEATBALL SAUCE

Try to make this a few hours before dinner. You can also serve the meatballs around a dollop of curry mayonnaise.

Combine:
3/4 cup sour cream
4 garlic cloves
1/4 teaspoons nutmeg (optional)
1 teaspoon dill
1/2 onion, chopped

Pour over the meatballs; do not boil.

CURRY TOMATO MEATBALL SAUCE

2 teaspoons tomato puree
1 teaspoon sugar, or more if the tomatoes are bitter
1 teaspoon lemon juice

Prepare a curry or add curry paste to stock or beer. Add ingredients (above). Heat and simmer five minutes. Pour over meatballs.

CRANBERRY SWEET AND SOUR MEATBALL SAUCE

1 cup whole cranberries, (or 1/2 cup raisins plumped 2 hours in 1/2 cup lemon juice)
1 cup mild chili sauce
1 medium onion, chopped
4 cloves garlic
2 beef bullion cubes
1 teaspoon Worcestershire sauce

Combine and simmer five minutes over low heat. Add meatballs and pressure cook eight minutes or sauté twenty minutes adding water as needed.

Lake Gatun, Panama

CHILI CON CARNE

Traditionally, chili meat is lean meat which has been finely chopped, rather than ground. Chili is a great place for fatty ground chuck (which is sautéed slowly over low heat, then drained), for lean, tough meat (which can be finely ground or beaten, then chopped), or canned meat. It's a good place to dispose of leftover miscellaneous meats, hot-dogs and even a bit of bacon. It is also a fine place to toss carrots and other vegetables which are nearing the end of their lives as the rich sauce dominates all.

Chili is a tomato base food which travels well. Make a load and pour meal-size portions, boiling hot, into a Ziplock bag and seal. Let cool, squeeze out air, refrigerate. Lasts a week in the refrigerator.

1 pound chopped or ground chuck
1 tablespoon cooking oil
1 large onion, chopped
1 can (28 ounces) Italian tomatoes, drained and chopped
3 teaspoons tomato paste
2 tablespoons vinegar
1 teaspoon sugar
1 large green pepper, chopped
2 cups kidney beans

The seasoning:
2 ounces (about 1/4 cup) chili powder
1 tablespoon cumin
2 teaspoons oregano
hot chilies or red pepper and garlic, as you dare

Sauté onions in oil until golden. Add meat, sauté over low heat until gray, then drain. Add all other ingredients except beans. Simmer twenty to thirty minutes. Correct seasoning: Add vinegar, sugar, salt, pepper to taste. Add cooking oil if too lean. Add beans, simmer five minutes more. Traditionally chili con carne is served over white rice and garnished with a generous portion of grated sharp cheddar.

KIMA

Curried ground beef and potatoes.

1 cup curry sauce
2 large potatoes, diced and parboiled for 3 minutes
3/4 pound ground beef
1 cup peas, cooked, preferably fresh
2 cups canned tomatoes, coarsely chopped, drained
1/2 cup red wine
1 can beef consommé
1 teaspoon each salt, pepper
2 bay leaves
1 teaspoon cumin
butter/oil
a *roux*

Make curry and reserve. Fry potatoes until browned. Add spices and beef. Cook until beef is gray, stirring frequently. Pour off fat. Add tomatoes and bouillon mixture. Simmer fifteen minutes over low heat, lid off. Add cooked peas, simmer five minutes. Thicken with *roux*. Serve over noodles or rice.

BRAISED GROUND BEEF

1-1/2 pounds ground beef oil
4 cloves garlic
1 teaspoon pepper
1 sliced green pepper
1 cup celery, well chopped
2 cups white rice, 15-20 minute variety
1 cup light beer, mixed with a beef bouillon cube

Add all ingredients to pressure cooker except beer and fry meat until it is gray. Drain. Add remaining ingredients, reserving some of the beer. Simmer for five minutes, lid off. Do not let the pan dry out. Add more beer as needed. Pressure cook for five minutes.

The following quick sauces may be served with the braised ground beef:

- Hot condensed tomato soup with a dash of Worcestershire sauce.
- Melted butter with Parmesan cheese. Do not cook. Spoon over each serving.

MEAT LOAF

1 pound ground chuck
1/2 cup bread crumbs
1 egg, beaten
1 small onion, chopped
2 celery stalks, chopped
1 can creamed mushroom soup
1/2 cup hard cheese, grated
1/3 cup water
salt and pepper

Mix all ingredients and half the soup. Place in greased pan and bake one hour at 375° F. or make into big patties and sauté over low heat in a greased pan until done. Mix the remaining soup, cheese and three tablespoons of drippings and heat as a sauce. You can add one tablespoon of tomato paste and a little lemon juice to make a pink sauce.

HAMBURGER RAREBIT

2 teaspoons butter
1-1/2 pounds ground chuck
1 cup celery, finely chopped
1 medium onion, sliced
1 cup dried mushrooms, reconstituted
2 cups red wine
1 teaspoon each: pepper, salt, Worcestershire sauce
1 can condensed tomato soup

Fry onions and celery in pressure cooker until onions are golden. Add mushrooms and sauté another two minutes. Reserve. Sauté meat in pressure cooker until gray. Drain. Add half the soup and all remaining ingredients to pot and simmer until thick. Pour remaining soup over all. Pressure cook for four minutes. Return vegetables to pot. Serve over toast.

PIGS IN THE BLANKET—GROUND BEEF IN CABBAGE

1 cup cooked rice
3/4 pound ground beef, or half pork or veal
1 medium onion
1 egg
1 teaspoon each: cumin, thyme, salt
1/4 cup capers
2 teaspoons vinegar
2 teaspoons brown sugar
1-1/2 cups catsup
1/4 cup water
cabbage leaves, whole, 1 for each "pig"

Blanch cabbage leaves. Combine ground beef, onion, beaten egg, thyme, garlic rice, salt, capers, vinegar, and brown sugar. Roll into twelve patties. Pan broil over high heat until brown all over. Wrap in cabbage leaf. Add catsup and water to pan; reduce to medium heat. Simmer twenty minutes. Baste occasionally until sauce thickens.

CUT BEEF

BRAISED STEAK IN WINE SAUCE

Ingredients per portion

1 tenderloin fillet or sirloin steak
2 tablespoons butter
olive oil
3 teaspoons chives or scallion ends, chopped
3 shallots or 1 small onion, chopped
1/2 cup good red wine
1 tablespoon balsamic or red vinegar
3 medium mushrooms, quartered
black pepper
1 teaspoon sage
soy sauce

Mix olive oil with butter and when sizzling add meat and mushrooms. Cook for seven minutes per side for medium rare. Keep the mushrooms cooking on the edge of the pan and sprinkle with a few drops of soy sauce. When done, set meat and mushrooms aside. Keep warm.

Add the shallots and sage and cook for about one minute. Add vinegar and wine. Bring the wine to a boil for a few minutes to reduce it. Add chives (saving a few for a garnish). Sauté one minute. Sprinkle on a little gravy flour, stirring furiously, to thicken. Serve sauce over meat.

TOURNEDOS ROSSINI

5 to 8 ounce fillet of beef
1 teaspoon celery salt
juice of 1 lemon
arrowroot or gravy flour
1 pate *fois gras* (duck liver pate) a slice 1/4 inch thick per portion of meat
1/2 cup Madeira, sherry or dry vermouth per portion
3 shallots or 1 small onion, finely grated

Pan braise fillet in a little oil and butter with pepper, about four minutes per side. When done, cover and set aside. Add the *fois gras*, minced onion and celery salt to the pan and brown pate for a minute or two over medium heat Reserve *fois gras*. Add and simmer wine and lemon juice for two minutes.

Mix arrowroot in a little cool wine and add to the pan, stirring briskly. Place the paté and onions on the steak and pour the sauce over all.

SWEET AND SOUR VEAL SHANKS

Easy pressure cooker meal serves four.

1/2 cup peanut oil
4 veal shanks, about 1/2 pound each
1/2 cup flour
10 garlic cloves, peeled
2 cups onion, chopped
2 cans (28 ounces) Italian tomatoes, drained and chopped
1 cup rice vinegar
juice of 1 lemon
3 teaspoons brown sugar

1 cup teriyaki sauce, or 1/3 cup soy and 2/3 cup beer
1/2 can beer
1/2 cup white wine

Heavily flour the shanks and brown in the pressure cooker over high heat. Set shanks aside. Brown onion and garlic. Add all other ingredients and simmer five minutes. Add shanks. Arrange the shanks so that they are not pressing tightly against each other, allowing sauce to surround meat. Pressure cook for fifteen minutes. Allow to cool. Thicken sauce if desired.

STIR FRIED BEEF AND PEAS IN SOY SAUCE

2 large onions, chopped
2 teaspoons oil
1 pound lean beef, cut into small cubes
1 cup each peas, chopped carrots, blanched
1/4 cup soy sauce
juice of 1 lemon
1 teaspoon sugar
5 cloves garlic
a roux
1 cup beer

Sauté onions in a little oil until brown. Add more oil to the pan and bring to high heat. Add beef chunks and stir fry until the meat is browned. Pour off pan juices as they accumulate to avoid stewing the meat. Make a *roux*. Add soy sauce, lemon juice, sugar, salt, pepper, garlic and beer. Stir until thick. Thicken and pour over the meat. Stir until the sauce thickens. Add vegetables and toss.

BEEF BRAISED IN BEER

1 pound cubed stew beef, well beaten
6 garlic cloves
2 teaspoons oil
3 potatoes, in walnut-sized pieces
3 carrots, in four slices each
1 onion, chopped
1 can beer (12 ounces)
1 bay leaf
4 cloves garlic
1/2 teaspoon pepper
1 teaspoon marjoram
2 teaspoons Worcestershire sauce

Brown meat and garlic in oil over high heat in pressure cooker. Add all other ingredients. Pressure cook for six minutes. Needs no thickening.

BEEF STROGANOFF

Beef Stroganoff is traditionally made from fillet of beef cut into one-half by one inch slices. There are many variations of this fine dish. We have divided our approach into two sections. First, the cooking of the meat, then several versions of the sauce, which is poured over the meat at the last moment. Beef Stroganoff is served over noodles.

The meat:
1-1/2 pounds chopped beef or hamburger
2 medium onions, sliced thin
1 teaspoon salt
2 teaspoons thyme
12 large mushrooms, caps whole, stems chopped
butter

Sauté onions and mushrooms in butter until golden. Add beef and brown over very high heat. Remove from pan.

The sauce:
a *roux*
2 teaspoons tomato paste
2 cups red wine
juice of 1/2 lemon
1/2 cup sour cream

Deglaze with red wine. Reduce. Thicken with a *roux*. Toss meat in sauce. Dollop sour cream, tomato paste and lemon on top.

STROGANOFF WITH GROUND BEEF

We aren't sure if it's Stroganoff, but it tastes good. Cook meat according to recipe; don't cook sauce and meat together.

RAGOUT OF BEEF

1/4 pound bacon, chopped
2 pounds tender beef, cut two-inch long strips
2 small onions, quartered
1 teaspoon flour
3 cloves garlic, chopped
bouquet garni
1 teaspoon rosemary
red wine to cover, or wine and stock
1/2 cup olives, sliced
1/2 cup dried mushrooms, reconstituted

Fry bacon and onions over low heat until onions are soft. Sear beef over high heat until browned. Sprinkle in the flour, stir, cook for two minutes. Add herbs and red wine to cover. Simmer ninety minutes over low heat. Add olives and mushrooms, stir for a few minutes and serve.

BACHELOR STEW

3/4 pound stew meat, cubed
2 boiling potatoes, diced
2 small onions, quartered
1 green pepper, chopped
3 sliced zucchini, 1/2 inch rounds
1 can (8 ounces) Italian tomatoes
1 teaspoon lemon juice
10 fresh mushrooms
4 cups red wine
salt and pepper

Brown meat. Pressure cook all ingredients for ten minutes. Sprinkle with Parmesan cheese before serving.

BEEF STEW

2 pounds stew meat, cut Into 3/4 cubes
3 teaspoons vegetable oil
a *roux*
2 cups red wine
2 beef bouillon cubes (dissolved in the wine)
3 cloves garlic, coarsely chopped
1 bay leaf
1 teaspoon each: thyme, salt, pepper
5 medium carrots, sliced
8 small onions, whole; or 3 medium onions quartered
4 medium potatoes, each In 6 pieces
1 cup canned corn, drained

In pressure cooker, brown meat, onions, and potatoes thoroughly in oil. Add potatoes first. Add remaining ingredients, except *roux*; pressure cook for eight minutes after first jiggle. Thicken with the *roux*.

BRITTANY TRAWLER HASH

We made the Portimão, Portugal breakwater late one night just wishing to give peace a chance. It had been one of those long, miserable days full of squalls, head winds at deadly Cape Vincente, broken halyards in the night, and an engine that ran more at its own choosing than ours.

The cape looked good on the chart. It proved to be one of those deep water coves ending in sheer rock cliffs against which the sea broke heavily, sending spray high into the air with a dull, booming sound. We were tired, but were afraid of getting caught against the cliffs with our sick engine, so we

pressed on. The spare jib halyard in some horrendous way held up a reefed mainsail, while the engine made uncertain, gasping sounds as we searched hungrily ahead in the darkness for the feeble Portimão breakwater light. We mistook some street lights for the breakwater, but realized our mistake, at the last moment, when the sounding lead showed shoal water. We finally found the light and the breakwater range markers. As we slipped through the surf-wracked, breaking inlet, we suddenly found ourselves in a calm pool of perfect silence, broken only occasionally by the hiss of a wave as it sluiced over the sea wall. Never was an anchor more gratefully lowered, taking our burden of fear with it as it slipped into the depths.

We slept the sleep of the grateful alive, but the instincts of the sea prevailed. Awakening at first light with a feeling that the tide had turned, I peered out the companionway to be sure that all was well. A fishing boat had moved into the anchorage nearby. When the tide had swung us, he had moved into an upwind position.

What lovely smells came from the galley! Mixed with the spice smell of the sea and the first cries of early gulls was an irresistible aroma. Seizing a bottle of wine (knowing that fishermen will drink wine at any hour), I jumped into the dingy and rowed over to find out what was in the pot.

Sitting around the main hatch were six hungry fishermen, indifferently clad against the chill morning air, smoking their roughly rolled cigarettes, and drinking coffee from old cans. They were a tired and unshaven crew; their cuts were wrapped with pieces of rag, their hip boots roughly rolled and patched. They thought the wine was just fine. The galley competed for space in the wheel house with the steering assembly and the skipper's birth. It consisted, in fact, of a two-burner propane range and a big pot.

The cook, Charlie, was an Englishman who had lived most of his life in Portugal, and owned a share of the boat. He gave me these recipes for Trawler Hash, a one-burner dish hefty enough to feed seven hungry fishermen, who had nothing to eat for their long night's work but a slice of bread with tomato paste and anchovies, and a big bowl of coffee. We have reduced the ingredients, which originally called for ten potatoes, to feed four hungry sailors.

BRITTANY TRAWLER HASH

1-1/2 pounds canned corned beef, coarsely diced
3 large potatoes, diced into half-inch cubes
1 large onion, diced
1 clove garlic, minced
1 teaspoon celery salt
2 teaspoons Worcestershire sauce
4 teaspoons butter/oil

Boil potatoes in salt water until firm; drain thoroughly, rinse. Sauté butter, garlic and potatoes until golden, turning often; add onions until golden. Remove half of the mixture from pot; cover remainder with a layer of chopped up corned beef. Sprinkle with celery salt and Worcestershire sauce. Repeat in several layers.

Cook over low heat, not stirring. If hash seems too dry, add a little red wine, beef stock, or water. Serve when hash is piping hot. Hash likes being browned, so you can brown one side, reverse onto a plate like an omelet and slide back into pan to brown other side.

Most everyone enjoys a fried egg or two on top of their hash. If the eggs are not your style, try a generous covering of mild, soft cheese, lightly browned in the oven.

BRITTANY TRAWLER HASH PATTIES

3/4 pound corned beef
2 large potatoes, grated
1/2 onion, finely chopped
8 slices bacon
4 teaspoons peanut oil
2 teaspoons horseradish powder
1 teaspoon thyme

Boil potatoes until firm; drain thoroughly. Fry bacon and onions until bacon is done. Drain and reserve. Combine and mix thoroughly all remaining ingredients, except bacon. Form mixture into eight patties. Dust with flour; sauté until lightly brown in oil. Drain; top with a slice of bacon.

A can of cream of mushroom soup, thinned with a little water, and seasoned with pepper and paprika, makes a fine sauce. Serve hash patties with hot apple sauce flavored with a touch of honey and cinnamon.

YACHT CORRINA EASY HASH

1-1/2 pounds canned corn beef

1 can beef soup
1 large onion, diced
2 large potatoes, diced into half-inch squares
salt and pepper to taste

Make layers of beef, potatoes, and onion in a casserole. Heat beef soup, thinned with a little water to consistency of light gravy. Pour gravy over casserole ingredients; cook in hot oven for thirty minutes or pan heat. If casserole becomes dry, add a little water. Serve with carrots or hot apple sauce.

SAILOR'S MASH

This pressure cooker meal is quite tasty foul weather fare. Since it cooks down to the consistency of lumpy mashed potatoes, it sticks to the plate as well as the ribs. It stays hot when the day is cold, and tastes better with some salt spray on it.

1 pound stewing beef, diced into half-inch squares
8 slices bacon
2 medium onions, well chopped
1 teaspoon each: dill, sage, salt, thyme
1/2 teaspoon peppercorns, crushed
1 teaspoon fennel, crushed bay leaf
1-1/2 cups water
3 potatoes, well chopped
4 carrots, sliced

Fry bacon in pressure cooker, lid off. Remove, drain and reserve bacon. Add onions and meat; fry until meat browns. Add remaining ingredients on top of meat, including the bacon, crumbled. Pressure cook for eight minutes after first jiggle. Stir together.

VEAL

OSSO BUCO

Osso Buco is made from small sections of **veal shin.** The bone is always left in for the little plug of marrow. Young veal, identified by the thin ring of bone and absence of heavy fat, is best for this dish but a beef shin is still okay. Osso Buco is a classic recipe that takes hours to prepare in the normal way. But we have created this pressure cooker version, the result of many attempts, each a small improvement over the one before. Same recipe is suitable for Lamb Shanks

2 pounds veal shin, cut into 1-1/2-inch strips
1 onion, chopped
3 teaspoons olive oil
1 chicken bouillon cube, crumbled
4 tomatoes, peeled, seeded, chopped; or 1 cup Italian tomatoes, drained, chopped
3 cloves garlic, chopped
1 teaspoon lemon rind, grated
1 cup dry white wine
flour
salt and pepper

Dip veal in seasoned flour; brown in olive oil using pressure cooker pot. Reserve. Add onion and sauté until golden. Add tomatoes, garlic, chopped lemon rind, and wine. Sauté a few minutes. Return meat to pot. Pressure cook for fifteen minutes. Serve over rice or noodles.

HEARTY VEAL STEW

1-1/2 pounds veal shank or shoulder, cut In two-inch long pieces
2 cups chicken stock
1 cup dry white wine
12 small white onions
4 cloves
2 cups mushrooms, caps whole, stems chopped
3 carrots, large slices
3 potatoes, diced
1 teaspoon each: marjoram, thyme, salt, pepper
1 bay leaf
1/2 teaspoon celery seed

Parboil veal in pressure cooker pot for five minutes; discard water. Add to pot all other ingredients; pressure cook for fifteen minutes. Add more salt and pepper, and a few drops of lemon juice, as desired. This stew is very good with black bread and cheese.

VEAL CUTLET SCALOPPINI

Veal is meat from a young calf, theoretically still milk fed. It is very tender, lean meat, pale in color. It can get amazingly tough and dry if it is overcooked. Since veal is considered done when it is white inside, judging its doneness is a bit tricky. We usually fall back on an old trick, flouring the meat and frying until browned.

If you have a broiler you may employ the technique used to make sole amandine—broil an oiled pan until really hot, slip in the veal and broil the top while the bottom fries.

4 veal cutlets, thin
seasoned flour
juice of 1/2 lemon
1/2 cup dark vermouth, or Marsala wine
a *roux*

1 cup dried mushrooms, reconstituted

Shake veal in seasoned flour. Sauté in butter until golden, about four minutes. Sprinkle on Marsala wine or dark vermouth. Simmer until wine thickens, about three minutes Remove veal. Add stock, mushrooms, lemon juice and wine. Simmer a few minutes. Thicken with a *roux*. Serve over rice or noodles. Absolutely delicious.

PORK

American pork is much leaner than it used to be and when grilled it should be treated like steak, cooked quickly over high heat. Cut pork chops or a pork tenderloin a half-inch thick, brush with oil and cook over a very hot grill for a few minutes per side.

Pork purchased in developing countries is usually very fatty. The meat should be chilled and the fat trimmed. Fatty pork should be cooked slowly on the grill or slow roasted until extremely tender.

Trichinosis in supermarket pork has been wiped out in America. Developing country pork should be cooked until white throughout but that does not mean white and dry. Just be sure the juice is clear and the meat is white, with no traces of pink. The meat should steam when an inspection slice is made. Thereafter, allow the meat to cool slightly to congeal juices which would run and be lost if the meat is cut piping hot. If you roast or cook over a rack be sure to skim the copious fat from the drippings before use.

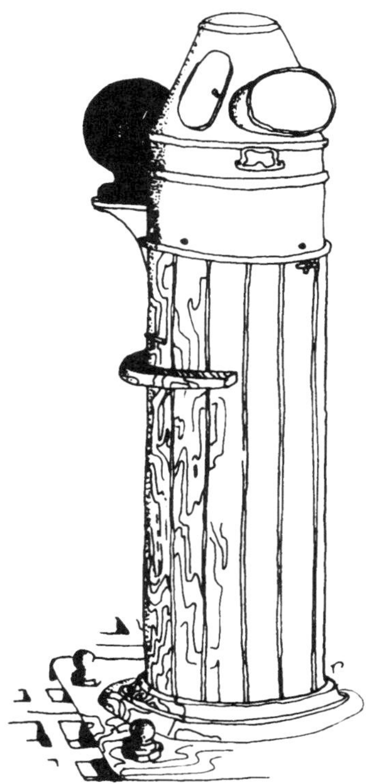

STORAGE: Store pork like beef. Keep cold. **Bacon**, which is naturally salty and full of preservative, may last for months if kept cold. **Country ham**, such as **Spanish ham** or **Italian Prosciutto** are similarly safe; they can be eaten without any cooking, and need no refrigeration, just coolness.

PRESSURE COOKING: Pork does not respond well to pressure cooking; it gets very dry. Baked pork recipes usually take a rather long time, and the crew does get very tired of fried pork chops. Grilled pork and stir frying are recommended.

ROAST PORK LOIN WITH APPLES

The tenderloin is a "best cut."

2 pounds pork loin, three-inch diameter or less
1/2 cup dried apricots, prunes or raisins
1/2 cup rum
1/2 teaspoon cinnamon
1/2 cup bitter orange marmalade
juice of 2 lemons
1 cup chicken stock or you can combine with cider or Calvados
3 apples, peeled and sliced
brown sugar

Plump the dried fruit for a few hours in rum, cinnamon and lemon juice. Sear the meat in an oven pot or skillet and add everything but the apples and raisins. Oven bake at 400° F. or simmer over low heat for thirty-five minutes. Spoon sauce over meat frequently. Add liquid as needed. Reserve meat, strain and skim sauce. Return sauce to pot and simmer with apples and raisins until apples are soft. Thicken with a *roux* if desired. Spoon over sliced pork. Serve with a medley of steamed vegetables.

PORK CHOPS AND CABBAGE WITH SAGE

4 large pork chops
2 onions, chopped

4 garlic cloves, crushed
1 cup white wine
1/2 cup heavy cream
1 cup chicken stock
2 teaspoons dried sage
1 white cabbage
1 teaspoon peanut oil
4 medium potatoes, peeled, quartered
3/4 cup Parmesan cheese, grated

Trim fat, sear the chops in a pan over high heat and reserve. Deglaze pan with wine. Add vegetables and simmer for a few minutes. Add stock, cream and sage. Simmer two minutes. Reserve. Quarter the cabbage and blanch in salted water for five minutes. Rinse in cold water. Add all the vegetables, half the sauce and the pork chops to the pan. Put cabbage on top. Simmer covered over low heat for about twenty minutes, basting frequently.

Remove pork chops, potatoes and cabbage and reserve. Strain pan juices, skim fat, combine with reserved sauce. Thicken if desired. Reheat. Core the cabbage and spread the leaves on each plate. Place chop on top. Place the potatoes, pour on gravy and sprinkle with cheese.

TRES REYES MEXICAN PORK CHOPS

4 pork chops, center cut preferred
2 teaspoons chili powder
5 teaspoons salad oil
3 teaspoons oil
2 cloves garlic
1 small onion, chopped
8 sausages
1 can (16 ounce) tomato sauce
1 can beef consume
1 green pepper, sliced
bacon drippings

Sprinkle chili powder on pork chops and brown in bacon drippings; remove from pan. Add to pan remaining ingredients; simmer five minutes. Add chops; simmer for thirty to forty minutes covered.

SEVERAL VARIATIONS FOR CANNED HAM

Canned ham is precooked and therefore easy to prepare. There are many sauces that garnish and enhance ham's taste; you probably have your own favorites. These are merely suggestions.

Without an oven, baked ham is made in foil that is set on a trivet in a fry pan, then covered and cooked over medium heat for twenty minutes. The surface of the ham is traditionally studded with cloves. Any one of the follow glazes adds variety. Cover ham with:

- Mustard; spoon orange marmalade over all.
- Mixture of raisins, honey, and cinnamon.
- Mixture of canned, crushed pineapple, honey, and lemon juice.
- Cranberry sauce and raisins.
- Canned pulped peaches, brown sugar, lemon juice, topped with raisins in butter.

BEANS 'N BACON DINNER

One-pot blue-water meal.

In large pot, fry:
1/2 pound bacon, chopped into bite sizes
1 small onion, chopped

When bacon is just brown, drain half the fat and add:
1 cup corn, cooked or canned
2 cups navy beans, cooked or canned
1 cup tomatoes, canned, chopped, excess liquid poured off
1 teaspoon paprika
1 teaspoon each brown sugar, chili powder
catsup (optional)

Simmer five minutes, stirring occasionally. Add catsup if desired.

PORK CHOPS IN SAUERKRAUT

4 pork chops, center cut
4 teaspoons oil
2 potatoes, quartered lengthwise
3 carrots, whole but peeled
1 pound sauerkraut
2 teaspoons caraway seed
2 ounces brandy
sage, salt and pepper to taste

Dust chops with sage and flour; brown in oil for six minutes, each side, or until juice runs clear. While meat browns, peel and parboil potatoes and carrots for three minutes. Remove chops from pan; deglaze pan with some of the kraut juice. Add kraut and potatoes; toss with caraway seed. Add all ingredients. Pour a good shot of brandy over all; steam for ten minutes. Salt and pepper to taste.

CHINESE SWEET AND SOUR PORK

In this traditional Cantonese recipe, crispy fried pork is covered with a rich sweet and sour sauce. The sauce can be made in advance, and will keep without refrigeration for months. This recipe makes more than twice the volume necessary for sweet and sour pork.

The sweet and sour sauce:
1 cup white vinegar
1 cup sugar
1/2 cup orange juice
1/2 cup pineapple juice
juice of 1 lemon
2 teaspoons brown sugar
pinch of cloves
1 teaspoon tomato paste
pinch of salt
arrowroot in water (thickener)

Combine all ingredients, except thickener; simmer ten minutes. Add thickener liquid slowly; thicken to consistency of honey. Add more sugar or vinegar to balance the taste as desired. While still hot, pour into a jar; keep lid loose to allow gas to escape. Store in a dark, cool place; it will last months.

The pork:
2 teaspoons oil
flour
1-1/2 pounds lean pork
3 teaspoons soy sauce
3 beaten eggs
2 onions, coarsely chopped
2 bell peppers, sliced
2 cups tomatoes
1/2 cup sweet and sour sauce (above)

Cut pork into bite-sized cubes. Sprinkle with three teaspoons soy sauce. Shake in seasoned flour. Put eggs in a plastic bag. Add pork and shake. Put pork back into the flour and reshake. Fry until brown, not more than three minutes, in very hot oil. Reserve. Add to pan and cook over high heat for one minute: onions, green peppers Add to pot and cook over medium heat: tomatoes, peppers, sweet and sour sauce. Serve with rice.

SWEET AND SOUR PORK RIBS SHANGHAI STYLE

Cut ribs apart, allowing a half pound per person. Dust the ribs in flour. Fry until brown in very hot oil. Remove ribs from pan, drain; deglaze with one cup sweet and sour sauce. Heat sauce; add browned ribs. Serve with rice.

CHINESE FRIED PORK WITH DRIED MUSHROOMS

1 pound lean pork, sliced into bite-sized pieces
4 teaspoons oil
flour
3 cups celery, leaves and stalks, well chopped
1 medium onion, in slivers
2 cups large fresh mushrooms; or dried mushrooms, reconstituted
6 garlic cloves, crushed
2 hot peppers, sliced (no seeds)
1/2 cup beer
2 teaspoons soy sauce
salt and pepper

Add onions, celery and stir fry over high heat. Add mushrooms and garlic and fry until mushrooms brown. Remove and reserve the contents of pan. Toss pork in seasoned flour. Brown pork all over; add hot pepper, stir until pork is browned. Drizzle in soy sauce, pinch pepper. Add mushrooms, sauté for another minute, tossing constantly.

SHANGHAI PORK WITH TURNIPS AND VEGETABLES

Vegetables, such as carrots, green beans, broccoli, peas, any or all, may be substituted for turnips. But if mixed, start long-cooking vegetables first.

1 pound lean pork, sliced into thin bite-size pieces
1/2 pound turnips (about 4 medium), peeled, sliced thin
4 garlic cloves
3 teaspoons soy sauce
1 teaspoon sugar
2 teaspoons vegetable oil

Add all ingredients, except pork; cook turnips until almost soft. Remove turnips, add oil; brown pork all over using high heat and stirring frequently. Add turnips; cook, tossing constantly, until turnips are soft.

CUBAN PORK SAUTÉ WITH BLACK BEANS AND YELLOW RICE

See Black Bean Soup.

COUNTRY STYLE PORK RIBS

This is a good recipe for fatty pork ribs. Cut ribs into "hands" of four "fingers." Parboil ribs for ten minutes in enough water to cover. Turn off flame; let fat accumulate on top, then pour off all liquid. Add chicken consommé to cover; then add:

2 pounds pork ribs, blanched
1 onion, chopped
1 cup celery
6 carrots, sliced
peppercorns and salt

Simmer for 1-1/2 hours until tender. Pour off liquid and skim. Serve with sauerkraut or red cabbage.

PAN BROILED PORK BARBECUE

Cut pork ribs as for previous recipe. In a large pot brown each set of ribs thoroughly in a little oil. Cook for not less than eight to ten minutes per set. Add one inch of water to pan. Brush ribs with BBQ sauce and stack upright in pot. Simmer over low heat for forty-five minutes, or until tender; baste occasionally with sauce. When ribs are almost done, stop basting with pan sauce that has become very oily. Use fresh sauce, and reserve some to serve at the table.

LAMB

Read more about cooking lamb in GRILLING.

A DELIGHTFUL LAMB STEW FROM BELGIUM

Our good friend, Franáoise Henkart, from the yacht *Hendriette*, made this very outstanding lamb stew large enough to feed six. The other two guests never showed up, and it was just as well. The meal was so delicious the four of us finished every last lick.

2 pounds lamb, cut up
oil
4 slices bacon, chopped
4 onions, chopped
1 bulb of garlic, chopped coarsely
1 teaspoon each: thyme, marjoram, savory, salt, pepper
2 cups stock
4 apples, peeled, chopped
1 cup canned Italian tomatoes, drained, chopped; or 4 fresh tomatoes, peeled
4 cups plain yogurt
3 teaspoons curry powder
corn starch in wine

In large pot sauté oil, bacon, onion. When bacon browns, add garlic, sauté for a minute. Reserve with drainer spoon. Add lamb and brown. Add seasonings. Add stock, apples, tomatoes and simmer thirty minutes. Add yogurt. Reduce flame to low and simmer for thirty minutes. Add curry powder. Simmer five minutes. Serve with rice cooked with raisins.

LAMB CURRY

2 pounds lamb
flour
2 onions, chopped
2 bay leaves
4 garlic cloves, chopped
3 teaspoons curry paste
1 quart beef stock
3 teaspoons tomato sauce
2 green apples
4 teaspoons chutney (optional)
grated coconut

Flour meat and brown over high heat. Add all other ingredients except apple, chutney, coconut and simmer about forty-five minutes until tender. Add the apples, simmer until hot. Thicken with corn starch in a little white wine.

LAMB AND RICE

3 cups lamb bits
flour
butter
oil/butter
1/2 cup long-grain uncooked white rice
3 tomatoes, peeled, seeded, chopped
1 cup tomato juice
1 cup chicken stock
2 onions, blenderized, squeezed
6 garlic cloves, chopped
3 teaspoons Worcestershire sauce

Brown the onions and meat in oil/butter over high heat. Reserve. Add white rice, more oil, Worcestershire sauce and garlic. Stir fry until lightly browned. Add all other ingredients and scrape pot bottom to degalze. Simmer over low heat for forty minutes. Add more liquid if needed.

SHEPHERD'S PIE WITH LAMB AND MINTED SWEET POTATOES

Mix and mash the following:
4 medium sweet potatoes or yams, peeled, sliced, boiled, mashed
1/2 cup light cream
3 teaspoons mint flakes

1/4 cup butter
salt and pepper

Parboil:
3 carrots, in thick rounds
4 stalks celery, chopped
1 medium onion, quartered

Add:
1/4 cup parsley, chopped
6 garlic cloves, chopped
1 medium onion, blenderized
1 green pepper, finely chopped
1 teaspoon each: thyme, nutmeg, pepper
2 cups meat stock
a *roux* (do not substitute another thickener)

Fry the parsley, garlic, onion, pepper and herbs until onion is golden. Add meat and simmer until hot. Add all other ingredients except potatoes. Simmer until hot. Thicken mixture with the *roux*. Add ingredients to a deep pie pan. Cover with mashed potatoes and bake at 350° F. for thirty minutes.

RABBIT

Read about rabbit selection at the end of this chapter.

RABBIT IN APRICOT SAUCE

1 rabbit
1 onion, chopped
2 cups rich red wine
1 bulb garlic
1 cup chicken stock
3-4 teaspoons butter
olive oil
rosemary, bay leaf, parsley

The rabbit we envision is a domestic one. If you cook a wild rabbit or a domestic hare cook longer. Avoid breaking the bones as they have sharp edges. Cut the meat from the rabbit into one-inch cubes and marinate for at least a few hours in one cup red wine, garlic, oil, and pepper. Toss often. Drain and reserve the marinade.

Pat the meat dry. Sprinkle liberally with flour. Brown chopped onions in a little oil, add the meat, rosemary and bay leaf. Sprinkle brown sugar all over. Set aside. Deglaze the pan with one cup of chicken stock or more red wine with powdered chicken bullion in it. Add the marinade:

6-8 cloves garlic
a handful of dried apricots and/or apples
juice of 1 lemon
2 teaspoons each brown sugar, rum
pinch of pepper

Simmer fifteen minutes. Add the meat and simmer thirty minutes at low heat. Remove the garlic and squeeze out the paste. Mix paste with butter or olive oil, chopped parsley, one teaspoon of steak sauce and pour over dished up rabbit. Serve over rice.

RABBIT BRAISED IN COGNAC

1 rabbit, quartered
1 onion, chopped
1 cup rich red wine
juice of 1 lemon
1-1/2 bulbs garlic, peeled
1 cup chicken stock
3 or 4 teaspoons butter
olive oil
1 teaspoon each rosemary, parsley
1 bay leaf
1/2 cup brandy
2 carrots, chopped into 4 pieces each
2 potatoes, cut into quarters

Cook rabbit as in previous recipe. Add a half cup of cognac sprinkled over all. Touch off with a match. This makes a fairly decent sized fireball and if that is a problem add the cognac a little at a time.

Deglaze the pan with the chicken stock to make a half-inch of liquid. Cover and simmer over low heat for twenty-five minutes. Add chopped potatoes, carrots, onion and a bay leaf. Cover and simmer over low heat for fifteen minutes, basting occasionally. Serve over cooked vegetables.

HASSENPFEFFER

1 hare or jack rabbit
1 cup spicy meat marinade
1 cup vinegar
1 cup flour
5 teaspoons butter/oil
1 cup hot water
1 teaspoon sugar
a *roux*

Cut up and marinate hare overnight in spicy marinade. Pat dry, dredge in flour. Fry until well browned. Add all other ingredients except sugar. Simmer forty-five minutes over low heat until tender. Add sugar slowly to taste. Thicken with *roux*.

Chaoen, Morocco

CORRECTING DEFICIENCIES IN MEAT

TENDERIZING: Most of the beef sold in the United States has been "finished" in a feed lot, a fenced area which is filled with cattle which are then fed as much corn and formulated food as they can eat. This adds fat and tenderizes the meat, making it delicious and full of cholesterol. **Range beef**, meaning animals which are raised entirely on grass, is what you usually find in developing countries. Range beef (and also lean cuts such as flank steak) is tough and lean (and much better for you). Lean meat can be of good flavor and very tasty if prepared properly.

THIN SLICING AND POUNDING: Slicing meat into thin sheets, then pounding with a meat hammer is an excellent way of tenderizing tough meat. Meat for the famous Mexican dish, **carne asada**, is usually made from thinly sliced flank.

MEAT TENDERIZER: Another method of tenderizing meat is to soak it or dust it with a commercial tenderizer containing pepsin, a derivative of the papaya plant. Use one teaspoon per pound of meat. While we admit that this procedure is much easier on the cook's muscles than pounding, the pepsin imparts a flabby, vaguely suspicious texture to the meat that we find unappetizing.

SLOW COOKING: On land, many a delicious stew has been made with tough meat by slow cooking it for hours, or over night, in a spicy sauce such as marinara or one containing prunes and other dried fruits.

The slow cooking breaks down the tough meat fibers and sauces with the ingredients just mentioned have natural tenderizing qualities. On a boat slow cooking has the major disadvantage of being fuel consumptive and necessitating a constant galley watch to guard against fire.

PRESSURE COOKING is a good way to break down tough meat, cooking it until tender in spicy sauce. The sauce conceals the somewhat depleted flavor of the meat which has been contributed to the sauce.

POUNDING AND ROLLING: Pounding breaks down the fiber in tough meat and, if that doesn't do the job, the next step is grinding. If you don't want hamburger, try pounding and rolling.

1. Pound a long, broad piece of meat such as a flank steak which is about three-quarters of an inch thick on both sides for a few minutes with a meat hammer until it becomes about a half-inch thick. It should be obvious that the consistency is more tender. Be careful to not break up the meat.
2. Marinate the meat in an acid marinade tenderizer plus soy sauce and rice vinegar for several hours or refrigerate overnight.
3. Pat meat dry.
4. Make seasoned bread cubes or use bread stuffing mix and soak in a mixture of olive oil, beer and a little vinegar. Squeeze dry. Add chopped scallions and chopped parsley. Add crumbled cooked bacon if desired.
5. Lay a quarter-inch of the softened bread on the meat and roll the meat into a cylinder.
6. Skewer the cylinder closed.
7. Cut into patties which should look like a thick burger. Grill quickly .
8. A rich sauce such as béarnaise with mushrooms or a spicy marinara goes well on top.

CORRECTING LEANNESS

If meat has good texture, but is excessively lean, there are several methods to correct this deficiency. The French **lard** meat with a larding needle. The hollow **larding needle** is as thick as a drinking straw with a sharp, hypodermic-shaped tip. It is thrust through a piece of fat and the resulting plug of fat is then injected into the meat. The fat used is usually salt pork, enhanced with garlic and fine herbs. If you are armed with a larding needle and a block of salt pork, by all means, use them. If not, try this:

Cut the fatty part of the bacon into strips a half-inch longer than the thickness of the meat, about two slices per steak. Punch holes in the meat with a marlin spike, then force the bacon through the cuts with a hemostat or something blunt like a bolt.

Hold the bacon when it emerges from the other side of the meat, and pull out the bolt.

An additional strip or two of bacon may be wound around the outside of the cut, and held in place with toothpicks.

MORE ABOUT CORRECTING LEAN OR TOUGH MEAT

PICADILLO

This should tenderize anything short of road kill. Put the Picadillo in tacos, over rice, or pasta. The meat is first sliced thin, as for carne asada, then pounded if needed. It is then further cut into small pieces and soaked in the Spicy Meat Marinade (page 282) for a few hours. All of these things go a long way toward tenderizing and improving flavor.

When it comes to consistency make firm for tacos and more sauce-like for rice or pasta.

3/4 pound meat
1 onion, chopped
8 cloves garlic, crushed, chopped
3 teaspoons oil
3 sliced hot peppers, seeds removed
1 cup tomato sauce
2 teaspoons lime juice, lemon juice or vinegar
1 teaspoon cumin
pinch cloves
chili powder to taste

Fry meat, onions and garlic in very hot oil for a minute or two. Add all ingredients, stir. Simmer thirty minutes. Sprinkle with cheese if desired.

SALVAGING A MISERABLE STEAK

Once a steak has been ruined—too dry or too tough to be palatable—there is no real cure for it as a steak. But the meat, mixed with half-cooked bacon or oil can be ground the next day, and made into seasoned sausage patties.

This sausage recipe adds missing fat, breaks down tough fiber, and adds a seasoning that will somewhat conceal the taste of the previously cooked meat. There is another secret, this one psychological: don't tell the crew they are eating last night's miserable steak until after they tell you how much they like the sausages.

MACHIAVELLI MISERABLE STEAK SAUSAGES

1 pound miserable, cooked steak, ground as fine as possible
6 strips bacon, cooked until fat is clear, then ground with steak
2 teaspoons olive oil
2 teaspoons steak sauce
pinch of red pepper
1/2 teaspoon marjoram
2 teaspoons sage
1 teaspoon thyme
1 teaspoon savory
2 teaspoons pepper
pinch of ground nutmeg (optional)

Combine thoroughly. Pan fry in oil over medium heat for three to five minutes. If the crew asks the name of this dish, just tell them "Sausage Machiavelli." Makes twelve patties.

MISERABLE MEAT CROQUETTES

Grind the meat. Add oil or butter if really dry. Add equal amount of mashed potatoes and some grated, lightly fried onion, chopped bell pepper. Flour and fry until brown.

SELECTING AND KILLING LIVE ANIMALS FOR CONSUMPTION

SENSITIVE CHEFS—DO NOT READ THIS SECTION: Food in developing countries is often sold "on the hoof." The most important thing when buying such critters is to not name them or pet them. A fast way to end up sailing solo is to kill cute little "Fluffy" in front of your date. Bring along some plastic wrap and little foam trays to make the critter look more acceptable when you bring it aboard. Use a marking pen. Write "Today's Special—$.49/pound" on the plastic.

PIGS: A nice pig weighs about four hundred pounds, so we are talking about a suckling pig weighing about ten pounds. Even a pig that size is too big for most galley stoves, so we're talking beach BBQ here. Suckling pigs are much more expensive than adult pigs per pound but they are handy and can be kept alive and therefore fresh.

Do not name or pet the pig but examine thoroughly for blemishes and be sure it is not too bony. Farmers love to sell the "runt", which is the smallest pig of the litter, and frequently the pig that gets left out when the sow is one tit short. Beware.

Pigs can be hobbled by tying the back legs together. This allows them limited mobility. If you do end up keeping the animal alive for a while, keep it hobbled and give it shade and water. Feed limited amounts of food once per day. The more you feed it, the more you clean up.

KILLING AND CLEANING: Resist the temptation to shoot the critter through the head because you or someone else may end up getting shot as well as the pig. If you don't do it right the pig will instantly emit an unending stream of loud, hideous screams and become a Super Pig with amazing strength, flailing about in all directions. I have known people who became instant vegetarians after experiencing such an event. If you insist on shooting your pig, straddle it and place the gun near but not against the back of the head where it joins the neck. Align so that the bullet goes forward and very slightly downward.

The best way to kill a pig is to slit its throat with a very sharp knife. If done properly, the critter hardly knows it's been killed. If done improperly the pig screams its head off, hardly comforted by the occasional severed human finger which joins it in eternity.

SOAKING THE ANCHOR TECHNIQUE: If the idea of throat slitting or shooting disturbs you, a quieter method is available. Tie a line securely around the pig. Tie the other end to an anchor. Drop pig and anchor in the water. Soak about four minutes or until struggles cease. Pull up and immediately cut the throat to bleed. After ten minutes, gut and save liver. Scorch skin and remove hair.

RABBITS: You are familiar with rabbits. Hares are big gray brown rabbit-like critters with huge ears. These guys can be mean, so handle with gloves. When you pick them up, grab them by the neck first. Avoid buying a fat rabbit as indicated by a big bulge of fat under the neck. If a rabbit is fat, it's fat all over and hell to defat. Rabbits sold cleaned are invariably skinned and the ends of the legs are chopped off. If you buy a cleaned rabbit, make sure it still has the head. Otherwise you might be buying a cat.

KILLING AND CLEANING: The best way to kill a rabbit is to first tie its hind legs (so it won't escape). Put your foot on its neck and hit it on the head with a hammer or stick. Some people grab it by the hind legs and slap its head against a wall. You can also weigh rabbits with an anchor like the pig.

Slit the throat and allow to bleed. Chop off ends of legs. Slit the skin from anus to breast bone. Pull off skin inside out like a glove toward the head. Gut immediately. Remove gall bladder. Save the delicious liver and pancreas. Hang upside down and cool.

LAMB, KILLING AND CLEANING: Tie a rear hoof tightly and secure the bitter end of the rope to a strong point. Tie a loop around the critter's neck. Have someone pull on that line until the tied leg and neck are extended. Remind this person to hold fast and keep pulling, even if the critter struggles. This stretches the lamb out, extending its neck. Slit throat. Or soak the critter with the anchor attached. Hang and allow to bleed for an hour. While it's hanging cut from breast bone to anus and gut. Save liver and pancreas. Skin. Remove head. The head can be baked for ninety minutes in a closed pot with a chicken stock. Include the hoofs and any spare bones to enrich the stock. Facial and eye muscles are extremely tender and delicious. Brains are mild flavored and quite tasty with a rich sauce. Neck meat is usually made into a soup or stew.

13 Chickens I have met and Et —and other birds

ABOUT CHICKEN

The Bermuda petrel may fly far out to sea, the Canadian goose may span continents, but to view a really well traveled bird—behold the chicken! It seems to exist everywhere, no matter how small the port, or how primitive the culture. These birds hold undisputed first place as available domestic protein.

SELECTION, COMMERCIAL CHICKEN: The bird should be bought whole to reduce the possibility of spoilage. Cutup parts have been handled and this introduces bacteria, which hastens deterioration. Cut up birds may be suitable for eating within a day or two but they do not travel well. The skin of commercial chickens is white or yellow but the taste is the same.

BROILER-FRYERS: Buy only young birds not more than four pounds for grilling or pan cooking.

ROASTERS: are older, a little tougher and weigh up to eight pounds which is a big bird. The skins should be white and unblemished, the breasts plump.

CAPONS are castrated roosters who have not spent their time running around trying to get laid. They have led an indolent life and are therefore large and tender. These are big birds, up to ten pounds and may be grilled or roasted like turkeys.

STEWING HENS are big chickens which are older than roasters. In this case the word "stewing" should be interpreted to mean "slow cooking" or "pressure cooking" since they are tough, stringy but loaded with flavor. They make great stocks.

BIRD SIZES AND PORTIONS

CHICKENS: Allow 3/4 pound/person
- **Broiler-Fryer**: 1-1/2 to 4 pounds
- **Capon**: 6 to 8 pounds
- **Roaster**: 3-1/2 to 6 pounds
- **Rock Cornish Hens**: 1 pound-feeds one
- **Stewing Hen**: 2-1/2 to 8 pounds

OTHER BIRDS
- **Duck**: 3-7 pounds; 1 pound/person
- **Goose**: 4-8 pounds; 1-1/2 pounds/person
- **Turkey**: 6-8 pounds; 3/4 pound/person

HOW MUCH SHOULD I BUY? A hungry sailor can eat a half a fryer and a potato. A medium fryer (3-1/2 pounds) feeds four normal people, which means each person gets a quarter. Six ounces of chicken meat is one portion. About forty percent of a dressed chicken is meat. A typical serving is three-quarters to one pound per person.

BUYING FREE RANGING CHICKENS

You really want a young, free ranging hen not more than two or three pounds. There are small, young, tender hens but there are also tough little old hens that had a hard life and had to run like hell after every grasshopper. It is important to know which is which. The differences are subtle.

Young birds have plump, smooth yellowish feet and legs, bright eyes. Older birds have legs which are stiff, more scaly and tinged with purple. Pinch a fold of skin near the throat. It should be thick, indicating a layer of fat. Fluff up the feathers and examine the skin. It should be white or yellowish without purple blotches or sores. Chicken lice are normal. Look at the hen's small comb. Be sure it is soft and pink, not hard and purplish. Depress the tip of the breast bone. It should be flexible and resilient. Older birds' breast bones are stiff. I will try to be as delicate as possible regarding the next part of the exam.

A young hen is more or less a "virgin" or does not have a long egg-laying history and this may be discovered by examining the place where the eggs come out. Hens sometimes do not like this exam, so get a grip on the pecking end before examining the other end. Let us just say that old hens who have been laying for a long time have big ones and young birds have little ones. To further familiarize yourself with this subject consult a butcher, a real butcher, not the meat man in a supermarket who may not know a cock's comb from a chicken's ass.

As is true of most birds, chicken takes on some of the flavor of whatever it eats. Birds which have been fed (in addition to whatever they can find) a steady diet of shredded coconut are particularly delicious. Birds which have been left to peck at fish skeletons taste a bit fishy. Keep this in mind and take a look around the barnyard or if the chicken has been cleaned, smell the body cavity.

FREE RANGING ROOSTERS: Farmers like selling roosters because they don't lay eggs and one rooster is capable of servicing a whole coop of chickens. The rest are redundant. A young rooster, up to three pounds, resplendent with gorgeous plumage, a small, pink, delicate comb, not a large, pronounced purple comb, is tender and tasty. An old rooster (sometimes politely called a "cock") is one tough bird. It is a mature gentleman, well laid but lean and stringy. I cannot imagine why such a bird is called a "cock", because it is clear that those days are over, which is why he is up for sale. If you are going to buy a rooster, buy a young one.

I once bought an old cock at a good price in the Azores, theorizing that his shortcomings could be corrected by a simmering for a few hours over low heat. I was wrong but I had a great sauce. I then theorized that pressure cooking the old gentleman for about an hour would tenderize him. I was wrong again. His drumsticks bounced on the plate. At least I had a great sauce. I poured it over an omelet!

KILLING: Tie the chicken's legs, place bird on the ground, hold body down with one hand near the base of the neck. Put head into the palm of your hand with the neck between the first and second fingers. Pull up sharply, twisting like you were using a corkscrew. This is called "wringing its neck." Some people just pick the chicken up by its head and whirl it around a bit.

CLEANING: Cut the neck veins or cut the critter's head right off, hang it by the feet and let it bleed. Immediately tie off the esophagus tubes with a rubber band to keep digestive juices from leaking onto the skin. Push down the neck skin and cut off the neck, being careful not to cut through the tubes. When the neck is removed, reach in and pull out the crop and tubes.

FEATHER REMOVAL: The bird is usually feathered before gutting to make handling easier and keep feathers out of the body cavity. Skin the bird immediately or remove all the easy feathers by pulling them off, cut off wing tips. It is better to do this away from the boat because of the chicken lice, which will not live on people but can cause itching and allergic reaction.

Singe off remaining pin feathers with a candle or over the burner. If you plan to eat the bird immediately you can pour boiling water over it to help remove pin feathers.

GUTTING: Slit the bird from the end of the breast bone to tail and around the vent. Place it on its back, reach far in and pull out the guts. Search for the knob-like gizzard and use it as a knob to draw out the organs. Be assertive and do not pull out the guts a little at a time since you do not want to break the gall bladder which is a greenish sack attached to the liver.

When you get the guts out, find the gall bladder, remove it and a bit of the liver without breaking the gall bladder. Do not let any of its juice touch the meat or liver as it will contaminate whatever it touches. This bitter flavor will spread through the meat as you handle it.

Feel around in the body cavity and pull out any loose matter which was missed when the bird was gutted. Do a good job. Just beneath the base of the tail is a small oil sack. Remove it.

CLEANING BODY CAVITY: Wash body cavity in water containing salt and vinegar, then rinse. Do not soak the bird. Scrub the backbone inside the body cavity with a light brush. Thoroughly dry inside and out with a clean towel. Store in a Ziploc with a piece of paper towel in the bottom to absorb juice.

STORAGE: We have eaten five day old chickens kept on ice. Frozen birds lose a bit of taste but may remain frozen or quite cold for a long time, adding at least several weeks to their storage life. Ducks are much more fatty than chickens and last longer. Rinse the bird before use and allow to warm up a bit. Birds stored with a **vacuum sealer** last much longer than traditional methods which allow air to surround the bird.

STORING LOOSE PARTS: Loose parts include the liver, giblets, feet, neck, wing tips and sometimes the skin. These parts are extremely perishable and should be cooked immediately or as soon as defrosted if frozen. Chicken liver is extremely delicious but high in cholesterol. If the liver of a small fryer has a yellow cast, discard it. If the gizzard is to be eaten, cut it open and remove the sack. Remove surrounding fat, blood vessels and clots from the heart. Heart fat is extremely high in cholesterol. Chopped giblets and livers make fine additions to gravy.

DIVIDING A CHICKEN INTO PORTIONS: All birds have **brittle bones** which leave sharp edges and bone chips if chopped. It is therefore prudent to divide a bird by cutting through its joints. The breast is usually deboned prior to dividing, either before or after cooking. For an illustration of how to divide a whole grilled bird or a raw one see GRILLING. If you use our method the body cavity bones are extremely easy to remove before or after cooking.

FREEZING A FRESH CHICKEN: Wash the bird in vinegar and water and dry to prepare for storage. Never use the original wrapper or tray for freezing; always use clean Ziploc bag or vacuum packet.

BUYING FROZEN BIRDS: Frozen birds are tougher than fresh ones and reduced in flavor but frozen birds can be dominated with a rich sauce. Examine a frozen bird for heavy **ice glaze** which indicates the bird has been **watered** before freezing to increase its weight. Glazed birds are usually dry and less flavorful. In general never buy a frozen bird which has not been bagged in heavy plastic as naked birds quickly dry out and become freezer burned, indicated by brownish patches of skin. If you are purchasing a frozen chicken in an isolated place, plan to use a high heat recipe, such as pressure cooking to kill any bacteria the bird acquired in its travels. A frozen chicken, if stored against a holding plate may stay frozen or at least will take several days to thaw, thus extending its travel time.

COOKING FROZEN CHICKEN: Frozen chicken parts take about fifteen minutes to cook in a pressure cooker. They can be added to brown rice and mixed grains and cooked together. If the recipe calls for chicken and lentils, boil the chicken for about five minutes, then add the lentils and pressure cook for an additional twelve minutes.

CANNED CHICKEN: The poor bird has been thoroughly cooked, and we find most of the flavor in the broth. The last thing this meat needs is further cooking. The goal with canned chicken is to get some flavor back into the meat without further cooking. This can usually be accomplished by making the recipes in this chapter which all call for stewing or sautéing. Delay the addition of the canned meat until the last minute. Canned chicken may also be used in croquettes, which call for cooked chicken anyway.

FAT REDUCTION AND SKIMMING: Commercially raised birds have a great deal of fat. Skim one-half to three-quarters cup of fat from the stock of a pressure cooked chicken. Most of a bird's fat is either attached to the skin or in lumps along the thighs and in the body cavity. These should be trimmed away. Grilling and roasting cooks out a great deal of fat but boiling, stewing and braising leave the fat in the juice. Obviously one can remove a great deal of it by removing the skin before cooking but of course the skin adds flavor. A second way which we often use is to pour off the pan juices into a narrow bottle or juice pitcher, allowing them to stand for a few minutes, then dip a cup into the liquid, carefully skimming off the fat. Or use your baster to suck the juice from beneath the fat.

WHEN IS IT DONE? Grilled or fried chicken is done when the skin is a dark golden color and the juice runs clear. The place to test is the thick part of the leg, which takes the longest to cook. Another good spot to examine is the leg joint. Fluid from the joint should be yellow, not tinged with blood. Grab the end of the leg with a towel to avoid burns. The leg should move easily up and down.

Stewed chicken can be opened and examined to be sure the flesh is cooked with just a few areas of blood near the bone, but no raw flesh. **Skinned, boned chicken** cooks faster than unboned, particularly the breast which can be painted with oil and grilled in eight to ten minutes.

Deboning: In general, fowl meat is *scraped* rather than cut from a bone, particularly the breast. **Stir frying** is a good way to cook **bite-sized pieces** of chicken in six to eight minutes.

COOKING TECHNIQUES

BAKING AND ROASTING mean the same thing as far as we are concerned, but some cookbooks say that baking is done at higher temperatures, say 400° F. instead of 325. Baking and roasting are favorite methods of preparing chicken in the home, but are not as popular on a boat because it takes forty minutes or more of oven time and heats up the cabin. Nevertheless, a chicken brushed with oil and garlic and sprinkled with herbs, then cooked at 350° F. results in a crisp, delicious bird which is lower in fat than if fried. Bake whole or cutup.

A typical 4-1/2 pound roaster takes about 1-1/2 hours to cook or 2-1/4 hours if stuffed. Actual time varies with size and the tightness of the stuffing. Cut up pieces usually take about thirty to forty minutes to cook. Cut up pieces are often dipped in milk/butter, then shaken in a bag with a breading mix.

Baste whole birds with oil every twenty minutes. After about an hour keep a good eye on the breast. If it darkens excessively or the skin begins to crack, cover with a foil tent or a piece of oiled rag. If the leg skin also seem to be cracking, do the same and also reduce the temperature. Roasted birds are usually placed on a rack in a pan which contains water, wine or stock. The drippings are used to make gravy.

LEMON-HERB BAKED CHICKEN

In this extremely delicious recipe a huge amount of butter is used to carry the aromatic flavor of herbs and garlic under the bird's skin. You can substitute oil but it is harder to work with. Almost all of the butter melts away so it is essential to place the bird on a rack with a pan containing chicken stock, vegetables, and beer. The juice is the base of the sauce. The butter and cooking juices drip into the pan. The herbs and butter somewhat insulate the meat so this bird takes longer to cook—but is worth the wait! When the bird is done, the juice is skimmed. A little of the butter is used to make a *roux* which is in turn used to thicken the juice into an extremely delicious gravy.

1 fryer, whole
juice of 1/2 lemon
2 cups parsley
2 shallots
2 tablespoons each thyme, marjoram
6 cloves garlic
1/2 cup cilantro
1 teaspoon each salt, pepper
1/4 pound butter
1 can chicken stock
1 teaspoon sugar
1 bottle beer
2 carrots, broken up
2 stalks celery, broken up

1 onion, quartered
loose chicken parts
cooking oil

Chop all herbs, garlic and shallots then add butter and combine to make a paste. Starting at the head end, slip a spoon under the skin, separating it from the meat. Work down into the drumsticks. Skip the wings. Adhere a spoonful of the butter to the spoon and slip it under the skin down to the leg. Keep the paste in place as you remove the skin. Rub the area to distribute the paste. Repeat until the entire bird is treated. Truss the legs and wings against the body. Add the stock, vegetables and loose chicken parts to the pan. Rub bird all over with oil. Bake for about 50 minutes until the skin is golden. Refresh the pan juice with more stock as needed. Keep in mind that a great deal of the juice is butter, so do not let the liquid beneath it disappear. Prick the leg joint to be sure the juice from the joint is clear or yellowish, not bloody.

Skim the pan juice and reduce to 1-1/4 cups. Make a *roux* from the pan oils. Add the skinned juice to make a sauce. You will love this recipe.

BRAISING: is a very good technique which is done after pre-frying. Chicken parts can be floured or dipped in breading mix, cracker crumbs or crushed Rice Crispies. Parts can also be double coated by dipping the floured pieces in egg/milk and reflouring. This adds body. The pieces are fried until golden. At this point the pan is drained of oil and a sauce is added. The sauce and the bird are simmered. The sauce **deglazes** the pan, drawing out delicious flavors. The **breading** thickens the sauce and bonds it to the chicken. On the land the simmering bird is occasionally finished in the oven.

BRANDY CHICKEN (MARENGO)

A quick, one-pot pressure cooker main course that can be served flaming on a platter. Does not taste like whiskey.

1 fryer, cut up in small pieces
2 teaspoons oil
1 large onion, chopped
1 tomato, peeled, seeded, chopped
3 teaspoons whiskey
1 teaspoon each thyme, marjoram
1 cup dried mushrooms, reconstituted
flour

Dredge bird in flour and fry in oil. When the chicken starts to brown, add onion. When chicken is brown, drain excess oil, add herbs, brandy. Sauté for ten minutes. Add tomato. Sprinkle with lemon. Add mushrooms, serve.

CHICKEN HEARTS BRAISED IN WINE

Serves four

1 pound chicken hearts
6 garlic cloves
1 cup white wine
1/2 cup chicken stock
a *bouquet garni*
1 cup dried mushrooms, reconstituted
flour
a *roux*

Remove the fat from around the hearts. Pressure cook hearts in a little stock for eight minutes. Drain. Dredge with flour and fry until browned. Add all other ingredients except *roux*. Simmer five minutes. Skim sauce (important). Thicken sauce with *roux*. Toss in mushrooms. Serve over rice.

CHICKEN FRICASSEE

1 chicken, cut up: breasts quartered, legs separated from thighs
4 teaspoons butter
4 teaspoons oil
flour
4 carrots, peeled and chopped
6 stalks celery with leaves
4 zucchini, in rounds
1 onion, chopped
2 leeks, chopped
1/4 cup parsley, chopped
1 teaspoon each: dill, salt, pepper
1 cup dried mushrooms, reconstituted
3 cups chicken stock
flour
1/2 cup cream

Dredge and lightly brown the chicken in oil. Pour off the fat. Use paper towel to pat off excess oil. Deglaze pan with stock and rub pan bottom hard to dislodge brown. Add half of vegetables and herbs except mushrooms and simmer thirty minutes. Remove chicken and reserve. Strain stock, discard vegetables.

Simmer stock and reduce by half. While broth is reducing, julienne, then sauté remaining vegetables until crisp, about three minutes. Add cream and stir. Add mushrooms. Add chicken and simmer until sauce bonds to crust.

BRAISED LIVER WITH VEGETABLES

1-1/2 pounds liver from a chicken, rabbit, goose, calf or kid
4 strips of bacon
1 cup flour
1 cup chicken stock
2 carrots, parboiled, sliced into rounds
2 green pepper, chopped
6-8 small onions, peeled, parboiled
salt and pepper

Flour liver. Fry bacon and reserve. Brown liver in bacon fat, no more than thirty to forty seconds per side using high heat. Drain. Blot liver. Pour combined vegetables on top. Add stock. Cover pan and simmer five minutes. Liver should be slightly pink inside.

CHICKEN LIVER LYONNAISE

Liver is extremely sensitive to overcooking and there are few things more awful than overcooked liver. Therefore, cook it fast over high heat, so that it is seared on the outside and pink on the inside. Chicken liver should be separated into individual lobes. Read more about liver on page 166.

1/2 pound liver from a chicken, rabbit, goose or kid
2 teaspoons butter/oil
1 cup seasoned flour
2 tablespoons butter
1 medium onion, diced
1 cup dried mushrooms, reconstituted, sliced
1 cup green pepper strips (optional)

Flour liver and reserve. Sauté onions, and mushrooms until browned over high heat. Reserve. Fry livers over very high heat until browned, three minutes, no more. Add onions, green pepper and mushrooms. Fry until hot, three minutes, no more. Add sweet vermouth, lemon juice to pan; allow to thicken. Toss once. Remove from heat and cool bottom of pan with a wet sponge.

BROILING is not a good technique on a boat since it usually smokes up the cabin.

FOIL BAKING means wrapping a bird in foil and baking it, a technique of which we are not fond as it produces a stewed bird with a rubbery skin. Foil is best used to protect parts of a roasting bird which threaten to become overcooked.

FRYING requires high heat. Get the oil very hot before adding the meat. Use peanut oil, it holds up to high heat best. Always use fresh oil. Drop a pinch of flour into the pan. If it skips on the surface and sizzles, the oil is ready. Divide breasts into at least four pieces for frying since whole breasts take longer to cook than the legs. Use a spatter screen or a lid left ajar, which should be wiped dry frequently to keep water from dripping back into the pan, reducing its heat. Alcohol stoves do not fry anything well as the temperature of the alcohol flame is too low.

Breading chicken: Parts can be floured or dipped in milk or egg and milk, then cracker crumbs, crushed corn flakes, cracker meal or breading mix. Bits of **ice** can be added to the breading mix. The ice vaporizes upon contact with the hot grease, producing a finish like **tempura**. Coating with flour helps seal in moisture, making the bird more succulent. Do not overload the pan as this will reduce the oil temperature.

DEGLAZING: After a bird has been fried you will notice crusty, brownish globs of residue attached to the bottom of the pan. These globs are intensely flavored and are the heart of many wonderful sauces and gravies. After the bird is removed from the pan, drain off the oil, carefully retaining the crusty residue. Add one-half to one cup of white wine, beer or chicken stock and scrape the pan with a spatula, freeing and liquefying the crust. The resulting liquid can be thickened with a *roux*, arrowroot or corn starch or it can be gently simmered until it becomes thick and syrupy. At this point it can be brushed on the cutup bird. You can also toss chopped, pre cooked vegetables into the pan and pour the coated vegetables over the bird.

SOUTHERN FRIED CHICKEN

The whole discussion regarding this recipe revolves around the breading mix, which can be cracker crumbs, crushed corn flakes in flour, bread crumbs, etc.

Make a dip consisting of:
2 eggs, beaten
1/2 cup condensed milk

Pat chicken pieces dry with a towel; dip pieces in egg mixture. Allow excess egg to drip off, then gently roll chicken pieces in breading mix. When all pieces are coated, set them aside on a paper towel. Wait a few minutes. Handling pieces very carefully, repeat dipping and breading.

Gently place pieces in a heavy fry pan containing: a half inch of very hot peanut oil. Add pieces slowly to avoid reducing oil temperature. Brown all over, turning once or twice with tongs; handle pieces as little as possible to avoid breaking off batter. Reduce heat after turning. Frying should take about fifteen minutes. Remove chicken pieces from pan, and pat off excess oil with a paper towel, or let stand on paper for a few minutes.

FRIED CHICKEN FRIED WITH ONIONS AND MUSHROOMS

1 fryer, cut up
1 large onion, julienned
1 teaspoon each marjoram, thyme
6 garlic cloves, chopped
2 cups dried mushrooms, reconstituted
3/4 cup dry vermouth or white wine
juice of 1/2 lemon
3 teaspoons flour

Fry chicken, mushrooms and onion in oil. When mushrooms and onions are browned, remove and reserve. Fry chicken until golden. Reserve chicken. Pour off excess fat. Add marjoram, thyme, garlic and sauté a few minutes. Sprinkle in gravy flour a little at a time, stirring furiously and make a *roux*. Add wine and lemon juice and stir. Simmer until thickened Add mushrooms and chicken. Toss and serve.

CHICKEN BREASTS WITH NUTS

Flatten breasts by either boning them or place in plastic bag, set tool box on top and jump on box lustily. This is a pan-fry recipe which can be improved by first par grilling your breasts using smoke chips. Either way, you will be glad you tried it.

4 chicken breasts, boned
3 teaspoons cooking oil
1 cup hard cheese, grated
3/4 cup cream or condensed milk
juice of 1/2 lemon
3/4 cup chopped pecans, walnuts, Brazil nuts
1 cup dried mushrooms, reconstituted, sliced
3 cups macaroni or twists, cooked
sweet vermouth
pepper

Sauté breasts in oil skin down using high heat to give the skin a golden finish. Sprinkle with sweet vermouth and lemon juice as you cook. Turn breasts, reduce heat to medium and cook until done. Set aside. Add mushrooms and sauté. Sprinkle several times with a few drops of vermouth.

Reduce to low heat. Let pan cool a bit. Add chopped nuts. Toss nuts golden. Add cheese, mix with milk. Add to pan. Toss in cooked pasta and mushrooms Put pasta on plate, place a breast on top, add sauce.

QUICK BREASTS

Serves two

2 chicken breasts
1/8 pound butter
4 teaspoons oil
1/2 cup walnuts or slivered almonds
3 cups fresh mushrooms
4 slices white cheese

Sauté walnuts in butter/oil over low heat. Remove and reserve nuts. Sauté mushrooms until golden. Reserve. Add breasts to pan, sauté fifteen minutes, spooning butter over breasts. Cover breasts with slices of hard cheese. Cover and let cheese melt. Place on plate. Sprinkle with nuts and mushrooms.

CHICKEN WITH PAPRIKA AND OREGANO

1 fryer, cut up
oil
6 cloves garlic, roughly chopped
1 teaspoon oregano
1 teaspoon celery salt
2 teaspoons marjoram
1 teaspoon paprika
1 cup tomato sauce or whole tomatoes
cayenne pepper

Fry chicken and onion until chicken is brown. Add other ingredients Simmer over medium heat for thirty minutes until tender.

GRILLING: We love chicken grilled. Read more about that on pages 51-52.

PRESSURE COOKING: Technique produces a delightfully succulent chicken as well as a quantity of wonderful stock. Half-fill the pot with stock, an onion, several carrots, celery, pepper, a bay leaf and some garlic. Pressure cook for fifteen minutes, no more. If the bird is underdone you can simmer it some more.

If you overcook the flavor of the bird will go to the stock. Remove bird immediately.

SAUTÉING: The bird is usually cut up and fried to give the skin a golden, crispy finish. The excess pan oils are drained off. Wine, beer, stock or another liquid plus herbs and seasonings are added and the bird is simmered in it.

CHICKEN CHASSEUR OF THE CAPTAIN

1 fryer, cut up
1 tablespoon bacon fat
1 cup rich, red wine
1 cup consommé
1 can (about 6 ounces) Italian tomatoes; or 1/2 cup tomato puree
2 cups skinned, sliced zucchini
2 carrots, chopped
1 green pepper, sliced
1 teaspoon each: basil, marjoram, chervil (optional), thyme, salt
2 cups mushrooms, sliced pepper to taste

In large pan fry chicken until golden. Add consommé, simmer for ten minutes. Add remaining ingredients, except the mushrooms. Add lid and simmer ten minutes. Add mushrooms, simmer five minutes. Serve over rice.

CHICKEN FLORENTINE

In this classic Italian dish, the chicken is first browned, then simmered in marinara sauce, and served on a bed of spinach. Fresh spinach is best, but frozen may be used. If no spinach is available use shredded, cooked cabbage. To make the dish heartier, serve it with a healthy layer of cooked noodles under the spinach.

1 fryer, cut up
3 tablespoons olive oil
flour
marinara sauce
1/2 pound fresh spinach, washed and cooked; or 1 package frozen spinach, squeezed
2 cups macaroni or twists

Dredge in flour, fry bird until golden and reserve. Make a marinara sauce. Add chicken; simmer for twenty minutes. When chicken is tender, make a bed of noodles, then add spinach, butter, salt, and pepper. Finally, add chicken, pouring sauce over all.

CHICKEN TARRAGON

1 fryer, cut up
3 teaspoons butter/oil
3 shallots or 1 onion, chopped
2 teaspoons tarragon
3 carrots, in quarters
6 cloves garlic, sliced
1 cup dry white wine
1 chicken bullion cube
3 teaspoons flour

In a large pan fry chicken until done. Add pinch tarragon, carrots and onions toward the end and fry until carrots are done. Reserve everything. Drain half the oil. Add more tarragon, garlic, wine and bouillon cube. Simmer and deglaze pan by scraping. Add flour, and thicken by frying. Add wine. Simmer over low for ten minutes to reduce by about half. Return chicken to pan and toss. Simmer ten minutes.

CHICKEN WITH ARTICHOKES

Use the marinated artichoke hearts packed with oil and spices in small jars. Avoid artichokes packed in water or vinegar. Their flavor will not contribute to this dish.

1 fryer, cut up
1 small jar marinated artichoke hearts
3 teaspoons oil from marinated artichokes
5 cloves garlic
1 onion, diced
1 cup white wine

Brown bird in a large pan using artichoke oil and olive oil. Add onions and garlic toward end. Add artichoke hearts last. Add white wine with dissolved chicken bouillon cube and simmer over medium heat, lid on, for twenty minutes. Add more wine or beer if needed. Serve over rice or noodles; sprinkle liberally with Parmesan cheese.

FIRST OFFICER'S CURRIED CHICKEN

1 fryer, cut up
1 cup curry sauce
3 cloves garlic, smashed
1 teaspoon ginger
2 teaspoons white vinegar
3 zucchini, peeled, chopped into 1/2-inch rounds
1/2 cup nuts
3/4 cup raisins
1 can tomato sauce, or blenderized Italian tomatoes

Fry chicken until golden. Add all other ingredients simmer ten minutes.

STEWING: In this technique the fowl may be partially fried for color but the basic recipe calls for slow simmering in a liquid which is usually not thickened at the end.

CHICKEN STEWED WITH VEGETABLES

1 broiler, cut up, skinned (use all parts)
4 teaspoons oil
3 carrots, quartered lengthwise
2 medium onions, quartered
3 potatoes, peeled and quartered lengthwise
1 cup water
2 chicken bouillon cubes, dissolved in a little water
1 cup dry white wine
1 teaspoon each: marjoram, parsley, sage
salt and pepper to taste

Brown chicken, onions and potatoes oil until potatoes brown slightly. Add all other ingredients, beginning with carrots; simmer over medium heat, covered, for thirty minutes (or pressure cook for fifteen minutes). Turn chicken several times; cook until chicken is tender. The cooking liquid may be thickened into a sauce with a *roux*.

MOROCCAN CHICKEN

1 chicken, cut up
3 teaspoons olive oil
6 cloves garlic, chopped
juice of 1 lemon
2 teaspoons cumin
1 teaspoon ginger
1 teaspoon each turmeric, paprika
pinch cinnamon
1 cup Greek olives, pitted
12 dried dates, chopped
1/2 cup raisins
1 apple, peeled, diced
1 cup orange juice

Combine all ingredients and half the orange juice and let stand an hour. Place in fry pan over medium heat and cover. Cook for twenty minutes adding a bit of orange juice now and then to keep up steam. Remove chicken, deglaze pan with orange juice and spoon over chicken. Or deglaze with rum. The Moroccans would never do this but I would.

STIR FRYING: See page 67-9.

STEAMING chicken parts is a tasty technique which produces a very tender bird. Steaming a whole bird takes a long time unless it is pressure cooked. Steam over stock and vegetables for about an hour or pressure steam for fifteen minutes.

STEWED CHICKEN

COQ AU VIN

This is a slow cook recipe for a stewing chicken and the wine helps break down and tenderize a big bird. Smaller birds should be cooked less as they will fall to bits if cooked this long. Traditionally, red wine is used in this dish which is unusual since birds are typically cooked in white.

1 stewing chicken, 5-6 pounds, cut into 10-12 pieces
3 cups pearl onions or chopped yellow onions
2 teaspoons butter
2/3 cup flour
2 teaspoons paprika
1 teaspoon each: salt, pepper, thyme, parsley
1/2 teaspoon sugar
1 pound mushrooms, sliced
6 slices bacon, or 1/2 pound salt pork
3 cups rich red wine

Boil half the onions in a large pot, reserve. Sauté pork and remaining onions. Sprinkle a little sugar on onions to brown them. Reserve and pour off half the fat. Mix flour, paprika, salt pepper and flour chicken. Brown chicken, until golden and also cook mushrooms. Remove mushrooms and onions when done. Add all other ingredients, except vegetables. Simmer over low heat forty minutes until chicken is tender. Add vegetables and simmer another ten minutes.

CHICKEN FRICASSEE

...or what to do with a big bird of questionable tenderness!

1 stewing chicken (about 5 pounds), cut up and skinned
3 tablespoons bacon fat
1 teaspoon parsley, chopped
2 bay leaves, broken into pieces
1/2 teaspoon nutmeg
1/2 pound bacon, chopped
2 cups mushrooms, sliced
2 egg yolks

stock to cover
1/2 cup condensed milk, unsweetened
1 chicken bouillon cube

Fry chicken in a pressure cooker until browned. Sprinkle with salt, pepper, and gravy flour (no lumps). Do not brown the bird, but turn it several times to fix the flour. Reserve, pat dry. Drain oil from pan. Add nutmeg, bay leaves, parsley, and bacon. When bacon begins to brown, cover with stock. Pressure cook for twenty minutes after first jiggle.

Remove lid; continue to simmer until tender, the length of time depending on the muscular fortitude of your bird. When chicken is tender, turn off heat. Let pot stand for five minutes. Reserve bird. Add egg yolks mixed with condensed milk; stir thoroughly, then return pot to very low heat.

The yolks will thicken the sauce to a creamy consistency, unless overheated, in which case, the egg jells. Take it slow and easy, removing the pot from the flame several times to keep the temperature low. This dish does not reheat well.

CHICKEN SALADS

Basic CHICKEN SALAD

The beauty of a chicken salad is that it utilizes leftover chicken in a tasty way. In addition, it is probably the very best dish for canned chicken. Pressure boiled and grilled chicken are particularly good for conversion into a salad, the former because it is very tender, the latter because of its wonderful flavor. Last, but not least, it is a fine hot weather recipe that may be used in sandwiches, hors d' oeuvres, or as an entree.

2 cups cooked chicken meat, chopped
1 cup potatoes, diced, boiled, but firm
1 cup cooked green beans, firm and cooled
3 fresh tomatoes (not canned), cut in wedges
1 cup (any or all): black olives, pitted capers, chopped anchovies, artichoke hearts, celery hearts
Vinagrette dressing (page 218)

Combine ingredients by tossing lightly: avoid smashing the vegetables.

CHICKEN SALAD NIÇOISE

Leftover chicken is cut into bite size pieces, rinsed and soaked in the Spicy Meat Marinade (page 282) for several hours. It is then dropped on a Salad Niçoise (page 225).

CHICKEN SALAD—AMERICAN STYLE

Combine:
1-1/2 cups cooked chicken, diced
1/2 cup celery, finely chopped
1/2 cup mayonnaise
3/4 cup potatoes, boiled, diced
3-4 hard-boiled eggs, chopped

Sprinkle with salt, pepper and paprika. Add French dressing on top.

MISCELLANEOUS CHICKEN RECIPES

CHICKEN A LA KING

4 cups cooked chicken or turkey, cubed
1/2 stick butter
3 teaspoons oil
1/2 cup cream
1/2 pound fresh mushrooms
1 red bell pepper, julienned
1 cup boiling onions
1/2 cup flour
2 cups sugar snap peas (or other tender vegetable)
2 cups chicken stock
4 chopped carrots
1 cup peas

Sauté and reserve mushrooms. Blanch vegetables. Make a *roux*, thin with stock and cream. Add all other ingredients and heat. Serve over toast.

HUNTER'S PIE

Make chicken or turkey a la king with a slightly thinner sauce. Place in pie shell, cover with mashed potatoes. Heat in oven at 350° F. for about thirty minutes until top browns lightly.

ABOUT DUCKS

Domestic ducks are larger than chickens but contain less meat, more bone and espe-

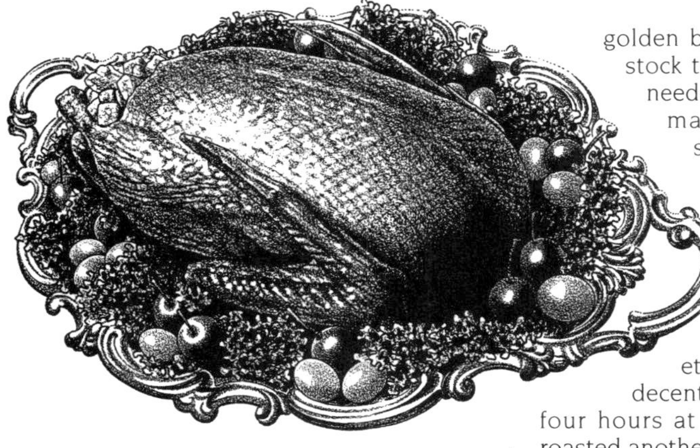

cially more fat. Duck cookery has a great deal to do with rendering out the four to five cups of fat which is contained in a typical bird. This may be done by slow roasting/grilling or by removing the skin and trimming the meat. Some people stuff ducks but the stuffing becomes very fatty. Duck is usually served with a mixture of long grain brown rice and wild rice which pressure cooks in about fifteen minutes.

HOW MUCH SHOULD I BUY? About twenty percent of a duck is meat. A six pound duck will provide about as much meat as a 3-1/4 pound chicken. A six pound duck will feed four normal people or two hungry sailors.

PAN FRYING PARTS: Skinning a duck prior to cooking has become quite fashionable because it results in a much leaner product—but the skin is very tasty and protects the meat from drying. **Unskinned breasts** and legs can be **pan fried** skin side down which helps render out the fat and brown the skin. The meat is usually **deboned after cooking** which makes it much easier to eat. Deboning prior to cooking shrivels the meat. A little fat, garlic and shallots can be added to the fry pan for flavor.

ROASTING OR GRILLING: See Chapter 4.

OVEN ROASTING WHOLE BIRDS: The duck can be opened and flattened as is described for chicken in GRILLING. The skin should be pricked all over to facilitate fat drainage and should be pricked throughout the cooking process. The bird can be roasted in the oven for an hour (eighteen minutes per pound) at 375° F. until the skin turns golden brown. Add a little chicken stock to the pan and replenish as needed. The resulting drippings make a fine sauce (once skimmed) or can be added to a pressure cooked stock.

MAKING A RICH SAUCE FROM THE CARCASS: In classic recipes the duck carcass, a *bouquet garni*, garlic, vegetables and a whole bottle of decent red wine are slow roasted four hours at 325° F. then strained and roasted another six hours to get a delicious sauce as thick as jelly. On a boat pressure cook for about an hour and reduce two-thirds by simmering. The rich stock is then strained and if desired thickened into a gravy or used as-is as a sauce. Three cans of chicken stock reduces to about one cup of rich sauce. Chop the heart, gizzard and neck meat to thicken the sauce. A nice variant is to toss a little orzo (pasta shaped like rice) into the stock thickening it and adding body.

QUICK ORANGE SAUCE FOR DUCK A L'ORANGE

1/2 cup bitter orange marmalade
juice of 1 lemon
2 tablespoons brown sugar
1/4 cup Gran Marnier or Triple Sec
pinch of ground clove

ABOUT GEESE

Geese are not birds of choice for the cruiser because they are long and not well shaped for the small heat sources on a boat. There is nothing tougher than an old goose except maybe a Big Tom (see: Turkey). About eighteen percent of a goose is meat, so you get much more meat per pound from other birds. On the other hand the **goose liver** is quite large and extremely delicious. A typical goose weights eight to twelve pounds. Don't buy bigger ones.

Geese are even more fatty than ducks and should roast for at least 2-1/2 hours at 300° F. or twenty-five minutes per pound at this low temperature. Geese can be cut up and roasted like ducks, or (much better) skinned, defatted and pressure cooked like a turkey;

or the breasts can be cooked like duck breasts (above). Prick whole, unskinned geese all over with a fork and keep on pricking as they cook. Expect to render several quarts of fat from a goose so be sure you have a sufficiently deep pan for them.

ABOUT TURKEYS

SELECTION: Turkeys are very popular in the USA where they are selected by weight, sex and preparation technique. **Hens** are a little fatter, more succulent and more expensive than **Toms**. The smaller the turkey the more expensive per pound. Some American turkeys have been injected with cooking oil to make them more succulent and retard drying. This is okay but you are paying turkey prices for the oil. Turkeys are more perishable than chickens and should be purchased quite fresh or quite frozen. Smell carefully. Measure your cooker. Buy a turkey which fits.

Turkeys are very popular in many isolated places since they are much bigger than chickens and therefore more capable of defending themselves against predators. Every flock of barnyard turkeys has at least one **Big Tom** which frequently weighs up to fifty pounds. Big Toms are extremely aggressive and will readily take on a fox, cat, dog, or a sailor. They are also extremely territorial, like geese, and make good guards. I have seen quite a few barnyard turkeys in developing countries that I would never confront unarmed. Never buy the Big Tom.

HOW MUCH SHOULD I BUY? A turkey contains about 45% meat. An eight pound turkey yields about 3-1/2 pounds of meat which will feed six.

COOKING: Turkeys six to eight pounds can be grilled on a rack in a pan on the barbie or roasted in the oven. Grilled birds cook much faster than oven roasted birds. Grilling takes about eight minutes per pound unstuffed, ten minutes stuffed. An eight-pound unstuffed turkey takes about an hour to roast. No more. In a 350° oven the time increases to twelve minutes unstuffed and fifteen minutes stuffed.

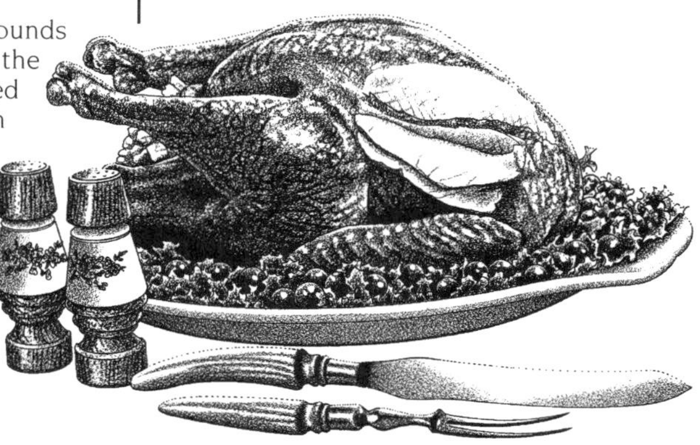

Ignore those dumb-ass little plastic temperature indicators one sometimes finds stuck in turkey breasts which only tell you that you have seriously overcooked your bird. Turkey parts also grill (roast) well in a pan with a rack. Baste frequently with oil or oily pan juices. We consider the piece done when the skin becomes golden brown, about thirty minutes.

Pressure cooked turkey parts are extremely succulent and delicious. Pressure cook about fifteen minutes in a little stock which will become a gravy, or in 1-1/2 quarts of stock to make turkey-barley soup or stew.

WILD BIRDS

FIELD DRESSING: In general the way wild birds are handled immediately after killing heavily influences their flavor as does their age and what they have been eating. Wild birds should have their throats cut and be hung upside down for a half-hour to bleed. The neck tubes should then be tied off, the neck cut off and the crop and tubes removed. The bird should be gutted immediately. The oil gland should be removed and the body cavity wiped dry. Remove feathers just before cooking to preserve moisture.

HANGING: An extremely ancient, safe process similar to aging beef which tenderizes and improves flavor. **Small birds** like quail and pigeons and medium sized birds like grouse and ptarmigan can be cooked immediately after killing. **Larger birds** such as pheasant, geese, wild turkeys or large Guinea fowl are usually gutted and hung by the legs. Wild birds can also be dressed, skinned, cut up and softened in an **acid marinade** for two or three days in the refrigerator.

HANGING TIME: One to three days, in a cool dry, airy place, wrapped in gauze, until the feathers in front of the tail pull out easily or the leg joints stiffen. After about three days a hung bird begins to, as some say, *smell*—but this is normal. Some wild game gourmets hang their birds until the head falls off but this is an acquired taste.

PREPARATION: Skin the bird and throw away the skin or **dry pluck** and singe off the small feathers just before cooking. Pinch up a bit of skin under the neck of your bird to judge fat content. If the bird is very lean skin it. If the bird was killed with a shotgun it behooves you to pick out all the shot before cooking. Shot can cause you to break a tooth or *give you a case of lead poisoning, pilgrim*.

COOKING: In general **only the breast of wild birds is served**. The legs, which contain tough tendons and all other parts are usually pressure cooked into a stock which is strained and reduced to a rich sauce. The breasts are then sautéed in the sauce. Traditionally a veal stock is preferred as a base but chicken stock will do. **Marinate** the breasts a few hours or overnight in an acid marinade before cooking. **Wild rice** and other mixed grains are traditionally served with the bird.

Herbs and Spices: The traditional spice for wild birds is sage. In many places where birds are hunted, wild sage can be picked and thrown on the coals or directly under the grilling bird to add flavor. Sage, marjoram and garlic are usually mixed with oil and brushed on the bird or added to the marinade.

Grilling: Wild birds are generally quite lean and need to be injected with a little cooking oil and covered with bacon or an oiled rag. The skin of lean birds invariably chars without a covering. Birds can also be roasted in a pan with a little oil and chicken stock to use for basting. Baste frequently.

Grill time varies, depending on the fattiness of the bird. Fat ones can cook up to eight minutes per pound, lean ones six minutes. Birds with dark meat breasts such as wild duck cook to a dark, rich red color with red juices. Light-breasted birds like grouse cook to a tawny color with clear juices.

Grilling small breasts: Pigeon and dove breasts can be wrapped in bacon, skewered and grilled for twenty minutes. Brush on oil, sage, thyme, garlic as the breasts cook.

Sautéing: Breasts are usually sautéed in a sauce or marinade. They produce very little drippings, so a sauce is important. The game taste of wild birds can be concealed with a rich, dominant sauce.

GROUSE AND PTARMIGAN

I hunted these birds in the Northern States and the Arctic. Natives call them Fool Hens although it is hard to imagine a critter dumber than a chicken. I had an old, grizzled cook who taught me the **Fool Hen Dance** which got us many a dinner. When he spotted one nearby he would immediately send me off to walk in front of them and do the Fool Hen Dance.

The dance consisted of shaking my arms, legs and head as though going into a convulsion while spinning slowly around uttering loud choking sounds. While I was doing the Fool Hen Dance he would take a piece of split log from the wood pile and sneak up from another direction. The birds were so engrossed in watching me they ignored him. When he got close enough he would suddenly half kneel and send the stick spinning toward the birds, close to the ground. That put quite a few birds on the table and they sure tasted better than **Spam** which I have consumed to excess. Potting at grouse with a slingshot didn't spook them, so I got a few in my own way. Maybe they are dumber than a chicken.

Immediately pick up the dead bird by the lower beak. If it breaks off you have yourself a **young roaster**. If not you have an **old braiser**. An old braiser should be hung up or cut up and marinated for a few days then sautéed in a rich sauce.

Roasters should go right on the grill. **Lard** the breast and legs with bacon strips slipped beneath the skin. Keep oiling the skin as it cooks. Cook for twenty to thirty minutes. No more. Thoroughly wash the **crop material** then dry. Sauté in generous butter with bread or biscuit cubes, some chopped celery, parsley, raisins or dried fruit. Makes a fine dressing.

FOWL GRAVY

The technique you use depends on how the bird was cooked.

FRIED FOWL GRAVY

4 teaspoons gravy flour
1-1/2 cups chicken consommé (double strength), or two bullion cubes
1 to 1-1/2 cups milk (optional)
1/4 cup heavy cream

Remove the bird from the fry pan and pour off all oil. Remove three teaspoons of oil and allow to cool. Mix flour with oil (or use vegetable oil) and return to pan. Heat flour and make a *roux*, rubbing the pan hard with a scraper to loosen brown matter and deglaze it. Add stock slowly, whisking furiously until desired consistency is achieved. If you are using bouillon cubes add milk instead of stock.

PAN ROASTED FOWL GRAVY

Baste bird as it cooks with chicken stock and white wine. Pour off the drippings (at least one to two cups) and skim. Make a *roux*, then pour in the drippings, whisking furiously. Add cream (optional)

GIBLET GRAVY

1/4 pound giblets, neck, wing tips, feet
2 cups chicken stock
a *bouquet garni*
drippings if any or fry pan brown stuff deglazed with wine

Pressure cook everything but the drippings or deglazed stuff for eight minutes. Pour off liquid, add drippings and skim. Chop giblets and reserve. Make a *roux* (about a quarter cup of flour) and add the liquid. Whisk furiously until smooth. Add giblets, sprinkle with parsley, salt and pepper and serve. Gravies can be thickened by adding crumbled hard-boiled egg yolk.

FOWL STUFFING

COUNTRY BREAD STUFFING

4 cups seasoned bread cubes
1 onion, chopped and fried
3 stalks celery, pared
1/2 cup raisins
1-1/2 cups mushrooms, chopped, sautéed
1 cup chestnuts, chopped (optional)
2 apples, peeled, cored, chopped
1/2 cup walnuts or pecans, chopped
1-1/2 sticks melted butter
3 teaspoons sage or poultry seasoning
2 eggs, beaten
1 cup fowl broth

Use some of the butter to sauté the vegetables. Mix everything together and stuff into bird or bake thirty minutes in a greased, covered casserole at 325° F. Uncover and bake ten minutes to make a crust. Makes enough for a small turkey

WILD RICE AND RICE STUFFING

1/4 cup each wild and brown rice, pressure cooked in 1 cup of chicken stock with *bouquet garni*
1 teaspoon sage
2 cups mushrooms, chopped, sautéed
1/2 cup each chopped celery, onion
1/2 cup slivered almonds
1/2 cup currants or raisins or 1 apple, peeled, cored, chopped; or use grapes
2 teaspoons butter for sautéing

Combine everything and stuff into bird.

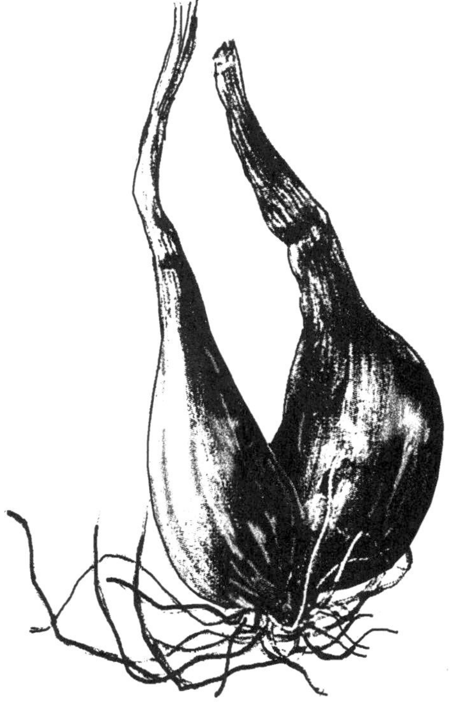

14 Pasta & Rice

Pasta and rice rank high on the list of fine cruising foods. They store well, are long lasting, cost very little, cook quickly, serve legions, and are a fine base for the sauce creations of the chef.

PASTA

Pasta is made from ground wheat and water. The best is made from the inner part of durum wheat which has a high gluten content. The gluten keeps the strands from dissolving as they cook. There is no difference in the content of dried versus fresh pasta, nor is there a flavor difference. There is a *texture* difference. **Dried pasta** cooks to a firmer consistency, called *al dente* in Italy, indicating some resistance to the teeth. **Fresh pasta** is more delicate and seems to melt in the mouth.

BUYING: Regardless of what kind of pasta you buy, examine the packages or boxes carefully. In some places, pasta has been on the shelf for years. Look for roach holes, chewed ends, black droppings, and hairs. Also check the ends of noodles or spaghetti for mold or mildew. Old pasta frequently takes on the flavor of its container.

STORING: Store in vacuum pouches or wide-mouthed plastic jars that have been washed in a strong solution of bleach, then dried thoroughly in the sun. The pasta is added, and the jar put in the sun for several hours with the lid on, but loose. The lid is then tightened, and the jar stored out of the sun. The air inside cools and forms a slight vacuum, which helps to preserve the pasta. Pasta thus stored will last four or five years.

WHAT KIND SHOULD I BUY? There are many different shapes of pasta. For convenience we use linguine, macaroni, short twists and orzo, which looks like rice. You buy what you like.

SERVING SIZE: Dried pasta, when cooked, doubles in weight and volume. A typical portion is four ounces dry. A typical package of dried pasta, one pound, plus a sauce, feeds four. An adequately large pot and plenty of salted water are the secret of successful pasta cookery. Two quarts of water per half pound of pasta is generous. Two teaspoons of salt should be added to raise the boiling temperature. Do not boil in sea water as it is too bitter.

ADDING OIL TO THE WATER: Add a generous tablespoon of oil to the boiling water before adding the pasta. The oil prevents the pasta from clumping or sticking to the bottom of the pot. The uncooked pasta should be added a little at a time to the briskly boiling water. This keeps the water at a high temperature and prevents clumping. Agitate the pasta as you add it.

ADDING PASTA TO BOILING WATER: Along shore a gallon of water is used to cook a pound of pasta. While this is a good rule, much less can be used with a little care. Add the pasta slowly and rinse it with a little fresh boiling water when it is cooked. In addition to oil, a certain amount of care must be exercised when adding pasta to boiling water to prevent it from sticking together or to the bottom of the pot. We usually break spaghetti in half and sprinkle it into the boiling water. Those who love long strands can hold a bunch in the hand and introduce it a few inches at a time, slightly agitating it. After adding the spaghetti to the water, agitate it with a fork. Drain thoroughly when done.

WHEN IS IT DONE? The Italians prefer their pasta *al denté*, not completely soft and offering a bit of resistance to the teeth. Taste the pasta frequently as it cooks since cooking time varies considerably according to the thickness of the pasta, its age, and the wheat from which it was made. When its taste suits you, it's cooked. Cooking time varies with thickness. Rice-shaped pasta (orzo) takes about four minutes to cook. Spaghetti usually takes eight to twelve minutes to cook. **Fresh pasta** takes three minutes to cook.

REHEATING COOKED PASTA: If you have leftover pasta, toss it with a little oil (to prevent clumping) and store in a tight Ziplock bag. Drop into salted, boiling water for a few minutes to restore.

MIXING PASTA: It is unwise to cook different types or brands of pasta together in one pot. Different pastas cook at different rates.

ABOUT PASTA CHEESES

When it comes to expensive ingredients, put your money into good cheese. Trust me. This is important. We do not even bother to purchase any sort of grated cheese, which is almost invariably of low quality, has a limited shelf life and quickly becomes rancid. Avoid it.

The best **Parmesan** cheese comes from Italy, usually from the Reggiano region. It is marked Parmesan-Reggiano. Parmesan dries and improves in flavor as it ages. The youngest Parmesan is aged ten months. It is chalky colored and clumps when pressed together, indicating excess moisture. Even this is far superior to canned, grated cheese but it is still below minimum standard for our table.

In Italy an ordinary table Parmesan cheese used for pasta is aged two years and a good one, often served with nuts and port wine for dessert is three years old. It is wheat colored, hard as a rock, very crumbly and crunches slightly between the teeth before dissolving in the mouth. It has a powerful, almost overwhelming flavor. It is slightly salty and never sharp or bitter.

Like Parmesan, good **mozzarella** cheese is in a class by itself. The cheap, tasteless mozzarella which comes in a block, is hard and rubbery. Quality mozzarella always comes packed in water and the best is very young, soft and unsalted. Always store mozzarella submerged in water. Be sure the water fills the container, without any air. Change the water as it becomes opaque, indicating bacterial presence (which is not dangerous).

Good mozzarella is sold in the form of balls. The large balls are about the size of a lemon. Their disadvantage is that you often cannot use the entire ball and the remaining portion has been exposed to contaminants by handling. Wash it off and put it back in water. Small balls are about the size of a walnut.

The gastronomic pinnacle of mozzarella cheese is made from buffalo milk and is called **buffo mozzarella**. Do not envision an American bison. We are talking domesticated oxen-like critters here. Buffo mozzarella is incredibly expensive in Italy because of demand but can occasionally be found at "reasonable" prices in the U.S. Fresh mozzarella will last a few weeks in the refrigerator.

When cheese is used in Italian cooking such as on pizza or in lasagna several types are often mixed together. When a pasta dish is served the cheese is usually served on the side. In Italy a block of Parmesan cheese and a small grater are served on a plate and each diner grates what he wants.

PASTA SAUCES

PESTO SAUCE

The dominant ingredient in pesto is fresh basil, but cilantro or parsley can be used as a substitute. In the classic recipe pine nuts are used but you can also use Brazil or macadamia nuts. The cheese of choice is Parmesan, the best you can find. Good quality cheese makes the sauce.

Pesto is classically used as a pasta sauce but can also be served over fish, shrimp, chicken or veal. Thin it a bit, add some lemon juice and it makes both a good marinade for skewered lamb and also a fine salad dressing. Some people cook the pesto but we prefer it uncooked. This is a blender recipe, so the quantity made will fill the blender two-thirds full when we are finished.

basil leaves, about 1 cup tightly packed
2/3 cup olive oil
3 cloves garlic
pine nuts: enough to fill the blender one-third full before chopping
1 cup Parmesan cheese, grated

Chop the nuts in the blender until they are aspirin sized. Reserve. Blenderize the oil and garlic. Pack the leaves in the blender until it is full. Pour on the oil and finely blend. Combine all ingredients and let stand several hours at room temperature. You can also add chopped sun dried tomatoes and chopped shrimp, scallops, or lobster. If you really want to be decadent add a dollop of sour cream on top before serving.

You can jar pesto, pour on a little olive oil to cover and refrigerate up to a week.

RED PEPPER SAUCE

This is a colorful, pink sauce that looks very good on seafood. Grill seafood and place in a pool of sauce. Garnish with colorful bell peppers and twists of lemon rounds.

2 red bell peppers, roasted and skinned
1 cup chicken stock
1 teaspoon corn starch
1 onion, chopped
1 teaspoon butter
1/2 cup cream
1/2 cup Parmesan cheese, grated

Sauté the onions in butter until soft. Chop and add the peppers Sauté until everything is hot. Add chicken stock and simmer a minute. Mix corn starch in a little water and add. Do not boil. When thickened add cheese, stir and blenderize. Add cream.

MEAT AND MUSHROOM SAUCE OF THE CAPTAIN

You will be making a great deal of this if you have a large crew of hungry sailors. Make enough for a few days.

3/4 pound ground beef
1 quart marinara sauce
2 cups dried mushrooms, reconstituted, sliced

Fry the meat until gray. Drain Add marinara sauce and simmer twenty minutes Add mushrooms, simmer for another ten minutes and serve. Sprinkle with a generous amount of grated Parmesan cheese.

Puttanesca Sauce

The distinct nature of this sauce derives from anchovies and olives. High quality fancy olives packed in water, oil and spices are recommended. Forget about those cheap, pitted, canned olives.

1/2 cup olive oil
1 can anchovy fillets
6 cloves garlic, crushed and ground in the oil
6 Italian tomatoes, skinned, seeded, crushed
4 tablespoons capers, rinsed
1 cup olives, chopped
salt and pepper

Mash oil, anchovies and garlic into a paste. Add one tablespoon oil to a pan and saute the tomatoes until soft. Add remaining ingredients and simmer over low heat twenty minutes, stirring occasionally.

DRIED MUSHROOM TUNA SAUCE

1 can tuna
3 garlic cloves, finely chopped
1/2 can cream of mushroom soup
2 hot peppers, sliced
1 cup slivered carrots
1 onion, chopped
1/4 cup olive oil
2 cups dried mushrooms, reconstituted
1/2 cup parsley, chopped

Sauté onions, garlic and hot peppers in oil until onions are golden. Add soup, simmer a minute until hot. Add remaining ingredients Mix thoroughly; pour over pasta.

PASTA WITH DRIED MUSHROOM SAUCE I

End of the passage recipe

1 cup dried mushrooms, reconstituted
1 medium onion, chopped
1/2 can cream of mushroom soup
1/4 cup sun-dried tomatoes, chopped
12 ounces marinated artichoke hearts, chopped
1/2 cup water
2 tablespoons sherry
3 tablespoons butter
2 tablespoons olive oil
salt and pepper

Sauté the onions in oil and butter until golden. Add mushrooms and sherry. Sauté another three to four minutes. Blend water with soup. Add all remaining ingredients. Sauté another five minutes.

PASTA WITH DRIED MUSHROOM SAUCE II

Make two cups béchamel sauce. Add Parmesan cheese. Add dried reconstituted mushrooms and some of their juice before serving.

SPAGHETTI SAUCE FLORENTINE

4 tablespoons butter
1 pound spaghetti, cooked
A *roux*
2 cups milk
1/2 pound ham, diced
1 cup Parmesan cheese
1 cup dried mushrooms, reconstituted
1/2 tablespoon each thyme, basil
1 teaspoon salt
1/2 teaspoon pepper
1 teaspoon Worcestershire sauce
1 teaspoon horseradish

Sauté meat until gray. Add milk; stir until thickened. Add remaining ingredients except cheese; simmer five minutes. Add cheese a little at a time, stirring constantly. Add mushrooms and cooked spaghetti.

SPAGHETTI CARBONARA

Courtesy of YACHT HENDRIETTEA oneburner, two-pot transatlantic meal. This lovely, easily prepared dish, is esteemed throughout Italy. I learned the recipe from a Belgian girl one cold, windy evening. We were harbor-bound in Estapona, a little port not far from Gibraltar, waiting for a vicious Levanter to blow itself out.

There was no fresh food left in the boat, the nearest store was a few miles away, and we really didn't feel like another evening of bacon and eggs. Then along came Françoise, whose very presence seemed to make that gloomy day brighter. "If you have bacon and eggs," she said, "Why not have spaghetti carbonara?" And so we did.

1/2 pound bacon
3 eggs, beaten
1 pound cooked pasta
1 cup Parmesan cheese, grated
1/4 cup cooking oil
6 cloves garlic, chopped

Fry bacon, cut into one-inch squares. Reserve. Boil and drain spaghetti. Combine all other ingredients and toss.

Broccoli, Mushroom Penne

3 cups broccoli, chopped
1 cup dried mushrooms, reconstituted
1 bulb garlic, peeled
1/2 cup olive oil
1/2 cup walnuts, chopped
1/4 stick butter
1 cup feta cheese, crumbled
2 cups Parmesan cheese

Cut the broccoli into small florets. Peel and chop the stems. Add two tablespoons of oil to pan and fry broccoli over high heat, drizzling in a little water. When the broccoli gets soft, add the garlic and brown. Add the nuts and toss for a few minutes. Add the penne, butter and remaining oil and toss. Add the feta and toss. Serve and sprinkle with Parmesan cheese. Delicious.

BASIC MACARONI AND CHEESE

This traditional dish is usually baked, and we have included baking instructions for those who have an oven. It can also be prepared on top of the stove. You can dump a can of tuna or salmon into this as a variant. Also add fried, crumbled bacon, ham, smoked oysters or shrimp.

1 pound macaroni, cooked
2 cups mild cheese such as American, cheddar, Gruyère or gouda, grated

Choen, Morocco

2 eggs, beaten into milk
1 cup milk
2 tablespoons butter
pinch of salt, pepper, paprika

Combine ingredients in pot: reserve some cheese for top. Mix thoroughly. Heat until just bubbling. Sprinkle with cheese and butter dots; bake until cheese is browned or heat until cheese melts.

If you do not have an oven, simmer over low heat, stirring frequently, for five minutes until cheese is melted. Do not let mixture thicken excessively; add milk if it does. Sprinkle generously with cheese and butter dots; cover until cheese melts.

CLAM AND TOMATO SAUCE

The Italians are extremely fond of this sauce which they make with small cockles or wedge shells. Served after a crisp green salad and helped along with a good bottle of Pino Grigio, well-prepared spaghetti della vongola is dangerously addictive. We came to know and love this sauce when our sloop, *Fire Witch* was moored for the winter in the Tiber River, about ten miles from Rome.

We visited the Club Nautico restaurant several nights a week just to have a plate of **spaghetti della vongola**. The restaurant was at the mouth of the Tiber river and the clams came from the delta. The club was at the end of a long and dark dirt road, muddy as a swamp when it rained (which was often), and full of holes. There was always a mean dog somewhere along its length which necessitated carrying an oar. In addition, motorists heading down this unlit quagmire held the popular Italian belief that the ride would be smoother if you just go fast enough to keep the tires out of the holes, say about 100 miles per hour. This meant that when we spotted headlights coming in our direction, the safest and possibly only way to survive was to hurl one's self into the tall, wet marsh grass that grew beside the road.

Consequently, we often arrived at Club Nautico wet, bedraggled, and ravenous. The clams were fresh and alive, living happily in a big pot full of sea water. They were speedily transformed into this Epicurean delight by the matron of the house while we sipped our Cinzano and tuned our appetites.

Then came the spaghetti, well covered at our request with the lovely vongola sauce. A lovely salad invariably followed, consisting of several kinds of lettuce, escarole, sliced fennel, onion, sweet olives, garlic oil dressing with slices of fresh Italian bread and mozzarella cheese on the side.

Walter, the waiter, always the paragon of diplomacy, would then saunter over with a huge, two-liter (one-half gallon) fiasco of wine and suggest we help ourselves. We always did. By the time we had our espresso, a dish of wonderful chocolate ice cream, and a generous shot of the sweet Italian anise liqueur, Sambuca, we were feeling no pain; even the mean dog on the long walk home could not ruin the night.

SPAGHETTI della VONGOLA (Red Sauce)

Any type of sweet, tender clam may be used; but if the meat is from a larger, tougher clam, grind it, reserving the liquid. Canned clams, including cockles, may also be used. Add them a few minutes before serving, cooking them just enough to warm the meat. Their flavor is definitely wounded in the canning process, but a few drops of lemon restores some of the loss. Small clams, such as wedge shells, may be added unshelled to the sauce, leaving the individual diner the fun of sucking the meaty morsels free.

2 pounds small clams, steamed, juice reserved
1/2 fennel bulb or a pinch of fennel seed
4 shallots or 1 large onion, peeled into leaves
8 garlic cloves, smashed
1/2 cup parsley, chopped
1 cup celery, chopped fine
4 tomatoes, peeled, seeded, chopped, squeezed
2 tablespoons tomato paste
1/2 cup clam juice
2 tablespoons butter
2 tablespoons each oregano, thyme, basil, dill
1/2 cup white wine

Fry onions, garlic, fennel in sauce pan. When garlic begins to turn golden, add all other ingredients except parsley. Simmer over low heat for fifteen minutes, stirring occasionally. Add clams. Simmer ten minutes, stirring occasionally. Garnish with parsley.

SPAGHETTI DELLA VONGOLA (WHITE SAUCE)

Same as above but omit the tomatoes, tomato paste. Add a few chick peas, thicken with a *roux*.

Chicken livers and tomatoes

1 pound chicken livers, chopped and dredged in flour with 1 teaspoon paprika
1/2 cup olive oil
6 Italian tomatoes, peeled, seeded, chopped
1/2 cup balsamic vinegar
1/2 cup chicken stock
1/2 cup dry red wine
1 teaspoon dried rosemary
3 cups penne or pasta twists, cooked

Sauté livers in oil over high heat until browned. Reserve. Add remaining ingredients except pasta and simmer ten minutes. Add livers and heat until thickened. Add pasta and toss.

LASAGNA

Lasagna is traditionally baked in the oven and you know our general preference for not baking things on a boat. On the other hand, lasagna ingredients are all precooked, so the oven's job is to heat them and marry the flavors. If you do not make a lasagna too thick it can be heated in a pan. We find that a two-layer lasagna made from hot ingredients and not more than one-inch thick will heat up over a low flame in about twenty minutes.

Meat Sauce lasagna

3-4 cups Captain's Meat and Mushroom Sauce (page 205)
1 cup marinara sauce
3 cups ricotta cheese
1 cup cooked spinach, chopped
1-1/2 cups each Parmesan and mozzarella cheese
1/2 teaspoon nutmeg
8 large lasagne noodles (to make two layers), cooked (about 12 minutes)
olive oil

Combine the spinach, Parmesan and mozzarella. Reserve. Oil the pot and add the tomato sauce, spreading it evenly over the bottom. Add the meat sauce. Add a layer of noodles. Add the spinach mixture. Add a layer of ricotta. Repeat, adding the tomato sauce last. Sprinkle with remaining Parmesan and mozzarella. Cover and bake forty minutes at moderate heat. Allow to rest ten to fifteen minutes before serving.

RICE

Rice is an essential in the cruising pantry because of its durability and long shelf life. Our favorite rice recipe calls for pressure cooked brown rice in a rich stock. After cooking, fried onions, mushrooms and vegetables are added. Any of the pasta sauces described in this chapter can be made with rice or rice can be mixed with pasta.

There are thousands of varieties of rice, but we are more interested in how to cook them, rather than their names, so we classify them as brown or white, long grain, round or short grain. Each has slightly different properties which are distinct.

TYPES OF RICE

Brown, long grain: Flavorful, chewy, slow cooking rice we use in side dishes or as a bed for meat, fish or fowl. We always pressure cook brown rice in stock.

Brown, short grain: Our favorite for soups and stews.

White, long grain: Bland, quick cooking, fluffy rice good for serving with highly spiced dishes.

White, oval: More meaty than other shapes, this is the classic Japanese rice, which they serve plain. We also add oval rice to soups and stews where it cooks into a mush and acts as a thickener.

White short grain: A fast-cooking rice popular in US oriental restaurants. It cooks quickly and is often made as a sticky rice ball (see pages which follow).

Wild rice: Wild rice is a grain which grows in a swamp or marsh. It has a distinct flavor which influences the taste if it cooks with other rice. Wild rice takes as long to cook as brown rice. It can also be cooked separately and mixed results in contrasting flavors.

Milling makes brown rice into white rice by removing its tough, golden-brown **husk**. Removing the husk greatly reduces cooking time and results in a lighter, fluffier dish, but the chewy husk adds body and is rich in vitamin B1. People who rely on rice as their principle food usually eat brown rice. Substitution of white rice in their diet causes a vitamin deficiency called Beriberi. The diet of most modern sailors rarely consists mainly of rice, so you can eat brown or white rice without any dietary consequences whatever.

PREPARATION AND STORAGE

CONTAINERS: Package rice in quart jars rather than gallon bottles to reduce the chance of losing it all to mold or insect pests. Stores well in a vacuum pack.

RICE PESTS: Weevils in the rice: immediately after purchasing rice, put rice in a big pan and bake it at 400° F. for about ten minutes, stirring occasionally or zap it in the microwave for a minute or two. This process kills the weevils and their eggs. These little devils lay tiny eggs, so examining the rice will not ensure they aren't there. Weevils make the rice taste bitter but they are not poisonous. Do not store bulk rice in large containers as it will all be lost if contaminated.

STONES: In developing countries rice, grains and beans will occasionally have small stones mixed in. It doesn't take many to ruin your meal, especially if you break a tooth. After purchasing, pour the rice into a tray or onto a table and examine it before storing. Stones usually migrate to the bottom of a sack. Check there. When you pour rice into

boiling water, listen for a "clunk," indicating the presence of a stone.

COOKING RICE

WASHING: Packaged rice, particularly white rice is coated with rice powder which thickens when cooked and makes the rice grains stick together.

Sticky rice is made by cooking unwashed white rice until its moisture is absorbed. The rice flour acts as a binder. Sticky rice is very popular because of its rubbery consistency and it is also easier to eat, particularly with chop sticks. Add two cups of water per three cups of rice. Simmer over low heat until water is absorbed, about twenty minutes. Turn off and allow to sit at least fifteen minutes. Do not stir.

If you want **fluffy rice**, wash it four or five times in hot water, or better, boil it in water for a minute or two, discard the water and rinse several times in cold water. You can use sea water for this process but do not cook the rice in sea water as it makes the rice taste bitter.

LIQUID REQUIREMENT: The cooking time and liquid requirement of each kind is influenced by age, the variety, and how much it has been milled. Most rice you will purchase requires **1-3/4 to 2-1/2 cups water per cup of rice**. Rice with a greenish tint is very fresh and needs 1-3/4 cups of water per cup of rice. Aged rice is very dry and needs more liquid. If excess liquid has been added you can (1) add pasta and cook, allowing pasta to absorb excess liquid (2) pour off the excess and allow to stand covered for twenty minutes.

BOILING TIME: **Brown rice** generally takes eighteen minutes in a pressure cooker or fifty minutes in a pot but every sack varies and you will soon know how long it takes to cook your particular rice. You can cook brown rice and small dry beans (except black beans) together and they will finish together. Lentils and split peas overcook before brown rice is done. Limas and big beans take longer to cook than rice. Their cooking time can be equalized by soaking overnight.

The boiling time of **white rice** varies tremendously but is normally about **twenty to thirty minutes**.

Instant white rice is partially pre cooked. Just pour it into boiling water, add the lid, turn off the heat and wait. Some packaged rice dishes contain slightly precooked rice and this reduces the usual boiling time. Follow the directions on the package. In addition, you will be stocking a quantity of rice and will soon know how long it takes to cook.

FRYING RICE: **Pre-frying** rice keeps the granules separate when they are boiled, producing a light taste. Thoroughly wash the rice and cover it with water. Allow to stand twenty minutes. Fry a chopped onion or a few shallots in generous oil/butter over high heat until the onion is well browned. Add the rice and cook over medium heat for five to ten minutes, stirring delicately. Add 2-1/2 cups stock and simmer or pressure cook.

Frying after boiling, usually with herbs and vegetables toughens the rice and changes its flavor. Frying in spicy or savory oil is an option. The rice is usually boiled for three-quarters of the normal time until *al denté*, then fried. Use a large fry pan and spread out the rice. This minimizes the amount of turning, which breaks the grains. If the rice is still a little too tough, keep sprinkling in water and allow to finish.

COOKING TECHNIQUES

Two approaches to fluffy rice: (1) add exact amount of water and thoroughly rinsed rice, cook until done; or, (2) add three cups water per cup of rice, cook until done, drain after cooking, wash with boiling water, return to the stove, close lid, heat for a minute or two and let stand for ten minutes.

Combination rice dishes contain rice, beans, stock, vegetables and herbs. We frequently combine a one-third mixture of small dry beans to brown rice and the combined grains finish cooking at the same time. This combination has nutritional advantages and also makes you feel more satisfied at the end of the meal if you are "vegging" it.

RICE WITH PASTA, MIXED GRAINS AND VEGETABLES

We eat some variation of this dish at least three times a week. In this recipe we make a stock the rice cooks in.

2 tablespoons olive oil
2 medium onions, chopped
1 cup long grain brown rice
1/3 cups small dried beans
1/2 cup pasta twists
1 can chicken consommé
1 beer
4 garlic cloves, chopped
1/2 pound chicken scraps
2 onions or leeks
3 carrots
4 stalks celery
1 cup dried mushrooms, reconstituted
soy sauce
large *bouquet garni*
1/4 cup cheddar cheese, grated

Sauté half the chopped vegetables in a pressure cooker pot. When soft, add the mushrooms, sauté a few minutes then dribble on a little soy sauce. Cook until soy is absorbed. Reserve.

Add all other ingredients and remaining vegetables except the cheese. Pressure cook eighteen minutes. Cool. Open pot, remove and discard chicken and vegetables. Add pasta and liquid if needed. Should be like gruel. Simmer until pasta is cooked. Simmer off excess liquid over low heat, lid off. Close, let stand five minutes. Add veggies and toss. Serve and sprinkle cheese over all.

Sometimes we throw two tablespoons curry powder in the pot

CURRIED RICE

2 tablespoons curry paste
1 onion, finely chopped
2 tablespoons oil
1 cup red peppers, chopped
1 cup tomatoes, seeded, chopped
3 hot peppers, seeded, chopped; or 2 tablespoons chili paste
2 tablespoons ginger, minced
1 teaspoon each turmeric, cumin
1 cup vegetables, chopped
6 garlic cloves
1 cup white rice
4 cups hot water

Combine all ingredients and bake in a 350° F. oven for 1-1/2 hours, stirring occasionally. You can also pressure cook for eight minutes. Use three cups water. Baking is better.

RISOTTO (Saffron) RICE

Golden-colored Risotto is a dish in itself or all kinds of vegetables, tomatoes, salami, chicken, duck, lamb, beef, cheese, nuts—whatever—can be added to create your own unique recipes.

1 cup white wine
1 cup dried mushrooms, reconstituted
1 large onion, chopped
1/2 cup olive oil
2 cups long grain rice
6 cups stock
1/2 teaspoon saffron
3 slices bacon, chopped, cooked, drained; or 1 tablespoon beef marrow
salt, pepper, Parmesan cheese

Simmer wine and reconstitute mushrooms in it. Reserve. Heat oil and sauté onions until soft. Add rice and half of stock and simmer adding more stock as needed. Add remaining ingredients and simmer, adding more stock as needed until rice is creamy. Total cooking time is about thirty minutes.

BASIC SPANISH RICE

6 slices of bacon, more If desired
1 cup white rice
1 onion chopped
1 -1/2 cups Italian tomatoes
1/2 cup chicken stock
1/4 cup white wine
3 cloves garlic, chopped
1 green pepper, chopped

Fry bacon until done. Reserve bacon. Add rice and stir until rice is slightly golden. Add tomatoes, wine, garlic, green pepper and stock. Simmer over low heat until rice is cooked. Examine pot but do not stir. Do not let dish dry out; add stock or water as needed.

RICE AND HAM CASSEROLE

1-1/2 cups white rice
1 pound ham diced
oil
2 eggs
1/2 can condensed cream of mushroom soup
1/2 cup milk
1 carrot, small dices
salt and pepper

Boil rice in chicken stock until done. While rice is cooking, dice ham. Brown in oil. Combine eggs, soup, milk , salt, pepper. Reduce heat to low. Add everything together and stir once. All to thicken.

RICE DESSERTS: See pages 274-275.

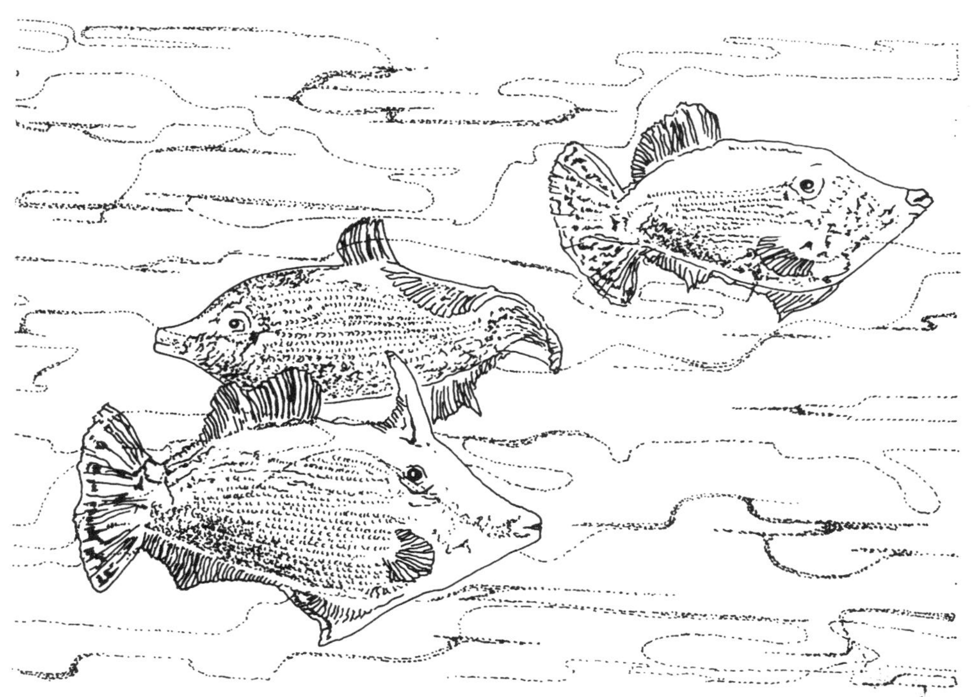

15 Salads

Webster defines a salad as "a dish of lettuce or other vegetables, herbs, meat or fowl, fish, eggs, fruit, etcetera, prepared with various seasonings or dressings." The "etcetera" explains more than all the rest. More informative, perhaps, is the location of this work in the dictionary, between salacious (which means lustful or lusty) and Saladin (who was a sultan). And that is exactly how we think of a salad, as a lusty etceteras fit for a king!

The word "salad" usually brings to mind a combination of lettuce, onions, tomatoes, and a dressing. But what happens when provisioning in some tropic port that has never seen a head of lettuce? Oh, yes, there are many places like that! Know the comfort, then, of the salads that can be created entirely without lettuce or tomatoes, salads that are possible on the last day of an ocean passage, crispy, delightful little nothings that sharpen the appetite and satisfy the soul.

As is true in the home, a salad requires some fresh ingredients but can also include canned items that may be added to fresh vegetables to enliven the dish and add variety. These include canned beans, artichokes packed in seasoned oil, pickled vegetables, olives, bottled mushrooms, and cooked pasta. In addition, tinned fish can turn a vegetable salad into a meal-in-a-bowl. When planning a voyage, don't forget to include these supplies.

EATING SALADS IN DEVELOPING COUNTRIES

"Be sure you don't eat the salads!" How many times we have heard that advice given to travelers. This may be good advice for developing country restaurant salads if the level of cleanliness is unknown—beware the eatery without running water—but we are certain that it need not apply to salads from your own galley. We have gone to some very humble vegetable markets in some very, very humble corners of the world and eaten the leafy vegetables that we bought there. We understand that vegetables sold in developing countries are invariably unwashed and should be thoroughly cleaned. The locals know this and so should you.

Separate lettuce or cabbage leaves before use and rewash them in chlorinated water, even if you washed the entire head before it came aboard. Thoroughly agitate the leaves in chlorinated water, then pat dry. Thin-skinned vegetables, such as tomatoes, should always be washed before use; and other types, such as onions may be skinned.

GROWING SALADS UNDER SAIL

No seagoing chef ever needs to feel that fresh salad makings are unavailable, even on the last day of a long ocean passage. Fast growing seed sprouts can make salads an every day affair. They may be combined with onions, beans, potatoes and/or pasta.

Alfalfa, and **mung bean sprouts** are sold at many U.S. supermarkets. Spicy **radish sprouts** are delicious. The seeds may be purchased in health food shops and some chandleries. They should be vacuum sealed or stored in a tight jar and placed in the bilge. They will last for more than a year this way.

SELECTION: Our favorite seeds are radish and alfalfa.

GROWING: Place several layers of paper towel in the bottom of a plastic storage tray about 8 x 12 x 3 inches. Moisten the towel and sprinkle with a layer of seed sprouts. Continue moistening for an hour. Lift the corner of the paper towel and add about a quarter inch of water. Let stand all day. Then drain off the water, if any; keep the seeds moist for two to four additional days.

The resulting growth produces a highly compact mass of tender, white shoots about an inch long. If kept moist, they will continue to grow at an amazing rate for four to five days and provide several fine salads for four.

END-OF-THE-PASSAGE BLUE WATER SEED SPROUT SALADS

2 cups sprouts
1 onion, sliced into rings
2-3 hard-boiled eggs, sliced
1 small jar artichoke hearts, packed in seasoned oil (add about 2 tablespoons of the oil)
1 teaspoon celery salt
1 can (7 ounces) tuna
3/4 cup mayonnaise
3/4 cup vinagrette (page 218)
1 cup tinned chick peas
1 cup macaroni, cooked and cooled
1/4 cup olive oil
3 teaspoons capers
2 cloves garlic, minced and chopped
salt, pepper, lemon juice

Arrange eggs, artichokes, onions and whatever else you like around the edge of the plate. Toss pasta, the artichoke oil, garlic and some of the mayo. Make an inner ring of the pasta. Make a bed of sprouts in the center. Combine with a few strokes: tuna, lemon juice, capers, salt, pepper, chick peas, mayo and olive oil. Heap tuna on sprouts. Pour vinagrette over all.

SALAD OIL

OLIVE OIL salad dressings have become very fashionable—and fine oil can be very expensive. Superior oil comes from tree-aged olives and this fact is never marked on the bottles. Tree aging coverts the watery juices into flavor, but also increases the risk that a storm will come along and destroy the crop. The risk increases the price.

Olive oil is extracted from olives by pressing them. The terms "**extra virgin, fine virgin, or super fine virgin**" have nothing whatever to do with virginity. They indicate that the oil is the first (virgin) pressing of a batch which will then be pressed again, much harder, crushing the pits, then harder again, using heat and chemicals to extract every possible drop of oil. The harder the olive is pressed, the more green, bitter and "oily tasting" the oil becomes.

Light tasting, delicious olive oil is golden in color and we find that the lighter the color, the finer the taste. Olive oil which is strong flavored can be improved by diluting a small amount of it with a large amount of corn or peanut oil, about one to ten.

NUT OILS, such as walnut and hazelnut are expensive and strong flavored. They are specialty oils which have limited use on a boat and we do not have any recipes which call for them. They do add variety to salads, and variety is the spice of life!

COOKING OIL: Corn and peanut oils are almost neutral in flavor and, as a result, act as a carrier of herb and spice flavors. We use them frequently and, if a recipe says "add 1 cup oil," it is referring to them.

GARLIC OIL: Some people add a few unpeeled cloves of garlic to a bottle of oil but we find that the garlic goes rancid quickly. Make small quantities and use promptly.

Regardless of what you use, remember that dressings are added to a salad just before eating. Tossing the salad and dressing long before the meal is ready produces a wilted salad. A classic method of mixing salad dressing is to pour it into the serving bowl, swirl it around to coat the bowls sides, then add the salad and toss.

VINEGAR

We recommend three types of vinegar for a cruise: balsamic, apple and rice.

BALSAMIC VINEGAR: This is a rich, aged wine vinegar, deep purple in color, whose price increases with the amount of aging. A really outstanding balsamic can cost more than a bottle of good wine. A premium balsamic is loaded with flavor and, if you are going to be a salad dressing dilettante, put your money here. Once you have tasted the intense flavor of balsamic vinegar, your pantry will never be without it. We usually keep a small bottle of balsamic with a big sprig of rosemary in it for added flavor.

APPLE VINEGAR is caramel colored, most commonly used for salads because of its mild flavor. When a recipe calls for an unspecified vinegar it is really apple vinegar to which we refer. White (clear) vinegar is used mainly for pickling and cleaning. It is far too strong for use in salad dressings.

RICE VINEGAR is a mellow, slightly sweet vinegar which we often use in a variety of recipes where we do not want vinegar's acidic quality to dominate.

HERB VINEGARS: Fresh herbs impart their flavor to vinegar and the acid in the vinegar retards decay. A quick swish of a fresh herb in boiling water improves longevity. Nevertheless, you are better off making small quantities to keep flavors fresh. Here are a few suggestions:

- Rosemary, mustard seed, garlic, whole peppers, hot chili peppers
- *Bouquet garni*: Marjoram, thyme, celery seed, several cloves garlic, oregano, bay leaf
- Basil, garlic, walnuts, mustard seed
- Dill, coriander, garlic

SPICY VINEGARS: In addition to herbs, hot peppers may be added to vinegar to make it more spicy. They are first swished in boiling water to kill surface bacteria and yeasts. Fresh peppers, three to four inches long, such as the Dutch red or the red or green Thai pepper can be lightly grilled before use to make it both spicy and smoky. Any of the small dried red peppers, especially the half-inch round Thepin pepper or the half-inch long Pequin peppers are excellent. Adding peppers to vinegar does not make the vinegar as hot as the peppers.

OTHER SALAD DRESSING BASES: yogurt, salsa, liquefied cucumber, lemon juice, tomatillo mush, tomato sauce and cheese.

SALAD DRESSINGS

MAYONNAISE: See page 41.

FIRST OFFICER'S BASIC Vinagrette (FRENCH DRESSING)

Makes about one cup

Combine and shake:
1/3 cup balsamic vinegar
1 teaspoon dry mustard
2 cloves garlic, chopped
3/4 cup olive oil
salt and pepper

Sprinkle with three teaspoons Parmesan cheese. Also add dill, basil or tarragon.

THE CAPTAIN'S ROQUEFORT DRESSING

Makes about two cups

Blenderize and serve chilled:
1/2 cup sour cream
1/2 cup Roquefort or bleu cheese, well crumbled
1 teaspoon Worcestershire sauce
1 clove garlic, minced
juice of 1/2 lemon
salt and pepper

Thin with oil if desired

Author's hotel in Tanjier

THE FIRST OFFICER'S AVOCADO DRESSING

Makes about two cups

Blenderize:
1 ripe avocado
1 teaspoon lemon juice
1/4 cup cooking oil
1/2 cup sour cream (or cream cheese and oil)
2 cloves garlic
pinch of cayenne pepper

YOGURT DRESSING

Combine:
1-1/2 cups plain yogurt
juice of 1/2 lemon
3 teaspoons honey
2 teaspoons dried dill
2 hard-boiled egg whites, grated
salt and pepper

CREAMY GARLIC DRESSING

This version of Spanish alioli was written in the late 9th century and the recipe is probably much older than that, possibly of Egyptian origin—the love of combining eggs, oil and garlic goes way back! The dressing is somewhat similar to fresh mayonnaise, but no attempt is made to create a mayonnaise consistency. Makes about two cups. Also see: Catalan Bombshell in Chapter 16.

Blenderize:
2 cloves garlic, minced
1 teaspoon lemon or lime juice
2 raw egg yolks

Dribble in one cup of olive oil over a period of two minutes. Add two teaspoons boiling water. Whisk furiously. Add salt and pepper to taste. Pour into a cold bowl and chill immediately

THE CAPTAIN'S SPECIAL SALAD DRESSING

Combine:
1 cup vinagrette
1 teaspoon each: oregano, thyme, cumin
1/2 teaspoon lemon juice
1 hard-boiled egg white, grated
1/2 cup cheese, grated
1 cup combined of any or all: chopped parsley, scallion ends, green pepper, black olives
pinch of sugar to taste
salt

Let stand at room temperature for a few hours and chill before use.

HOT GOAT CHEESE NUT DRESSING

This is a good general dressing that goes particularly well over a combination of romaine lettuce, endive, arugla and apples.

1/3 cup cooking oil
juice of 1 lemon
1/4 cup pine nuts, sliced almonds or chopped macadamias
1/2 cup goat cheese, crumbled
2 cloves garlic

Sauté nuts and garlic in oil for two minutes. Remove from heat and allow to cool five minutes. Add remaining ingredients and toss. Use immediately while still warm.

SALAD INGREDIENTS

APPLES can be stored for a long time and are recommended for the long lasting base supply. Apples sold in U.S. supermarkets are waxed and refrigerated. The waxing reduces evaporation, extending the life of the fruit. Waxed apples are shiny and if you buy dull, unwaxed apples you can coat them with banana wax to extend their life.

There are many varieties of apple so choose the one you like best. We like Pippins, which are tart and often used for pies. Because Pippins are tart they make good salad ingredients and can be heaped with all kinds of tinned items such as artichoke hearts, beans, pickled beets, hard-boiled eggs, boiled potato slices, pasta curls and served with a vinagrette.

AVOCADOS are one of our favorite foods and they are rich in vitamins, particularly vitamin C, but they are also the fattiest of all fruits and more than 70% of the calories in an avocado come from fat.

There are many varieties of avocado and the tastiest in the U.S. is the Haas, distinctive because of its granular skin. Other avocados are often more mushy and this is why the **Haas** is popular.

Haas avocados are light green when immature and dark green, almost black when ripe. A dark Haas which is soft to the squeeze is overripe. The ripening process can be retarded for a week or more with refrigeration but longer storage results in a woody texture which is unpleasant. The ripening process can be accelerated if the avocado is stored in a paper bag at room temperature. When buying hard avocados for a voyage, examine them particularly carefully for bruises. Bruised hard avocados invariably rot before ripening.

When an avocado is cut it rapidly begins to turn brown, so cut just before use. Otherwise you can retard the browning of cut pieces by tossing in lemon juice. If a portion is unused surround it tightly with plastic wrap.

KILLER GUACAMOLE

In addition to being great as a dip or a salad dressing guacamole also makes a great fish sauce. Contrary to popular belief, retaining the pit of an avocado in the guacamole will not prevent it from turning brown, but pressing a layer of plastic wrap over the surface will.

Blenderize:
3 cloves garlic
4 teaspoons cooking oil

Then add and thoroughly blenderize:
2 avocados
1/2 cup cream cheese
juice of 1/2 lemon
1 teaspoon salt
hot sauce or taco sauce to taste

CUCUMBERS: Most U.S. cucumbers are sold waxed to retard moisture loss—I will never forget the cucumbers sold in the Abaco Islands (Bahamas) which were grown there, shipped to New Jersey to be waxed, then imported to the Abacos for sale. The secret of selecting a good cucumber is to look for a thin one. Fat ones have big, well developed seeds. Should this not be possible, you can split a cucumber lengthwise and gouge out the seeds with a spoon. Pickling cucumbers make great pickles but they have tough flesh and don't do well in salads.

GARLIC: See page 242.

LETTUCE is one of those ingredients that really must be refrigerated or it will rot within a few days. On the other hand, if you carefully remove all dead or damaged leaves, soak in chlorinated water, air dry, then wrap in a damp towel and store in a plastic vegetable bag, a head of lettuce can last for weeks. **Iceberg** lettuce lasts longest and may survive for two to three weeks in the refrigerator. **Romaine** is the second most durable and **butter lettuce** will just make it through the week.

Escarole is not a lettuce, but it is a tough customer which will survive as long as iceberg lettuce. Escarole is bitter and the dark green part should be trimmed away, leaving the lighter part for the salad. Escarole goes well with apples, fruit and walnuts which mellow its bitterness. A rich, somewhat sweet dressing like Russian or Thousand Island goes well over all.

As a general rule, wash the separated leaves of lettuce before making the salad to remove grit and contaminants. Press the leaves in a towel to dry them.

CAESAR SALAD

Dressing ingredients (combine):
2-3 cloves garlic, crushed, then chopped
l/2 cup olive oil
2 egg whites
1 teaspoon salt
1/2 teaspoon pepper
6 anchovy fillets, crushed
3 teaspoons vinegar
1 teaspoon Dijon mustard
1 teaspoon Worcestershire sauce

Other ingredients:
1/2 cup Parmesan cheese, grated (serve immediately)
2 cup croutons (use breading mix recipe but do not crush)
1 head lettuce
juice of 1/2 lemon

Pour dressing into bowl and whisk. Break lettuce into bite-sized pieces and add to bowl. Sprinkle on a dash of lemon juice and toss. Garnish with croutons. Sprinkle on cheese.

ONIONS: Read more about onions in Chapter 16. No vegetable family is more widely represented in the modern kitchen than the onion. Garlic is a member of the same family, as are chives, shallots, leeks, scallions, and the many varieties of the common onion. Garlic and the dry onion are the most important for the sailor since they are among the longest lasting and most easily stored fresh vegetables.

Both texture and flavor of onions are considerably altered when they are cooked. Strong flavored onions are preferred for cooking since the mild ones, such as Bermudas, become mushy and bland. Marinating onions in vinegar for a day makes them mild, crunchy and extremely delicious. This is useful if your onions are too strong to eat raw.

A most common cooking error is to add raw onions to simmering food. This technique is often used in stews that call for pearl (or boiling) onions, and the result is a mushy, boiled onion whose flavor you know. A mushy boiled onion is OK in the right place but not everywhere. In most recipes, onions should be sautéed in a little oil or butter, until translucent or golden. This toughens them and preserves flavor.

PEELING: Onions are easy to peel, especially in quantity. If they are dipped in boiling water for a few seconds the skins slip off easily. If you get "soap opera eyes" when chopping onions, we can recommend two techniques: chill the onion, but don't freeze; second: wear a diving mask when peeling. Many a bowl of onion soup has been produced in our galley this way.

HEARTS OF PALM: Almost everyone who has tasted hearts of palm has had them canned. Considering how well canned palm hearts are received and the fancy prices that some restaurants charge for them, imagine the superb taste of fresh palm heart. The heart of the palm is the tree core at the top where the green fronds are growing. The heart of a mature palm is about three feet long and four to six inches thick. It is white, tender, and crunchy like celery heart, and very solid. A big heart might weigh twenty pounds.

Should you find a tree overturned by a storm or cut down, seize this fine opportunity to sample one of the gastronomic pinnacles of the salad world. Use an ax to chop away the tough exterior. You know that you've arrived when the white interior begins to be chewable. It will be worth the trouble.

Palm hearts have a very delicate, somewhat nutty flavor. They are excellent in a salad of fresh mung bean sprouts with chopped onion and green pepper, seasoned with lime juice and oil. In a ceviche, they are absolutely delicious. Another extravaganza is to have them as a substitute for water chestnuts in Cantonese recipes. They are delightful with raisins, cinnamon, and a honey-lime dressing. Cooked with cuts of fish in coconut butter and lime, they are a delight. Palm heart is so delicious and easy to store that no vigilant galley gourmet should miss an opportunity to try it.

BELL PEPPERS are served peeled, unpeeled or roasted. The skin is slightly chewy but colorful. The skin also helps hold the shape. **Whole peppers** can be julienned or shredded to make a garnish. **Peeled peppers** are added to cooking food for flavor and color.

Roasted peppers taste different and are soft, almost slimy, but delicious. They need no further cooking. They are usually added at the last moment to cooking food or (more frequently) added to salads for both flavor and taste. Roasted peppers suck up the flavors of a marinade and therefore convey flavor. An extremely delicious red pepper marinade can be found on page 56.

If you love roasted peppers as much as we do you will roast a batch and keep the leftovers covered with olive oil in a little jar. The secret of roasting peppers is to flatten them and broil or grill them quickly over very high heat until the skin blackens, then cool them quickly, skin up on a counter top or on a damp towel. Steam from the cooling pepper raises the burned skin. It peels easily. You can also buy them this way in jars and they are usually quite good.

ROASTED BELL PEPPER SALAD I

This recipe may be served as a side salad or a can of tuna, salmon and chopped hard-boiled eggs can be added to make it into a delicious cold plate meal.

5 bell peppers, preferably of different colors, roasted and skinned
6 medium carrots, quartered lengthwise and blanched in boiling water five minutes
6 cloves garlic, chopped and crushed
1 apple, peeled and sliced thin, brushed with lemon juice
1/2 cup walnuts, chopped
1/2 cup black olives
1 tomato
1 avocado, or 1 cup red beans
1/4 cup walnut or olive oil
1 teaspoon powdered oregano
4 tablespoons spicy vinegar

The peppers: Slice peppers into long strips about a half-inch wide. Pat dry. Add peppers, carrots, oil, garlic, oregano and spicy vinegar. Add salt and pepper to taste. Marinate a few hours, if possible. Arrange the peppers on individual plates, add the other ingredients using the apple as an artistic garnish.

The dressing: Mash a soft cheese, preferably a goat cheese into a half-cup of oil. Add juice of half of a lemon and a pinch of sugar. Add the walnuts and olives. Salt and pepper to taste. Stir vigorously. Pour over all. Sprinkle with balsamic vinegar.

ROASTED BELL PEPPER SALAD II

Add to a sauce pan and simmer ten minutes:
2 cups rice vinegar
1 teaspoon whole peppercorns
1 bay leaf
1 teaspoon hot chile pepper paste
1 teaspoon mustard
2 cloves
1/2 cup sugar
1 apple, skinned and cut into thin slices
3 large red bell peppers, cut into strips
1/4 pound bleu or gorgonzola cheese, crumbled
juice of 1/2 lemon
soy sauce

Simmer the vinegar and seasonings ten minutes, then add apples and peppers. Immediately remove from heat and pour into a shallow pan to cool. Chill. Arrange on plate, sprinkle with chopped walnuts. Add a mound of bleu or gorgonzola cheese sprinkled with a little soy and lemon juice.

TOMATOES: Most supermarket tomatoes are picked green, stored under refrigeration for ages, ripened with ethylene gas and are therefore useful only as decoration. Vine-ripened tomatoes are much more perishable. They cost more but taste better. Tomatoes going on a sea voyage should be of the thick-skinned variety and unblemished. Read more about tomatoes in Chapter 16.

ITALIAN TOMATOES are normally used for cooking since they are much firmer and less juicy than the salad variety. Fresh marinara sauce is made with Italian tomatoes.

USING TOMATOES IN SALADS: Pare away the stem eye and the core beneath. Taste the skin and see if you like it. Some skins are very tough, others tasty and delicate. If you don't like what you taste, peel it off with a parer. We cut the tomato in half and squeeze out most of the seeds and juice which detract from the salad.

TOMATO SALADS

SALAD NIÇOISE

This popular Mediterranean salad requires lots of fresh ingredients, but is a fine change from the usual tossed salad. There are many variations; feel free to add small pieces of raw cauliflower, fresh uncooked green peas, dices of salami or ham, crumbled blue cheese, cooked asparagus tips, or anything that suits your taste.

3 tomatoes, peeled, quartered
1 cucumber, peeled and thinly sliced
8 anchovy fillets, chopped
1 cup pitted black olives
1 cup potatoes, cubed cooked
2 cups lettuce (mixture if available)
1/2 teaspoon pepper

Toss lightly and pour Vinagrette dressing over each portion.

TABOULI SALAD

This Near Eastern dish is a salad of tomatoes, cucumbers and onions served with a mound of seasoned **bulgar wheat**. Bulgar is cracked, processed and precooked. The beauty for the sailor is that the wheat is easy to prepare, stores well and is seasoned with dried herbs. It adds considerable bulk to a salad and is quite satisfying. You can also add tinned tuna and a variety of vegetables to this dish to make it a complete meal.

There are numerous prepared Tabouli mixes on the market which are quite convenient and you may enhance the spicing of them as you wish. Keep in mind that the wheat swells to almost four times its original volume and that one cup of wheat will garnish four to six side salads.

The wheat mixture:
1 cup bulgar wheat
1-1/2 cups boiling water
2 teaspoons salt
1 teaspoon pepper
juice of 1 lemon or 2 limes
2 teaspoons garlic, minced
1/2 cup scallion ends, chopped

4 teaspoons olive oil
2 teaspoons dried mint flakes
1 cup parsley or cilantro, chopped

The tabouli: Combine the wheat, salt, pepper, mint, olive oil in a bowl and toss occasionally for twenty minutes. Add all other ingredients and toss, let stand about an hour at room temperature before serving. You can also refrigerate three to four hours before serving but we prefer the mix at room temperature.

The tabouli salad: Arrange diced, seeded tomatoes and cucumbers around the edges of a large plate. You can also include olives, artichoke hearts, parboiled carrots, red peppers, summer squash, hard-boiled eggs but they are not traditional. Put the tabouli wheat mix in a cup and press it slightly. Invert it quickly over the plate so that it keeps its shape. Fluff up the top of the wheat and sprinkle with a garnish of parsley.

The tabouli salad dressing: Traditionally the salad dressing is garlic crushed into a good olive oil and lemon or lime juice. We have developed a taste for a mustard mayonnaise dressing poured in a few quick ribbons over the vegetables.

MORE SALAD SUGGESTIONS

END-OF-THE-PASSAGE RUSSIAN SALAD

Canned vegetables may be used, but we urge you to include as many fresh ingredients as possible. By garnishing with thinly sliced ham, salami, cheese, or hard-boiled egg halves, this becomes a one-course meal.

Dice and combine: cooked carrots, chilled boiled potato, diced beets, artichoke hearts, olives, pickled onions, etcetera. Garnish with julienned ham. Serve with a vinaigrette or a mayo-based dressing.

CREAMY COLESLAW

Unlike lettuce, cabbage is a vegetable that lasts a week or two without refrigeration and several months in the refrigerator, especially if it has been soaked in chlorinated water and dried. I usually cut the stem to clean it, wrap the head in a damp towel and make sure there is a little towel pad near the fresh-cut stem to give the head moisture. Cabbage is a good source of vitamin C.

The dressing:
1 cup mayonnaise
6 scallions, chopped (green end only)
dash hot sauce
2 teaspoons rice vinegar
juice of 1/2 lemon
2 teaspoons sweet relish
pinch salt and pepper

The salad (toss together):
1/2 medium cabbage, shredded or thinly sliced
1 green pepper, julienned
2 carrots, shredded

CARROT-RAISIN-NUT SALAD

The dressing is traditionally sour cream with lemon juice. Vinaigrette or mustard mayo can also be used.

The salad (combine):
4 carrots, pared into peels
1/2 cup raisins
1/2 cup pecans or walnuts, chopped
2 teaspoons lemon zest

PICKLED BEET SALAD

2-1/2 cups canned chilled pickled beets
1/2 cup white vinegar
1/4 cup beet juice
1 green pepper, julienned
1 small onion
1/2 teaspoon horseradish or dried mustard
salt and pepper
pinch of clove
pinch of sugar

Combine liquids and simmer a few minutes. Cool and pour over beets.

FRESH FRUIT SALAD

If you are short on fresh fruit, this dish may be expanded with drained, canned fruit.

Chop and combine:
4-6 cups mixed fruit
4 teaspoons brown sugar
juice of 1 lemon
1 teaspoon cinnamon

Let stand an hour in refrigerator.

POTATO SALAD NIÇOISE

This is a European version of potato salad. Every open air restaurant along the Mediterranean coast has a big plate of it ready for instant action. It's a sort of emergency ration since the service is often slow.

4 cups potatoes, cooked firm, peeled, diced
1/4 cup rice vinegar
1 cup cooked green beans
3 peeled tomatoes, seeded, chopped
3 teaspoons capers
1/2 cup small black (Greek) olives, pitted
1 cup vinaigrette dressing
3 hard-boiled eggs

Parboil potatoes until firm. Drain water and immediately add vinegar and toss. Cool. Chill other vegetables. Toss and pour Vinaigrette dressing over each portion. Crisscross each portion with four to six anchovy fillets. Garnish with hard-boiled egg and tomatoes.

AMERICAN POTATO SALAD

We love potato skins but not in a potato salad. Traditionally small red potatoes are boiled until firm, after which the skins slip off easily. Boilers resist crumbling and do not become mushy as easily as other varieties. The secret of success is to not overcook the potatoes. People occasionally use leftover boiled potatoes for this recipe, but leftovers are usually too mushy for good results; leftover boiled potatoes do best as hash browns. This salad can be extended with cooked pasta if desired.

3 cups red boilers, boiled firm
3/4 cup vinaigrette dressing
3 hard-boiled eggs, whites chopped, yolks crumbled and reserved
2 cups of any or all: olives, celery, cucumbers
1/4 cup capers
juice of 1/2 lemon

Boil potatoes, skin and immediately marinate in vinaigrette dressing while still warm. Add egg whites, capers and toss. Refrigerate. Combine other vegetables in separate pot and toss in lemon juice. Cool. Pour potato mixture on plate, add dollop of mayonnaise, then add vegetables, combine all with a few quick strokes. Garnish with crumbled egg yolk.

GREEK EGGPLANT SALAD

1 medium eggplant, pricked all over and greased
3 cloves garlic, chopped
1 onion, chopped
juice of 1/2 lemon
1/2 cup olive oil
1/4 cup balsamic vinegar
1/2 teaspoon sugar
1 teaspoon oregano
1/2 cup parsley, chopped
1 tomato, squeezed and chopped into irregular pieces
Greek olives and feta cheese garnish

Grill the eggplant, turning frequently until it is charred all over. Allow eggplant to cool, then peel away the charred skin. Chop the eggplant into small pieces. Cool to room temperature. Combine everything except the garnishes. Add a sugar to balance.

Mound on serving plate. Chill. Sprinkle the tomato around the edge of the plate. Serve with olives and feta cheese.

The Tropic Bird

Ethereal ocean nomad with a tail longer than its body and a cry similar to the human voice. The male courts its mate in flight by stroking her with his long tail. The tropic bird comes to land only to mate and rear its young, then flies off to spend the rest of its time at sea. There is no event more dramatic than to have a tropic bird fly close to the ship's surging rail, look at you and cry its haunting call.

16 Fruits & Vegetables

HAVE YOU HUGGED YOUR VEGETABLES TODAY?

If you love your fruits and vegetables they will love you back. Visit them frequently and try to make them happy. Choosing fruits and vegetables is like choosing a mate. After all, you were meant for each other and will soon be one. When it comes to close relationships, ask yourself *what would my mother say*? Your mother would tell you first of all to choose carefully and not rush into anything. She would hope the Chosen One would not only have good prospects but that he or she was also attractive, smelled good and was sweet. Your mother is right and you'd better listen to her.

FRESHNESS

In developing country markets you usually get what you see. If it looks fresh, it probably is fresh. It was probably picked at four a.m. that morning and brought to market on a donkey. In first world supermarkets deception is a normal part of the selling strategy. Fruits and vegetables are frequently big, gorgeous, inviting—but may be older than some of your children and often have miserable flavor. All kinds of things have been done to reduce spoilage and improve looks but most of those "improvements" benefit the seller, not you.

Since you are buying for a sea voyage you must be much more careful than normal in selecting fresh food. Once the vessel leaves the dock you can't make exchanges! Everything must be smelled, tasted and examined before you buy. Think of plastic wrappers as containers, not deterrents. Dive right in and check things out. Don't be a sissy, you're an adventurer! Become a fruit and vegetable guerrilla; wage war against indifferent taste.

SELECTING FRUIT

GENERAL ADVICE: Fruit can frequently be purchased "green," a few days or a week away from ripening. Most green fruit can be held in the refrigerator for an additional week or two without excessively sacrificing flavor. **Blemished green fruit** usually rots before ripening. Almost without exception fruit should be washed in chlorinated water (1 cap of bleach per bucket of water) and sun dried to kill surface mold prior to storage.

APPLES

Cut open, taste, smell and squeeze. Fresh apples are aromatic and juice should run from the cut surface when squeezed. Avoid apples with soft spots or blemishes. Shiny apples usually indicate that they have been waxed. This prevents drying out. Wrap apples in aluminium foil to extend their life.

APRICOTS

Purchase firm, not rock hard. Rub skin and smell. No smell, no buy. Avoid blemishes.

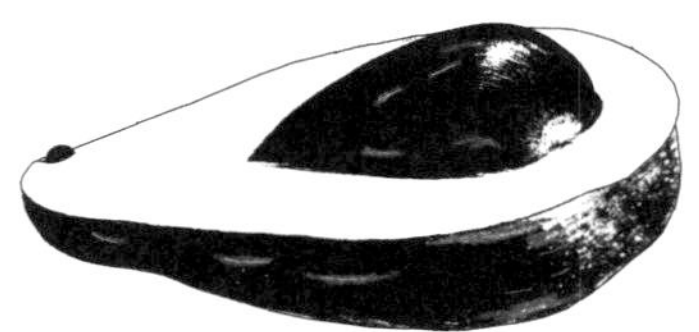

AVOCADOS

Purchase rock hard, as large as possible and unblemished. Allow some to ripen and refrigerate the rest. Avocados held more than about a week in the refrigerator become woody and will not ripen properly.

BANANAS

Bananas purchased in the United States are just a few days away from ripening because they have been subjected to a ripening gas. When bananas are purchased in their country of origin they are incredibly cheap and can take a week to ten days to ripen. When green they can be boiled and eaten like a potato.

Bananas come in many different varieties. The long thin **Cavendish** is the one most commonly found in U.S. supermarkets. The short, fat **Cuban** banana with a reddish brown skin has a more intense banana flavor. All are similarly selected. As bananas ripen the skins develop brown mottling which does not affect their taste. Avoid bananas with soft spots or mold around the stalk. Be sure that they are showing at least some yellow otherwise they may be immature, intended for use as a starchy vegetable, and may never ripen.

Submerge your bananas in water before bringing them aboard. Banana bunches are a favorite hiding place for spiders, especially tarantulas, mice and small snakes. In Africa and Asia they can also conceal much nastier critters, poisonous centipedes and several really dreaded lethal vipers.

Bananas make a joyous sight hanging from the backstay but many get bruised, since they swing madly in a seaway. You are better off cutting them into hands and storing them in a cool, dark place. Accelerate ripening by placing in open paper bag in sun. Refrigerate only after ripening.

BERRIES

Berries must be purchased ripe and should have a pronounced berry smell. No smell no buy, even if big and attractive. Squeeze the box and smell the aroma.

CHERRIES

Cherries when hard and very red are immature and will not ripen before spoiling. Dark red, somewhat softer cherries are mature and ready to eat. Be sure most are mature and examine them for mold. Taste one.

CITRUS FRUIT

Heft the fruit to judge its weight. Imagine the potential weight of a globe of water of similar size. Don't buy light citrus fruit. Skins may be blemished but not moldy. Wash in chlorinated water, sun dry, wrap in aluminum foil.

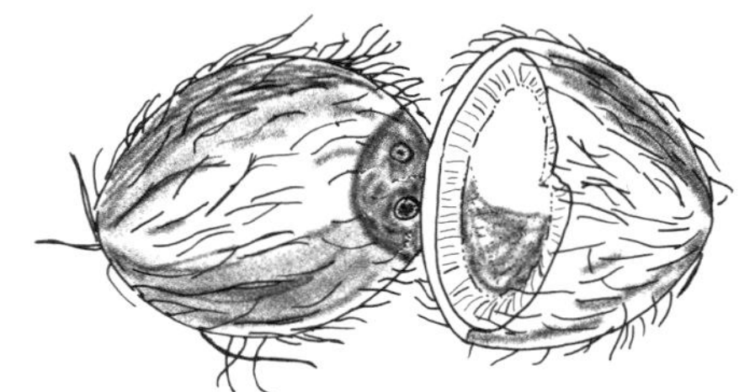

COCONUTS

Green unhusked (white husked) coconuts should be heavy and full of juice with a gelatinous meat. The sloshing sound should therefore not be pronounced since that would indicate a partially filled interior. If there is no sloshing sound at all and the unhusked nut shows no signs of yellow the fruit may be immature.

Brown-husked or unhusked coconuts have a firm flesh which has a pronounced coconut smell. The interior must at be least a third full of juice. The eyes should be dark brown but not black and should be hard. Soft eyes indicates decay. Dry nuts (no sloshing sound) which are sprouting make fine salad. Dry nuts which are not sprouting are inedible. The meat is called *copra* which is used to make soap and confections.

Coconuts travel extremely well and may be stored under the dinghy or in the bilge if it is clean. If possible, coconuts should be obtained green. They may be consumed this way or allowed to turn a mottled yellow which is a sign of maturity. Coconuts with brown husks are quite mature and somewhat past their prime as food.

Green coconut juice: Green coconuts are full of a tart, flavorful, slightly effervescent water which always seems to be cool. It is extremely thirst quenching but has a laxative effect when drunk to excess. Two nuts per day per person is the maximum.

Green coconut meat is gelatinous, mildly flavored, extremely delicious and just begging to be cooked into something like a custard or a chicken stew. Mixed with chopped fruit, honey, lemon, cinnamon with a touch of rum, it is a fine dessert. Added to cooked rice, it imparts its own subtle flavor. Stirred into sauces such as Hollandaise or sour cream, it makes a new creation.

Eating green coconuts: Green coconuts are traditionally eaten "on the half shell." The top is whacked off with a machete, a small spoon-like edge of husk is removed to help eat the delicious jelly. The water is drunk, then the nut is opened to finish the snack.

Coconut milk is a mixture of coconut cream and coconut water. It is the essential heart of good a curry sauce. Coconut milk also comes in powdered form which is very good and also in cans which is naturally sweet and should never be purchased with sugar, except to make drinks. Coconut milk plays an essential part in island cuisine.

Coconut cream: The entire husked nut can be baked for twenty minutes at 350° F. (drain first) and the meat is then grated for use in cooking or desserts. Grated coconut meat is mixed with coconut milk, then squeezed to make coconut cream, which is the heart of a good curry. It can also be purchased canned or freeze dried.

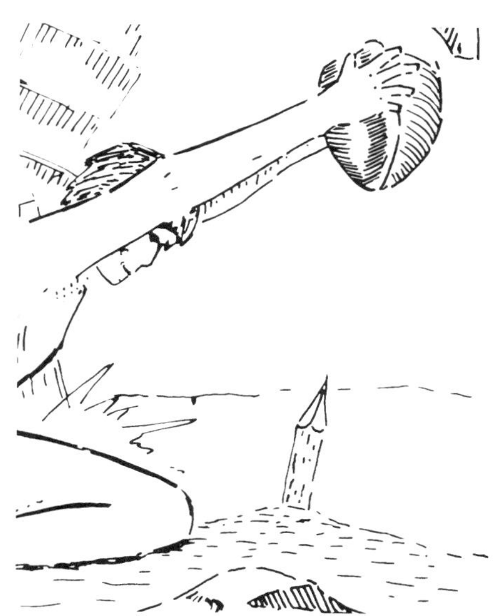

Opening coconuts: Coconuts are hard to open and I do not know a truly effortless method to do so. The Caribbean natives drive a stake into the ground at a forty-five degree angle. The projecting end is sharpened. The stake is straddled; the nut is raised high above the head using both hands. With a hard swing, the nut is brought down onto the point of the stake. I have seen a coconut husked in about three seconds this way but always thought I might need my fingers for typing, so I never tried it myself.

A safer method is to first drill out two eyes and drain the juice. Then, whack the nut as hard as possible with a machete, going with the grain. Use the machete imbedded in the husk as a hammer smashing the nut on the ground again and again or hit the machete with a hammer until the nut splits. Another method is to just keep pounding it on the nearest big stone. If you know a better technique, write to me.

GRAPEFRUIT

See Citrus Fruit.

GRAPES

Grapes are covered by a velvet film of yeast which cannot be washed off. Bunched grapes at their peak are still attached to the vine, are firm and bursting with juice. When you find many loose grapes around a bunch this is a sign of maturity. Examine the fallen grapes. The stem spot should not be oozing and be surrounded by healthy-looking skin.

Wash in chlorinated water and sun dry. Cut into bunches. Jam a grape on the stem of each bunch. Store in damp towel or vegetable bag and refrigerate.

LEMONS

See Citrus Fruit.

MANGOS

Mangos must be purchased in the tropics or semi-tropics, they do not like northern latitudes. They dry out and do not ripen if picked green and held in a refrigerator. Buy big ones and wrap in aluminum foil. Refrigerate when ripe, not before.

MELONS

Cantaloupe and similar melons: Rub the stem spot and smell. No smell no buy. Shake the melon and listen for a sloshing sound. Sloshing indicates that the melon is overripe. An old farmer's adage is *always pick an ugly melon*. I don't know why this works but it does.

Watermelons are sounded with a knuckle and sound hollow when mature but I do not know how to convey the sound to you in print. Bonk, bonk. The white spot (where the melon has rested on the ground) has a yellowish cast when the fruit is mature.

PEACHES AND PEARS

Peaches do not travel well. Ripe peaches have a short shelf life. Immature peaches bruise easily and often rot as they ripen.

PLUMS

Plums travel better than peaches or pears and are less easily bruised. Rock hard plums are immature and probably will not ripen. Firm plums are within a few days of ripening which can be retarded by refrigeration. Cut one open before buying and look for brownish discoloration. That is a sign of either refrigerator burn or bruising.

PINEAPPLES

Buy them large and green, wash thoroughly and dry. Store a few in the fridge, others in a dry place. Ready when about two-thirds yellow. From hard green to yellow ripe can take a week unrefrigerated and several weeks if refrigerated.

PRICKLY PEARS

Prickly pears are the seed pods of a cactus, similar in character to pomegranates. Prickly pears are fiery red when ripe. The surface of the fruit is covered with clumps of tiny spines which should be washed away with an abrasive sponge or pared off as they easily lodge in tender gum tissue and the tongue. The meat of the fruit is bright red, extremely flavorful, sweet and tart. Traditionally the fruit is eaten including the seeds which are then spit out.

Sailors occasionally find vast fields of prickly pears on deserted islands which may be harvested by the bucket-full. Keep in mind that prickly pears are the favorite food of wild boar. As the fruit rots it ferments and the boar become quite drunk and extremely aggressive. One would not wish to encounter one—unarmed—while hip deep in cactus.

ABOUT VEGETABLES

PREPARATION FOR STORAGE: Some vegetables should be soaked and agitated for a few minutes in chlorinated water (one cap of bleach per bucket of water) and sun dried. This reduces loss to rot and retards the taste of mold which is associated with long storage. Other vegetables are best stored dry and some prefer being dirty, meaning with the soil still clinging to them. Vegetables should usually be sun dried for a few hours before storage. This exposes the skin to x-rays which kills mold and the sunlight evaporates lingering moisture which may harbor bacteria.

STORAGE: If the vegetable has a stem, re-cut it exposing a fresh cross section and rest it on a damp towel. When moistening a towel for this purpose dissolve an aspirin in a cup of water and use the acidified water which discourages decay. Towels dampened with acidified water can be wrapped around many vegetables to cool them and reduce moisture loss. This also extends their life.

FRESH HERBS can be stored with their stems in a jar of acidified water. Bunches of herbs and many vegetables can be wrapped in a damp towel and layered in a tray to prevent their drying out.

REFRIGERATED VEGETABLES last much longer than those stored at room temperature. Therefore unrefrigerated vegetables should be eaten first. Plastic vegetable bags have little holes in them to allow the venting off of gasses generated by the vegetables. This reduces loss caused by mold and rot. If vegetable bags are unavailable leave bags open or prick them.

COOKING PHILOSOPHY: In days gone by people often overcooked vegetables. I have vivid memories of my grandmother's brussels sprouts, which arrived at the table in uninviting shades of gray-green, mashed to a pulp, mixed with over-boiled pearl onions and topped with a heart-stopping lump of butter.

We prefer to serve vegetables "al denté," which means offering a bit of resistance to the teeth. To achieve this we prefer to **stir-fry** or **sauté** vegetables very quickly in a very hot pan. **Pressure cooking** has long been recommended as a vegetable cooking technique because it uses very little water and the vegetable cooks very fast. Pressure cooking delicate vegetables is impractical since it is difficult to estimate their brief cooking time. Less delicate vegetables are prime candidates for pressure cooking.

COOKING TECHNIQUES: There are four general techniques for cooking vegetables: steaming, stir frying, braising, and baking. The first three techniques are the fastest and therefore generally preferred. **Boiling** has fallen out of fashion because it produces a mushy product and causes vitamin loss. **Blanching** means boiling for a few minutes to half cook the vegetable, preparing it for finishing in some other way.

STEAMING requires the vegetable to be above boiling water. The vegetables rest on a steam tray or trivet. Steaming achieves the cooking effect of boiling without dissolving out vitamins.

STIR FRYING is a favorite because it is quick and preserves food value but it requires high heat. To stir fry we carry a ten inch propane burner ring designed to melt lead. With the valve wide open the ensuing flame envelopes the pan. This is the kind of heat real chefs love! Vegetables are cut into small pieces to decrease their cooking time. The vegetable is usually blanched, then stir fried in peanut oil which can stand high heat. Never stir fry with butter or margarine because they burn .

Stir frying consists of cooking the sliced vegetable in a scant amount of very hot vegetable oil (1 or 2 teaspoons). The vegetables are tossed frequently to avoid burning. Stir frying cooks vegetables in 3 to 5 minutes and retains their crispness. A fine mixed vegetable dish can be created if vegetables are added to the pan in the proper order, the most delicate added last.

BRAISING in oil is an uncommon but excellent technique similar to stir frying. The vegetable is first fried in a little oil/butter to firm it, frequently with garlic, herbs or spices. Then a little water is added, a spoonful at a time and the pan tightly covered. This creates an atmosphere of superheated steam.

FREEZE DRIED VEGETABLES are often as tasty and nutritious as frozen vegetables. Peas, green beans, and carrots taste best, last longest, need no special handling, and are easily cooked. They are expensive if purchased in outdoor stores as yacht or trail food, but the cost for commercial quantities is significantly less.

SAUCES: A variety of excellent sauces and mayonnaises can be found in Chapter 3 which can be served with vegetables. Tomato salsa and cucumber dressing, both discussed in this chapter, make fine low-cal vegetable sauces which are also very low in fat. Salad dressings also make good sauces.

VEGETABLES A TO Z

The vegetables in the following sections are those which are most commonly available throughout the temperate and semi-tropical climates of the world—the warm, lovely places where most sailors cruise. Each section has been arranged to discuss the selection, preparation and storage of each vegetable. All of these subjects are condensed into the word "about" (as in Artichokes, about) in the index. The "about" section is followed by recipes in which the particular vegetable dominates. Consult the index for other suggestions.

ARTICHOKES

PURCHASING: Artichokes with dark, shriveled stems are old. If a choke looks old it is old. Over mature 'chokes are open and have a spongy feel. If the stem cut looks fresh the choke is usually fresh. Buy the biggest chokes as they have the biggest hearts. **Baby artichokes** are immature and the hairy choke inside is not developed. Small chokes are typically braised whole in a little oil.

JARRED: Artichokes are sold packed in oil and spices and are succulent. Tinned artichokes are packed in water are bland. Jarred chokes are very good in salads and also in pasta dishes. They can also be baked.

STORING: Artichokes will last a week at room temperature and two weeks if refrigerated. Sun dry to retard mold. Recut the stem with stainless knife exposing a fresh cross section. Keep stem moist with acidified water. Chokes should be stored upright in a cool, dark spot. Examine the stem pack and add more water as needed.

COOKING ARTICHOKES

1. Cook in non-stick or stainless pot as iron discolors choke. Pack chokes together in pot to avoid rolling.
2. Pull off any brown or leathery leaves near bottom before cooking.
3. Place stem down in a pot with a half to three-quarters of an inch of water. Squeeze a lemon over them. Add pinch of salt. Add more water as needed.
4. Steam for about thirty to thirty-five minutes until a fork pushes easily into the stem. Leaves should resist slightly when pulled off. A sickly green color and leaves which fall off to the touch indicates overcooking.
5. Remove from pot and allow to drain.

EATING ARTICHOKES: Most of the choke is tough and inedible. Only the heart (the bottom and stem) and the small lump of flesh at the base of each leaf are tender and delicious. Small, white or purplish (inedible) transparent leaves at the center of the flower conceal hairs which if eaten will make you—choke. The hairs have little hooks which can catch in the throat and are very irritating. The outer leaves are usually tough, and at least one or two rows should be discarded. The remaining leaves are pulled off one at a time, dipped in sauce, and the little lump of flesh on the inside base of each leaf is eaten. This is accomplished by placing the base of the leaf in your mouth, holding it with the teeth, then pulling it out. The flesh remains in your mouth while the rest is discarded.

The heart of the artichoke, located at its base, is tender and very delicious. Scrape or cut away the immature leaves and the hairy choke. Be sure to remove all of the hair. Rinse heart. Dip in sauce and enjoy. Artichokes can be cooked, then the transparent leaves and choke removed (with a grapefruit knife or spoon) and the hollow stuffed with whatever—such as fish salad.

ARTICHOKE SAUCES: The classic sauce is made by mixing your own combination of hot, melted butter, lemon, grated Parmesan cheese. Other outstanding sauces are: Hollandaise, fresh mayonnaise, mustard or garlic mayonnaise, vinagrette, or good old melted butter. Another outstanding sauce consists of sour cream, dill and lemon juice.

ASPARAGUS

Asparagus when fresh is bright green, crisp and breaks with a snap. Limp stems, shriveled stalks, a khaki color, opening tips or a spongy consistency are a bad sign. Also, rub the tops and smell. Should not smell rotten. Look for hints of slime in the buds. **Thin asparagus** is tender and delicious but does not store well. **White asparagus**, usually found in Europe, has been protected from the sun while growing by heaping cinders around the stalks. It is delicious but expensive. **Thick asparagus** is usually tough but can be made very tender by paring before cooking.

STORING: If properly prepared, asparagus will last a week without refrigeration. Refrigeration makes them last several weeks. To prepare for storage, tie bunch with a string for ease of handling. Do not wash but sun dry. Cut off the bottom of each bunch, exposing a live cross section. Store the bunches upright in a glass of water or on a damp cloth.

PREPARING: Trim to about six inches in length. Thick asparagus has a tough outer rind which should be pared away before cooking. Peel from bottom toward top. Peel bottoms more.

COOKING: Asparagus is best if cooked until crisp, no more. **Simmer** in butter/oil, garlic and a few dribbles of water. Add more water a dribble at a time to prevent scorching. **Steam** using a cooking trivet to keep vegetable above water. Bundle individual servings with a rubber band. If you have the right pot, cook upright with stems down. Takes about three minutes for thin ones, five for medium and eight for thick. Remove from pot instantly as soon as done as they overcook easily. **Stir-fry** with julienned carrots or squash in peanut oil with a dash of soy sauce, hot sauce, butter, garlic. **Blanch** two minutes before stir frying. Garnish with scallions.

SAUCES AND GARNISHES: Butter with lemon juice, sautéed sliced almonds, reconstituted or fried fresh mushrooms, ginger, capers, olives, Hollandaise sauce, fresh garlic mayonnaise.

BEANS (GREEN)

SELECTING: fresh beans are dark green and snap crisply. Green beans with a pronounced "string" are over ripe. Beans in developing countries often have "strings" which must be removed before cooking. Hybridized beans as are found in the U.S. do not need to be de-stringed. Break sample bean and taste. Should not be bitter or dry. Freeze dried green beans aren't bad. Thin green beans are called *haricots verts* (which is French for green beans). They are quite delicious but expensive and do not store well. Canned green beans are awful.

STORING: Wash and sun dry. Store in vegetable bag and refrigerate up to three weeks or place in tray and cover with a damp towel if stored at room temperature.

COOKING: Pan steam like asparagus or steam for five to eight minutes and serve with butter, hollandaise, cheese sauce, fried bacon and bread crumbs, nuts sautéed in butter or sprinkled with Parmesan cheese.

Serve cold, in a salad when mixed with onions, black olives, anchovies, sautéed mushrooms, and cheese. They improve canned corn and are a welcome addition to several canned soups, such as chicken noodle, minestrone, and split pea. Cooking in sea water makes them bitter.

GREEN BEAN SUGGESTIONS: Parboil green beans for three minutes, then sauté with chopped onions, carrots, a pinch of marjoram, salt, and pepper. Marinated green beans: Parboil four minutes, marinate overnight in vinegar, thyme, celery seed, garlic and oil with chopped, raw onions.

Author in Algiers

GREEN BEAN, BACON, ONION AND POTATO CASSEROLE IN CHEESE SAUCE

1 pound green beans, blanched 3 minutes
4 onions, sliced
2 red or green peppers, chopped
3 medium baking potatoes, peeled, sliced into 1/8-inch rounds, blanched 3 minutes
3 teaspoons butter
6 slices bacon, chopped
1-1/2 cups milk with 1 teaspoon salt and a pinch of pepper added
1/2 cup Parmesan or sharp cheddar cheese, grated

Fry bacon in baking pot, reserve bacon, rub pot sides with fat. Drain excess. Blanch beans and potatoes Layer vegetables in pot, covering each layer with milk/cheese. Bake at 375° F. for about forty minutes until sauce bubbles for about eight minutes. Sprinkle with bacon and serve.

PAN ROASTED BEANS AND POTATOES

3/4 pound green beans
1 pound small boilers, quartered
1 teaspoon each celery seed, salt
pinch of fennel seed, pepper

Blanch beans and potatoes for four minutes in fry pan and reserve. Oil the pan and fry the beans, potatoes and herbs until potatoes begin to brown

BEANS (LIMA)

Fresh baby lima beans with salt and butter are a real treat. We are not fond of dried limas which are bland and mushy. Fresh lima beans may be hulled by slitting the edge of the pod. The beans pop out easily. The pods account for almost fifty percent of the weight. Baby limas may be steamed in a little water for fifteen minutes or pressure cooked for just two minutes.

LIMA BEANS IN TOMATO SAUCE

2 cups lima beans
1 cup canned Italian tomatoes
2 cloves garlic, chopped
1 cup olive oil
water to cover

Simmer ingredients, lid off, until liquid thickens, about twenty minutes. Add to the pot: two teaspoons butter, a teaspoon celery seed, a pinch each of salt and pepper. Simmer until beans are soft, adding water if necessary. Season to taste.

BEETS

SELECTION: buy big ones which last longer, or small ones which are more tender. Buy them dirty if possible. Do not wash. Beets are very delicate. Never buy bruised beets and handle with care. Beets with greens attached are fresher. Beets without greens should have a stump, otherwise they have bled and go stale quickly. Do not cut flush. Yellowed leaves are a sign of age. Fresh beets bleed when cut and appear very moist.

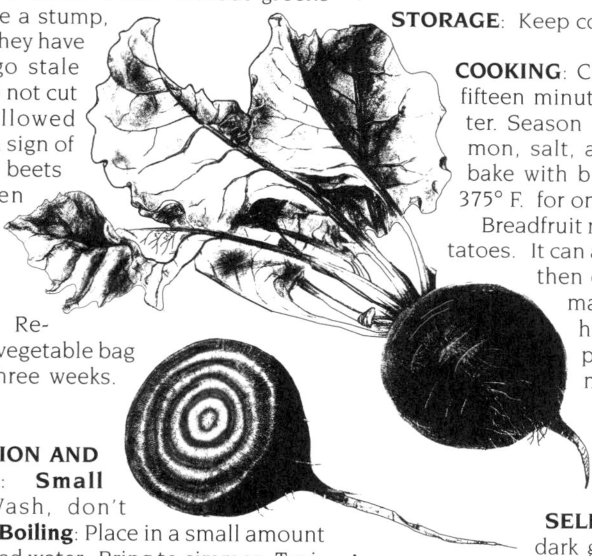

STORING: Refrigerate in vegetable bag for up to three weeks. Keep dry.

PREPARATION AND COOKING: **Small beets**: Wash, don't break skin. **Boiling**: Place in a small amount of cold, salted water. Bring to simmer. Typical 1-1/2 inch beet cooks in about thirty minutes. Large ones may be **pressure cooked** for ten minutes. Do not pierce with fork to test. Remove one from pot and squeeze. Should be slightly soft. Cool in cold water or if used in a salad, refrigerate before skinning. Cool beets bleed less when skinned. Skins slip off easily.

Large beets: Peel and slice. Cook in a small amount of water containing brown sugar, white sugar and lemon juice to taste. The water becomes the sauce. Serve hot with butter or cold in a salad with cucumbers, apples, nuts, in vinaigrette or with soy and mint. **Baking** or **foil steaming** on the grill is better than boiling since the juice concentrates. Blanch in pressure cooker eight minutes. Foil wrap. Bake at 350° for thirty minutes or grill. Test with fork in top. Don't stab to death.

BREADFRUIT

Bread fruit meat is slightly fibrous, light yellow in color, and somewhat sweet. Breadfruit with seeds may be eaten raw and the seeds roasted like chestnuts. Seedless varieties must be cooked. The tough core is usually removed, either before or after cooking. Mature fruit has a bit of green color. Avoid blemished or pulpy textured specimens.

STORAGE: Keep cool and dry.

COOKING: Cut and pressure cook for fifteen minutes in 1-1/2 cups of water. Season with butter and cinnamon, salt, and pepper or cut and bake with butter and cinnamon at 375° F. for one hour.

Breadfruit may be mashed, like potatoes. It can also be French fried and then dipped into **poi**, a dish made from **taro root** that has been baked, pounded, and fermented.

BROCCOLI

SELECTION: Fresh color is dark green in tight bundles. Spongy head is bad. Mottled yellow buds are a sure sign of over maturity.

STORAGE: Wash and sun dry. Cut stem to create fresh cross section. Cover stem with paper towel held with rubber band. Keep towel damp. Refrigerate in vegetable bag. Lasts about two weeks.

COOKING: Pan roast with garlic and oil. Delicious and classic. Cut into small florets and steam. Drop into boiling water for three minutes. Stems are delicious and may be the tastiest part of the broccoli. Peel vigorously to remove fibrous sheath, slice and stir fry. Broccoli is also good with other vegetables or served cold as a salad with vinaigrette. Broccoli can also be blanched for two minutes, then baked in a cheese sauce consisting of milk, cheese, lemon juice, salt and pepper. After cooking a pot of broccoli add butter, cheese, hot peppers, mushrooms, sautéed nuts or fried onions and toss.

BRUSSELS SPROUTS

SELECTION: Fresh sprouts are brilliant green, rock hard and have fresh, unblackened stems. Overripe sprouts are large, pale or yellowish and spongy. Small sprouts are best.

STORAGE: Do not wash, store dry in vegetable bag. Best if used within a few days. Brussels will last for weeks but get tougher and more bitter as they age.

PREPARATION: Pare stems, remove withered leaves before cooking. Make deep cuts in stems of big sprouts so the core finishes when the leaves are cooked.

COOKING: Steam six to ten minutes depending on size. Test with fork. Toss with butter, garlic and cheese. Pan roast halves. Use chicken stock instead of water. Toss in butter, garlic oil, hot sauce, etcetera.

BRUSSELS SPROUTS IN WHITE SAUCE

1 quart brussels sprouts, blanched ten minutes
3 cups white sauce (flour, chicken stock, milk)
pinch of nutmeg
juice of 1 lemon
1 cup white cheese, grated

Make the white sauce and thin with milk to a consistency of heavy cream. Bring to a boil and add all ingredients. Reduce heat and simmer until sprouts are done, about five minutes. Serves four.

CABBAGE

WHITE (SAVOY) CABBAGE is highly respected in the galley because of its general availability and long shelf-life. It is an important source of vitamin C, which is more concentrated in cabbage than orange juice. When eaten, raw cabbage supplies roughage, which is particularly important on long passages when other sources of roughage are gone. Sautéed in oil or butter cabbage makes a tasty addition to any meal.

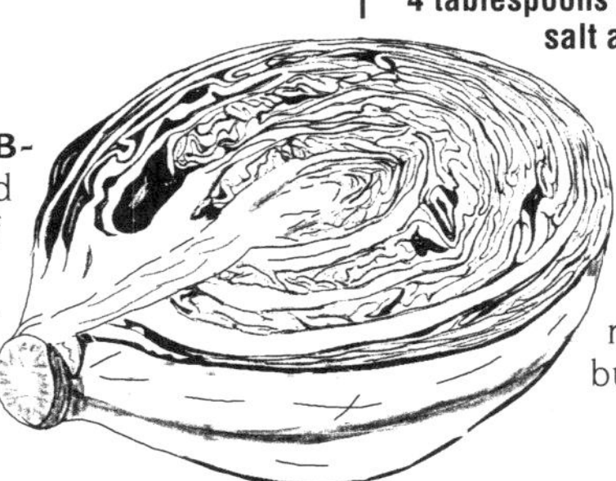

SELECTION: Bigger is better because bigger lasts longer. Should be rock hard and unblemished when outer leaves are pared away.

STORAGE: Do not wash before use. Remove outer leaves with clean hands. Will last a week or two "as is" if kept cool. If refrigerated, pare stem, and place a damp towel pad beneath it. Can also be wrapped in a damp towel. Store in a vegetable bag. Cabbage will live happily in your refrigerator for a month or more if it is examined weekly and the outer, deteriorating leaves pared away.

RED CABBAGE has a shorter shelf life than white cabbage.

PREPARATION: Cut into wedges and remove core or shred.

COOKING: Steaming or pressure cooking are both techniques that minimize the loss of water soluble vitamins. Shredded or chopped cabbage may be added raw to all of the legume soups just when they are finished cooking. The internal temperature of the soup will cook the cabbage "al dente," in this case half raw, a very pleasing effect and quite nutritious. Cabbage is usually cut into wedges and steamed. Boiling really reduces food value. Steaming takes about twenty to thirty minutes. Check with fork for tenderness.

BASIC CABBAGE

1 medium cabbage, cored, chopped coarsely
4 tablespoons butter
salt and pepper

Bring a large pot of water to a rolling boil, add cabbage and cook for five minutes. Wash in cold water, drain, break up or flake cabbage and reheat. Turn off flame and add butter and salt to taste.

FLEMISH CABBAGE

1 medium cabbage (red)
4 tablespoons butter
2 apples
1 teaspoon vinegar
1 teaspoon sugar
3 teaspoons water
salt and pepper

Quarter the cabbage, remove the core and slice finely. Melt the butter in a pan, add everything but the apple and simmer over low heat for an hour. Peel and slice the apples, add to the pot and cook for a half hour.

SWEET AND SOUR CABBAGE

See MEAT.

GRAND BANKS DELIGHT (CABBAGE, POTATOES AND HAM)

This is a recipe that goes back to the days when Grand Banks fishermen spent years away from home, wintering in Greenland or northern Canada, returning to the Grand Banks the following Spring until their holds were full of salted cod. Rare, indeed, was the dinner of a Grand Banks fisherman that did not consist of cod, cod, and more cod. Fishermen grew so sick of cod they sometimes ate raw fresh mackerel—which was carefully rationed for use as bait.

This recipe (which does not contain cod) although quite basic, was a favorite of the Portuguese fisherman. It must have seemed like heaven itself after six long months of cod. It is particularly useful to the long-distance cruiser because it is made with long-lasting non-refrigerated supplies. It is also a fine way to use leftover canned ham.

1 medium cabbage, quartered
3 large potatoes, pared and halved
2 cups chicken stock
1/4 cup butter
2 tablespoons dry sherry (optional)
caraway or celery seed
1/2 pound canned ham or smoked ham

Boil potatoes and cabbage twenty minutes. Peel potatoes; slice into half-inch rounds. Flake cabbage. Shred ham, or slice finely and chop. Put a layer of cabbage in the bottom of a buttered pot. Sprinkle with salt and a pinch of caraway or celery seed.

Add a layer of potatoes; dot with butter. Then add a layer of ham. Repeat this process until all ingredients are used. Pour chicken stock or bouillon over all and, if desired, dry sherry. Warm over low heat until bubbling.

CORNed BEEF HASH AND CABBAGE

1 medium cabbage, whole
1 can corned beef, minced
3/4 cup onions, chopped and satuéed
1 cup cream or evaporated milk
1 teaspoon thyme
1 cup chicken stock
2 cups corn flakes, crushed
4 tablespoons butter
1 can cream of mushroom soup

Simmer whole cabbage about thirty minutes until barely tender. Cut half open and scoop out enough of the inside to house the corned beef. Mix corned beef, onions, herbs, and stuff into cabbage. Pour cream over hash. Push cabbage together. Put cabbage into a buttered pot and mash down. Moisten with chicken stock. Sprinkle with buttered corn flakes. Pour mushroom soup over all. Heat at 375° F. for about fifteen minutes to reheat.

SAUERKRAUT is shredded, fermented cabbage. Some families have clay crocks which contain fermenting bacteria and the crocks are never washed, just wiped clean. Shredded cabbage is added and a weight placed on top. Mother Nature does the rest.

In the eighteenth century, captains fed their crews sauerkraut believing that it would prevent scurvy, a disease caused by chronic vitamin C deficiency. Unfortunately the fermenting process destroys vitamins. It took that great humanitarian, daring explorer and navigator, Captain Cook, to prove that lime juice and fresh vegetables, rich sources of vitamins, are all that is needed to prevent this dreaded disease. On his second voyage of exploration, which lasted more than three years, Cook did not lose a single man to scurvy.

The best sauerkraut is uncooked, freshly fermented, low in salt and refrigerated. Canned sauerkraut doesn't have much food value but it does make a nice side dish and a tasty garnish. Serve hot or cold.

SAUERKRAUT AND TOMATO CASSEROLE

1 can sauerkraut
1 onion, chopped and sautéed in bacon fat until golden
1 teaspoon caraway seed
1 can Italian tomatoes, well chopped
4 strips bacon, quartered, fried, reserved
1/2 cup brown sugar
1 teaspoon black pepper

Combine all ingredients and bake in 375° F. until bubbling. Garnish with bacon.

COLESLAW

See page 224.

CARROTS

SELECTION: Bigger last longer, smaller are more tender. Really big ones are suitable for long passages. Attached greens is a sign of freshness. Reject cracked ones or those with blackened stumps at top.

STORAGE: If purchased dirty, leave dirty. Do not bruise. Otherwise wash in chlorinated water and sun dry. Refrigerate in plastic bags (not vegetable bags) to preserve moisture. If unrefrigerated store in dry in a dark, cool spot. Moistening induces sprouting, which spoils their taste. Carrot greens should be removed before storage; cut them back if they reappear. Carrots become limp and woody after about two to three weeks without refrigeration; but last months in the refrigerator.

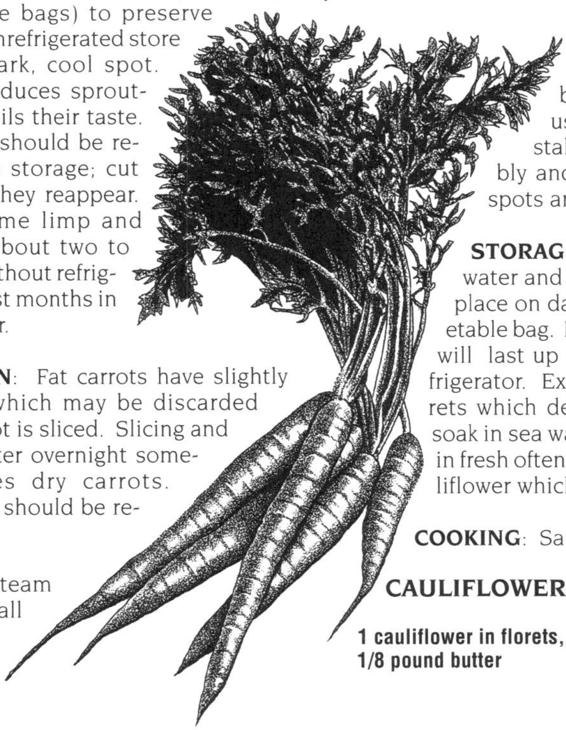

PREPARATION: Fat carrots have slightly bitter cores which may be discarded when the carrot is sliced. Slicing and soaking in water overnight somewhat restores dry carrots. Flabby carrots should be rejected.

COOKING: Steam or stir fry. Small carrots may be cooked whole and unpeeled. Peel and slice large carrots. Small whole carrots steam in fifteen minutes. Pressure steamed slices take two minutes at fifteen pounds; larger cuts, like quarters, take four minutes. Carrots roast beautifully in a pan on the grill with chicken or meat. Whole carrots roast in about forty minutes. Blanch slices before stir frying. Boil quartered carrots about ten minutes.

CARROTS WITH EGG SAUCE

1/2 pound new carrots
4 tablespoons butter
2 teaspoons flour
1 cup milk
2 egg yolks
1/2 cup parsley, chopped

Simmer the carrots in three-quarters of a cup of water until crisp. Reserve carrots and liquid. Make a white sauce with the flour, buttermilk and carrot water. Simmer twenty minutes. Add the carrots and simmer. Turn off heat. Mix egg yolks with a little milk and stir into the sauce. Salt and pepper to taste.

CAULIFLOWER

SELECTION: Heads should be rock hard, pure white and unblemished. Cauliflower usually rots before going stale. Old heads are crumbly and brown-tinged. Black spots are rotten.

STORAGE: Wash in chlorinated water and sun dry. Cut stem and place on damp pad. Store in vegetable bag. Needs refrigeration and will last up to several weeks in refrigerator. Examine and cut out florets which develop black spots. A soak in sea water followed by a rinse in fresh often extends the life of cauliflower which is developing mold.

COOKING: Same as broccoli.

CAULIFLOWER POLONAISE

1 cauliflower in florets, blanched 5 min.
1/8 pound butter

4 teaspoons olive oil
1 cup bread crumbs
1/2 cup chopped parsley
2 hard-boiled egg yolks, grated

Melt the butter/oil in a pan and sauté the bread crumbs two minutes. Add the cauliflower florets and toss. Sauté a few minutes, tossing occasionally. Add the egg yolks and toss. Add the cheese and toss. Sprinkle with parsley and serve.

CAULIFLOWER AND RICE CASSEROLE

1 pound mushrooms, chopped, sautéed in butter
1 large onion, chopped
1 large cauliflower in florets, blanched 4 minutes
3 cups cooked brown rice
3 cups sharp cheddar or whatever cheese
4 cloves garlic, chopped
1/2 cup milk
butter, salt, pepper

Add all ingredients to greased baking dish and bake for thirty minutes at 350° F. or pan sauté over very low heat until cauliflower is tender. Do not boil.

CELERY

Celery is an important staple in the galley. It is a standard part of any stock, as are carrots and onions. We use lots of celery. Celery lasts several months in the refrigerator and a week or more without refrigeration.

SELECTION: Celery must be firm, bright green, unwilted. Yellow leaves are a sign of age. Best celery are thick heads. Outer stalks are bright green, stringy and tough. Inner stalks are lighter in color and tender. Hearts are green-gold and very tender. In the USA, unlike third world countries, most bunches are sold with outer stalks removed.

STORAGE: Agitate thoroughly in chlorinated water and sun dry upside down, shaking occasionally. Do not remove leaves. Cut bottom and place on damp pad. Store upright in refrigerator in plastic bag.

PREPARATION: Pare strings off outer stalks. Be aggressive. Rinse thoroughly before use.

CORN

SELECTION: Corn is a mid to late summer delight and is pretty tasteless the rest of the year. Supermarket corn has frequently traveled far and lost most of its flavor. You are better off with frozen or canned corn.

Canned white corn is definitely the sweetest. **White corn** is usually sweeter and more tender than yellow but freshness and selection, regardless of color, is everything. Fresh corn will have light green husks, willowy golden yellow silk, which is not dry or blackened, and a fresh cut stem, not black and moldy. The husk will be slightly damp. The kernels should be plump and bursting with juice. Break off an end kernel. It should taste markedly sweet. No taste, no buy.

STORAGE: The shelf life of unrefrigerated corn can be extended to four or five days if it is soaked in ordinary tap water for an hour, then kept damp with a sprayer or damp towel. Refrigerated corn can be husked and packed in a plastic bag. It will last several weeks although its flavor diminishes steadily.

COOKING: To grill (our favorite method), just toss on coals in husk and blacken all over. A few charred kernels add to the flavor. To boil or steam use scouring pad to remove last of silk before cooking. Steam or boil in scant amount of water for fifteen to twenty minutes, turning several times.

Southwestern Spicy Corn Casserole

4 ears white corn, boiled or grilled (better), cut from cob, or use canned corn
1/2 red pepper, chopped
1 can kidney beans
1/2 cup milk or light cream
1-1/2 cups very sharp cheddar, shredded (smoked cheese optional)
1 ounce chili powder
1/4 stick butter or oil
3 teaspoons each powdered oregano, thyme
6 cloves garlic, chopped
jalapeño peppers to taste, chopped
salt to taste

Mix and heat in 400° F. oven for about thirty minutes or until cheese is melted. Just get hot. Sprinkle a little more cheese on top and brown if desired.

JALAPEñO CREAMED CORN

Pieces of grilled chicken or shrimp can be added to make a main course.

6 ears of corn, cooked, kernels removed from cob
2 cups white sauce
2 jalapeños peppers, cooked, seeded, chopped
1 red pepper, chopped
1 cup white cheese, grated
3 teaspoons cooking oil
3 cloves garlic
juice of 1/2 lemon
1 red pepper julienned, blanched 2 minutes
1 teaspoon salt

Add garlic, pepper, oil to blender and liquefy. Combine all ingredients and heat. Delicious.

CORN FRITTERS

This is a typical fried food recipe that requires high heat, otherwise the fritter is oily. Blot the fritter thoroughly as soon as it comes from the pan. Serves six.

1 cup water
1 teaspoon sugar
1/2 teaspoon red pepper or 2 jalapeños, cooked and liquefied (better)
1/4 pound butter, melted
1 cup white flour
1/2 cup corn meal
1-1/2 cups corn
2 eggs
peanut oil to fry

Combine all ingredients except water. Whisk and add water slowly until mixture is between a dough and a porridge. Whisk thoroughly until smooth. Drop golf ball sized globs into very hot oil. Remove one at a time when cooked and replace with fresh dough. This process keeps oil hot. Drain and blot.

ROASTED CORN SALSA

Serve as a vegetable or snack.

5 ears corn, lightly roasted, cut from cob
1/2 cup dried mushrooms, reconstituted, chopped
1/4 cup olive oil
2 large Anaheim, Plobano or medium-hot chilies
2 teaspoons marjoram
4 cloves pan-roasted garlic, chopped
1 red bell pepper, chopped
1 teaspoon chile sauce
1 teaspoon tequila
1 teaspoon sherry
juice of 1 lime
1/2 teaspoon kosher salt
1 teaspoon chile powder

Dry roast the corn a little at a time for about five minutes, until smoky-brown. Add everything except mushrooms and toss and sauté until bells are soft. Add mushrooms and season to taste. A sauce consisting of bleu cheese, dash of soy sauce and sour cream goes great.

CUCUMBERS

SELECTION: Pick long, thin cucumbers since fat ones have well developed seeds. If you find prominent seeds, split cuke and scrape them out. Fresh cukes are plump. Don't buy any that show the least signs of shriveling. Never buy blemished or damaged cukes. Most cukes in the USA come waxed which retards mold and moisture loss. If the skins are dull, oil them. They may last a week or two in the refrigerator. Long thin English cucumbers have few seeds and are very tasty, but do not store well. Pickling cukes have bumpy skins but do not make a great salad vegetable.

PREPARATION: Waxed cukes should be peeled as the skins are tough and get tougher with storage.

COOKING: This vegetable is usually eaten raw but can be blanched and served in a vinaigrette. A cuke, onion salad is good with just a little rice vinegar on it. Cucumbers, onions and beets with lemon and sugar is delicious and very refreshing. Dill, lemon juice and sour cream is also good on top. Cucumbers can also be liquefied and used as a salad dressing base.

CUCUMBER LOW FAT SALAD DRESSING

1 teaspoon lemon zest
juice from 1/2 lemon

2 teaspoons rice vinegar
1 teaspoon sugar
2 teaspoons honey
1 teaspoon dry mustard
1 teaspoon port wine
salt to taste

EGGPLANT

Globe Eggplant (above)

Japanese Eggplant (right)

SELECTION: All eggplants should be absolutely unblemished and have undamaged skins. They should be plump, hard and lustrous. Reject any which are spongy or have black, withered tops. Baby eggplant is tender and free of seeds but tedious to peel. **Globe eggplant:** buy thin ones as the fat ones have pronounced seeds. **White eggplant** is smaller, firmer and slightly sweeter than the purple variety. **Japanese eggplant** is long and thin. This is the "best buy" as they have no seeds.

PREPARATION: Wash in chlorinated water, sun dry and refrigerate in paper bag.

STORAGE: Eggplants are delicate. Handle with care. Wrap in paper and store in refrigerator. They will last no more than a week, shrivel and get very bitter as they age.

FRYING: Sliced eggplant absorbs huge amounts of oil as it cooks and the resulting slice is mushy. **Leeching**: Prior to cooking, slice the skinned eggplant into rounds about 3/4 inches thick, then thoroughly salt each slice. The salted slices are stacked and pressed several times, with increasing pressure over the course of an hour. The salt leaches the water from the slices and reduces the cooking time. It also toughens the fiber preventing the slices from falling apart during cooking. The thickness is reduced to about a quarter inch. Salted slices must be thoroughly washed in very hot water before use and tasted to be sure the salt is removed. This is very important. Then pat dry. Cooking time is reduced and the slice absorbs two-thirds less oil as it cooks.

FRYING/SAUTÉING: Salt and leech , dip in egg and seasoned flour or fry as is.

GRILLING: produces a light, fluffy vegetable that is fat free and suitable for use in salads, buttered as a side dish. Toss eggplant on grill. Turn frequently. Purple eggplant is grilled until charred. Japanese eggplant is grilled until it bursts or gets soft and limp. May also be sliced into rounds, painted with olive oil and grilled.

BAKING: Bake at 400° F. in slices (fifteen to twenty minutes) as bigger pieces take too long to cook. Brush with oil before baking.

EGGPLANT PARMESAN

This is one of my favorite recipes which I often make in a fry pan. Thin slices of breaded, fried veal may be layered into this dish or aged ham can be slipped in after the dish has been cooked. Cooking the ham toughens it. The eggplant can be floured before frying if desired. Serves four.

2 medium purple eggplants or equivalent, peeled, sliced, leeched, fried, blotted
1 quart marinara sauce (see BASIC STUFF)
3 cups Parmesan cheese, grated
2 cups mozzarella cheese, grated (combine with Parmesan)

Pour a quarter-inch of sauce into an oiled baking dish. Add layer of eggplant, then sauce, then cheese. End with layer of sauce. Bake at 350° F. for thirty minutes. Sprinkle with layer of cheese and melt, then brown under broiler (quickly) if desired.

To make this dish in a pan heat the sauce and make just two layers. Cook over low heat for twenty minutes, add cheese and melt.

ROASTED EGGPLANT SALAD

(see page 225)

MARINATED EGGPLANT AND ROASTED PEPPERS

1 medium purple eggplant or equivalent, peeled, sliced, leeched, dipped in milk, then seasoned flour and fried until golden
2 red or green peppers, roasted, cut thick slices
1 cup vinaigrette, with extra garlic

Layer eggplant and peppers, sprinkling with sauce between each layer. Let stand several hours at room temperature or refrigerate overnight. This extremely delicious dish is served as an appetizer, cold salad or as a sandwich.

RATATOUILLE

This is a popular dish to which fried rounds of Italian sausage may be added.

1 medium purple eggplant or equivalent, peeled, leeched, cut into 1-inch chunks
2 cups potatoes, peeled, diced, blanched
4 teaspoons olive oil
1 each red and green roasted bell pepper, cut into 1-inch slices
1 onion, chopped
4 cloves garlic, roughly chopped
4 medium tomatoes, squeezed, chopped
1 teaspoon each: salt, pepper, thyme
1-1/2 cups feta cheese, diced
3 teaspoons oregano
1/2 cup fresh basil (if available)
1/2 cup parsley

Fry eggplant and potatoes in olive oil. When eggplant is soft, add onions and garlic. When onions are soft add tomatoes. When juice of tomatoes is cooked down add all remaining ingredients except cheese. When everything is bubbling add cheese, cover and turn off heat. Let stand five minutes and serve.

LEFTOVER FRIED EGGPLANT

Leftover fried eggplant makes the most delicious cold appetizer. Sprinkle each round with garlic, salt, wine and vinegar. Cover with layer of tomato paste. Top with a mushroom half, pre-fried in butter (optional). Put in large dish and cover with olive oil. Let stand overnight in refrigerator or at room temperature.

TUNA AND EGGPLANT SANDWICH

1 medium eggplant, peeled, sliced into rounds, leeched, dipped in egg, then milk and floured
1 cup tuna salad
1 large tomato, sliced

Fry floured eggplant rounds until browned. When the eggplant is browned, blot it, then cover with a spoonful of tuna salad and place another eggplant round on top. Add a tomato garnish on top. Delicious! Goes well with apple sauce.

GARLIC

I love garlic and I am unashamed. Love me, love my breath. In addition to its culinary properties, garlic is reputed to deter vampires and I can attest it did drive off at least one Vamp whom time proved to have been an unwise choice.

Garlic can be subtle or domineering depending on how it is prepared. **Unpeeled cloves** whose juice is held in check by the skin are mild and sweet. They are often added to bottles of oil as flavoring to be used in pasta or for cooking lamb or chicken. Unpeeled cloves are often roasted and used as a spread (see below).

Peeled whole cloves give oil or sauces a more pronounced garlic flavor but whole cloves are sweet and delicious when stewed. **Slicing, chopping, or blenderizing** garlic brings out the juice—and a much more aggressive flavor. **Mincing, crushing and grinding**, frequently with salt as an abrasive lets the full beast loose, producing a harsh flavor guaranteed to dominate. Garlic flavor is quickly transmitted through oil, especially if the garlic is crushed in oil. **Mincing** is accomplished by placing the flat of a knife over a clove, then smashing the knife with your fist. **Cooking modifies the taste.** Cooking garlic makes its flavor more mild. If a strong garlic flavor is desired add garlic during the last few minutes of cooking.

SELECTION: Good garlic bulbs are big, fat, rock hard and heavy. The cloves should be large and bulging. Never buy sprouting garlic. Squeeze each bulb hard and reject those with soft cloves. Examine skin for traces of black mold. In some countries garlic is sold woven into strands. Examine the bulbs carefully to be sure they are fresh as strands are often sold for decoration. Elephant garlic, whose bulbs are two or three times the size of the normal variety, is too mild to do its job.

STORAGE: Garlic stores well at room temperature for more than a month, even longer in the fridge, so when you find high quality garlic, stock up. Store in cool, dry place. Allow air to circulate. Do not store in plastic.

PREPARATION: **Skinning** garlic is accomplished by first cutting off the root end of the clove, covering with a towel, then smashing with the flat of a knife or hitting with the palm. The skin slips off a smashed garlic clove easily. To skin a whole bulb, slice off the entire root end, place in a plastic bag, place knife flat over bulb and smash hell out of it. Then peel.

COOKING: **Roasting whole bulbs**: Remove loose skin, lightly smash the bulb to slightly separate the cloves, brush with thyme/olive oil, cover and bake at 350° F. for forty minutes. Uncover and bake ten minutes. Cool, squeeze out mush, mix with butter/olive oil and spread on bread. Four bulbs produce about a half cup of cooked garlic "meat." Sautéing, frying or boiling garlic greatly reduces and modifies its potent flavor.

Frying: Chopped garlic in combination with finely chopped shallots or onion can be fried in oil until light golden, then small pieces of precooked meat, shellfish or chicken stir fried for a minute or two. This imparts a mild garlic flavor and the garlic bits are crunchy and delicious.

GARLIC BREATH: The residual aroma created by eating garlic may be somewhat dispelled with lemonade, by eating parsley or taking a few good belts of brandy, after which you won't really care whether you smell or not. Fingers may be washed in lemon juice or baking soda.

GARLIC AS AN AVENGING ANGEL

If God allowed us but one seasoning in the world, our vote would be solidly for garlic. How much do we like it? We once asked a Mexican waiter who spoke no English for a garlic dressing for our salad. He seemed confused and finally brought out a bowl of what turned out to be a huge load of finely chopped garlic covered by peanut oil (for lightness) and a little olive oil (for flavor). This mixture was used in the kitchen for cooking. We were now as confused as the waiter, but decided to put a daub on the tomatoes and give it a try.

The result was so extraordinarily delicious that we ate the whole pot of garlic, wiping up the last bits with pieces of bread. We returned home with a garlic halo that lasted for days, made the dog whine and hide under the bed, turned friends into strangers, and made the postman wince. But it was worth it.

GARLIC SAUCE—CATALAN BOMBSHELL

This dressing won't make the dog whine and hide under the bed, but it's not for the timid. Strap on your pacemaker and dive right in! The secret here is to first crush and then chop the garlic, not blenderize it. Not for the timid or anyone working in the dental profession.

1 bulb garlic, crushed and chopped
1/2 cup olive oil
1/2 cup cooking oil
juice of 1/2 lemon
salt

Combine garlic and oil and whisk for a few minutes. Let stand overnight. Stir a few times. Serve over onions and tomatoes. Sprinkle tomatoes and onions with lemon juice, salt and pepper. Spoon on oil and garlic mush.

LEEKS

Leeks look like big scallions but are really a variety of Lily root. They are much too tough to eat raw. They have a sweeter, different flavor than scallions. Leeks, in addition to onions and potatoes, are the heart of a great vichyssoise.

SELECTION: Buy the fattest as they last the longest. The root should be unblemished white, green part should be light green, not yellow.

PREPARATION: Trim green but leave a few inches. Leave roots on or do not further trim. Wash in acidified, not chlorinated water as root is sensitive. Leeks are grown in gravel and need thorough washing.

STORAGE: In vegetable bag. Leeks will last a week in refrigerator.

COOKING: Boil until tender, about ten minutes. Steam about fifteen minutes. Sauté sliced. Cook until browned.

A classic French snack is made by cutting leeks into three to four inch sections, brushing with olive oil, grilling slightly, then packing in a tight dish and covering with vinaigrette. As the leek cools the sauce gets sucked into it. Serve chilled. Very tasty.

MUSHROOMS

Fresh mushrooms are delicate and short lived. They do not cruise well since they do not store well. **Button mushrooms** are the ones most commonly sold in groceries in the USA. **Portobellos** are huge, flat, brown and are longer-lasting than buttons. **Shitakes** look like smaller portobellos and are our favorite. **Morrels** are considered a gastronomic pinnacle but are quite expensive. **Enokis** are string like mushrooms that grow in a bunch. They store well and make a dramatic presentation grilled or fried in a single bunch. **Wild mushrooms** are extremely delicious but eating the wrong ones will get you dead.

STORAGE: Do not wash. Store in open paper bag in refrigerator. Enokis may be stored in a plastic bag and have a longer shelf life.

PREPARATION: Wash and allow to thoroughly air dry over several hours as the underside holds water. Portobellos and big, mature mushrooms need to be skinned and sliced. Shiitake stems are tough and should be cut away. Slice or chop as needed.

COOKING: **Sauté or stir fry** in peanut oil over very high heat, tossing frequently. This toughens the mushroom and improves texture. We do this even if we plan to add the mushroom to a stew later. Low heat allows water to leach from the mushroom into the pan, resulting in flabby, stewed mushrooms. If this happens, tilt pan and absorb water into a paper towel which can also be tossed into the pan and stirred around. When the mushroom browns, sprinkle in a bit of soy sauce a little at a time. Greatly enhances the flavor. Add a hot pepper, garlic or seeds such as caraway or dill to the fry pan as desired as these spices impart their flavor to the mushroom.

GRILLING on a skewer: Marinate a half-hour in the mushroom marinade. Larger mushrooms should be quickly browned on top then turned and grilled until moisture stops dripping from the underside when squeezed, fifteen minutes for medium sizes, twenty-five for big Portobellos.

BROILING: brush all over with marinade and broil three to four inches from flame, turning a few times with tongs. Let underside broil at least ten minutes.

GRILL/BROIL MARINADE: Use oil, soy sauce, chopped garlic, hot sauce, cumin and salt. Dip or paint lavishly with mixture. Allow mixture to sit, bottom, up for twenty minutes.

DRIED MUSHROOMS: While their shriveled and small unappetizing looks seem to promise little, dried mushrooms possess incredible flavor and many gourmets use them in preference to fresh mushrooms, including myself. Most varieties are available, such as morels, black Chinese, cepes, and the well known mushroom relatives, truffles. All are much cheaper dried than the fresh. Learn to use them.

STORAGE: Pack in Ziplocs or in tight jars. Jars are better for long-term storage. Lasts for years.

PREPARATION: Reconstitute by soaking them for a half-hour in hot water or hot soy sauce. Add the liquid a little at a time and toss until fully reconstituted. Don't just dump on the liquid. They will soften, swelling to a respectable size full of a pronounced mushroom flavor. Even the juice is powerfully flavored. They require no cooking.

USE like fresh mushrooms, adding them to a recipe last as they do not need cooking. Add directly to soups, such as mushroom and barley, or in omelets, stews, stuffings, and anything else that tastes delicious with fresh mushrooms. No gourmet galley is complete without a good supply of dried mushrooms.

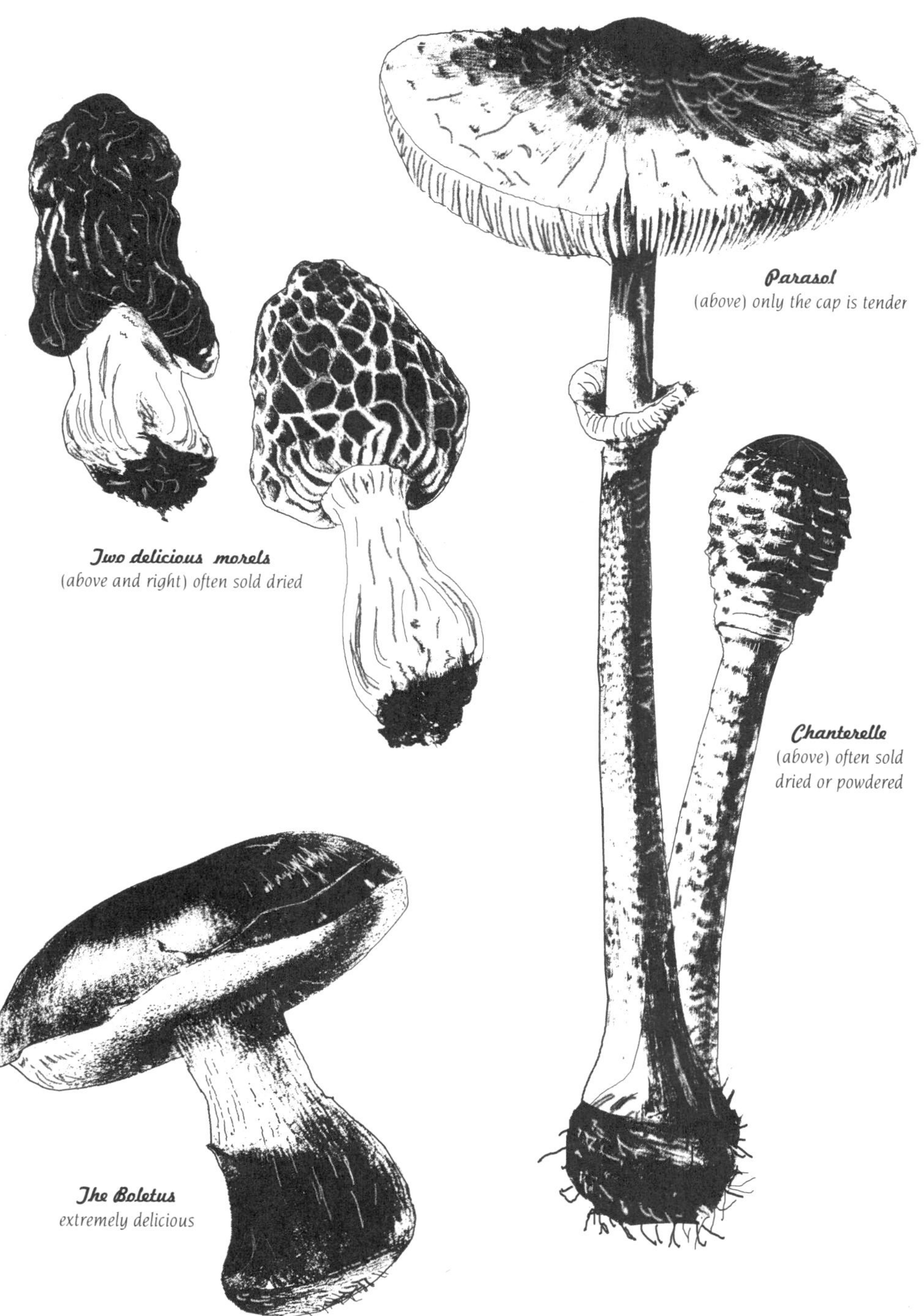

Two delicious morels
(above and right) often sold dried

Parasol
(above) only the cap is tender

Chanterelle
(above) often sold dried or powdered

The Boletus
extremely delicious

Edible mushrooms

MUSHROOMS IN WINE SAUCE

Sauté the mushrooms in a generous amount of butter/oil with a sprinkle of lemon juice. When cooked, remove from pan. Add a half cup of dry white wine, salt and pepper and reduce until thick. Add the mushrooms and toss. Garnish with parsley.

PURÉE OF MUSHROOMS

Cut mushrooms into small pieces and sauté in butter/oil with salt, pepper and a dash of lemon juice. You can add chopped walnuts, almonds, pine nuts or macadamias if desired. When soft, add a béchamel sauce and serve over meat, chicken or fish.

ONIONS

This section includes **shallots**, which are small onions used for their pronounced flavor; yellow (Cepa) onions (described below), **pearl onions** which are short-lived and hard to peel, the **red onion** which is sweet and mild, used in salads; **Bermudas** (flat) and **Spanish** (big and round), which are stronger flavored than reds but more mild than Cepas and are often eaten raw, as on burgers or in salads; finally there are "sweet" onions—**Maui**, **Vidalia** and **Walla Walla** which are not bitter at all—and also very expensive.

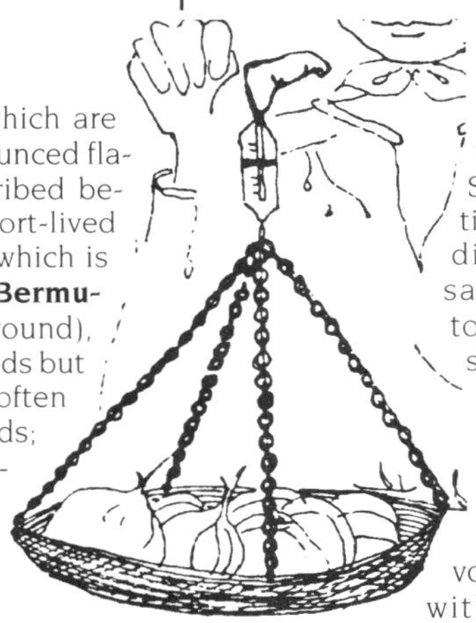

SELECTION: Buy select large yellow cooking onions with undamaged golden skins. Bigger is better. Bermudas or Spanish onions are tasty but do not last as long. Reject any onion which is beginning to sprout or is damaged. Fresh onions are rock hard. Squeeze hard to detect soft cloves. Cut one in half and examine center for rot.

STORAGE: Store in a dry cool, dark or shady place where the onions will not roll around and bruise. Adequate air circulation is important to prevent mold. Check onions weekly and remove sprouters. Young sprouts can be pared away, but if stalks get more than a few inches long the onion is ruined although the sprout can be grown longer and eaten. Unrefrigerated onions will last about six weeks depending on temperature.

PREPARATION: Skin just before use as skinned onions deteriorate quickly. Slice through root, grab skin flap and pull toward head. Then cut through head, grasp skin and pull toward root. Pull off remaining skin. To skin many onions blanch, then cool or refrigerate. Skin slips off easily. To chop, cut in half, slice out root core first. If your eyes are sensitive to onion juice, peel under water. To rid hands of onion smell, rub with salt and vinegar or lemon juice.

IMPROVING CANNED FOOD: Adding cooked onions to canned vegetables or stews greatly improves them and reduces their canned quality.

GRILLING: We love cutting onions into thick rounds, brushing with olive oil and grilling until browned on both sides. A fat slice of grilled tomato goes well on top. Sauté chopped onion until soft, or golden over medium heat. Long, slow sautéing over low heat toughens onions and destroys their flavor. BURN slightly by first sautéing until golden, then cooking briefly over high heat without stirring. This produces a dominating flavor. BROWN by sprinkling with a little flour, this strengthens their flavor.

BOILING: We have no boiling recipes although many an onion has been boiled into a stock, then discarded.

ROASTED: Onions added to a roasting pan are delicious. Skin, brush with oil and rest in a little liquid.

MARINATED ONIONS

Slice a large onion into thick rounds and soak in heavily salted water for several hours. Drain, soak in balsamic vinegar for an hour.

ONION RINGS

Onion rings are a special end-of-the-passage delight, but are just as good in port.

3 large onions
1 cup milk
1 egg

2 cups flour
1 teaspoon each salt and pepper

Slice onions about a quarter-inch thick; separate into rounds. Soak the whole lot in a mixture of egg/milk. Remove onions and allow to drain. Place seasoned flour in a large plastic bag, add onions and shake. Dump onions onto counter and shake off excess flour. Fry until golden in hot peanut oil. Drain in colander and serve.

PEPPERS, BELL

See pages 221-222.

THE WONDERFUL WORLD OF HOT PEPPERS

The thermonuclear qualities of hot peppers is determined by the concentration of the chemical **capsaicin** in the pepper's skin and flesh. In general, the smaller the pepper, the hotter it is. I, of course, had to learn this the hard way. I found this cute, little, delicate, Jamaican, orange-yellow fellow about the size of a walnut in an open air market in Port Antonio. I was not a complete fool and asked "how hot?" I was honestly told "oh, very hot, sir, very hot indeed. Just use a little of the skin in a stew." I found out shortly thereafter exactly what *very hot indeed* meant.

I thought I would be ever so careful and test the pepper's strength before using it in the stew, so I just pricked the skin with my fingernail and touched the nail delicately to my tongue—how much more conservative could one be! My entire mouth instantly exploded in pain, within a half-minute I was on the deck, I went into immediate allergic shock, had trouble breathing, broke out in a rash, had intense shooting pains in the hand that touched the pepper and developed a deep blister on my gum. To make matters worse, I accidently touched the contaminated finger to my face and was rewarded with a fingernail-shaped burn on my cheek. I had to get a Benedryl shot and was laid up for several days. I had tasted a **Scotch Bonnet**, a little devil which is fifty times hotter than a jalapeño. For this reason we have included a pepper ID chart on the next page, and you'd better take a good look at it. Because of my experience I now like to minimize my risk. I buy dried peppers and when I find one which suits me I stock up, so that I do not have to take another risk for awhile!

PEPPER WISDOM

- *Chile* is the Spanish word for pepper and is used interchangeably in this book.
- If you are handling very hot peppers wear rubber gloves and wash them before removing. Capsaicin tenaciously sticks to skin.
- Pepper seeds and the vein are the hottest part of the pepper.
- Pepper skins are tough and are often roasted until blackened, then allowed to cool after which the skins shuck off easily. Be sure to prick the pepper with a fork several times before grilling to prevent the pepper from bursting. After the pepper is skinned cut off the top and wash away the seeds.
- Starchy foods such as grains or rice somewhat neutralize the potency of hot pepper.
- The more hot peppers you eat the more the body adjusts to them.
- The capsaicin in hot peppers does not damage internal organs. It may burn you going in, in the middle and going out, but the problem will pass.
- Drinking alcohol while eating hot peppers makes them seem hotter, increases their absorption, promotes sweating and stimulates the heart. This process cools the body.
- Drinking milk after eating hot peppers reduces the burning effect and helps to settle pepper indigestion.
- Roasting hot peppers brings out their flavor but makes the skin bitter. It should be removed. To scorch skin use a torch, a grill or high heat and blacken quickly. Do not wash after skinning as this reduces flavor.
- A pepper is just as hot after drying. Buy only whole dried peppers. Do not buy crumbly, dusty peppers or ones with mould or white spots. Store in a tight jar for up to six months.
- Most dried peppers should be roasted and rehydrated like dried mushrooms

before use.

- Adding both dried and fresh peppers to food makes the taste more complex and interesting.
- If you have handled hot peppers, be sure to **wash your hands thoroughly** before answering **nature's call**, or you will be sorrier than you ever dreamed possible.

SELECTION: Buy mature chiles which are dry to the touch, firm and heavy, unblemished and have lustrous skins.

STORAGE: If dirty leave dirty. Otherwise, wash in chlorinated water, sun dry and store in a paper bag in the refrigerator. Do not store in plastic or leave unrefrigerated.

If I had followed the vendor's advice I would not have damaged myself quite so severely. Cooking somewhat diminishes the potency of a pepper and in any event spreads the heat into the food. If you buy a pepper which is too hot, boil it, wash, and seed it to get a milder flavor.

REHYDRATING DRIED PEPPERS: Cut peppers open, remove seeds and veins (important). Get a dry fry pan very hot, press peppers (one at a time) onto pan until they smoke. Do both sides. Soak peppers in hot water for about 30 minutes. Blenderize and strain.

CHILE (PEPPER) POWDER is the main ingredient in **chile mix**. A fresh powder is much more flavorful than canned. It should have a deep, rich color and not be too dry. Clumps of powder indicate that it is very fresh and rich in oil. Fresh chile should stain the fingers when rubbed. Chile powder is not fiery hot. The heat is achieved by adding other peppers, such as red pepper to the mix. You are much better off buying chile powder, rather than chile mix and adding pepper, salt, sugar, cumin and garlic to your taste.

QUESADILLAS

4 flour tortillas
4 Anaheim chiles, roasted, skinned
1 red pepper, roasted, skinned
1/2 pound of cheddar or a white cheese, grated
1 cup guacamole or sour cream

FRESH AND DRIED PEPPER HEAT INDEX

Name	Units of Capsaicin	Relative Heat
MILD (Fresh)		
Bell/Pimento/Sweet Banana	0	0 - 1
Cherry/Mexican Bell/ Cherry	0.1 - 0.5	2 - 3
Big Jim/Anaheim/N.Mexico/Poblano	0.5 - 1.0	3 - 4
Ancho/Pasilla/ /Casacbel	1 - 2.5	4 - 5
MEDIUM HOT (Fresh)		
Jalapeño/Huachinango	2.5 - 5.0	5 - 6
Serrano/Peter/Peruvian	5 - 15	6 - 7
De Árobol/ Rocotillo/Thai	15 - 30	7 - 8
PREFLIGHT PHYSICAL REQUIRED (Fresh)		
Piguin/Cayenne/Tabasco	30 - 50	8 - 9
Ají/Tepín/Jamacian Hot	50 - 100	9 - 10
OH, VERY HOT INDEED (Fresh)		
Habañero/Scotch Bonnet/Macho	150 - 300	10+
DRIED (ONLY)		
Guajillo/Mulato/New Mexico Miniatures		2 - 4
Chilhuacle/Green Pasilla		3 - 4
Chipotle/Red Pasilla/Pepperoncini		5 - 6
Cayenne		8

hot chiles, roasted, skinned, minced, added to cheese (optional)

Heat the tortillas, sprinkle on cheese, heat until just melted, cover with Anaheim and red pepper slices. Heat until peppers are warm. Remove, allow to cool slightly and cut into triangles.

PLANTAINS

Plantains look like big bananas but are almost invariably eaten cooked as a vegetable, either satuéed in butter or oil or cooked like a potato into a stew. Plantains

POTATOES

Potatoes are the cruiser's best friend and were, in fact, introduced in Europe by that famous sailor, Francis Drake. We can't even tell you how long a potato will last because we have never been on a cruise long enough to see them all go bad. Our longest sea voyage was 54 days.

Potatoes are nutritious and about as fattening as a piece of fruit. The calories in a potato come from all that lovely butter, sour cream, and crumbled bacon that we dump on top. The skin of the potato contains most of the non-carbohydrate nutrition, including several vitamins and minerals, not to mention the roughage. Think twice before throwing it away.

SELECTION: Don't buy just any sack of potatoes for a long sea voyage. Select only mature baking potatoes, preferably large, smooth, thick skinned, even textured ones, even if they cost a little more. Examine each and every one. Reject those which are bruised or are sprouting. Mature baking potatoes are best because their thick, tough skins are more resistant to bruising and mold than new or boiling potatoes. Other types, sweet, delicious new potatoes with delicate skins and red boilers, are just fine for short voyages but aren't long distance cruisers.

HOW TO INSPECT POTATOES:

1. Cut several potatoes open on the spot to be sure that they have not been frozen. Frozen potatoes are gray or black just beneath the skin and are worthless. They won't last a week.
2. Cut a potato into quarters and look for pest holes or worms. If you find one, there will invariably be more.
3. Count the eyes on three to four sample potatoes. If they have more than three eyes each, they have been sitting around for a while and will soon sprout.

INSTANT POTATOES: The flavor may be improved by adding whole or condensed (not powdered) milk and lots of butter. Instant potatoes should be purchased in foil packets as the potato powder is hygroscopic and absorbs moisture from the air. It spoils quickly if packed in a cardboard box.
Instant mashed potatoes make a good topping for stews: making a beef stew, for example, into a beef pie, a particularly handy way to stretch leftover food.

STORAGE: If dirty, leave dirty. The skins are surrounded with bacteria resistant toxins that inhibit spoilage. If there is any doubt regarding their freshness, wash thoroughly in the fruit and vegetable dip, twist off all eyes. Eyes are a bad sign, indicating aging. Store in fruit trays or dish drainer trays, not in a big box or sack where the bottom ones might be damaged by the ship's motion. The damaged potatoes will decay and spoil the ones above. Frequent inspection and immediate use of bruised potatoes will help to prevent an epidemic. If immediate use is not possible, remove bad spot and refrigerate. Some potatoes can be refrigerated for long storage. Otherwise, do not refrigerate as this spoils the potato's consistency.

PRESSURE COOKING: for ten minutes, quartered; whole potatoes for six minutes.

BOIL (in salted water) quartered large potatoes for twenty to thirty minutes, small new potatoes for fifteen minutes; diced potatoes for five minutes. Drain, place towel over pot for five minutes, add butter, salt, pepper, herbs and garlic. Toss and serve.

OVEN BAKING whole potatoes in 400° oven forty-five minutes. Prick all over to allow steam to escape. Accelerate cooking by driving nails into ends. Make baked French fries (less oil) by blanching and placing on an oiled piece of foil. Brush with oil and salt. Bake at highest temperature until browned.

STOVE TOP BAKING on a trivet in a large covered pot. Cooking is accelerated if a large nail, marlin spike, or screw is pushed into the ends. Cook over medium heat for forty minutes for large potatoes, thirty minutes for small ones. Push a fork into the potato to test it. After the initial resistance of the skin, the fork should slip easily to the center.

GRILL in foil and prick the potato through the foil in many places to allow the steam to escape. Test with fork.

FRYING: Cut into strips and blanch five minutes until just soft. Bring peanut oil to high heat and add blanched, drained potatoes. USE CAUTION! Fry over high heat until browned.

POTATO PANCAKE DELIGHT

These potato pancakes are an absolute delight. The secret of success is to make them small, starting with a golf ball-sized glob. The fried exterior has the most flavor and the interior is somewhat bland. The thinner you make them, the quicker they cook and the better they taste.

4 large, mature potatoes, grated, squeezed dry
2 large onions, grated, squeezed dry
2 teaspoons baking powder
2 eggs
4 teaspoons flour
2 teaspoons salt

Combine the mixture thoroughly; shape into golf balls. Work quickly as potato discolors in open air. Smaller pancakes are better. Drop in very hot oil, and mash flat. Fry over high heat in peanut oil, enough to half cover. Turn several times until crisp, golden brown. Drain on paper. Serve with apple sauce or cold sour cream.

MASHED POTATOES

This recipe screams for a blender as hand mashing is a pain.

4 large baked potatoes
4 tablespoons butter
2 egg yolks (optional)
2 teaspoons salt
3 cups milk

Bake or boil potatoes until done. Slip off skins under running water; chop. Drop in blender until half-full. Make several batches as needed. Add butter, egg yolks to pot and start motor. Add milk slowly until desired consistency is achieved.

POTATO Soufflé

Make mashed potatoes and include the optional egg yolks. Whip the egg whites stiff, combine with grated sharp cheddar cheese and a chopped, boiled onion using a few quick strokes. Fold roughly into the potatoes and place mixture in a buttered baking dish. Cook at 350° F. for twenty minutes, then broil for a minute until surface is browned.

HASH BROWNS

Dice and parboil potatoes for five minutes. Add to large oiled skillet and bring to high heat. Add to the pan: large onion, chopped, salt, pepper and paprika. Cook over high heat, tossing occasionally with spatula and adding more oil, if necessary, to prevent drying out. Cook until golden brown.

STRAW POTATOES

Peel potatoes and pare them into long strips. Wash, squeeze and dry with a towel. Drop them into very hot oil, tossing constantly for a few minutes until brown.

PAN BROILED GRATED POTATOES

This approach is becoming popular because it's easy and the skins, rich in food value, are also used. The recipe is somewhat similar to potato pancakes but much less oil is used for cooking.

Grate and thoroughly squeeze baking potatoes, skins Included, blanch two minutes, drain and pat dry. Mix in an onion and an egg. Bring an oiled pan to high heat. Make a tight ball of grated potato, drop into pan and press down hard with a spatula. Peek under the potatoes but do not fool with them until they are well browned. Then flip.

SMASHed FRIED POTATOES

4 medium baking potatoes
1 bulb garlic, roasted
1/4 cup cilantro or parsley
1/4 cup cooking oil
3 teaspoons butter
1 teaspoon each: dry mustard, pepper, paprika, salt

Peel and cut the potatoes into rounds, boil until firm. Drain, fry in oil over medium heat until golden. Drain, blot. Make a paste of the butter, spices, garlic and cilantro. Stir into potatoes with a spatula, chopping and breaking up the potatoes.

CREAMED POTATOES

4 peeled, sliced, potatoes, blanched 4 minutes
2 cups white sauce
2 large onions, grated
1 cup white cheese, grated
butter

Butter a baking dish and add a little white sauce and layer it with potatoes and onions, adding more sauce to each layer. Do not cover the last layer. Heat in 350° oven for thirty minutes or until everything is bubbling nicely. Add a final layer of white sauce, sprinkle with cheese and melt.

FRENCH FRIES

French fries should be crisp and golden on the outside, mealy on the inside something only achieved with high heat. We don't think good fries can be made on an alcohol burner since the heat is too low. Blanching greatly reduces cooking time. Unblanched are tastier and if you have the time just soak for fifteen minutes in hot water and dry. Adding animal fat or coconut oil makes the fries taste much better but it is not good for you.

Cut potatoes into strips and blanch five minutes in large pot of water. Dry. Bring enough vegetable oil to almost cover potatoes to very high heat so that a test potato, dipped in the oil instantly begins to fry. Drop fries a few at a time into hot oil, being careful of spatters. Fry potatoes without turning them until golden brown. Remove from oil; drain on paper. Salt and serve.

SWEET POTATO OR YAM

The very word yam in Senegal means "to eat" and in most West African countries there are several varieties to choose from. The soft, moist variety is unquestionably the most tasty, but hard, gnarled yams last longer and are nearly as good. About five days without refrigeration is tops for the soft sweet potato but the tough ones usually survive a month.

SELECTION: Buy only very large, rock hard, heavy, unblemished, unbroken yams as they last longest. Blemished yams rot

CANNED YAMS are quite good. We like mashed, canned yams mixed with pineapple, dried fruit, or raisins, and this fine dish goes quite well with a candied canned ham.

STORAGE: See potatoes.

COOKING: Like potatoes. Baking time depends on size. Bake at 400° F. on foil as they drip. Prick all over or they burst. A delightful curry sauce is made with a yam base.

MASHED YAMS WITH FRUIT

Peel and simmer yam rounds until soft. Blenderize with a little milk and butter. Mix with one or two of the following: pineapple, raisins, dried apricots, carrots or prunes. Add, if desired, cinnamon honey.

CANDIED YAMS

You can also cut thin slices of apple, blanch for two minutes and add to this dish. Peel yams and cut into half-inch thick rounds. Sprinkle with brown sugar, honey, or maple syrup and lemon juice. Sauté over low heat, lid on, until sugar melts. Spoon juice over all. Add raisins and let sit for five minutes. Sprinkle with cinnamon if desired.

SWEET POTATO PIE

3 cups cooked sweet potato, pureed
1/2 stick butter
3 egg whites, beaten stiff
1/2 cup sour cream (optional)
juice from 1/2 lemon
1/2 teaspoon each: cardamom, allspice, ginger
1/2 cup brown sugar with pinch powdered clove
cracker crumb pie shell

Combine potato, sour cream, lemon juice and herbs except clove. Fold in egg white with a few strokes and place mixture in pie shell. Shake to settle. Combine clove and brown sugar. Dust on top. Sprinkle with lemon.

SQUASH

Winter squash is hard and is harvested in the fall. Summer squash is soft, quite delicate and will actually grow all year anywhere where the temperature is mild. Winter squash is tough, durable and immortal. Many end up in decorative baskets rock hard and dry. There are many varieties of both summer and winter squash but we will not further classify them here.

WINTER SQUASH, SELECTION: Fresh winter squash is hard, shiny, heavy and should be unblemished. Old squash is much lighter and often (but not always) has become dull rather than shiny. Old squash can be cut, soaked overnight in water and reconstituted but fresh squash is tastier.

STORAGE: Same as potatoes. Do not wash. Shelf life-immortal.

PREPARATION: Cut open and gouge out seeds with spoon.

COOKING: The classic spices for winter squash are brown sugar, butter, lemon juice, cinnamon, allspice and clove. It is also served with a dollop of sour cream. Vegetables associated with winter squash are boiled onions, parsley and rutabaga.

PRESSURE COOK pieces ten to fifteen minutes.

BOIL twenty minutes.

BAKE: Split, paint with butter, dust with brown sugar, sprinkle with lemon juice in buttered pot one to 1-1/2 hours at 375° F. The hollow can be filled with creamed spinach, Swiss chard, julienned ham, sausage.

SUMMER SQUASH, SELECTION: Should be fairly hard, heavy, unblemished and shiny. Light, spongy ones should be rejected.

STORAGE: Wash in chlorinated water, sun dry, store in paper bag in refrigerator. Vegetable bags are a second choice. Ziplocs make them rot.

COOKING: Summer squash is delicate and is often served raw in salads or as a garnish. It requires only the slightest cooking.

SAUTÉ for a few minutes in butter or oil.

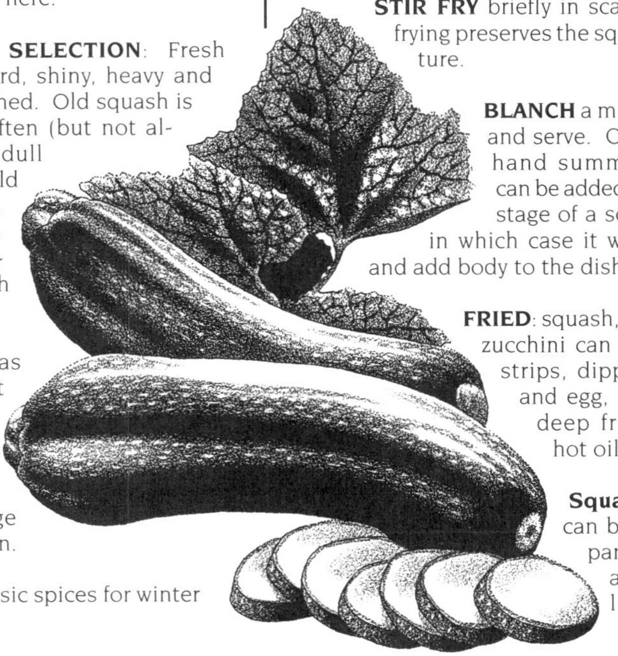

STIR FRY briefly in scant oil. Stir frying preserves the squashes' texture.

BLANCH a minute or two and serve. On the other hand summer squash can be added at the early stage of a soup or stew in which case it will dissolve and add body to the dish.

FRIED: squash, particularly zucchini can be cut into strips, dipped in milk and egg, floured and deep fried in very hot oil.

Squash flowers can be dipped in pancake batter and cooked like a pancake. The flowers can be stuffed with precooked ground meat such as lamb, greased and baked.

TOMATOES

Tomatoes are really a fruit but are treated as a vegetable. There are many varieties and many of them are much tastier than the three which make good cruising food. The ones not mentioned are, unfortunately quite delicate, bruise easily and do not travel well. The good travelers are the **globe** or **salad tomato** which is smooth, round and has a tough skin. Buy the biggest as they last the longest. The **Italian** tomato is smaller, oval, firmer, less juicy and used in cooking. They may be purchased almost green and rock hard. The small **cherry** tomato's tough skin protects it and prevents drying. Tomatoes are called an "acid fruit" which implies that food with a tomato base resists spoiling and, if canned, requires less pressure cooking.

SELECTION: The tastiest tomatoes have been vine ripened and never refrigerated. For cruising buy green tomatoes which show pronounced red. Totally green tomatoes will never ripen. Purchase tennis ball-sized globe tomatoes. Examine them carefully. Any with bruises or dark spots will rot before ripening.

CANNED TOMATOES: We recommend whole canned Italian tomatoes rather than globe tomatoes, tomato sauce or puree. Whole tomatoes can be blenderized into any thickness desired by draining water and liquefying. Canned Italian tomatoes are full of water and should be squeezed before adding to soups or stews.

STORAGE: Wash fresh tomatoes in chlorinated water and sun dry. Wrap in aluminum foil to prevent moisture loss and retard ripening. Keep cool, examine frequently after a week. They will last several weeks this way. Refrigerating tomatoes damages their flavor but extends their shelf -life. Refrigerate only ripe tomatoes.

PREPARATION: Skinning: Most tomatoes can be peeled with a sharp paring knife. You can also blanch tomatoes for a minute in a big pot of boiling water, then allow to cool. Dropping into ice water works best. The skins slip off easily. You can also squeeze out the seeds and toss a whole tomato into a stew. The skin may be pulled off as the tomato cooks. **Improving texture**: Tomatoes are extremely liquid. Their texture can be improved by squeezing, skinning, chopping, heavily salting, resqueezing, then washing to remove the salt. The toughened product holds up better in soups and stews.

COOKING: Tomatoes are usually eaten raw or cooked as an ingredient. Tomatoes can be brushed with oil and **grilled**, often on a skewer. **Baked, stuffed**: Select a large tomato, cut off the top, scoop out the inside, brush the outside with oil, stuff, set on a greased pan and bake fifteen to twenty minutes at 350° F. Stuffing may be whatever—tuna salad, bacon and spinach, shrimp and onions or shrimp salad. The ingredient is usually precooked. The stuffing may also be added after the tomato is cooked and cooled in which case a ball of foil is often inserted in the hollow to prevent the tomato from collapsing. **Raw stuffed**: Cut off top, scoop out interior, stuff with tuna, shrimp, crab, chicken salad.

STEWED TOMATO

This is a little different from marinara sauce (see Basic Stuff) and can be served as a side dish or over pasta with a little basil, goat cheese and garlic.

4 large tomatoes, skinned, seeded
2 teaspoons butter
1 medium onion, diced
1/2 cup celery, chopped
1 teaspoon sugar
1 teaspoon dill
1 teaspoon oregano
pinch salt and pepper

Sauté the onion, celery, herbs in butter until onions are soft. Add all other ingredients and simmer over low heat until just bubbling. Serve at once.

KILLER FRESH TOMATO SALSA

A tomatillo is not a tomato. It is a green berry covered with a leaf. You'll just love this.

3 serrano peppers, chopped (makes medium hot)
2 cups chopped tomatoes, peeled, seeded, drained

1 cup tomatillos (look like small green tomatoes)
1/2 cup red onion, diced, squeezed
3 cloves garlic, minced
1/2 cup cilantro, chopped
1/2 cup rice vinegar
1/4 cup olive oil
juice of 2 limes
1 teaspoon sugar
2 teaspoons salt (most will be lost)

Blenderize garlic, peppers, salt and tomatillos into a pulp. Add the onion and cilantro and blenderize ten seconds. Add the tomatoes and blenderize to the desired consistency. The resulting goo will be dull red with a greenish cast and look unappetizing. Do not despair.

Drain in a sieve, forcing out as much liquid as possible over about an hour. The salt will help pull out the water and the two run off together. The mush will lose about half of its volume. Add the oil slowly while stirring until the sauce glistens. Add the lime juice and rice vinegar slowly, to taste.

Salt to taste. Let stand one hour. Drain off excess liquid before serving. If you want the sauce "chunky" don't blenderize the tomatoes, chop them and add last.

TOMATO, OLIVE, CAPER CASSEROLE

4 large tomatoes, peeled, squeezed, sliced
2 cups white rice, blanched 5 minutes
1 leek, blanched, sliced
1 onion, sliced
1 cup celery, chopped
2 cups Greek olives, pitted, chopped
1/4 cup capers
1 cup feta cheese, diced
4 teaspoons olive oil
2 teaspoons oregano
1 teaspoon each: thyme, marjoram, salt, pepper

Combine all ingredients in a greased casserole, cover, bake at 350° F. for forty minutes.

TURNIPS AND RUTABAGAS

SELECTION: Bigger is definitely better and last longer. Should be rock hard, unblemished with unbroken skins.

STORAGE: If dirty leave dirty. Otherwise wash in chlorinated water and sun dry. Store in vegetable bag in refrigerator. Lasts weeks.

COOKING: May be eaten raw in salads.

ROASTED: Pare, quarter, add to pan like potatoes.

STEAMED (about fifteen minutes) or blanched and stir fried. Pare away skin, slice or chop. When steaming watch carefully as they overcook suddenly and become mushy and bland. They are very tasty blenderized like mashed potatoes. Particularly good mashed in combination with apples and potatoes.

YUCCA

Yucca root is a sort of tropical potato which grows in latitudes which are too hot for potatoes although their ranges overlap. If you go cruising you will be eating yuccas. They can be cooked and eaten like a potato: boiled, baked mashed or fried. Traditionally, after cooking, yuccas are covered with a mixture of oil, garlic, lemon juice salt and pepper. Yucca is very good French fried in very hot oil and tastes similar to French fried potatoes. It is particularly good fried in coconut oil, although the oil contains cholesterol. Yucca can also be used as a thickener in soups and stews. The central core is fibrous, so the yucca is usually quartered lengthwise and the core is removed.

Fresh yucca has a dry flaky skin but is sometimes dipped in wax to reduce moisture loss and make the root less perishable. I did not know this and tried to bake a waxed yucca—with dramatic results. When the wax got hot it smoked so fiercely it smoked us out. We had eat out!

YUCCA IN TOMATILLO SAUCE

2 pound yucca
8-10 ounce tomatillos
2 jalapeño peppers, seeded
4 cloves garlic
1/2 cup cilantro
1 red onion
olive or vegetable oil

Peel, then rinse yucca. Quarter lengthwise and remove core. Roughly chop. Add to salted, boiling water and simmer twenty minutes until tender. Blenderize or mash until fluffy. Add a little oil or butter if desired. Reserve. Blenderize remaining ingredients. Squeeze out excess water. Add oil until mixture glistens, about a quarter cup. Salt and pepper to taste.

ZUCCHINI: See summer squash

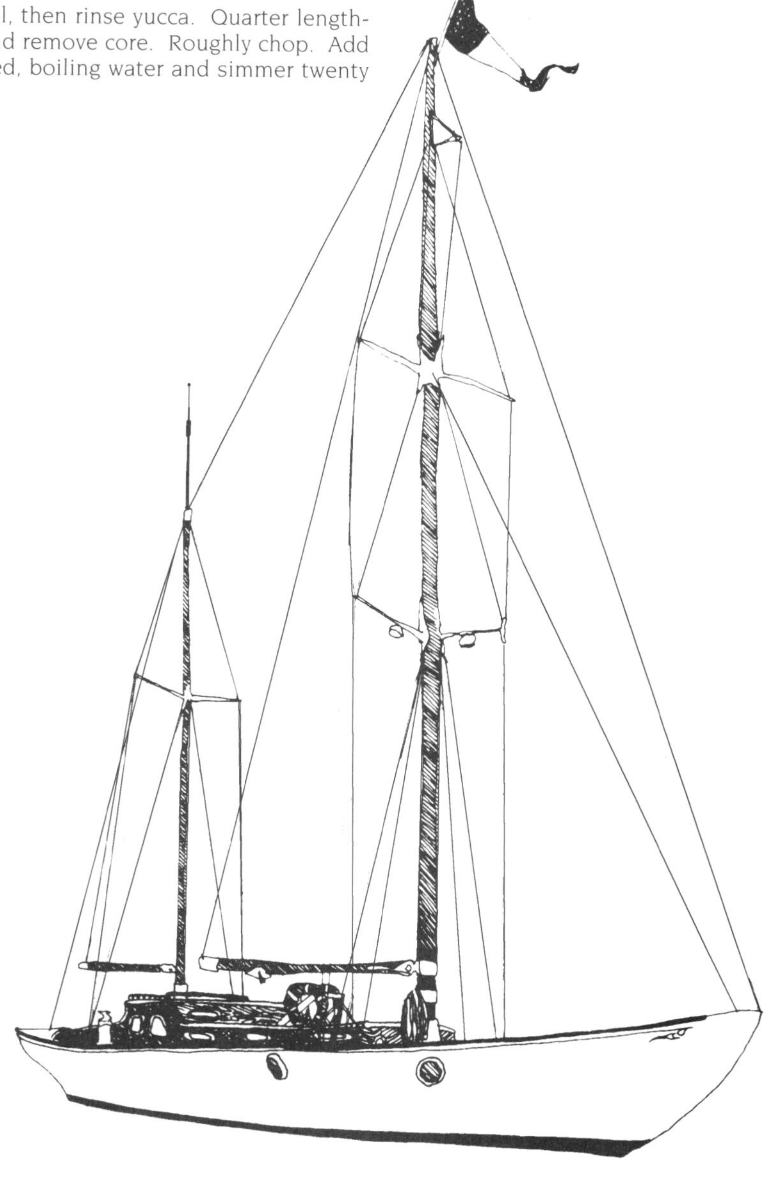

Barcarfolle

Atlas Mountain Bakery

17 The Bakery

Bread baking is not complicated and can be a very sensual experience—all that squeezing and kneading—but for me it is an art better suited to the home than a boat. There are bread baking devotees who live aboard and make fresh bread several times per week—but I am not among them. I have other things to do with my cruising time, like exploring and diving! If I cannot buy bread ashore I occasionally make quick pan breads, but more often than not, I just open a packaged pizza shell and heat it up, eat crackers or Melba toasts or fill that wheat-loving hole in my gut with pasta.

When it comes to baking bread, there is no substitute for a good oven which keeps a steady heat. The best ovens I ever saw were huge African beehives made of mud and stone, the size of small rooms. Some had been in operation for centuries. They were heated by packing the interior with wood and firing it off. This transferred the fire's heat to the oven walls, which then radiated pure heat, uncontaminated by fuel gasses. The fire's ashes were removed and bread was baked on the hot oven floor.

Boat ovens are notoriously poor bread baking devices, the very antithesis of the African beehive. They are small and poorly insulated, with little heat holding capacity. Opening the oven door greatly diminishes temperature, so one must develop a second sense to know when the bread is done. Nevertheless, such is the spirit of man that good bread can be baked even in them.

Alternate ways to make bread: You can bake bread in a **pressure cooker** or create a **Dutch oven** by placing a baking pan (containing the dough) on a trivet in a **large, nonstick pot** which is preheated over a medium flame. A **flame diffuser** beneath the pot further distributes the heat. **Potato bakers** or **portable ovens** can also be used. If a **fry pan** is to be used for baking, it is better to make relatively flat breads than to try to make raised, light golden loaves.

A medium propane or kerosene flame produces **baking temperature approximately 375° F.** You will have to experiment to get the correct baking time. Use a nonstick surface baking pan for best results.

PREPARATION: Consider the different recipes in this chapter before you set sail. Experiment, using the same materials as will be on board, until you find the dough that fits your needs.

BREAD AND CAKE MIXES

While packaged mixes are more expensive than "from scratch" recipes, they are convenient and consistent. The long shelf life of these products and the handy unit compensates for the difference in price. Mixes are easy to make. Most call for the addition of an egg, a little milk or just plain water.

PURCHASING: Packaged mixes should be purchased from stores with a rapid turnover of stock. In more isolated groceries where the volume of sales is low, packaged mixes may sit for years. After a while, they lose their flavor and ability to rise.

Examine the outside of the carton and reject those which seem to have been around for a long time. Check carefully for roach or ant holes, crushed ends, or signs of mold in the corners of the carton.

STORING: Remove package mixes from their box and **vacuum seal** with instructions. This will reduce the deterioration due to moisture and prevent the carton from flavoring the mix. Packaged mixes, flour, and other grains are among the few items that may be stored in a rather warm spot, such as the engine compartment.

ABOUT LEAVENING (RISING)

We expect full cooperation from our dough and no nonsense. Prima Donnas, Sometimes Risers, and fancy dressers have no place in a cruising oven. For this reason, we are inclined toward the use of **baking powder as a rising agent**.

Girl winnowing wheat

BAKING POWDER is a chemical which reacts with dough to produce **carbon dioxide** which is the **rising gas**. The process begins as soon as the ingredients are mixed with water. **Baking soda** accelerates this process. Baking powder is a fast acting, extremely reliable rising agent and that is its virtue. Baking powder bread is more crumbly than yeast breads producing a biscuit-like texture and that is its limitation. On the other hand, biscuits are well suited for a boat as they are quicker and easier to make than bread.

YEAST is a living organism which is rehydrated when mixed with water. It is sold as either a powder or a cake, which are interchangeable. Yeast eats the sugar and starches in the dough and produces carbon dioxide, which makes the bread rise. Yeast doughs rise slower/take longer than baking powder doughs but the result is a more chewy, more durable loaf. **Quick Rising Yeast** accelerates the rising process by about 50 percent.

Accelerators: Eggs add protein to dough and help it to rise. Yeast also likes **sugar** but too much sugar accelerates the rising process and can make the dough too hot. If the day is cold and the yeast slow, sprinkle a little sugar with the flour when the dough is kneaded. Salt, oil and cold **retard** rising.

Problems: The quality of yeast varies from place to place. It is sensitive to moisture and becomes unreliable with age. In places where the people eat unleavened breads (such as tortillas) packages of yeast may sit on the market shelf for years. Take a supply, vacuum seal it in small batches and store in the bilge. Yeast is not the best sailor. It does not like dampness, cold, or a falling barometer.

Temperature: Yeast doughs are happiest at eighty to eighty-five degrees. Excessive heat kills the yeast. Cold inhibits its action. In cold climates dough is often placed in an unlit oven with a large pot of hot water beneath it to keep the dough warm. Dough also loves freshly slept-in beds.

Speaking of beds, I knew a guy from Anchorage who claimed he put his dough in a cloth bag—and used it as a pillow. I wanted to know more, particularly the part about sleeping with hot dough, but didn't care to probe too deeply into the relationship. **Refrigerating dough** preserves it for several days. It should be kneaded and punched down once or twice. Refrigerated dough takes much longer to rise.

Punching down and **kneading** are processes essential to make yeast bread rise. Flour your hands first. Give the dough a good whack. Drop it onto a floured surface. Roll and push with the heels of your hands, then give the dough a half turn, fold over and repeat the process.

When kneaded, wheat proteins form **gluten** chains which lock in the carbon dioxide. Punching and kneading strengthen the strands of gluten, prevent them from breaking and improve flavor.

Crust finish: Crusts can be made soft and shiny by brushing the dough with butter prior to baking. Brushing with a mixture of egg and milk produces a crisp, glossy crust (see French Bread page 260).

ABOUT FLOUR

WHITE FLOUR is made from milled wheat. The heavy, tough (but flavorful) husk has been ground away. This makes the flour lighter and that is what makes white bread lighter than whole wheat or bran bread. Plain white flour does not produce a pearly white, ultimately light bread (which we call Bimbo bread) but it has a better taste. Plain white flour should be sifted before use.

Bleached flour is white flour that has been subjected to chlorine gas. It is used in the lightest breads and rolls. **Gravy flour** is bleached, coarsely ground, and has very low gluten. It is designed to resist clumping in hot liquids. It is fine for gravy and as a thickener but does not make good bread. **Pastry flour** is more finely milled than ordinary white flour and has less gluten. It produces crumbly flakes.

All-Purpose flour is a white flour mixture used for making dough. It is a combination of bleached flour and malted barley flour which improves yeast baking. All purpose flour is also **enriched** with several vitamins removed by milling, so the nutrition lost when the wheat is husked is restored.

WHOLE WHEAT FLOUR is a combination of both the wheat grain and its husk. It is more flavorful than white flour but the husk makes it a little heavier. It contains more gluten than white flour and is quite determined about yeast rising. White and whole wheat flour can be mixed together.

MIXED GRAIN FLOURS produce heavy bread because most of the other grains are oily and do not generate gluten. Mixed grain bread sold in supermarkets usually contains very little grain and is therefore similar to white bread. Real whole grain bread is delicious but usually breaks too easily to use for sandwiches.

SELECTION FROM BULK: (1) Examine the barrel and surrounding area for insect hairs and droppings. (2) Smell the flour for mold. (3) Pick up a pinch and rub it between your fingers. It should not feel gritty, indicating a quantity of sharp husk particles, or form clumps indicating dampness.

PREPARATION: Flour bought in remote places should be heated in an oven or fry pan before storage to kill mold, insect pests and their eggs.

STORAGE: All flour can get stale and whole grain flour contains oil which can become rancid. Therefore buy just what you need and refresh your supply frequently. Store in recipe-sized portions. A typical bread recipe (two loaves) requires about seven cups of flour. Vacuum seal.

YEAST-BREADS

BASIC WHITE BREAD

This basic, reliable recipe produces the classic white bread. It is a little heavier than Bimbo bread but has a nice texture and a delightful yeast smell. It requires about 2-1/2 hours to make or two hours if you use **quick rising yeast.**

You can add many ingredients such as nuts, vegetables, seeds, even fruit to the basic recipe. Our favorite is to add a handful of small dices of sharp cheddar, and a half cup per loaf of chopped, sautéed jalapeño and Anaheim peppers. This recipe makes two loaves.

The starter:
1/4 cup tepid (110° F.) water
2 cups tepid milk
1 package (1 tablespoon) yeast
2 tablespoons sugar

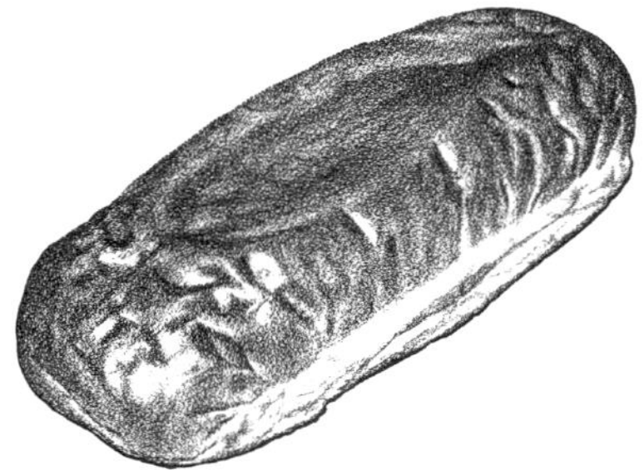

1 teaspoon honey
2 cups all-purpose flour

The mix:
2 tablespoons melted butter
1/3 cup honey
1 tablespoon salt

The final flour:
3-1/2 cups white all-purpose flour (or 50:50 white and whole wheat)

The glaze:
milk mixed with a beaten egg in it

BASIC INSTRUCTIONS FOR ALL YEAST BREADS

1. Add the yeast and a pinch of sugar to the water and let stand five minutes.
2. Beat in the rest of the starter, cover and let stand a half-hour.
3. Beat in the mix. Let stand fifteen minutes.
4. Add two cups of the final flour a little at a time. Toward the end, use your hands to knead the dough as it thickens. It should be firm, feel springy and moist but not sticky with a consistency thicker than bedding compound. Roll out onto a floured surface. The remainder of the final flour is picked up by the dough from the work surface.
5. Knead the dough for fifteen minutes, adding more flour a little at a time as needed to prevent stickiness. Coat the inside of a bowl with butter. Drop in the dough and roll it around to coat it with butter. Let stand until doubled in volume, about one hour.
6. Punch down, roll out and knead for fifteen minutes.
7. Divide into two loaves, roll and pull into shape to fit pan and place in buttered pans. Be sure to butter the pan corners. Cover and let rise until doubled.
8. Glaze with butter or milk/egg if desired.
9. Preheat oven. Bake forty minutes 375° F.
10. Test for doneness by tapping top of loaf. A hollow sound means the bread is baked. Steaming should cease.
11. Remove bread from pan and cool .
12. Allow to cool at least thirty minutes.

FRENCH BREAD

Makes two loaves

The starter:
2 packs yeast
2 cups tepid water
1-1/2 teaspoons salt
2 cups flour

The mix:
none

The final flour:
3-1/2 cups all-purpose flour

The separator:
corn meal

The glaze:
egg white (add a little water, whisk until frothy)

Follow instructions for white bread. Roll dough into two ten by fifteen inch rectangles. Roll rectangles into long loaves. Place on a greased baking sheet sprinkled with corn-meal. Make three or four diagonal cuts about a quarter inch deep across the dough with a sharp knife. Bake twenty minutes. Remove from oven, brush with egg white and water. Bake an additional fifteen to twenty minutes. Raise final oven temperature and reduce final baking time slightly for more crust.

PRESSURE COOKER BREAD

A simple and reliable salt water bread made in the pressure cooker.

The starter:
1 cup lukewarm water
1/2 cup sea water
2 teaspoons powdered yeast
1 teaspoon sugar

The mix:
2 tablespoons butter
1 teaspoon sugar
1 cup flour

The final flour:
2-1/2 cups unbleached flour

The separator:
1/3 cup corn meal

Optional additions to dough:
handful of raisins
2 tablespoons cinnamon
2 tablespoons brown sugar

1. Combine the starter. Let stand in temperate spot for five minutes. Add mix.
2. Sift and work in flour. Knead, roll out twice. Let stand covered in temperate spot until dough doubles in volume.
3. While dough is rising, thoroughly grease pressure cooker pot with cold butter. Add corn meal to pot as a separator. Close lid and shake vigorously to coat pot with meal. Leave loose meal in pot.
4. When dough has doubled in volume, punch down, knead, and allow to rise again. When dough has increased in volume by fifty percent, punch and knead again, then shape into a ball. Roll in butter and drop into pressure cooker pot. Let stand for fifteen to twenty minutes, then close lid and cook with valve off for forty-five minutes over a moderate flame. Use a flame diffuser.

YACHT CORRINA BRAN BREAD

This is a flat loaf that is relatively failure-proof and will retain its freshness for days. Makes one loaf.

The starter:
1/4 cup warm water
1/2 cup brown sugar
2 packs yeast

The mix:
2 cups warm milk
1 cup all-bran cereal
1 cup mixed, dried fruit (like raisins and chopped apricots)
1/2 teaspoon salt

The final flour:
2 cups all-purpose flour

Combine starter and allow to stand five minutes. Add mix, stir ten minutes; let stand in temperate spot for one hour. Add final flour; combine quickly with a minimum of beating. Bake in moderate oven for one hour; cool before serving.

WHOLE WHEAT BREAD

Makes two loaves

The starter:
1/3 cup brown sugar dissolved in 1-3/4 cups hot water (allow to cool)
1 pack yeast
3 tablespoons butter
2 cups all-purpose flour

The mix:
1 teaspoon salt
2 cups whole wheat flour

The final flour:
2-1/2 cups whole wheat flour
1/2 cup toasted wheat germ or miller's bran

Follow directions for white bread. Make a moderately stiff dough by adding the final flour a little at a time while kneading. Bake forty-five minutes in a 375° F. oven.

QUICK (BAKING POWDER) BREADS

YACHT KUMBAYA OATMEAL BREAD

This is a heavy, tasty bread that lasts for many days without going stale. Makes two loaves.

The mix:
2 cups white flour
1-1/2 teaspoons baking powder
1/2 teaspoon baking soda
3/4 teaspoon salt
1-1/2 cups quick oats

Other ingredients:
1/3 cup shortening or oil
2 eggs, beaten
1/2 cup maple syrup or molasses
1 cup yogurt
1/2 tablespoon lemon rind, grated
2 tablespoons lemon juice
4 tablespoons butter, melted

1. Preheat oven to 375° F. Grease pans with cold butter.
2. Cook and blenderize oats. Spread out and let cool to lukewarm.
3. Combine the mix and make a well in its center. Pour all other ingredients into

well, mix and knead. Roll out and re-knead.

4. Let rise for an hour, punch down and knead. Place in pan, paint with butter, let rest thirty minutes.
5. Bake for 50 minutes at 350° to 375° F. Test with toothpick.
6. Cool in pan ten minutes. Invert pan and drop on counter to free. Should come out clean. Cool an additional half-hour.

CLASSIC SHIP'S BISCUIT

Classic seventeenth century ship's biscuit was made to last for years. It was sold packed in soldered metal boxes or wooden barrels. The classic recipe lacked salt, which attracts moisture and enables mold to develop. When packed in barrels it usually became weevil-ridden after opening. Sailors would sometimes patiently tap the biscuit on the table, encouraging the weevils to depart.

This "food" was too hard and dry to eat by itself and was usually soaked in drippings, or crushed, pounded and mixed with cooked salt pork and split peas, producing a porridge-like mush. It could be very tasty (see our split pea soup recipe) but usually wasn't. Blue water cooks in those days relied on strong spices to conceal poor quality.

This same biscuit has been eaten by many an explorer. I made it many times in a campfire heated reflector oven and also made it on hot stones in the Sahara. This is a recipe for adventurers. It will serve you well. Learn it by heart.

This basic baking powder biscuit is virtually failure-proof and is much better salted and fresh than whatever came out of those barrels. It can be made in a fry pan or an oven. The secret of success is long beating—give everyone in the crew a turn. The product is a crumbly, chewy cake. This recipe makes eighteen biscuits.

Sift together:
2 cups bleached flour
1/2 teaspoon each salt, sugar
1 teaspoon baking powder

Combine with:
1/2 cup shortening or oil
1/2 cup water

Work in slowly to make a stiff dough. Beat at least five minutes, then roll out. Repeat two or more times. Roll out to half-inch thickness; cut into eighteen squares. Let rest one hour. Bake at 350° to 375° F. for twenty minutes on greased sheet without opening. Test for doneness with toothpick. If the tip pulls out dry, the biscuits are done.

FRYING PAN CORN BREAD

Makes one pan bread

Sift together:
1/2 cup white flour
2 teaspoons (heaping) baking powder
2 teaspoons sugar
1 teaspoon salt

Add:
1-1/2 cups yellow corn meal

Stir in:
3 teaspoons melted butter
1 egg, beaten with cooled melted butter
3/4 cup milk

Stir briefly; this bread does not like excessive handling. Grease fry pan and sprinkle with corn meal. Pour batter into cold pan. To prevent burning, never use more than a quarter-inch layer of batter in the bottom of a pan. Cook over low heat for twenty to thirty minutes, lid on, but loose. Test with toothpick; when toothpick pulls out dry, bread is done.

FLAT BREADS

SYRIAN PAN BREAD

This almost foolproof pancake-like bread is raised with baking powder and soda. The dough is rolled into a pancake not more than an eighth inch thick and then cooked in a lightly greased pan. The bread is browned on one side, then flipped just like a pancake. It rises to about three-quarters of an inch in thickness. Takes about fifteen minutes.

Sift together:
1-1/2 cups whole wheat or unbleached flour
1/4 teaspoon salt
1/2 teaspoon sugar
1 teaspoon baking powder
1 teaspoon baking soda

Combine and mix with dry ingredients:
1 egg, beaten
1 cup milk

Combine quickly and do not beat excessively. Let stand one hour. Take a lemon-sized ball of dough and roll out into a thin pancake not more than an eighth-inch thick. Work on a floured sheet and be sure that the dough is floured when placed in the pan.

Wipe a fry pan with an oily rag and heat until a test drop of water jumps from the pan before evaporating. Be careful that you do not let the grease smoke. Add dough. Reduce heat to medium, bake with lid on until browned, then flip and brown the other side.

INDIAN POORIE—FRIED PUFF BREAD

Poorie is a sort of fried soft cracker. It contains no leavening and therefore does not rise. It may be eaten hot from the pan, smeared with garlic, mustard and oil but we also like it sprinkled with confectioners sugar, cooled, served for breakfast. It keeps beautifully in a plastic bag. We cannot even begin to tell you how long it will last because good poorie has a tendency to disappear quickly, particularly at night. It makes a fine snack.

1 cup whole wheat flour
1 cup white flour
1/4 cup shortening or oil
1/2 teaspoon baking powder
2 teaspoons water, or a bit more as needed to make a pliable dough
cooking oil for pan

Knead until smooth; let rest for 1 hour. Shape into walnut sized balls and roll flat. Fry in eighth inch of hot fat. Cook until edges look just dry, not brown; flip and cook until golden. If sugar is to be sprinkled on, add when bread is hot from the pan.

TORTILLAS

There is no substitute for fresh tortillas but this well-known Mexican pan bread is available canned and isn't too bad.

1 cup flour
1/4 teaspoon salt
1-1/2 cups cold water
1/2 cup yellow corn meal
1 egg, beaten

Combine and beat until smooth adding water gradually to get desired consistency of light pancake batter. Spoon three teaspoons of batter onto a moderately hot, greased griddle to make a thin six-inch pancake. Turn when edges look dry, not brown. Tortillas may be bent while still hot and used to hold chili, chopped onions, peppers, and grated cheese. They may also be sprinkled with crumbled, fried bacon and a layer of hot baked beans.

SWEET BREADS

MY MOTHER'S BANANA BREAD

This is a heavy, sticky, extremely delicious dessert or breakfast bread which is more like a heavy cake. My mother used to bake it for me in coffee cans to make it immortal and utterly indestructible. She capped the cans while the bread was still hot, which kept it sterile and trapped moisture. To remove, cut open the bottom and forced out the loaf.

My mother would ship banana bread to me at the various ends of the earth which I called home. I received several by parachute and quite a few by float plane. A few arrived in diplomatic sacks and many, many came addressed "Post Restante" (General Delivery). My mother's banana bread has traveled more miles than most sailors. Learn this recipe, it will serve you well. Makes one loaf.

Combine:
1/3 cup butter
2/3 cup honey
1/3 cup sugar
2 teaspoons baking powder
1/2 teaspoon baking soda
2 cups flour

Add and beat until blended:
2 eggs beaten
1 cup mashed bananas (approximately 3 small)
1/3 cup water
1 teaspoon vanilla
1 cup milk

Mix separately, then combine with other ingredients:
1 teaspoon salt
raisins and walnuts to taste, up to 1-1/2 cups

Bake 350° F. for one hour until a toothpick inserted in center comes out clean. Remove from pan. Cool thoroughly and refrigerate overnight.

You can also make a zippy quick frosting by combining:
3/4 cup sugar
1 teaspoon lemon juice
2 tablespoons orange zest
1/2 teaspoon cinnamon
3 egg whites, beaten stiff

FRYING PAN SWEET BREAD

This fry pan cake is a reliable riser. Use corn meal as a separating agent. Makes one small cake.

Combine and let stand for one hour:
2 teaspoons (heaping) baking powder
1 teaspoon (heaping) corn flour
Enough sifted flour added to above ingredients to make 1 cup
1/2 cup brown sugar
1 egg in 1/2 cup of water beaten with brown sugar until foamy

Cook, lid on, over low heat for twenty minutes. Resist the temptation to look under the lid. After twenty minutes, test for doneness with toothpick. Plunge it into cake in several spots; it is cooked when toothpick pulls out dry. Cool cake.

Make icing from mixture of:
2 teaspoons butter
1 cup honey
juice of 2 lemons
1/2 cup confectioners sugar
pineapple juice to thin

DEEP FRIED COFFEE CAKE

Sift together:
2 cups all purpose flour
2-1/2 teaspoons sugar
1 teaspoon double-acting baking powder
1/2 teaspoon salt

Make a well in the center of the above ingredients and add:
1-1/4 cups milk
2 eggs, beaten with milk

Fold and turn ingredients until smooth. Heat one-inch of vegetable oil in deep fry pan until test drop of water jumps on surface. Put three-quarters cup of batter into a bowl, then pour into oil making a tight spiral. Deep fat fry for about three minutes on each side until golden Serve with confectioners sugar and cinnamon, or cinnamon and honey.

MISCELLANEOUS

GARLIC BREAD

This is not a bread recipe, but a nice way to salvage stale bread, dry ship's bread, or even to enliven packaged toasts.

Melt in pan:
4 teaspoons butter
1/2 cup olive oil

Add to pan:
3 to 4 cloves garlic, minced
1 teaspoon rosemary

Heat until garlic just simmers and add:
1 teaspoon thyme or oregano
optional: fresh chopped cilantro, parsley, basil

Heat for another minute. Brush mixture on slices. Sprinkle in a bit of Parmesan cheese if desired. Wrap loosely in foil. Cook over low heat until bread begins to brown. Serve piping hot.

PANCAKES

Pancakes and simple pan breads are more at home in the galley than good oven breads and they are more reliable. Pancake batters don't like excessive beating and should sit for a half hour before use to obtain best results. Don't worry about a few lumps; they will disappear when cooked. The batter should run like thick porridge. A little flour or milk may be added at the last moment to correct the consistency.

Never make a huge, thick pancake. Pancakes should not exceed a diameter of four to five inches and must be thin to be light and fluffy. Pancakes are not fried. The grease used should be just enough to keep the cake from sticking. Good non-stick pans need the barest suggestion of light oil. Apply by wiping with a greasy paper towel.

Pancakes are not lovers of heavy weather. When the barometer is falling or the sea is rough, they usually end up heavy and doughy. In addition, the rising process is not effective if the ingredients are cold.

GRIDDLE HEAT is of considerable importance. A sure test for correct heat is to sprinkle a few drips of water on the heated pan. If the water jumps a few times before vanishing, the temperature is correct. If it sits there and boils, the pan is too cool; if it instantly disappears, the pan is too hot.

PANCAKE BATTER is not poured onto the griddle; it should just run off the tip of a big spoon. This assures a round and thin cake. A few moments before the first side of the cake is cooked, bubbles appear on the uncooked surface. The cake is ready for turning when the larger bubbles begin to break.

The bottom of the pancake should be inspected just before turning to see that it is sufficiently browned. Flip the cake and cook until the second side is golden brown, two to three minutes. Steaming ceases just before the cake is finished.

BASIC PANCAKE BATTER

Makes sixteen pancakes, 3-1//2 to 4 inches

Sift together:
1-1/2 cups flour
3 tablespoons sugar
1 teaspoon salt
2 teaspoons baking powder

Combine:
1 egg
3 tablespoons butter, melted
1-1/4 cups milk

Quickly combine all ingredients, mixing for a minute or so. Leave in a few lumps. Allow to stand for an hour or two before cooking for best results.

WHOLE WHEAT PANCAKES

Make as above, but use fifty percent whole-grained flour. Add two teaspoons molasses to batter and handle as above.

CORN FLAPJACKS

Combine:
1 cup white corn meal
1/3 cup white flour
3/4 teaspoon baking soda
1-1/2 teaspoons salt

Combine and blend with dry ingredients:
2 cups buttermilk or sour milk
2 eggs
1/2 cup butter, melted

CREPES

Crêpes are a special type of pancake used for desserts or stuffed with a variety of meats, poultry, fish, or cheese to produce an elegant main course. The basic crêpe may be cooked in advance and quickly warmed in a pan just before serving. Learning to make a good crêpe is like learning to sail. There are a few tricks, but learn once and future success is automatic. The recipe for basic crêpes follows. Dessert crêpes are included in the dessert chapter.

The following basic pancake recipe may be endlessly varied by rolling up with jelly, chopped and sautéed fruit, honey, cinnamon, raisins, chopped dates, even mashed bananas. Makes about 12 pancakes.

Blenderize until smooth:
3 eggs
1 cup flour
1-1/2 teaspoons sugar
1/3 cup water
1 cup milk
pinch salt

If the crêpe is to be used "as is," the batter is now complete. If the crêpe is for dessert you may optionally add:

2 tablespoons powdered sugar
1 teaspoon vanilla
2 teaspoons orange or lemon zest, grated

Let batter stand a few hours. Wipe bottom of hot seven inch skillet or crêpe pan with butter, just enough to make an oily film. Use a nonstick skillet if possible. Pour about four teaspoons of batter into hot skillet; give skillet a few gentle twists to spread batter and make the crepe quite thin.

Brown crêpes about forty-five seconds over a moderate heat, turn and complete in about fifteen to twenty seconds. Be careful edges do not become dry and leathery. Immediately remove from pan to a cool plate.

Main course crêpes may be stuffed with seafood au gratin or whatever. Or while the crêpe is still in the pan, add a generous dab of grated, mild cheese. After the cheese melts, fold the crêpe in half. Another nice version is to fold in precooked pork sausage, braised beef, or sautéed vegetables with one of the sauces given in the sauce chapter.

DOUGHNUTS

The secret with doughnuts is to have the oil in the pan very hot, but not smoking. If the oil is too cool, it will penetrate the dough and make it oily. If it is too hot, the crust will be too hard and may burn. Don't try to cook too many doughnuts at one time. The cool dough reduces the temperature of the oil. Doughnuts should cook for about 1-1/2 minutes per side. Add each doughnut at fifteen to twenty second intervals. It is helpful to have a crewman cut some of the dough and sugar the cooked doughnuts. Makes 16 doughnuts.

Combine:
1 egg, beaten
1/2 cup sugar
2 teaspoons melted butter or shortening

Sift together:
2 cups sifted flour
1/4 teaspoon cinnamon
2 teaspoons baking powder
1/4 teaspoon salt

Mix the wet and dry ingredients. Roll out to half-inch thickness; cut and fry in deep fat.

FRITTERS

In this book two types of fritters have been included: **corn fritters** that are similar to a fluffy pancake, and **seafood or vegetable fritters** that are more like seafood fried with a coating. The batter for seafood and vegetable fritters is similar to a simple pancake batter; but like crepes, it must stand for a while before cooking or the result will taste gluey.

The onshore recipes for fritter batter call for it to stand six to twelve hours, but, of course, this is usually not possible on a yacht. Our fritter secret is threefold: 1) minimize the amount of beating or stirring; 2) use warm beer instead of water because the yeast in the beer helps to lighten the batter; 3) use eggs as specified but only half of the whites because batters heavy with yolks crust better and stay light and fluffy inside. Let the batter stand at least an hour or two, even overnight.

FRITTER BATTER FOR SEAFOOD OR VEGETABLES

Batter for three cups of ingredients

Combine in large mixing bowl:
1 cup beer
1 teaspoon salt
1/2 teaspoon pepper
1 teaspoon cooking oil
1 egg, well beaten

Combine thoroughly and add one tablespoon at a time:
1-1/2 cups sifted flour

Combine each addition with a few strokes of a whisk. The final batter should have the consistency of heavy motor oil. To test, batter should hang about two inches off the spoon before breaking. Add more or less flour as needed, but do not beat the batter with more than about twenty strokes. Let the batter sit for an hour or two, then use it to coat chunks of your favorite seafood or vegetables.

SANDWICHES

PEANUT BUTTER SANDWICHES

No bread chapter would be complete without a few sandwich suggestions, and no sandwich suggestions would be complete without peanut butter. Peanut butter is extremely nutritious, but hard to digest if consumed in quantity. Go easy when you spread it.

Everyone knows about peanut butter and jelly sandwiches. Jam or jelly is, of course, made from fruit. To cut down on sugar, we make a fresh fruit compote to use in place of jam. Just sauté a firm, seasonal fruit, such as apples, with a chopped orange and a little honey. This makes a fine combination with peanut butter.

We also enjoy peanut butter sandwiches made with bacon, tomato, and lettuce, or fried sliced ham, or sliced hard-cooked egg, lettuce, tomato, sliced cheese and onion.

TUNA SANDWICHES

To make tuna sandwiches more interesting, try flaking the tuna, sprinkling with a few drops of lemon juice, and adding any one of the following combinations:

- Onion, mayonnaise, mustard, and dill weed (optional)
- Onion, chopped celery, and mayonnaise
- Hard-boiled egg rounds, onion, and mustard
- Chopped green pepper
- Tomatoes, sweet pickles, and mayonnaise or thousand Island dressing
- Chopped parsley and sliced cucumbers
- Pimento, green olives, and mayonnaise

FRENCH TOAST

French toast is particularly useful on a boat because it can be made from stale bread if fresh is not available.

Soak bread slices in mixture of:
2 beaten eggs
1/2 cup milk
1 teaspoon salt
pinch pepper

Fry over medium heat in butter. Fry until toast is golden brown. Serve with butter and syrup. For lunch or supper, French toast may be served with several different sauces, such as cheese, marinara, or rarebit.

MODIFIED FRENCH TOAST

Thoroughly combine:
2 eggs
1/4 cup condensed milk
1/2 cup condensed tomato soup
1/2 teaspoon salt
pinch pepper

Mix and proceed as for regular French toast.

GRILLED CHEESE SANDWICHES

Lightly toast bread. Spread with butter, then with thin slices of cheese. We like sharp cheddar. Broil or heat in pan until cheese begins to melt. Be careful. The consistency of cheese breaks if overheated. Turn off flame and allow to stand until cheese is thoroughly melted.

For variety, try adding any of the following to your next grilled cheese sandwich:

- Fried salami
- Fried onions
- Ham slices, sausage or bacon

SARDINE PATÉ SANDWICH

What do you do after the fresh meat is gone, the cheese has gotten moldy, and someone has thrown a bag of tools on the tomatoes? The crew of the *Fire Witch* recommends this delightful sardine paté made from the long-lasting stores.

Soak two pieces of chopped white toast or stale bread in:
1/2 cup white vinegar
1/2 teaspoon sugar
2 teaspoons salt
6 dashes tabasco

Mash thoroughly:
2 cans sardines, drained
2 medium onions, chopped
4 hard-boiled eggs
3 tablespoons mayonnaise

Mix ingredients thoroughly. Tastes better the next day. Serve at room temperature on bread or crackers. Sardine paté also makes an excellent dip.

MONTE CRISTO SANDWICH

Dip one side of each rye bread slice in a beaten egg and add:
canned ham, sliced thin

mustard (in the middle)
cheese (Cheddar, Swiss, American), sliced thin

Fry dipped side out, in a little butter until egg browns a bit. Serve with sliced onions. Delicious!

REUBEN SANDWICH

Layer on buttered rye bread:
corned beef or thinly sliced ham
sauerkraut
Swiss cheese

Cook open face in fry pan or under broiler until cheese melts. Add mayonnaise and catsup, mixed one to one. Close with another slice of buttered toast.

SALAMi SANDWICHES

Try grilled salami slices, our favorite, on pan toasted bread with any of the following.

sliced mild cheese, mustard, and onion
sweet pickles, onion, and mustard garlic mayonnaise
sauerkraut and mustard
sliced cucumbers, sweet pickles and onions
cooked, curried lentils, sweet pickles, and mustard

CREAM CHEESE SANDWICHES

We can't decide which of the following is our favorite with cream cheese.

sauce and onion on black bread
black olives on whole wheat bread
anchovies on whole wheat bread
avocados on whole wheat bread
cucumber and onion on white bread
bean sprouts, oil, and cold peas

BACON SANDWICHes

In addition to the traditional bacon, lettuce, tomato, and mayonnaise on toast, try adding one of following to your next bacon sandwich.

cooked lentils, sliced onion
mustard, peanut butter, lettuce, and tomato
fried egg with mayonnaise
baked beans on toast
tomato, avocado, and French dressing
sliced chicken and crumbled Roquefort cheese

HAM SANDWICHes

ham, Swiss cheese, onions and sweet pickles, rye bread
ham, onions, mustard, and mayonnaise, white bread
ham, sliced hard-boiled eggs, and thousand island dressing on toast
ham, steamed cabbage, and mustard, rye toast
ham, fried egg, and catsup on white toast
ham, fried egg, tomatoes, and butter on whole wheat toast

CANNED CORNED BEEF SANDWICHES

Add any of the following to hot, flaked corn beef:
grated mild cheese, melted on the sandwich
sweet pickle, onions, and mustard on rye bread
tomato and mayonnaise on white bread
baked beans with curry powder on rye bread
fried egg, open face on whole wheat bread

EGG SANDWICHES

For sandwiches, the traditional "over easy" egg is fried a bit more than usual so that the yolk is somewhat gluey to make it easier to eat. A second technique is to break the yolk when you turn the egg; we never have any trouble doing that!

A hot fried egg on buttered whole wheat or an English muffin tastes delicious with any of the following:

grilled ham, mustard, and mayonnaise
grilled tomato, lettuce, butter, and scallions
baked beans, mild grated cheese, mustard, and butter
marinara sauce and Parmesan cheese
fried onions and anchovies
onions deviled ham and black olives

EGG SALAD SANDWICH

Mix lightly and spread on toast:
3 hard-boiled eggs, chopped
1/2 small onion, well chopped
1/2 teaspoon celery seed
1/2 teaspoon dill
2 stalks celery, finely chopped
3 teaspoons mayonnaise
1 teaspoon mustard
1/2 teaspoon salt and pepper
juice of 1/2 lemon

OPEN FACE SANDWICHES

FISHERMAN'S SANDWICH

We have seen this sandwich eaten by fishermen in so many different places that it is impossible to guess its origin. The bread of tradition is white, rough, crusty, and usually a day old. The dryness of slightly stale bread makes it soak up the flavors of the pan.

Fry until light golden:
1 onion, finely chopped
4 cloves garlic, peeled
1/4 cup olive oil

Pour off half the oil into another pan. Add to onions:
1 teaspoon basil
1 teaspoon each thyme and oregano
2 teaspoons tomato paste
2 Italian tomatoes, peeled, seeded, chopped, squeezed

Simmer for ten minutes. In remaining oil, fry four large slices of bread until lightly toasted. Turn bread; fry one minute, then pour on sauce and continue cooking for five minutes. Crisscross each portion with anchovies and serve.

THE POOR BOY, HERO, OR ZEP

Cut in half lengthwise:
loaf of crusty bakery bread

Spread both slices with:
mayonnaise

On the bottom half, arrange layers of any or all of the following:
sandwich meat
shredded ham
sliced salami
spam
bologna
pepperoni
cheese slices (provolone, Swiss, American)
tomato
pickles
boiled egg slices
sauerkraut
lettuce
onion
anchovies

Spread generously with mustard. If desired, sprinkle lightly with oil and vinegar or vinaigrette. Cut into manageable portions.

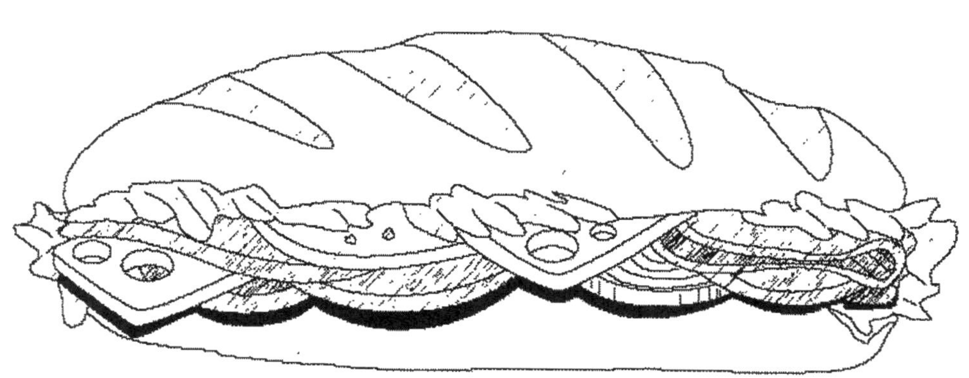

18 Desserts

Wise chefs know that dessert is the most important part of the meal, or as the old saying goes "leave them gasping." A good dessert is a delight but it can also somewhat dim the memory of any shortcomings in the meal. This may be devious but it works! We have presented here only quick, simple, surefire absolutely delicious recipes which we have tested many, many times. We are great devotees of simple desserts. "Dessert" as my old grandmother used to say, "should be a little something sweet in the mouth."

DESSERT OMELETS

Somewhat neglected in the dessert world, light and lovely dessert omelets seem to be made just for the cruising chef. A hearty salad followed by a dessert omelet is a complete meal. Desert omelets are nourishing, easy to make, and sweet enough to be satisfying. They are thin and light, similar in many ways to a crêpe. The pan is brought to high heat, the egg poured in, and the flame immediately reduced. The hot pan gives the omelet some color, but it must be cooked slowly thereafter or it will be tough.

BASIC DESSERT OMELET

Serves two

Combine and beat for twenty seconds:
3 egg yolks
2 egg whites
3 teaspoons cream or condensed milk
1/2 teaspoon sugar
1/4 teaspoon vanilla

Add to large, slope-sided fry pan a generous tablespoon butter and heat until sizzling. Pour in egg mixture and reduce to medium heat. The omelet should take about four minutes to cook. It is done when the top is just set and still glistening.

OMELET FILLING

The filling can be poured in a band across the center of the omelet in which case the edges are folded in. It can also be poured on one side. The fry pan is then tilted and shaken so that the empty side of the omelet shakes onto a plate and the filled side is flipped on top.

APPLE FILLER

Serves three

Sauté over medium heat:
2 teaspoons butter
2 apples, cored, peeled and chopped
1/4 cup raisins
1/4 cup rum
pinch cinnamon
3 teaspoons brown sugar

Stir frequently to avoid burning. Sauté until apples are soft.

QUICK FRUIT PRESERVE FILLER

Any good quality preserve with lots of fruit pieces may be used. Serves three.

One cup finely chopped fruit, such as bananas, mangos, peaches, or canned fruit, such as cherries or apricots. Add squeeze of lemon. Add to preserves. Heat until mixture bubbles. Spread in a broad band across middle of omelet; fold edges. Sprinkle top with powdered sugar.

THE CAPTAIN'S FRUIT FILLING

I save this one for special days in the middle of a long passage. That is a good time for occasional culinary wonders. Firm fruit, preferably fresh (not citrus), must be used for this filling. Apples and bananas make a good combination. Serves three.

1/4 cup raisins soaked in enough rum to cover for 2 hours

Sauté until soft:
1 ripe banana, sliced
4 teaspoons butter

Add to the pan:
3 teaspoons rum (from raisins)
1 teaspoon Grand Marnier or other liqueur
1-1/2 teaspoons lemon juice
1/4 cup brown sugar
3 teaspoons white sugar
1/2 cup fruit juice with mixed with 1 teaspoon arrowroot

Add arrowroot slowly, stirring constantly. Add raisins. Simmer until liquid is like syrup, stirring constantly. Do not allow to boil

CRÉPES

CRÊPES SUZETTE AND CRÊPES REBECCA

Christmas, mid-Atlantic, 20°36' N, 55°00' W, a fond hello and "Season's Greetings" to Ocean Station Echo, U.S. Coast Guard at 35°06' N, 48°00' W. Hell hath no fury like a woman scorned or a wife used to a big Colorado Christmas who must spend her holiday at sea. Tears. Sulking. Too many cigarettes smoked. Silence. But then dinner time came and we had a candied ham with sweet potatoes that couldn't be beat, and I whipped up these lovely crêpes from materials at hand.

Crêpes Suzettes are used to emergencies. They were invented by the great chef, Henri Carpentier for Prince Albert of Wales. Henri accidentally set fire to the delicate crêpe sauce literally under the prince's nose, much to everyone's horror. Never daunted in the face of disaster, Henri quickly poured the burning liquid over the pancake and served at once, hoping, we guess, to minimize the damage. The effort was a resounding success and Henri, as much a politician as a chef, named the dish Crêpes Albert. But there was a young lady present and the prince, a master himself at diplomacy, asked if the lovely dish could be renamed after the lady. We have followed suit.

The Suzette sauce (make in advance):
1/2 cup butter
1 teaspoon orange rind, shredded
1/2 cup orange juice
1/4 cup Grand Marnier or Triple Sec
1/4 cup brandy
1/3 cup sugar
6 crêpes

Simmer sugar, Gran Marnier, orange rind, orange juice in small pot until thickened. Pour the brandy into a small sauce pan and warm just before use. Do not boil.

Combining the crêpe and the sauce: paint both sides of the crêpe in sauce. Fold crêpe into a triangle and place in large skillet. Warm. As a last, extravagant touch, add a pinch of brown sugar on top of each crêpe, flame the pot of brandy and pour over all. Turn down the oil lamps, me hearties, serve at once!

CRÊPES REBECCA

Crêpes Rebecca includes a spoonful or two of the **Captain's Fruit Filling** inserted into the Crêpe Suzette before it is flamed. A slice of sautéed banana is a garnish.

NUT AND CURRANT DUFF

Serves four

Combine:
6 teaspoons sugar, granulated
3/4 cup milk
2 teaspoons baking powder
1 cup currants/raisins, or 3 heaping teaspoons jam
1/2 cup walnuts, chopped
2-1/2 cups flour

Place in greased casserole and bake for thirty minutes at 350° F.

CUSTARDS

ZABAGLIONE

This delicious light custard is the essence of simplicity. It takes about six minutes to make. It is made like a hollandaise sauce but the butter has been replaced with Grand Marnier. How delightfully decadent! Like hollandaise sauce, it can be ruined easily by fast cooking. Use a double-boiler. Bring water in the boiler to a fast simmer, not a rolling boil. Serves four.

Beat until light, then add to pot:
6 egg yolks
1/2 cup sugar
1/2 cup cream
ginger to taste

Whisk furiously. When mixture begins to foam and thicken, slowly add:
1/2 cup Grand Marnier, warmed and flamed

Continue to beat constantly until mixture thickens and has consistency of very soft ice cream. This process cannot be accelerated by turning up the heat, which would scorch the ingredients. Pour into large wine or sherbet glasses; chill or serve warm.

The egg whites may be beaten stiff and folded into the custard which expands it or use as a topping when combined with:

1/4 cup confectioners sugar
1 teaspoon freshly grated orange rind
1/2 teaspoon vanilla extract

END-OF-THE-PASSAGE ORANGE CUSTARD

The process for making this quick dessert is quite similar to that of the previous recipe for Zabaglione. It takes only seven to eight minutes to cook; be sure all the ingredients are ready for instant use. This custard may be served hot or cold. Serves four.

6 eggs
1/2 cup sugar
1 teaspoon orange rind, grated
1 cup warm milk
1/2 orange, chopped, drained

Combine yolks, sugar, and orange rind. Heat mixture in double boiler. Stir constantly until liquid foams slightly and begins to thicken. Then add milk slowly. Stir constantly until mixture turns into custard.

Remove from heat and add:
2 oranges, well chopped and seeded
1/2 ounces Grand Marnier (optional)

Combine:
3 egg whites, stiffly beaten
1/2 teaspoon vanilla
1/2 cup confectioners sugar
1-1/2 teaspoons lemon juice

Fold into custard. Chill.

CHOCOLATE CUSTARD

This dessert is in no way similar to instant commercial chocolate pudding. It takes two pots and about eight minutes to cook. Serves four.

Combine over low heat, stirring constantly until chocolate is dissolved:
1-1/2 cups condensed milk, or half & half (better)
6 ounces milk chocolate bars, grated

Thicken in double boiler:
5 egg yolks
3 teaspoons sugar
1 tablespoon rum

Slowly add the melted chocolate, a little at a time, stirring constantly until each addition thickens. Serve hot or cold.

MOUSSE AU CHOCOLATE

The above recipe becomes mousse au chocolate by first chilling the custard

Fold in:
3/4 cup whipped cream
1/2 teaspoon vanilla
1 teaspoon brandy

BAKED LEMON MOUSSE

Serves four

1/2 stick butter
1/2 cup lemon or lime juice
1/3 cup brown sugar
2/3 cup sugar
4 egg yolks
2 teaspoons lemon zest
4 egg whites with a pinch of salt, beaten stiff

Butter four oven bowls and sprinkle with brown sugar. Combine butter, lemon juice, half of both sugars and simmer, then remove from heat. Add egg yolks, one at a time stirring furiously. Add lemon zest and stir furiously over low heat until mixture thickens, about five minutes. Allow to cool. Mix custard and remaining sugar with egg whites, folding in with a few strokes. Bake in 400° F. oven for about fifteen minutes until puffy. Serve hot.

BERRY MOUSSE IN GELATIN

Serves six

1 packet gelatin
1 lemon zest
2 teaspoons water
1-1/2 pints of berries
4 teaspoons Grand Marnier or Triple Sec
2 egg yolks
1/2 cup sugar
2 cups whipped cream

Mix gelatin and water. Add zest, lemon juice, 2/3 of berries and 1/2 of liqueur and bring to rolling boil. Cool. Beat egg yolks and sugar and cook in a double boiler until thick, about ten minutes, whisking furiously. Cool. Combine berry mixture with eggs and pour into serving bowls. Chill until set. Cover with whipped cream. Cut remaining berries, toss in remaining liqueur and use as a garnish.

FLAN

No desert chapter would be complete without Flan and Creme Brulée. You can add orange or lemon zest to this recipe to modify it. Serves six.

The caramel sauce:
1/2 cup sugar
3 teaspoons water
Vanilla (optional)

The custard (combine)
1 cup orange juice
6 whole eggs, lightly beaten
1/2 cup sugar
3 teaspoons whipping cream
1 teaspoon Grand Marnier (optional)
1/ 2 teaspoon vanilla

Make **caramel sauce** by heating sugar/water in a sauce pan until bubbling. Pour into six oven cups and swirl to coat sides. Allow to cool. Add **custard mixture** to cups and bake at 350° F. about thirty minutes until set. Refrigerate or let stand at room temperature until cool.

CREME BRULÉE

You can also add fresh berries, lemon or orange zest to this custard as a variation. Pour berries, lemon juice and sugar in bottom of cup, then cover with custard. Serves four.

Mix:
1-1/2 cups half & half
3 teaspoons sugar
2 whole eggs
1/2 teaspoon vanilla
confectioners sugar

Combine everything but milk. Heat milk almost to boil. Reduce to low heat. Stir in eggs, whisking furiously. Remove from heat and cool when mixture begins to thicken. Cool pot bottom with sponge. Pour immediately into four oven cups. Place cups in pan and fill pan with water to two-thirds height of cups. Bake at 350° for about thirty-five minutes until inserted toothpick comes out clean. Cool for several hours.

PUDDINGS

END-OF-THE-PASSAGE RICE 'N RAISIN PUDDING

This old favorite is made from long-lasting ingredients. Steam in a double-boiler for about thirty minutes. Serves four.

1 cup rice, cooked
3/4 cup milk (condensed)
3 teaspoons sugar, or 4 tablespoons brown sugar
2 eggs beaten
1/2 teaspoon lemon rind, grated
1 teaspoon lemon juice
1/2 cup raisins
1/4 cup chopped almonds, walnuts, or hazelnuts
2 teaspoons rum

Combine all ingredients and stir thoroughly. Grease a double boiler with butter; cook pudding for about thirty minutes or until set. Sprinkle each serving with cinnamon.

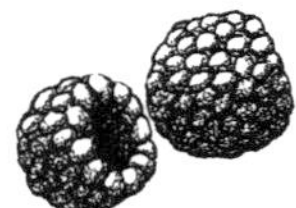

ENGLISH RICE PUDDING

A simpler recipe than the one above.

2 cups hot milk
1/2 cup white short grain rice
1/2 cap-full of vanilla
2 egg yolks
1/4 cup sugar
1/2 cup cream

Cook milk, white rice, vanilla in a pot (do not pressure cook) until rice is quite soft. Add more milk as needed. Combine remaining ingredients and add slowly to pot. Put in an oven dish and brown under broiler. Allow to cool.

TAPIOCA PUDDING

Tapioca stores well, cooks quickly, and makes a fine base for a variety of desserts. A double-boiler should be used; the water should be boiling when the tapioca is added. Serves two.

Combine:
3 teaspoons quick tapioca
1 egg, beaten
1/2 cup sugar
1/2 teaspoon vanilla
a pinch of salt

Cook without stirring for seven minutes. Stir a few times and cook for an additional five minutes. Cool. Try adding alone or in combination with any of the following: almond extract, grated orange or lemon rind, cinnamon, honey, shredded coconut, chopped nuts, canned fruit, chopped fresh fruit, chopped raisins, chopped dates and/ or chopped figs.

FRESH FRUIT FOR DESSERT

FRESH FRUIT COMPOTE

In this example we use strawberries but you can use apples, bananas, mangos, berries, peaches, or plums.

1 pint strawberries
1/2 cup orange juice
juice of 1 lemon
4 teaspoons brown sugar
1 teaspoon white sugar
1/4 cup rum

Pick out the ugliest strawberries and thinly slice, then chop to make one cup. Quarter the remaining strawberries and place them in bowls. Simmer all liquids until they are reduced to a syrup. Add chopped strawberries and simmer one minute. Spoon this mixture over the berries in the bowls and serve.

GLAZED APPLES

Since apples are part of the long lasting base supply you can count on this recipe to yield a fresh dessert even at the end of a long passage. It can be served on French toast or on top of key lime custard.

Combine with a half-cup orange juice:
1 teaspoon corn starch
dash of rum (optional)
2 teaspoons orange zest (minced bitter skin of orange)
1/2 cup brown sugar
1 teaspoon lemon juice
2 pinches each cinnamon, allspice
3 apples, peeled and sliced
2 teaspoons butter

Sauté apples in butter until golden. Sprinkle with spices and a little lemon juice while cooking. Remove and reserve apples. Add all other ingredients and thicken. Arrange apples on plate or over French toast, pancakes, muffins, etc. Pour sauce over all.

STRAWBERRY ICE

Make a larger quantity of the fruit compote described above. Add to blender and fill blender two-thirds full of strawberries. Liquefy and pour into a plastic bag. Place in freezer or against holding plate until frozen. Try to freeze so fruit mixture is flat. When ready to serve, slice strips with a sharp knife and serve over flambéed bananas (below).

BANANAS FOSTER (BANANA FLAMBÉ)

Learn this recipe, it will serve you well. Slice one banana per person lengthwise and sauté in butter. Let flat side brown, then turn.

Add to pan:
1/2 cup orange juice
2 teaspoons brown sugar
1 teaspoon white sugar
pinch cinnamon

Sauté over low heat until the sauce thickens or add one teaspoon arrowroot dissolved in a little orange juice. As the sauce thickens, **pour on and flame**:

1/4 cup Grand Marnier, rum or Triple Sec (orange liqueur)

Place bananas on plate and add sauce.

PEARS GRENADINE

4 pears (not too ripe), peeled, cored
2 tablespoons Grenadine
3/4 cup brown sugar
2-1/2 cups fruity wine
1 pinch cinnamon
juice of 1 lemon

Place ingredients in a covered pot, simmer for about twenty minutes. This produces a tasty but firm pear. To cook until soft, simmer about one hour. Remove pears, simmer until reduced to one cup. Pour over pears and chill. Delicious. Makes four portions.

FRUIT SALAD

Cut up enough fruit to make six cups. Do not use citrus fruit. Serves four.

Add to bowl:
1 teaspoon lemon juice
2 teaspoons brown sugar
1 teaspoon white sugar
2 teaspoons rum, Grand Marnier or Triple Sec

Toss lightly and refrigerate.

BERRY FOOLS

2 cups fresh berries
1 teaspoon sugar
1/2 cup berry preserve or jam
1 teaspoon lemon juice
2 cups whipping cream
1/2 cup Grand Marnier or Triple Sec

Whip the cream and sugar until stiff. Fold in jam with a few quick strokes. Heat the Gran Marnier in a small pot until it bubbles. Toss in the berries and simmer one minute. Ignite and allow to flame out. Cool mixture Place a dollop of berries in bottom of each dish. Sprinkle with lemon. Pour cream mixture on top and refrigerate.

DRIED FRUIT

No cruising galley is really complete without dried fruit. It lasts for months, is very nutritious, and can be made into a variety of desserts. Since dried fruit weighs about eighty percent less than when fresh, a little goes a long way. It can be eaten as is for a snack or "plumped" by simmering for fifteen minutes in all sorts of delightful liquids such as liqueur, lemon juice and sugar, or wine, cinnamon and cloves. Reconstituted in this way, dried fruit makes a fine filling for a dessert omelet or, mixed with a bit of honey, a fine syrup for pancakes.

DRIED FRUIT DELIGHT

Soak 1-1/2 cups dried fruit overnight in:
1 cup water or rum
juice of 1 lemon
pinch cinnamon
3 tablespoons of your favorite liqueur (optional)

Bring to simmer and sweeten to taste with honey or brown sugar. Add liquor.

FRIED FRUIT WITH FRESH CITRUS

Citrus fruit usually lasts several months and adds zest to dried fruit. Soak dried fruit for a few hours in citrus fruit juice and brown sugar. Simmer for fifteen minutes. Eat as is or serve over cake. Delicious!

DESSERT CHEESE

Hard cheese, such as provolone, aged Romano, or sharp cheddar served with nuts, olives, and crackers makes a fine dessert. After-dinner wines, such as port and sweet sherry, add the finishing touch. Hard cheese can be made into a dessert spread by mixing grated cheese, a little butter or cottage cheese and a dash of flavoring, such as vanilla, almond extract, brandy, or Grand Marnier. Grated hard cheese mixed with cream cheese is delicious.

The truly hard, aged cheeses, such as old provolone, Romano, and very sharp cheddar, last a long time without any sort of preservation. Soft cheese such as Montrachet can be placed in a small canning jar, covered with oil and seasoned with a pinch of herb such as thyme. The cheese will last many months this way without refrigeration.

UNCOOKED PIES

The recipes below call for a store-bought cracker crumb pie shell which feeds four, so we are just providing stuffing recipes below. None of these pies is baked and the stuffing is solidified by refrigerating.

BANANA CREAM PIE

Bake three bananas in their skins for thirty minutes at 350° F. or until soft. Place in bowl, add the juice of a half lemon and mash the bananas into the juice. Blenderize three egg whites until stiff. Blenderize three-quarters cup whipping cream until stiff.

Add to the whipped cream:
1/4 cup white sugar
1/2 teaspoon vanilla
1 teaspoon orange zest
the banana pulp

Fold in the egg white with a few strokes and place in the pie shell. Refrigerate.

Quick Key Lime Pie

1 can condensed, sweetened milk, chilled
3 eggs, yolks beaten stiff
1/2 cup lime juice
3 teaspoons sugar (or to taste)
1 teaspoon lime zest
pinch of salt

Combine milk and lime juice. Beat whites stiff and add lime zest, a pinch of sugar, adding sugar slowly until quite stiff. At last minute combine ingredients and pour into cracker crumb crust. Chill and serve.

BOSTON BANANA CREAM PIE

2 bananas baked until soft and mashed with juice of 1 lemon
6 egg yolks
1/2 cup whipped cream
1-1/2 cups sugar
3 cups milk
1 teaspoon butter
1 teaspoon vanilla extract
2 teaspoons brown sugar
1/4 cup pecan bits

Heat the egg yolks, sugar and corn starch until thick. Do not boil. Add all other ingredients except whipped cream and pour into pie shell. Spread whipped cream on top, sprinkle with nuts and brown sugar

QUICK OVEN CHEESE CAKE

Here are several incredibly simple dessert extravaganzas which fill a cracker crumb pie shell.

SOUR CREAM CHEESE CAKE

The filling:

1-1/2 pounds cream cheese
1/2 cup sugar
juice of 1 lemon
2 teaspoons almond liqueur or Triple Sec
1/2 teaspoon vanilla
3 eggs

The topping:
2 cups sour cream
1 teaspoon sugar
2 teaspoons lemon zest
1/2 cup sliced almonds or walnuts (to garnish)

Preheat oven to 350° F. Combine filling and pour into shell. Bake about forty-five minutes until top begins to crack. Allow to cool completely. Add topping, bake at 375° F. for fifteen minutes. Allow to cool and sprinkle nuts on top.

Philaropes

19 Sauces

VEGETABLE SAUCES

ANCHOVY BUTTER AND ALMONDS

Melt **two tablespoons butter** in a sauce pan. Fry until golden **three tablespoons almonds**, chopped Add: **four to six anchovies**, chopped. Sauté for a few minutes. Toss vegetables in this mixture; add salt and pepper to taste.

BREAD CRUMB AND ONION SAUCE

Melt in a sauce pan and fry until golden:
2 tablespoons butter
1 small onion, well chopped

Add four heaping tablespoons **bread or cracker crumbs**. Sauté until golden. Add one tablespoon **marjoram**, salt and pepper. Toss vegetables in the mixture.

QUICK CHINESE SAUCE

3 tablespoons butter
2 tablespoons bread crumbs
1 tablespoon each: mustard, vinegar, Worcestershire sauce

Melt butter. Add and sauté bread crumbs until golden. Add remaining ingredients. Also optionally add hot sauce. Pour over vegetables

MEAT, FISH, FOWL SAUCES

BUTTER SAUCES

Here are several combinations of herbs and spices which beat well into soft butter for use on meat or fish. After mixing the butter can be chilled and decoratively cut.

garlic, parsley, pepper, sage
garlic, minced sun dried tomato, rosemary, lemon
garlic, soy, dry mustard, blue cheese

Mix with vermouth or white wine, simmer until reduced. Add butter and serve or make a *roux* with the butter and add milk.

ORANGE SAUCE

For ribs and duck

3/4 cup sugar
1/4 cup honey
3 tablespoons rum
1-1/2 cups fresh orange juice
juice of 1 lemon
2 tablespoons orange zest
4 cloves garlic, minced
1/2 tablespoon each: dry mustard, pepper, ginger

Put sugar in a skillet, add the rum and caramelize over low heat until golden, cool a few minutes. Add remaining ingredients and simmer over low heat fifteen minutes. If you wish to thicken remove some of the sauce, add 1-1/2 tablespoons arrowroot and simmer until thick. Do not boil. Serve cool.

QUICK ORANGE SAUCE

3/4 cup bitter orange marmalade
1-1/2 cups fresh orange juice
3 tablespoons rum
juice of 1 lemon
1 tablespoon brown sugar

Combine, warm and serve.

Jalapeño CREAM SAUCE

For chicken or seafood

2-4 jalapeños cooked, seeded and chopped (handle with rubber gloves)
1 cup hard cheese or hard and goat cheese, grated
1/4 cup olive oil
3 tablespoons flour
1/2 stick of butter (2 ounces)
6 garlic cloves, chopped
1 cup milk

Fry the flour in butter and oil until light golden. Add all other ingredients and half the milk. Keep adding milk until the desired thickness is reached.

ROASTED GARLIC CREAM SAUCE

We have yet to find a meat, fish or fowl that does not do well in this sauce. You can cut up grilled chicken or shrimp, add to the sauce and pour over pasta. Also it is delicious over boiled potatoes.

This delicious sauce is usually made while grilling or using the oven. Roast a bulb of garlic in a 350° F. oven for twenty minutes or wrap the bulb in aluminum foil and place at the edge of the grill for about a half-hour. Use a toothpick to test. Should be soft.

1 bulb roasted garlic, squeezed out, minced
2 tablespoons butter
2 shallots, or 1 medium onion, minced
1 can chicken consommé
3 cups heavy cream or evaporated milk
1 tablespoon each salt and lime juice
pinch of pepper

Cook shallots in butter until translucent. Add other ingredients and simmer over low heat until reduced as thick as you like. Makes about two cups which means you are reducing by one-third.

BÉARNAISE SAUCE

1 cup white wine
1 tablespoon vinegar
2 shallots or 1 small onion, blenderized
1 sprig parsley
pinch pepper
1 tablespoon each tarragon, chervil
3 egg yolks beaten
1/2 cup butter
1/2 cup oil

Simmer everything but egg, butter and oil over high heat until reduced by half. Cool slightly and strain. Mix eggs, butter and oil. Add to pan, whisking furiously. Simmer over very low heat or use a double boiler. Allow to thicken. Have a wet sponge standing by to cool pan bottom.

UNIVERSAL SAUCES FOR MAIN COURSES

WELSH RAREBIT SAUCE

This classic sauce can be just served over toast, over rice, pasta, hamburger or even poached eggs. Delicious.

3 tablespoons butter
1 tablespoon oil
3 tablespoons flour
1 tablespoon dry mustard
1 can beer
1 pound sharp cheddar cheese, grated
1 tablespoon horseradish (optional)
dash of Tabasco sauce, salt, pepper

Melt the butter and oil, sprinkle in the flour and dry mustard, sauté over low heat until golden Add the beer, whisking furiously. Cook five minutes until thickened. Add all other ingredients and simmer over very low heat for ten minutes. Garnish with apples.

HUMMUS

We love this as a sauce or paté and it also makes a great sandwich spread. We would be less than fair however if we did not give you two warnings: This is extremely fattening and it is unwise to remain in an enclosed area with friends after consuming it.

1-1/2 cups canned chick peas
3 tablespoons tamari
juice of 1 lemon
3 cloves garlic
1 cup sour cream
1 teaspoon black pepper
1/2 cup chopped scallions

Blenderize everything except scallions. Add them last and stir in. A nice variation is to add a jar of artichoke hearts and blenderize.

EGG AND CHEESE SAUCES

FONDUE

Add to a saucepan over low heat:
2 cups dry white wine
1/4 cups Kirsch
2 tablespoons cornstarch

As mixture starts to simmer, slowly add:
1/2 pound Gruyère cheese, grated
2 cloves garlic, minced
pinch of nutmeg
1/2 tablespoon salt
1/2 teaspoon white pepper

Add more cheese as the mixture melts. Do not simmer. Serve with toast or crackers.

HOLLANDAISE SAUCE

Hollandaise is an absolutely delicious sauce with a wide variety of uses. It is well known served over vegetables but is just as delicious over poached fish, eggs and veal. There is always another use for a good hollandaise sauce and many possible modifications to make it even more versatile.

BLENDER HOLLANDAISE

Heat a half cup of butter until it is crackling but do not burn. Blenderize. With the blender running, add 1-1/2 teaspoons lemon juice and four egg yolks. That's it!

HANDMADE HOLLANDAISE

Handmade hollandaise is traditionally made in a double boiler which limits pan temperature to 212° F. This is the faster, riskier way.

Have a large wet sponge or towel nearby. This will be used later to arrest the pot's heat.

Melt a half cup butter, three tablespoons light oil until crackling. Remove pot from heat and add four egg yolks. Whisk furiously. If the sauce does not completely jell put it back on the flame for not more than twenty seconds at a time.

If the sauce starts to overcook and looks like bits of scrambled egg, quickly add 1-1/2 teaspoons lemon juice (or a lump of cold butter) and set the pot on the wet sponge. Stir frantically. Further rapid cooling can be achieved with cream. Salt to taste. Use white pepper.

MODIFIED HOLLANDAISE

Hollandaise can be "cut" with sour cream. Grated cheese is an excellent addition, particularly Romano. Cheese can also be quickly shaken into the sauce to arrest its cooking. Sautéed slivered almonds make a good addition and create a fine fish sauce. Hollandaise can be sweetened with sugar, flavored with rum and cinnamon and served on a sautéed banana for dessert or mixed with heavy cream and combined with fruit. As a fish sauce it can be modified with a bit more lemon juice and finely chopped dill. A large amount of very finely chopped parsley will make hollandaise into a green sauce for shrimp or fish.

CRANBERRY SAUCE

Delicious with meatballs or burgers.

Combine and heat:
1 can cranberries, crushed
juice of 1 lemon
1 teaspoon cornstarch diluted in 1/2 cup beer
sugar to taste

Simmer over low heat stirring constantly until the sauce thickens.

QUICK SAUCES FROM CANS

Quick MUSHROOM CREAM SAUCE

Heat:
1 can condensed cream of mushroom soup
1/2 cup condensed milk
1/2 cup Parmesan cheese
salt and pepper to taste

QUICK CHICKEN CREAM SAUCE

1 can condensed cream of chicken soup
1/2 cup chicken stock
2 tablespoons butter
pinch of celery salt and pepper
squeeze of lemon juice

QUICK TOMATO SAUCE

1 can tomato paste
2 tablespoons onion, grated
1/2 tablespoon sugar
juice of 1/2 lemon
1 large can Italian tomatoes, chopped, squeezed

Blenderize. Simmer fifteen minutes. Add chopped green peppers, olives, capers, pickled onions, etc.

MARINADES

A marinade is a seasoned liquid in which poultry, meat or fish are steeped. A marinade impregnates flavor, stabilizes color, adds moisture to grilled food and frequently tenderizes. A very spicy marinade, like a dominant sauce, can also improve bland food. Most marinades are used to prepare food which is to be grilled or braised in a pan.

A marinade consists of three parts: an **acid** like lemon or fruit juice, vinegar, wine or soy; **oil**; and **flavorings**. In an oily marinade the oil dominates. Acid is a tenderizer and also begins the cooking process, especially for fish. Ceviche is, after all, fish which has been "cooked" or "pickled" with lemon juice. Marinades are steeping liquids but they can frequently be used as basting sauces while the cooking is in progress.

MARINADE TIPS

1. Never add salt to a marinade as this leaches juice from the meat
2. Make marinade in a mixing bowl then pour into a freezer bag. Drop in the meat or fish, squeeze out air and seal. Kneed occasionally.
3. Marinating time depends on the size of the meat. Large roasts- six to twenty-four hours; steaks and chops two to six hours; shish kabob two hours; brochettes one hour; fish fillets in soy twenty minutes, without soy one hour; chicken parts one to four hours.
4. When tenderizer is added to a marinade the meat is usually served with a dominating sauce.
5. Chill while marinating, warm to room temperature before cooking.

MEAT MARINADE

1/2 cup olive oil
1/2 cup red wine
juice of 1/2 lemon
6 garlic cloves, crushed, chopped
1 tablespoon each, any, all or none: oregano, thyme, sage, pepper, cumin, powdered mustard

SPICY MEAT MARINADE

1/2 cup olive oil
1/4 cup lemon juice
1 tablespoon sugar
1/2 cup hot sauce or chili paste
1 tablespoon powdered mustard, oregano
2 tablespoons powdered sage
8 cloves garlic, chopped
variation: add 4 tablespoons chili powder, chopped hot peppers to taste

ACID-FRUIT MARINADE FOR PORK

You can marinate tender pork for a few hours or soften tough or dry meat by chilling overnight with an acidic marinade like this one. The sour marinade can then be sweetened with honey and brown sugar to make a glaze.

1/2 cup white vinegar
3 cups chopped fresh pineapple
1 cup chopped dried fruit
1 cup orange juice
1 or 2 cloves

Variation: use canned, drained pineapple plus a half cup lemon juice.

FISH SAUCES

SOY MARINADE FOR FISH

4 tablespoons soy sauce
1/4 cup white wine
1 tablespoon powdered ginger
1/2 cup sesame, walnut or olive oil
4 cloves minced garlic
juice of 1/2 lemon

CURRY MARINADE FOR FISH

This is a simple recipe which produces a curry flavor less dominant than most sauces.

1 cup coconut milk
juice of 1/2 lemon
2 tablespoons curry powder
1 tablespoon ginger powder
1 tablespoon turmeric
1 tablespoon sugar
pinch of pepper

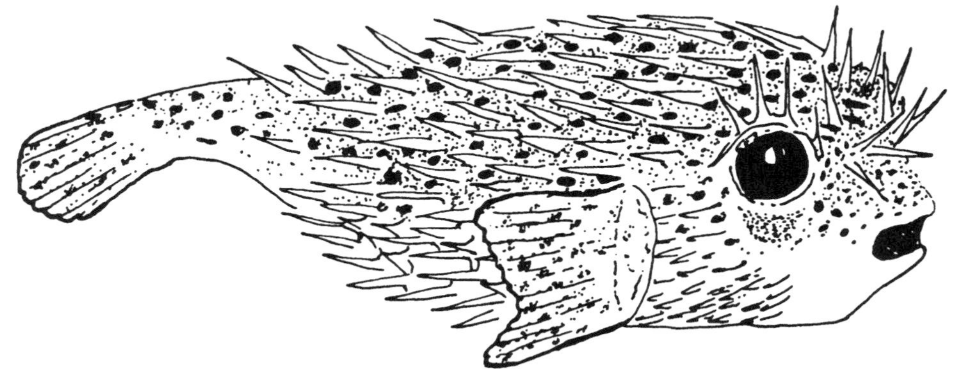

20 Night of Falling Birds

"That's where the *Sweet Marie* broke up, about ten years back, come Christmas," our crewman Shep said. He pointed toward a spot far out on the Abaco reef, where the black water wells up suddenly from the depths and crashes heavily against white coral.

"It was sure a sad thing," he continued, shaking his head. "We all watched it from right here on the hill—hid behind the light keeper's shack for a bit to keep dry. The Little Harbor beacon there . . .," he said, pointing aloft, "it blew right off the tower and was gone. Even here, on this hill, so far from the sea, the air was full of spray and blown sand. Ya' couldn't hardly breathe. And the noise! Between the crashing of the waves and the palm fronds all beatin' together—we finally got inside the light keeper's shack for relief but there was no relief for Capt'n Marcus. We could see him out there on deck, fightin' the storm the whole time, waves breakin' over him every few minutes. It was terrible to watch, I can tell ya'," Shep said with a sigh.

"Capt'n Marcus was a fool to go out that afternoon, with the seas in such a rage. The Little Harbor beacon here just disappeared in the night. Never even found the globe. A few pieces of the lantern turned up as far away as the Bight of Old Robinson, can ya' beat that? And the roof of this shack took off like a bird and landed in the bay. That alone should have been enough for him—the bar was breaking so hard, white sea smoke was rising from it like fire; enough to chill the blood. But that old fool had the money from twenty-six Haitians heavy in his pocket, paid in advance to make Cap Haitian before Christmas. Oh, how he smiled that morning, thinking of all the presents he could buy, maybe even an engine for the *Sweet Marie*. He could only think of the money and didn't give a damn about the rage."

"Why didn't the others stop him?" I asked.

"Capt'n Marcus wasn't the kind of man you could stop once he'd made up his mind. Besides, those blacks had been building the highway up in Marsh Harbor for maybe a year. A year's a long time for a man with a family. All they could think about was hoppin' in the sack with Mama. They couldn't read the signs or just didn't care. Or maybe the sea just called them.

"Maybe Capt'n Marcus just got too good. He'd run that bar many a time in rough seas—used to delight in it. He didn't give a damn about rough seas or anything else once he got the tiller in his hand. He was always daring that police cutter to follow right behind. They never did and I think they were smart. They could never go where Capt'n Marcus went, no sir. The sea woulda' got 'em for sure. But Marcus always made it, slicker'n a cat. No sir, he didn't give a damn about rough seas, but this is what we call a Great Rage, when the sea wants blood, it's a great killer storm that will eat all living things—fish and birds and ships and men.

"Well, Capt'n Marcus had an onshore breeze to boot, damn fool—but he run the *Sweet Marie* way up on the inside, above North Bar Channel to get a good run through the reef. Oh, that fool, that ol' smackboat could never beat into a gale at her best, let alone loaded with thirty men. Yes, thirty men with the crew and a forty-six foot boat with no engine.

"The *Sweet Marie* went through the breakers like a shot, disappeared into that howling smoke on the bar and we all thought she was gone. But she came through all right, sailed past the breaker line, water running like crazy off her decks, half drowned but still movin' with Capt'n Marcus standin' tall at the tiller. We had to give it to that old fool for guts then, but that wasn't the end of it. He must have parted his jib halyard or somethin'—couldn't set the jib for a bit. And that was the end. He couldn't beat past Elbow Reef. He had to tack back to the south. Not much hope after that. He was caught on a lee shore with the only chance of escape dead to windward into that storm.

"Well, Marcus wasn't thinkin' right at all that day—I guess the time for clear thinking was past. I could hardly think myself, with all the noise an' wind, and I was safe on shore! Capt'n Marcus could have turned right then and driven her down on the beach, but it probably never occurred to him—he was a fighter. He tacked back and forth all afternoon, not losin' much ground, but not gainin' any either—tackin' back and forth between the reefs, hopin I guess for a shift in the wind.

"About six that evening, gawd, it was a dreary sunset, like it was the end of the world. It was just about dark and there'd be no hope then, tackin' back and forth in the night, waiting for the reef to take him. Just then, I suppose Capt'n Marcus thought he saw his chance. From up here on the hill, by the wreck of the lighthouse, it looked for a bit like he made it all right. We was just ready to go down and have a few drinks to celebrate.

"I don't know if he ever saw the coral head he hit—it was getting pretty dark—or maybe he saw it and hoped to slip by on the wave crest. We saw the ship strike. Then the masts went over the side. We stood and listened to the cries of the men as they drowned. Too bad. That big head was the last bad spot before the deep water. After that, Capt'n Marcus could have run around Cherokee Point and been gone."

"The Greeks would say he sailed off despite the omens," I said.

"Ol' Marcus didn't know about omens," Shep replied. "He just spent so many years on that old smackboat, always walkin' on the thin edge of danger, just stickin' his toe over the line now and then to bait the devil—drunk Saturday nights—he'd stumble into church, Sunday morning, late as usual, still high as a kite, but very repentant. I'd have to bite my hand to keep from laughin'. Yep, he used to repent 'til the bar opened. It was straight downhill after that," Shep said with a quiet laugh.

"But I guess you're right," he said, looking at the distant breakers, "Marcus sailed so far in the *Sweet Marie*, ran in so many loads of beer, so many illegals, got so good in her I guess he finally thought there weren't nothin' he couldn't do. Didn't read the 'omen' as you say. He lost his fear.

"That night, when the bodies floated ashore, that was a bad time. Big sharks and other things we never seen before swam the shallows, glowing all green in the darkness. We found squid twenty-five feet long in the surf an' other things too ugly to mention. It rained that night; black mud and dead birds fell from the sky. We was glad enough to be lying snug in Little Harbor with three anchors down and a big warp tied to a coconut palm. I don't know much about omens, but I'll tell you no man living had the courage to go out that night and look for Capt'n Marcus."

"Did anyone survive?" I asked.

"Nope, we found six bodies in the surf the next day. The masts and doghouse roof came up with them. You can still see a few pieces of iron ballast down there on the bottom. Not much, though. She was an old boat and didn't have much metal in her. Even the kids who went down to look at her a few days later didn't find much—just an old pair of Marcus' shoes and a small silver cross—musta' been a present fer someone. Yup, even the gulls got more than those kids—how the birds screamed over that spot! The sea got the rest—the hull and thirty men. Marcus' body washed up a couple of days later. He looked kinda' calm. Some folks said it served him right, blasphemin' the way he did. But I don't know; he wasn't all that bad. He was a big talker but he was a real sailor. Maybe in his heart he'd made his peace with the sea."

Smugglers Moon over Gibraltar

21 The Great Polvoronis Smuggle

"We need a man with a boat who can operate at night and doesn't mind taking a few risks. It's worth 500 pounds for a night's work with no questions asked." Our onboard visitor was a small man with broad shoulders, swarthy skin, and a fine handlebar mustache that pointed proudly toward the sky. His arms were disproportionately large with a deceptive flabbiness that often conceals the strength of a boxer. He had a thick neck and bulldog face with heavy jowls that quivered when he talked. He held a Moroccan pipe in his teeth, and as he talked, smoke wafted from his mouth, filtered through his great mustache, then drifted upward to obscure his face in a gray cloud. His words were intoned with a unique accent: a mixture of Moorish, Spanish, Arabic, and English that identified the native Gibraltarian.

Spanish authorities had closed the border several years before making the tiny peninsula a political island—a symbol of British tenacity, not an actual fortress. The Gibraltarians, long accustomed to siege, have since tightened their belts a little and increased trade with Morocco by buying foodstuffs, raw materials, and unskilled labor. Because of increased trade by sea and the strategic location of the rock, smuggling flourishes. Cigarettes, whiskey, and television sets are smuggled out: jewels, hashish, and hard drugs are smuggled in.

As for our nameless messenger, he stood right in the middle of our companionway, completely blocking it with his stocky frame, as though to prevent escape.

"Well, what do you say?" he asked, looking fiercely at Rebecca, my first mate, and me. His offer was almost a demand.

Five hundred pounds is a tidy sum. A tidy sum indeed for an evening's work. It was nearly Christmas, and the extra "quid" would go a long way toward making it festive. Rebecca could buy lovely clothes, and I could outfit our 39-foot sloop with a set of new sails. But what kind of cargo was worth that much money? Surely it had to be heroin or raw opium to be worth 500 pounds per run.

"What's the load?" I demanded, determined to be just as stubborn as the dark stranger who confronted us.

"No questions are part of the deal," he replied. "You just be at a certain spot down the coast and a boat will come out to load you up."

"What's the cargo and quantity? If you can't give us answers, we aren't interested," I said, already dismissing the possibility of an agreement. The man looked thoughtfully at us for a moment, pulled a tobacco pouch from his pocket, reloaded his pipe, and fired it with great care. Smoke reeled overhead and swirled around a kerosene lamp giving the tiny cabin a softer hue. We could almost see his mind swaying like a pendulum, and soon it polarized.

"It's Polvoronis and Spanish hams from Tarifa. About 15,000 polvoronis and as many hams as the boat will hold to top off the load," he said.

"Polvoronis? You don't mean Spanish Christmas cookies?" I said incredulously.

"That's it," he replied.

"What kind of a fool do you think I am, expecting me to buy a fairy tale like that? You're running junk or hash or refugees, something really seamy I'll bet, and you think that by whispering a few words in my ear I'll go floating off down the coast to give you a hand. Well, just hop on up those steps behind you and flit off." I was furious—sure by his answer that his game was dope.

"Shut your gab, wind your neck in, and I'll tell you a few things, my friend," he said with a patient smile; he was not at all disturbed by my words. "Most of the people in this town are Spaniards or, at least, have some Spanish blood in them. It was once the tradition around here for men to go to Spain, usually Algeceris or San Reque, and find a wife. Many families around here speak Spanish and eat Spanish food...or at least they did until the blockade. When Spain closed the border, they also embargoed all exports, particularly food, hoping to force the Spanish people off the rock. Well, it takes more than that to break the people in this place," he said, gesturing upward toward the huge, craggy cliffs that rose from the bay behind us. "But people certainly do miss their 'cafe con leche' in the morning. English coffee is vile. It tastes like boiled tires! You know if you've ever tried the local variety. And they also miss their cheese, like Roncal or Burges, light fluffy tortillas like Hueves a la flamenca, and sweet little nothings like bizcocho. Then the wine ran out," he said, a little sadly. "The Alella was the last to go," and a hopeful gleam of remembrance flickered in his eyes. "Ah, it was so light and sharp. It crept into your soul like a little devil and made you both sad and happy at the same time.

"We have Portuguese wine now. It tastes like rabbit droppings. Well," he said drawing himself up proudly, "it takes more than that to make us knuckle under. But now it's Christmas and that nasty Northwester has been blowing for a whole week. It's too rough for the fishing boats that normally do a little 'free trading' with friends in Estapona. So the little bit of nice cheese and wine that we used to bring in are gone. But that's okay. We can do without. But now it's Christmas and we have no polvoronis." A sullen look came into his eyes. "The English, they ship us the flour and the nuts and so forth and all the shops try to make it, but it comes out like dirt with little cinders in it. The ingredients are all wrong. And then there is the ham. What is Christmas without a nice ham? Our ham comes from Italy and it's not too bad, but it's Italian ham; they don't age it in nice, cool caves like the Spanish ham. No, my friend, it's very different. Christmas will be very sad indeed without the Polvoronis and the ham. Very sad." He mumbled to himself as he turned to leave.

"Wait!" I cried. "Maybe we'll give it a try. By the way, what's your name?"

"Call me Nicholas," he replied.

The sky was the color of boiled lead and the barometer was still dropping as we pointed the bow of the *Fire Witch* toward the Strait of Gibraltar. The Northwester had been hurling gusts of up to sixty knots through the mouth of the strait, lashing the water into a fury, creating huge overfalls, columns of water which shot out of the sea like the blast from a volcano, flinging everything in its path aside. Rebecca manned the tiller. I stood watch up forward with a pair of binoculars and was often covered to my waist by the frothing sea. That 500 quid was beginning to look smaller and smaller as the *Fire Witch* bucked the turbulent sea. Night rolled over us like a miasmal cloud; we tried to stay in the lee, hugging the northern shore precariously close to those watchful eyes in Spain. Huge super tankers lumbered by, virtual mountains of steel and speed, loaded so heavily with crude oil that only a few feet of their incredible freeboard could be seen. The skipper of one once told me it takes eighteen miles just to stop the brutes—in an emergency! So, regardless of the "rules of the road," we avoided them with scrupulous care.

Finally, we heard the mournful siren on Pointe del Tarifa long before we saw its red and white flash flicker through the gloom. It took us six hours to make the twelve miles from Gibraltar to Tarifa, so it was well past midnight when we received the recognition signal from the little fishing vessel that chugged out to meet us.

Although it was impossible to see more than a few hundred feet in the turbulent darkness, we were so close to the lighthouse that I felt naked and trapped every time the light flashed. The *Fire Witch* rolled drunkenly on the swells—first one rail under, then the other. The fishing boat eased slowly and cautiously nearer, then was caught on a breaking wave and smashed violently into us crushing a rub rail and scraping our side. With curses and shouts in many languages, lines were flung and made fast, tires were dropped between the boats to reduce damage, and Rebecca jockeyed our now appended *Fire Witch* to face the storm.

Then the loading began; it was a murderously dangerous job in rough seas. Each box of Polvoronis became an evil personality on those tossing decks. Each box, safely loaded, became a major triumph. We filled the entire forward compartment then started loading hams. They were in sacks, so a well timed heave got them aboard quickly. We must have loaded two hundred before the first rays of dawn put an end to our struggles.

With the wind behind us the *Fire Witch* fairly flew toward home. Now all we had to do was slip past the Spanish patrol to be 'longshore in no time, with a long, hot shower and a big breakfast in the offing. We sped down the strait with the gale behind us, flogging the *Fire Witch* with every foot of sail that we dared. But we had tarried too long loading the hams, for I spotted a Spanish E-boat plowing water behind us. She was making great speed and threw a huge bow wave as she thundered ahead.

Our engine came to life with a roar making the poor *Fire Witch* shudder as we fairly flew along at fifteen knots, surfing on the crests of the waves. But I knew it was a losing race, for the monster machine behind us could do twice our speed. It was fascinating to watch her approach as that ugly hull became ever more distinct through the spray. Then she slowed perceptively, maintaining her distance, and I realized they were waiting for us to get closer to Gibraltar so the people there could see our capture. The *Fire Witch* continued to give us her best, and soon the rock loomed above us. Then, as the E-boat gunned her engines and began to close the gap, the first shot from her bow cannon roared toward us and erupted water a scant hundred yards away. Were they trying to sink us without the usual warning shots? It seemed so. And the rock was so near; so near we could see buildings plainly and cars moving along narrow streets in the morning's early light. The second shot thunked into the sea, much closer this time, throwing a huge, greasy water column high into the air to shower us with spray.

I gave Rebecca the helm and started cutting the lashings on the life raft. Perhaps we could abandon ship before the Spaniards found us with their gun. Then, from behind the rock came an eerie sound: whoop, whoop, whoop and a gray destroyer appeared, starboard rail awash in a tight turn around the rock, searchlights trained on the E-boat. She was easily making thirty knots as she roared toward us. But the E-boat had increased its speed and was moving in to board us. Without reducing speed, the destroyer slid between us and the Spaniards, shuddering as she came, her engines full in reverse. As she slid to a stop abeam of us, I read her name on the bow—*Protector.*

They were all waiting for us on the sea wall. Thousands of people, some dressed in Moroccan jalabas, some in heavy, dark fishing garb, even pretty girls in scanty miniskirts. They were all waving and cheering as we tied up at the dock just behind *Protector.* Still a bit weak in the knees and queasy in the gut, I walked over to the big boat to give the captain our thanks. I stood there on the bridge shaking his hand surrounded by grinning sailors.

"By the way," I asked the Captain, "What piece of luck put your vessel in a position to aid us?"

"Well," he said thoughtfully, "we received a call on the radiotelephone that you might be in trouble. The chap called himself Saint Nick, or something like that. So, we decided to have a look. Lucky we did."

Rebecca and I walked down the wharf, that December 1971, with everyone slapping us on the back and talking in many languages. Never again, I vowed. One smuggling run is enough for a lifetime. But then, what's Christmas without a little Polvoronis?

طنجة
86
TANGER

22 Equivalents 'n Things

SYMBOLS AND ABBREVIATIONS

Can Size	Description	# Cups
1/2	fish and meat products	1
1	fruit, usually pineapple	1
1-1/4	fruit, usually pineapple	1-1/2
1-1/2	usually holds fruit	2
2	small fruit juice or fruit	2-1/4
2-1/2	can or glass jar	3-1/2
10	largest can	6-1/2–8 lbs
46	large juice drink can	6
211	tall can, holds drinks	1-1/2
300	holds vegetables, or juice	1/4
303	can or jar for vegetables	2
6 ounce	juice drinks	3/4
12 ounce	vegetables or meat	1-1/2
picnic	vegetables or meat	1-1/4
tall buffet	vegetables or meat	1

LIQUID MEASURES

60 drops	= 1 teaspoon	
3 teaspoons	= 1 tablespoon	= 0.5 ounce
2 cups	= 1 pint	= 0.53 liters
2 pints	= 1 quart	= 1.06 liters
4 quarts	= 1 gallon	= 4.221iters

METRIC CONVERSIONS

1 ounce	= 28 grams
1 pound	= 454 grams

LINEAR MEASURE

1 inch	= 2.54 centimeters
1 centimeter	= 0.39 inches
39.37 inches	= 1 meter

SUBSTITUTIONS & EQUIVALENTS

Cornmeal	3 cups = 1 pound = 12 cups cooked
Egg Whites	8-11 whites = 1 cup
Egg Yolks	12-15 yolks = 1 cup
Flour, all purpose	1 pound = 4 cups sifted
Flour, wh. wheat	1 pound = 3-1/2 cups unsifted 3/4 cup = 1 cup all purpose
Milk, condensed	1 cup condensed + 1 cup water = 2 cups whole
Milk, powdered	2/3 cup powdered + 1/3 cup water = 1 cup whole milk
Milk, dry, whole	4 teaspoon powdered + 1 cup water = 2 cup whole
Mushrooms	1 ounce dry = 4 ounces fresh
Peas, dry, split	2 cups = 1 pound (5 cups cooked)
Macaroni	1 cup = 4 ounce (2-1/4 cups cooked)
Noodles	1 cup = 2-2/3 ounces (2 cups cooked)
Spaghetti	2 cups (1/2 pound) = 4 cups (1 pound cooked)
Rice	2-1/2 cups = 1 pound (8 cups cooked)
Tapioca	2 tablespoons quick = 6 teaspoons cooked

RECONSTITUTED EQUIVALENTS

Apples	1 lb dry = 3-1/2 pounds fresh
Apricots	3 cups = 1 pound dry
Beans/Legumes	2-1/2 cups = 1 pound (6-7 cups cooked)
Corn meal	1 cup = 5 ounces (4 cups cooked)
Eggs, dried	2-1/2 tablespoons egg + 4-1/2 tablespoon water = 1 whole egg
Gelatin	1 ounces powder makes 1qt.
Lemon	1 squeezed = 2-1/2 tablespoons juice

Index

D

E

F

G

H

N

O

P

Q

R

S

More Books from Paradise Cay Publications...

2001 NAUTICAL ALMANAC *22.95*

The Nautical Almanac is the cornerstone for all sight reduction. Lists the positions of the sun, moon, stars, and planets that are used for navigation. This edition contains the exact same data as the edition published by the U.S. Naval Observatory, as well as the last two months of the previous year.

GREEN FLASH *14.95*

by L.M. Lawson

Sailors and non-sailors alike will enjoy this passage into the world of boats and foreign ports. Set in the tropical heat of the Mexican cruising community, tensions rise when Jessie and Neal Fox choose to give the video camera they salvage to the authorities rather than its insistent owner - a recent widower.

KING SALMON: A GUIDE TO SALMON FISHING IN CALIFORNIA *27.50*

by Greg Goddard

Go fishing with Greg Goddard in this entertaining and very informative book. Greg takes you from the dock to the dinner table in this comprehensive how to book. A complete guide including charts of every popular salmon fishing region in the Golden State, charter and guide service phone numbers, and bait shops.

TWENTY SMALL SAILBOATS TO TAKE YOU ANYWHERE *19.95*

by John Vigor

In this fascinating book, well-known boating author John Vigor turns the spotlight on twenty seaworthy sailboats that are at home on the ocean in all weather. All are small - from 20 feet to 32 feet overall - but all have crossed oceans. And all are cheap.

If you have ever dreamed the dream, this book can help you turn it into reality.

HEAVY WEATHER TACTICS USING SEA ANCHORS & DROGUES *19.95*

by Earl Hinz

In this book, Hinz sets out the operating principals, designs details, and tactics of use for both sea anchors and drogues applied to sail and powerboats up to approximately 100 feet.

DESTINATION MEXICO *15.95*

by Carol & Bob Mehaffy

This book tells you everything you need to know about getting yourself and your boat ready for a cruise of weeks or months in Mexican waters. You'll find advice on clothing and provisions, recreational and galley equipment, and toiletries and medical aids.

COST CONSCIOUS CRUISER *29.95*

by Lin and Larry Pardey

In this book Lin & Larry discuss topics ranging from making your getaway plans to finding a truly affordable boat, keeping your outfitting costs and maintenance time in control, then learning to feel confident as you cruise farther ahead.

Their chart of the gear considered necessary by many shoreside experts will give you a convenient checklist to gauge whether you are buying true necessities or overloading your budget and boat with high-tech items.

THE CAPABLE CRUISER *32.00*

by Lin & Larry Pardey

The Capable Cruiser illustrates how successful cruising is the result of a combination of factors including a homogeneous crew, proper preparation, solid gear, regular maintenance and exemplary seamanship. This is indeed the global bible of cruising sailors.

CARE & FEEDING OF SAILING CREW 29.95

by Lin & Larry Pardey

Expanded by more than 30%, this book tells not only how to buy, provision and stow food for local cruising and extended voyages, but also how to take care of all the other aspects of crew comfort. Sleep, outfitting galleys, keeping warm and dry, medical considerations, building an efficiently insulated freezer/fridge/ice chest, water and watermakers plus one of the most innovative gimbaled stoves afloat.

CARE & FEEDING OF THE SAILING CREW VIDEO 29.95

by Lin & Larry Pardey

Although this video works as a companion to Lin's book of the same name, it also stands on its own to show you how to provision for passages, but more immediately, how to make your crew more comfortable afloat. 59 minutes.

DETAILS OF CLASSIC BOAT CONSTRUCTION: THE HULL 49.95

by Larry Pardey

Building a wooden hull is discussed in detail, step-by-step with illustrations including 600 photographs and 178 diagrams, vital information for potential builders, repair specialists, designers and owners of wooden hulls.

CRUISING IN SERAFFYN 16.95

by Lin & Larry Pardey

This cruising tale is full of the sights and sounds, the fragrances and native customs of foreign lands, especially Central America and the Caribbean.

SERAFFYN'S EUROPEAN ADVENTURE 16.95

by Lin & Larry Pardey

Join Lin and Larry while they winter in England working to pay for the next leg of their journey into the Baltic, Denmark, Sweden, Finland, and Germany.

SERAFFYN'S MEDITERRANEAN ADVENTURE 16.95

by Lin & Larry Pardey

Lin and Larry Pardey spent 11 years cruising the world in their backyard-built, 24-foot cutter Seraffyn. *Seraffyn's Mediterranean Adventure* covers three years of their cruising life, in and around the Mediterranean, where they explored the Spanish Coast and then worked their way back down to the African coast and the Arab world.

SERAFFYN'S ORIENTAL ADVENTURE 16.95

by Lin & Larry Pardey

In this book, fourth of the *Seraffyn* series, the Pardeys have reached a turning point in their lives–halfway around the world, eight years into a meandering voyage. The underlying theme of *Seraffyn's Oriental Adventure* is the demands of passage making as they sail up through the China Seas and across the North Pacific.

VOYAGING: UP-GRADING YOUR CRUISING BOAT VIDEO 29.95

by Lin & Larry Pardey

Cost effective ways to transform your cruising boat for offshore voyaging. How to convert your dinghy into a sailing-like raft, back-saving methods of lifting the dinghy on board, abandon ship, self-steering advice, original storage ideas. 54 minutes.

CRUISING: CONSTRUCTIVE ADVICE & HINTS ON FITTING OUT A CRUISING BOAT VIDEO 29.95

by Lin & Larry Pardey

Simple, easy adapted ideas for fitting out your own cruising boat: storage ideas, simple-to-build, truly watertight hatches, a dining table for port at sea and more. Over 50 useful tips and ideas. 56 minutes.

THE SELF-SUFFICIENT SAILOR 29.95

by Lin & Larry Pardey

This book is what the title says. It is the distillation of what the Pardey's have learned in 150,000 miles of sailing on board their two cutters, *Seraffyn* and *Taleisin*, and on scores of other boats they have delivered or raced. Lin and Larry tell how they have sailed in comfort and safety on a pay-as-you-earn-as-you-go plan and by simplifying.

STORM TACTICS HANDBOOK: Modern Methods of Heaving-to for Survival in Extreme Conditions 19.95

by Lin & Larry Pardey

Modern methods of heaving-to for survival in extreme conditions. Trysail and para-anchor technology for all types of boats and sailors.

THE CHINESE SAILING RIG: DESIGNING & BUILDING YOUR OWN 15.95

by Derek Van Loan with Dan Haggerty

This is a practical handbook which emphasizes adapting western hulls to a Chinese rig. Its "take a hammer in one hand and a nail in the other" approach leads the amateur designer/builder through all the steps from dream to voyage. The emphasis here is on "practical."

SURVIVOR 26.95

by Michael Greenwald

Required reading for all sailors! Caught in the eye of the hurricane, sudden disaster in the night, attacked by killer whales, shipwrecked in the dead of winter on an Alaskan island: these are a few of the many adventures described in *Survivor*, a boat disaster anthology so gripping you won't be able to put it down. True stories of the struggle for life in tiny survival craft, or cast up on an uninhabited coral atoll, stark photos of castaways, daring rescues, tragic failures, and a wealth of solid survival lore make *Survivor* a sailor's manual, required reading for those who go to sea.

CRUISING GUIDE TO THE HAWAIIAN ISLANDS 29.95

by Bob and Carolyn Mehaffy

In this book, boaters will find the most comprehensive guide to the Hawaiian Islands ever published, with detailed coverage of 68 harbors and anchorages in the Islands, including Midway Atoll. *Cruising Guide to the Hawaiian Islands* is an essential companion for all boaters who plan to cruise in the Hawaiian Islands, whether by powerboat or by sailboat.

CRUISING GUIDE TO SAN FRANCISCO BAY, 2ND ED. 29.95

by Bob & Carolyn Mehaffy

In this updated and expanded second edition, this comprehensive cruising guide includes four more destinations outside the Bay: Pillar Point Harbor, Drakes Bay, Bodega Harbor, and Tomales Bay. For the more than 70 destinations covered, the authors give detailed instructions on how to get there safely, where to anchor or tie up, and what to do there.

BREATHTAKING – ONE MAN, ONE WOMAN, ONE BOAT: TWO HAPPY DAYS 12.95

by J.P. Valdury

Nick knew better than to buy a boat, but that didn't stop him. He bought a boat because Claire- Anne wanted it, needed it, dreamed about it, went electric with excitement when she talked about it... And Claire-Anne was very beautiful when she was excited.

A good humored romp.

ON THE BOULEVARD OF GALLEONS 14.95

by Wallace B. Farrell & Sandra J. Burns

On the Boulevard of Galleons is the account of a two-year sailing adventure retracing the paths of Spanish treasure ships and buccaneers in the New World. The voyage sweeps along the stark Bala peninsula and down the unspoiled Gold Coast to Acapulco.

TAKING TERRAPIN HOME: A LOVE AFFAIR WITH A SMALL CATAMARAN 14.95

by Mathew Wilson

An exciting account of crossing the Atlantic in a small sailboat by Mathew Wilson, a noted lecturer who used his adventure as the subject for this, his first book. *Terrapin's* route took her across the English Channel, through France to the Mediterranean before turning to cross the Atlantic. This is a good story.

THE COMPASS BOOK 12.95

by Mike Harris

The magnetic compass is one of the most ancient of navigational instruments, and even in these times, it remains a vital piece of gear for any boat.

The Compass Book is an introduction to the principles of compass work. It is a guide for those wanting to carry out as much of their own repair and maintenance work as possible.

THE STAR FINDER BOOK 12.95

by David Burch

A comprehensive book explaining the use of the 2102D star finder, and the many applications it offers in planning navigation. Its numerous examples and diagrams make it a most definitive treatment. This book is an indispensable companion to the star finder itself.

100 PROBLEMS IN CELESTIAL NAVIGATION 19.95

by Leonard Gray

Noted author Leonard Gray treats us again with this potpourri of celestial navigation exercises, each designed around a specific journey; New York to Lisbon, Anchorage to Hilo, Hungnam to Akita to name a few.

NAVIGATION RULES (RULES OF THE ROAD) 9.95

Required on board all vessels 12 meters or more in length. *Navigation Rules* is one of the items a Coast Guard boarding officer will ask for during a routine "safety" inspection. The rules are presented in a convenient format emphasizing distinctions between inland and international rules.

DRUG TESTING 12.95

by Captain Alan Spears Esq.

Captain Spears examines the procedures prescribed in 46 CFR Part 16 and 49 CFR Part 40 as they pertain to the collection of drug test specimens from licensed mariners. Drug testing explains random, reasonable cause, and pre-employment testing procedures; analyzes legal cases; and discusses employer-generated pre-termination (discharge) hearings.

LANDFALL LEGALESE - VOLUME I: THE PACIFIC 29.95

by Captain Alan Spears Esq.

VOLUME II: THE CARIBBEAN 24.95

by Captain Alan Spears Esq.

If you are going cruising in the Pacific or the Caribbean, and you are interested in previewing the required customs and immigration forms prior to arrival, *Landfall Legalese* is a must. Together, Volumes I and II comprise a compendium of the legal requirements and protocols for entering and clearing the majority of popular cruising ports throughout the Pacific and the Caribbean.

SHIPPING OUT 12.95

by Captain Alan Spears Esq.

An exposé of commercial and recreational shipboard jobs. A practical reference for job-seeking mariners describing various methods of finding work in the industry.

For a free Paradise Cay Publications catalog, call 1-800-736-4509, or visit our web site at www.paracay.com